APPLIED SOCIO-ECONOMICS AND PUBLIC POLICY

AHMED RIAHI-BELKAOUI

To Hédi J. Belkaoui

CONTENTS

Preface	xi
1. Prolegomenon to Socio-Economic	3
2. Corporation and Society: Toward and Economic Paradigm	21
3. The Corporate-Society Relationship: Toward a Rectification Paradigm	44
4. Corporation and Society: Toward an Ethical Paradigm	69
5. Economics of Social Issues	93
6. Micro Social Economics Proposed Approaches	114
7. Micro Social Economics Concepts and Measurement	189
8. Macro Social Economics	230
9. Social Auditing	260

Preface

This book represents the beginning foundations of a new approach to applied *socio-economic* accounting and public policy. As we move into the last decades of the twentieth century, it becomes increasingly apparent that we have to lay aside narrow and short-term considerations and work together to achieve new forms of reporting that take into account the environmental effects of organizational behavior. That is exactly the aim of applied socio-economic: to improve the quality of life and to measure and disclosure such improvement in various forms of "social reports." These social reports would identify, evaluate, and measure those aspects essential to maintain an adequate quality of life for all the members of organizational units, both firms and nations, as defined by appropriate social goals. This arithmetic of quality and the eventual production of social reports in conformity with social goals at both the firm and the national level is the main purpose of socio-economic accounting. It is a call for the measurement of the total performance of economic and governmental units and their contribution to the quality of life of all the members of a nation.

The objective of this book is to provide the reader with a thorough exposure to the various paradigmatic thoughts and avenues emerging from the social sciences and defining the emerging field of applied socio-economic. The paradigmatic thoughts, including the commitment to social welfare, the new environmental paradigm in sociology, the ecosystem perspective, and the sociologizing mode, are presented in Chapter 1. The avenues identified include the needs for an economic paradigm (Chapter 1), a rectification paradigm (Chapter 3), an ethical paradigm (Chapter 4), an economic remedy to social issues (Chapter 5), social economics (Chapters 6-8), and social auditing (Chapter 9).

No book can be written without the help of numerous individuals and organizations. I am particularly indebted to those who influenced the book by their stubborn resistance to see the potentials for a humane and social approach to management and economics.

A special note of appreciation is extended to my research assistant Elizabeth Alvarez for her cheerful and intelligent assistance.

Finally, I thank all the individuals and organizations that gave me permission to reprint part of their works in this book.

APPLIED SOCIO-ECONOMICS AND PUBLIC POLICY

1
PROLEGOMENON TO APPLIED SOCIO-ECONOMICS

Following World War II, most of the economies of the Western countries, some of the socialist countries, and even some of the emerging countries have experienced constant growth and increasing strength and have produced new arrays of goods and services intended to meet people's high expectations and living standards. What was asked from the economy was an improvement in the quality of life. To most people this concept meant more than the provision of goods and services. It is rather a state of the world depending on a satisfactory resolution of all social issues: ecology, technology, pollution, urban blight, education, housing, crime, energy, urban congestion, poverty, population growth, monopoly power, consumer problems, discrimination, high national debt, and so forth. All the sectors of the economy moved at one point or another to tackle these issues and improve the quality of life. The *result has been far from perfect*. A. W. Clausen ventures the following explanation: "I submit that a major reason for our inadequate response is that we find the quality of life issue confusing- and that the prime cause of that confusion is a lack of even the crudest form of measurements of 'quality.'"[1]

It is easy to concur with the above statement and suggest that the confusion may be cleared with the development of an "arithmetic of quality" leading to an eventual "social report."[2] Such a social report would identify, evaluate, and measure those aspects essential to maintain an adequate quality of life for all the members of a nation as defined by social goals. Daniel Bell rightfully argues that these social goals should deal with the "ability of an individual citizen to establish a career commensurate with his abilities and live a full and healthy life equal to his biological potential, and include a definition of the levels of an adequate standard of living and the elements of a decent physical and social environment."[3] The arithmetic of quality and the eventual production of social reports in conformity with social goals at both the firm and the national level is the purpose of applied socio-economics. Applied *socio-economics is a call for the measurement of the total performance of economic and government units and their contribution to the quality of life of all the members of a nation*. Most people would enthusiastically espouse this goal. There are, however, various individuals who might object to this concern with the quality of the environment. The most disturbing example of this type of individual is reported by A. W. Clausen as follows:

Some quite literally don't give a damn about the quality of the environment. In a recent speech before Bank of America managers, Louis Banks, Editorial Director of Time Inc., described a vivid recollection of lunching in an elegant Manhattan apartment, surrounded by priceless impressionist paintings, and hearing one of Wall Street's venerable geniuses remark: "I think the city is past saving, and I think my responsibility is to sit back and figure out how I can profit from its decline and fall." Mr. Banks went on to say he regretted to report that particular Nero is still fiddling- and still prospering.[4]

Luckily, this particular Nero is among a minority with the wrong vision of truth. He failed to understand that the quality of life around him is heavily dependent on the quality of life of all the individuals in the nation. Prosperous individuals, firms, or nations in a troubled and spoiled environment may be able to shelter themselves in a ghetto of economic well-being but may not be able to secure the best quality of life given the interrelated social issues that define the quality of life. That is why a measurement of the total performance of economic and governmental unites and their contribution to the quality of life. That is why a measurement of the total performance of economic and governmental unites and their contribution to the quality of life of all the members of a nation is an important task; that is why we should be interested in the prolegomenon to applied socio-economics.

1.1 Early Reference to Applied Socio-economics

Applied socio-economics as a word is a relatively new phenomenon. It is sometimes confused with social accounting, which is an established field of accounting and economics. Social accounting was first introduced by J. R. Hicks of Oxford University in *The Social Framework: An Introduction to Economics*, published in 1942.[5] The accounting research of the time interpreted it as the whole system of accounts and balance sheets of a nation or a region, the price and quantity components of these accounts, and the various considerations to be derived therefrom.[6] Social accounting was basically associated with national income accounting. An examination of the early publications in the accounting literature proves that point. A general theme in the early literature is the failure of the accountant to be involved in social accounting, as evidenced by the following statements:

Although social accounting applies the same double-entry rules as business accounting applies the same double-entry rules as business accounting, and makes use of the accounting professors in American universities.[7]

Thus, while the principles and procedures of accountancy have benefited private enterprise over the years, in recent times it has become increasingly apparent that accounting data promote the effective direction of the entire economy. The major possibility today for increasing the social usefulness of the profession lies in the development of business enterprise accounts with attention to the widest possible use of these accounts, and the summarization of overall figures covering capital employed, wages, costs, interest, and rent for use in the administration of the economy.[8]

There were few noticeable involvements in the area of social accounting. The American Accounting Association, for example, created a Committee on National Income, which issued a report in 1952 on Aspects of National Income. The members of this committee worked on independent projects of their own choosing. Notable examples include "The Classification of Sectors in the Social Accounts," by Julius Margolis, and "Use of Accounting Data in National-Income Estimation," by Carl L. Nelson.[9] Other attempts examined the role of accounting in social accounting.[10] M. E. Murphy summarizes this role as follows:

A system of social accounts provides an historical record of a country's economic operations, measures the efficiency with which its economy functions, and affords a periodic inventory, that is, an indication of the economic position of a country. These three functions correspond to those of business accounting, the chief difference being that business accounting is conducted exclusively on one level set by the legal structure of the locale.

Social accounting, on the other hand, must be calculated on two levels: first, the combination of existing accounts in accordance with prevailing business methods, and second, the combination in recasting of these accounts to conform with a set of standard rules derived from economic theory. The two levels are designated as "national business accounting" and "national economic accounting." They coexist at any given time.[11]

The interest of researchers in the field of social accounting in general and national income accounting in particular has, however, declined over the years and was left to economists and social statisticians. Any resurgence of interest in applied socio-economics would definitely spur more involvement by researchers in the field of social accounting. In fact, as will be evident in Chapter 7, the renewed interest in social measurement in the mid-1960s has spurred research for the development of "social indicators," "social accounting," "measuring the quality of life," "monitoring social change," and "social reporting."[12]

1.2 Nature of Applied Socio-Economics

The recent interest of researchers in expanding the scope of accounting and economics beyond the business enterprise established the area of applied socio-economics as a full-fledged discipline of interest to social scientists. Various definition of socio-economics were offered in the literature. Let's examine some of these definition before proposing a definition befitting the paradigmatic theme of this book. David F. Linowes proposes the following definitions:

Socio-economic... is intended here to mean the application of accounting in the field of the social sciences. These include sociology, political science and economics.[13]

As I see it, socio-economic accounting is the measurement and analysis of the social and economic consequences of governmental and business actions on the public sector.[14]

Sybil Mobley offered a definition in 1970 that gives broadest scope to socio-economic accounting:

[Socio-economics refers to the ordering, measuring, and analysis of the social and economic consequences of governmental and entrepreneurial behavior. So defined, socio-economic accounting is seen as encompassing and extending present accounting. Traditional accounting has limited its concern to selected economic consequences- whether in the financial, managerial, or national income areas. Socio-economic accounting expands each of these areas to include the social consequences as well as economic effects which are not presently considered.[15]

Steven C. Dilley rightfully observed that Mobley's definition is broad enough to include any extensions of accountants' responsibilities and proposed instead to categorize the various types of social economic accounting into five general areas as follows:
1. National social income accounting
2. Social auditing
3. Financial/managerial social accounting for nonprofit entities
4. Financial social accounting
5. Managerial social accounting[16]

Each of the above-cited definitions offers one or several aspects of the nature of socio-economics as viewed in this book. Put together, they provide a more exhaustive definition of socio-economics as follows:

Socio-economics results from the application of measurement in the social sciences; it refers to the ordering, measuring, analysis, and disclosure of the social and economic consequences of governmental and entrepreneurial behavior. It includes these activities at the macro and micro level. At the micro level, its purpose is the measurement and reporting of the impact of organizational behavior of firms on their environment. At the macro level, its purpose is the measurement and disclosure of the economic and social performance of the nation. At the micro level socio-economics includes, therefore, financial and managerial social accounting and reporting and social auditing. At the macro level socio-economics includes, therefore, social measurement, social accounting and reporting, and the role of accounting in economic development.

Given this definition, the next objective is first to rationalize and motivate this expansion of the scope of measurement, and second to present the avenues for socio-economics. The expansion of the scope of measurement to cover the goals of applied socio-economics may be rationalized and motivated by some of the new paradigmatic thoughts in the social sciences, namely, the commitment to social welfare, the new environmental paradigm in sociology, the ecosystem perspective, and the sociologizing mode. The avenues for socio-economics include the need for an economic, an ethical, and a rectification paradigm, a micro and macro social accounting, and, finally, a need for social auditing.

Paradigmatic Thoughts Favorable to Socio-Economics

The literature in the social sciences in general and in sociology and social work in particular is witnessing a resurgence of new paradigms challenging the early focus on individual welfare and encouraging a more general focus on social welfare, the environment, and a total ecosystem perspective. These paradigms may be used as a justification for the expansion of the scope of conventional measurement to include the social measurement, reporting, and verification aspects of socio-economics. These paradigms include a *commitment to social welfare paradigm*, a *new environment paradigm*, an *ecosystem perspective*, and *ecosystem perspective*, and a *sociologizing mode of management*. In what follows, each of the paradigms.

TOWARD A COMMITMENT TO SOCIAL WELFARE

An examination of the history of mankind shows that human survival has been possible only through cooperation. Consider for example the following insight by Stewart C. Easton, a historian:

It used to be thought that man in a state of nature was forced to compete with all other human beings for his very subsistence, or, in the famous words of Thomas Hobbes, that his life was "solitary, poor, nasty, brutish, and short." We have no record of such a way of life, either in early times, or among present-day " primitive" men. And it no longer seems as probable to us as it did in the nineteenth century, under the influence of the biological ides of Darwin, that human survival was a matter of success in the constant struggle for existence, if this struggle is conceived of as a struggle between human beings. It now seems much more probable that survival has always been due to successful cooperation between human beings to resist the always dangerous forces of nature.[17]

More recently, with the concern with ecological preservation and with the protection and promotion of human life, the cooperation has taken the form of social welfare programs and services as important answers to the various personal and social perils threatening human life. A good definition of social welfare is provided by Friedlander and Apte's statement: "Social welfare is a system of laws, programs, and benefits which strengthen or assure provisions for meeting social needs recognized as basic for the welfare of the population and the functioning of social order."[18] Thus, social welfare includes all programs for meeting the basic social needs; it has its roots in religion, humanitarianism, and compassion. It calls for the creation of social structures or social agencies that have been appropriately described as the institutionalization of the philanthropic impulse and love of mankind.

The rationale for social welfare depends on two views, whether social welfare is needed for emergency situations or as a permanently needed function of society. Wilensky and Lebeaux put it his way:

Two conceptions of social welfare seem to be dominant in the United States today; the *residual* and the *institutional*. The first holds that social welfare institutions should come into play only when the normal structures of supply, the family, and the market, break down. The second, in contrast, sees the welfare services as normal, "first-line" functions of modern industrial society.[19]

It is rather evident that both views constitute an acceptable rationale for social welfare, although the institutional approach is the one that will eventually prevail in the future as a way of *continuously* answering the various personal and social perils that threaten the delicate balance of human life and the fragility of human security.

THE HUMAN EXCEPTIONALISM PARADIGM VERSUS THE NEW ENVIRONMENT PARADIGM

For a long time the human exceptionalism paradigm (HEP) dominated the environmental discipline in sociology before the emergence of the new environment paradigm (NEP). The HEP views humans as unique among earth's creatures with a culture that can change infinitely and more rapidly than biological traits and with human differences as the result of acculturation, not biology. The NEP views the humans as but one among many species interrelated by cause-and-effect linkages and bounded by a world with finite limits on economic, social, and political growth. The NEP is a result of the interest in societal changes not explainable by traditional sociological theories. It in turn has led to emergence of environmental sociology.

The numerous competing theoretical perspectives in sociology-e.g., functionalism, symbolic interactionism, ethnomethodology, conflict theory, Marxism- all focus on men's relations with themselves rather than with the environment. This *anthropocentric* view represents the HEP. William R. Catton Jr. and Riley E. Dunlap presented the following assumptions underlying HEP:
1. Humans are unique among the earth's creatures, for they have culture.
2. Culture can vary almost infinitely and can change much more rapidly than biological traits.
3. Thus, many human differences are socially induced rather than inborn, they can be socially altered, and inconvenient differences can be eliminated.
4. Thus, also, cultural accumulation means that progress can continue without limit, making all social problems ultimately soluble.[20]

As a result of this position the ecosystem dependence of human systems was for a long time neglected in the sociological literature on economic development. The belief was that there were no limits to technological improvement, growth, and abundance.

The NEP emerged as a result of a new literature highlighting the problems for human society that may arise from the limitations of the ecological world. This literature included the works of Rachel Carson, Barry Commoner, Paul Ehrlich, and Garret Hardin.[21] The NEP led to the acceptance of environmental variables as a legitimate area of inquiry for sociologists and the emergence variables as a legitimate area of inquiry for sociologists and the emergence of a new set of assumptions different from those of HEP. They include the following:
1. Human beings are but one species among the many that are interdependently involved in the biotic communities that shape our social life.
2. Intricate linkages of cause and effect and feedback in the web of nature produce many unintended consequences from purposive human action.
3. The world is finite, so there are potent physical and biological limits constraining economic growth, social progress, and other societal phenomena.[22]

These assumptions point clearly to the importance of environmental facts to understanding and explaining social facts. It is evident that human beings, as truly as other species of the organism, cannot ignore ecology or leave the ecology scene and are therefore engaged in what mathematical biologists can describe as the game of "existential Gambler's Ruin," wherein the optimal strategy in human encounters with environmental selection pressures is to minimize the stakes.[23] The environment is to be perceived as a factor that may influence and in turn be influenced by human behavior.

One tangible outcome of NEP is the emergence of *social impact statements* which consider the total impact of a project on the environment.

THE ECOSYSTEM PERSPECTIVE

Everyone is being exposed to speeches, literature, and other media on ecology and the "environmental crisis." Both topics are presented either as matters of fact or as the beginning of the imminent extinction of life on earth. In either case the global ecosystem is threatened, and the source of the problems remains to be clearly identified. Is the crisis due to the failure to limit growth as dictated by market-oriented policies? If it is, then the ecological crisis is nothing but a crisis in the economic organization of the global ecosystem as much as a new social and political crisis. Natural environment is then not the problem, it is the economic organization dictating its use that is the problem.[24] The damage is further aggravated by the nature of some of the relationships in the ecosystem:

1. The ecosystem processes are interlinked, and small changes in one process may produce large and unexpected effects and disturbances in other processes.
2. Most of the ecological changes are irreversible.
3. There is no complete scientific theory to deal with the complexity of ecosystemic processes and relations. Anthony Wilden warns as a consequence that "the inability of present theory to deal properly with these and mother much more complex interactions means that *every ecological statement we read about is inherently and necessarily much more conservative in its estimates and predictions than the probable future state of the reality it is describing.*"[25]

Given these problems, a kind of ecosystem understanding and perspective is needed to protect human future.[26]

To adopt this perspective, a position has to be taken concerning the ideology of growth. More explicitly, are there limits to growth and hence a solution to the ecological crisis? The publication of the Club of Rome's *Limits to Growth* provides one possible answer to the question.[27] The *Limits to Growth* is based on a cybernetic and systemic world model as a basis for computer simulations of the future development of the global socio-economic system and as such includes in the simulation various factors and combinations of factors such as population growth, capital growth, available land for agriculture, pollution, and renewable resources. The results of the simulation point to a definite exhaustion of the world's natural resources over the next one hundred years. The authors conclude by identifying an "ideal" program for a stable world system with the following policies to be introduced beginning in 1975.

1. The stabilization of population by equalizing the birth and death rate.
2. The stabilization of industrial capital by equalizing the deprecation and the investment rate, beginning in 1990.
3. The reduction of the consumption of natural resources to one-fourth of the 1970 level per unit of industrial output;
4. The shifting of economic preferences in society away from material goods forward services, such as education;
5. The reduction of pollution per unit of industrial output to one-fourth of its 1970 level;
6. The diversion of capital to food production with the goal of providing food for all people and overcoming traditional inequalities in distribution;
7. The diversion of a part of agricultural capital toward soil enrichment and preservation to avoid soil erosion and depletion;
8. An increase in the lifetime of industrial capital to counteract the low final level of capital stock resulting from the first seven policies.

The *Limits to Growth* is a call to some international intervention to ensure human future. It is also an ideological statement for checking and limiting growth, in brief, it is an ecosystem perspective.

The necessity for an ecosystem perspective is more evident when uncontrolled population growth and the environmental problems are analyzed in terms of "the tragedy of the commons."[28] Men attempt to maximize their gain. In the absence of controls, Hardin argues, they are driven by rational calculations of self-interest to overexploit or abuse the commons, whether it is a pasture shared by herdsmen or the earth's atmosphere. "Freedom in a common brings ruin to all."[29] Given the absence of technical solutions to the problem, Hardin suggests the use of stringent controls ("mutual coercion, mutually agreed upon") to escape the "remorseless working of things" that characterizes the logic of a free commons.[30]

THE ECONOMIZING VERSUS THE SOCIOLOGIZING MODE

The economizing mode and the sociologizing mode are two extreme perspectives suggested within which the actions of the corporation can be estimated and judged.[31]

Economizing results from the collaboration of the engineer and the economist to determine the best allocation of scarce resources among competing ends. Economizing is basically concerned with reaching a level of efficiency in the use of resources. It relies on engineering for designing the machines and determining the optimal way to use these machines in order to produce a maximum output within a given physical layout. It relies on economics to find the optimal mix of men and machines in the organization or production.

With economics, comes a rational division of labor, specialization of function, complementarity or relations, the uses of production functions) the best mix of capital and labor at relative prices), programming (the best ordering of scheduling of mixed batches in production, or in transportation), etc. The words we associate with economizing are "maximization," "optimization," "least cost," in short, the components of a conception of rationality.[32]

Economizing relies naturally on the market system and the resulting price system to evaluate the firm's allocation of resources. And more importantly, the economizing mode focuses on individual satisfaction as the unit for which costs and benefits are recognized and measured.

Unlike the economizing mode, the sociologizing mode focuses on the society's need in a coordinated fashion and taking into account a notion of the public interest. The sociologizing mode addresses two fundamental issues: the conscious establishment of social justice by the inclusion of all persons into the society; and the relative size of the public and the private sector. Both these issues will be addressed in Chapter 3.

Which of the two modes is more appropriate for the business corporation of today? The trend is clearly toward the sociologizing mode, mainly as a reaction to the increasing criticism toward the corporation reinforced by the feeling that corporate performance has caused the quality of life in society to deteriorate. Daniel Bell illustrates the new situation when he states that the "sense of identity between the self-interest of the corporation and the public interest has been replaced by a sense of incongruence."[33] The best evidence of the shift toward sociologizing is the increase in corporate participation in providing social benefits to their employees.[34]

The Need for an Effective Paradigm
THE ECONOMIC PARADIGM

Corporation-society relationships are governed by the economic principles espoused by the government and the nation. These same principles determine the role of the corporation in society and define the nature of its activities. The continuum of economic principles goes from the extreme right libertarianism to the extreme left of radical economics. In between these views fall the institutional and the social economists.

Both libertarianism and radical economics center on extreme views concerning the preeminence of either the market or the state and present rigid solution to complex economic and social problems. The social and institutional economists present a more reasoned approach to corporation-society relationships. The social economists may be identified by their deep commitment to human welfare and social justice. The institutionalists may be identified by their commitment to pragmatism and reliance on empirical observation and inductive logic as a way of analyzing economic and social problems. Both the social economists and the institutionalists work at the social level of generalization to analyze social organization and process and avoid the atomistic analytical units used by conventional micro-economics.

The interest in human and social welfare in social economics and the interest in a pragmatic approach to problems by the institutionalists may be strengthened by a synthesis of their approaches. Such a synthesis would serve to improve corporation-society relationships in a manner beneficial to both.

The economic paradigm governing the relationships of corporation and society need not be the role or importance of the market and/or the state in the libertarianism or the radical economics but a clear statement of national and social goals based on a commitment to human welfare and social justice and experimentation with institutional arrangements to solve economic and social problems.

This synthesis of social and institutional economics is at the heart and within the spirit of socio-economics as defined in this book. It calls for every organizational unit, including the government, to define goals compatible with human welfare and social justice and to look for institutional arrangements suitable to their realization. Accordingly, Chapter 2 will present the institutional, social, radical economics' approaches to corporation-society relationships and will argue for an economic paradigm more favorable and supportive of business' social involvement in general and applied socio-economics in particular.

THE RECTIFICATION PARADIGM

We live at a time when there are increasing tensions about the nature of the social contract and the inadequate provision of public goods, economic inequality, and social injustice. Because the corporation is an active market and social agent, its activities can either worsen or correct some of these problems. Thus, the corporation's relationships with society are by definition affected by its role in dealing with the sources of those tensions. The options open to the corporation are on a continuum from complete indifference to an active role in rectifying some of these social problems. Complete indifference would definitely be harmful to the long-term interests of the firm. Involvement in some forms of rectification is a way of ensuring mutual acceptance by society and a role in securing social order and affluence.

Socio-economic accounting is by definition compatible with a rectification paradigm. It even implies that rectification is necessary to reassess and improve business' social conduct. Accordingly, Chapter 3 will argue for a rectification paradigm to motivate and/or explain the corporation's role in reducing social tensions and to create an atmosphere more favorable to and supportive of business' social involvement in general and socio-economics in particular.

THE ETHICAL PARADIGM

The activities of business corporations have a tremendous effect on their environment in terms of both social costs and social benefits. Indeed, not only is a business corporation first of corporate citizen but it should be a good corporate citizen. This view of the world presents the business executive with a new set of choices. There are generally two opposite views on the role of management. One, the strict constructionism school, criticizes the social responsibility advocates and argues mainly that profit maximization is the only acceptable objective of business corporations. The other, the social responsibility school, argues that businessmen should be involved in correcting some of the social ills of society. Both have generated a debate in the corporate-society literature.

Socio-economic accounting is by definition more favorable to the social responsibility school. It even implies ethical guidelines to reassess and improve business' social conduct. Accordingly, Chapter 4 will argue for an ethical paradigm of the corporate-society relationship more favorable to and supportive business' social involvement in general and socio-economics in particular.

AN ECONOMIC REMEDY TO SOCIAL ISSUES

For the market to produce an efficient level of output, the private marginal benefit must equal the social marginal benefit and the private marginal cost must equal the social marginal cost. With respect to both the conditions, sources of market failure such as imperfect information, consumer ignorance, external economies and diseconomies, and monopoly render the market allocation unlikely to result in an efficient level of output. Similarly, the market fails to provide an equitable distribution of the level of output given the presence of poverty, inequality, and discrimination.

The failure of the market to provide and efficient and equitable level of output for most of the social issues requires some form of government intervention either by directly providing the good or service, by regulating the market, and/or by imposing a system of taxation/subsidization.

Government intervention has not necessarily met the criteria of efficiency and/or equity in most of the social issues. Experimentation may be needed before finding the type of economic organizations most adequate to deal with each of the social issues. For example, the voucher programs in education and in housing, the negative income tax proposals for inequality, and the Health Maintenance Organizations (HMOs) in health care are indicative of the type of experiments needed. *The controversy of market versus nonmarket solutions seems to obscure the real issue, which is to correct some of the social and unfair ills of society.* Experimentation in various forms of economic organizations coupled with the measurement and audit of their social costs and benefits is the key. Socio-economic accounting, with its emphasis on measurement and audit of costs and benefits, may help choose the type of economic organization needed to deal with each of the social issue. Accordingly, Chapter 6 will present the externality problem and the economics of selected social issues before emphasizing the experimentation needed to choose the best economic organizations to deal with the social issues.

SOCIAL ACCOUNTING

The previous calls for a synthesis of social and institutional economics, a rectification paradigm, an ethical paradigm, and an economic remedy to social issues may only be implemented by an effort at the micro and macro levels to identify, measure, and disclose the total performance, economic and social, of al the economic and social units of a nation. Such is the objective of micro and macro social economics. Micro social economics will deal with the measurement and disclosure of the social performance of micro-economic units, while macro social economics deals with the same tasks for the macro-economic units. Micro and macro social economics will constitute an expansion of social accounting to deal with the effects of organizational behavior on the total environment. To accomplish these objectives, theories and techniques of social economics need to be constructed, verified, and used by micro and macro economic and social units. Accordingly, Chapters 6, 7, 8 will examine the different approaches used for micro and macro social economics in the literature and in practice.

SOCIAL AUDITING

Public demand for socially oriented programs of one kind or another and for measurement and disclosure of the environmental effects of organizational behavior will create pressure for a form of social auditing of the activities of corporations. Given the novelty of the phenomenon and the lack of generally accepted procedures, social auditing tends presently to take forms to accommodate the various views about the ways firms should respond to their social environment. However, as the need for social measurement and reporting increases with a greater acceptance of socio-economic accounting, social auditing may become as standard and as rigorous as financial auditing. The professional "social auditor" will be involved in the social audit and be asked to examine the validity of the social data prepared by the firm.

Socio-economics relies heavily on social auditing for an appraisal of the total performance of profit and not for profit entities. Accordingly, Chapter 9 will provide a general definition of social auditing and clarify the difference between the various forms of social audits advocated in the literature and in practice. These types of audits include social process/program management audit, macro-micro social indicator audit, social performance audit, social balance sheet and income statement, energy accounting and auditing, comprehensive auditing, environmental auditing, human resource accounting, and constituency group attitudes.

Conclusion

This chapter has explored the beginnings and nature of applied socio-economics. This new discipline is to be accepted as a full-fledged discipline given the various paradigmatic thoughts emerging from the social sciences and favorable to this expansion of the scope of accounting. The paradigmatic thoughts identified in this chapter include the commitment to social welfare, the new environment paradigm in sociology, the ecosystem perspective, and the sociologizing accounting. The avenues identified in this chapter include the needs for an economic paradigm, a rectification paradigm, an ethical paradigm, an economic remedy to social issues, social accounting, and social auditing. Each of these avenues will be examined thoroughly in this book.

Notes

1. A. W. Clausen, "Toward and Arithmetic of Quality," *The Conference Board Record* (May 1971): 9.
2. U.S., Department of Health, Education and Welfare, *Toward a Social Report* (Ann Arbor: University of Michigan Press, 1970); Daniel Bell, "The Idea of a Social Report," *The Public Interest* (Spring 1969): 78-84.
3. Daniel Bell, "Social Trends of 70's, "*The Conference Board Record* (June 1970).
4. Clausen, "Toward an Arithmetic of Quality," p. 9.
5. Published by the Oxford University Press. The American edition was prepared by J. R. Hicks and A. G. Hart and issued under the title, *The Social Framework of the American Economy* (New York: Columbia University Press, 1946).
6. Milton Gilbert and Richard Stone, "Recent Developments in National Income and Social Accounting," *Accounting Research* (January 1954): 1-31.
7. John P. Powelson, "Social Accounting," *The Accounting Review* (October 1955): 651.
8. Mary E. Murphy, "The Teaching of Social Accounting: A Research Planning Paper," *The Accounting Review* (October 1957): 630.
9. Julius Margolis, "The Classification of Sectors in the Social Accounts," *The Accounting Review* (April 1953): 178-186; Carl L. Nelson, "Use of Accounting Data in National Income Estimation," *The Accounting Review* (April 1953): 186-190.
10. E. L. Kohler, "Accounting Concepts and National Income," *The Accounting Review* (January 1952): 50-56; Wilson L. Farman, "National Flow of Funds: An Accounting Analysis," *The Accounting Review* (April 1964): 392-404; Wilson L. Farman, "Some Basic Assumption Underlying Social Accounting," *The Accounting Review* (January 1951): 33-39; Wilson L. Farman, "Social Accounting in Subsistence and Family-Production Type Economies," *The Accounting Review* (July 1953): 392-400; A. C. Littleton, "Socialized Accounts," *The*

Accounting Review (December 1933): 267-271; A. C. Littleton, "Socialized Accounts (II)," *The Accounting Review* (March 1934): 69-74.
11. Mary E. Murphy, "Socialized Accounting," in Morton Backer, ed., *Modern Accounting Theory* (Englewood Cliffs, N.J.: Prentice-Hall, 1966): 466-472.
12. Eleanor Bernert Sheldon and Wilbert E., Moore, "Toward the Measurement of Social Change: Implications for Progress," pp. 185-212, in Leonard H. Goodman, ed., *Economic Progress and Social Welfare* (New York: Columbia University Press, 1966).
13. David F. Linowes, "Socio-Economic Accounting," *The Journal of Accountancy* (November 1968): 37.
14. David F. Linowes, "The Accounting Profession and Social Progress," *The Journal of Accountancy* (July 1973): 37.
15. Sybil C. Mobley, "The Challenges of Socio-Economic Accounting," *The Accounting Review* (October 1970): 762.
16. Steven C. Dilley, "Practical Approaches to Social Accounting," *The CPA Journal* (February 1975): 17.
17. Stewart C. Easton, *The Heritage of the Past* (New York: Holt, Rinehart and Winston, 1964), p. 4.
18. Walter A. Friedlander and Robert Z. Apte, *Introduction to Social Welfare* (Englewood Cliffs, N.J.: Prentice-Hall, 1974) p. 4.
19. Harold L. Wilensky and Charles N. Lebeaux, *Industrial Society and Social Welfare* (New York: Free Press, 1965), p. 60-62.
20. William R. Catton, Jr., and Riley E. Dunlap, "Environmental Sociology: A New Paradigm: *The American Sociologist* 13 (February 1978): 42.
21. Rachel Carson, *Silent Spring* (Boston: Houghton Mifflin, 1962); Barry Commoner, *The Closing Circle* (New York: Knopf, 1971); Paul R. Ehrlich and Ane H. Ehrlich, *Population, Resources, Environment* (San Francisco: Freeman, 1970); Garrett Hardin, "The Tragedy of Commons," *Science* 162 (1968): 1243-1248.
22. Catton and Dunlap, "Environmental Sociology," p. 42.
23. Lawrence B. Slobodkin and Anatol Rapoport, "An Optimal Strategy of Evolution," *Quarterly Review of Biology* (September 1974): 181-200.
24. Anthony Wilden, "Ecology and Ideology,: in Ahamed Idris-Solven, Elizabeth Idris-Solven and Mary K. Vaughan, eds., *The World as a Company Town* (The Hague: Mouton, 1978), p. 74.
25. Ibid., p. 76. Emphasis is mine.
26. Ibid., pp. 78-79.
27. D. H. Meadows et al., *Limits to Growth* (New York: Universe Books, 1972).
28. Hardin, "The Tragedy of the Commons," pp. 1241-1248.
29. Ibid., p. 1244.
30. Ibid., p. 1243.
31. Bell, Daniel, "The Corporation and Society in the 1970's," *The Public Interest* (Spring 1969).
32. Ibid, p. 10.
33. Ibid., p. 7.
34. Ibid., p. 23.

Bibliography

Bell, Daniel. "The Idea of a Social Report." *The Public Interest* (Spring 1969): 78-84.
---. "Social Trends of the 70's." *The Conference Board Record* (June 1970).
Buttel, Frederick H. "Environmental Sociology: A New Paradigm?" *The American Sociologist* 13 (November 1978): 252-256.
Carson, Rachel. *Silent Spring.* Boston: Houghton Mifflin, 1962.
Catton, Wiliam R., Jr. "Carrying Capacity, Overshoot and the Quality of Life." In J. Milton Yinger and Stephen J. Cutler, eds., *Major Social Issues: A Multidisciplinary View.* New York: Free Press, 1978.
--- and Riley E. Dunlap. "Environmental Sociology: A New Paradigm." *The American Sociologist* 13 (February 1978): 50-53.
---. "Paradigms, Theories and the Primacy of the HEP-NEW Dimension." *The American Sociologist* 13 (November 1978): 256-259.
Clausen, A. W. "Toward an Arithmetic of Quality." *The Conference Board Record* (May 1971): 9-13.
Commoner, Barry. *The Closing Circle.* New York: Knopf, 1971.
Daly, Herman E., ed. *Toward a Steady State Economy.* San Francisco: Freeman, 1973.
Dilley, Steven C. "Practical Approaches to Social Accounting.: *The CPA Journal* (February 1975): 17-21.
Dunlap, Riley E. and William R. Catton, Jr. "Environmental Sociology: A Framework for Analysis.: In T. O'Riordn and R. C. d'Arge, eds., *Progress in Resource Management and Environmental Planning.* Vol. 1. Chichester, England: Wiley, 1979.
Ehrlich, Paul R. and Anne H. Ehrlich. *Population, Resources, Environmental.* San Francisco: Freeman, 1970.
Fairfax, Sally. "A Disaster in the Environmental Movement." *Science* (February 1978): 741-748.
Farman, Wilson L. "National Flow of Funds: An Accounting Analysis." *The Accounting Review* (April 1964): 392-404.
---. "Some Basic Assumptions Underlying Social Accounting." *The Accounting Review* (January 1951): 33-39.
Finterbusch, Kurt. *Understanding Social Impacts: Assessing the Effects of Public Projects.* Beverly Hills, Cal.: Sage, 1980.
--- and C. P. Wolf, eds. *Methodology for Social Impact Assessment.* Stroudsburg, Pa.: Dowden, Hutchinson and Ross, 1977.
Frendenburg, William R. and Kenneth M. Keating. "Increasing the Impact of Sociology on Social Impact Assessment: Toward Ending the Inattention.: *The American Sociologist* (May 1982): 71-80.
Friedlander, Walter A. and Robert A. Apte, *Introduction to Social Welfare*, Englewood Cliffs, N.J.: Prentice-Hall, 1974.
Friesema, H. Paul and Paul J. Culhane. "Social Impacts, Politics, and the Environmental Impact Statement Process." *Natural Resources Journal* (April 1976): 339-356.
Gilbert, Milton and Richard Stone. "Recent Developments in National Income and Social Accounting." *Accounting Research* (January 1954): 1-31.
Hardesty, Donald L. *Ecological Anthropology.* New York: Wiley, 1977.
Hardin, Garrett. "The Tragedy of Commons." *Science* 162 (1968): 1243-1248.
Kohler, E. L. "Accounting Concepts and National Income." *The Accounting Review* (January 1952): 50-56.

Linowes, David F. "The Accounting Profession and Social Progress." *The Journal of Accountancy* (July 1973): 32-40.

---. "Socio-Economic Accounting." *The Journal of Accountancy* (November 1968): 37-42.

Littleton, A C. "Socialized Accounts." *The Accounting Review* (December 1933): 267-271.

---. "Socialized Accounts (II)." *The Accounting Review* (March 1934): 69-74.

Margolis, Julius. "The Classification of Sectors in the Social Accounts." *The Accounting Review* (April 1953): 178-186.

McEvoy, James, III and Thomas Dietz, eds. *Handbook for Environmental Plannning: The Social Consequences of Environmental Change*. New York: Wiley, 1977.

Meadows, D. H., et al, *Limits of Growth*. New York: Universe Books, 1972.

Michelson, William, *Man and His Urban Environment: A Sociological Approach*. Reading, Mass.: Addison Wesley, 1976.

Mobley, Sybil C. "The Challenges of Socio-Economic Accounting." *The Accounting Review* (October 1970): 762-768.

Murphy, Mary E. "Socialized Accounting," pp. 466-510. In Morton Backer, ed., *Modern Accounting Theory*. Englewood Cliffs, N.J.: Prentice-Hall, 1966.

---. "The Teaching of Social Accounting: A Research Planning Paper." *The Accounting Review* (October 1957): 630-645.

Neidinger, Errol and Allan Schnaiberg. "Social Impact Assessment as Evaluation Research: Claimants and Claims." *Evaluation Review* 4, (1980): 507-535.

Nelson, Carl L. "Use of Accounting Data in National Income Estimation." *The Accounting Review* (April 1953): 186-190.

Ophuls, William. *Ecology and the Politics of Scarcity*. San Francisco: Freeman, 1977.

Powelson, John P. "Social Accounting." *The Accounting Review* (October 1955): 651-659.

Stretton, Hugh. *Capitalism, Socialism and the Environment,* Cambridge: Cambridge University Press, 1976.

U.S. Department of Health, Education and Welfare. *Toward a Social Report*. Ann Arbor: University of Michigan Press, 1970.

Wilden, Anthony. "Ecology and Ideology." In Ahamed Idris-Solven, Elizabeth Idris-Solven and Mary K. Vaughan, eds., *The World as a Company Town*. The Hague: Mouton, 1978.

---. *Ecology and Ideology: The Structure of Domination in Western Society*. Londong: Tavistock, 1973.

Wilensky, Harold L. and Charles N. Lebeaux. *Industrial Society and Social Welfare*, New York: Free Press, 1965.

Wilke, Arthur S. and Harvey R. Cain. "Social Impact Assessment Under N.E.P.A.: The State of the Field." *Western Sociological Review* 8 (1977): 105-108.

Wolf, Charles P. "Getting Social Impact Assessment Into the Policy Arena." *Environmental Impact Assessment Review* (March 1980): 27-36.

2
CORPORATION AND SOCIETY: TOWARD AN ECONOMIC PARADIGM

The large corporation and its leaders generate ambivalent attitudes among the various populations of the world. The aspects of the corporation that contribute to a betterment of the standard of living on the whole generate admiration, respect, and even awe. These aspects refer to the productivity, efficiency, rapid technological advances, and image of strength conveyed by the large corporation through various media. However, other negative aspects generate distrust, dissatisfaction, hostility, and a questioning of the corporate role in society. These aspects include the power and the impact of the social, economic, and political environment. This ambivalence creates chronic tension between the large corporation and the rest of society. As a result it has become more and more acceptable to challenge business leaders' economic decisions as interfering with the "public interest" and to ensure through various social actions that these leaders follow new lines of action compatible with societal values. Naturally this is not a widely held position. Other well-intentioned individuals are ready to question the technical competence and social legitimacy of any efforts by business leaders to include and take into account "the public interest" in their decision making. These and other positions have colored the nature of and the literature on corporate-society relationships.

    The nature of the large corporation and its relationship to the economy and to the larger society is of importance to an understanding of its present and future role and behavior. The large corporation evidently affects through its actions the society in general, posing the above-mentioned questions of whether they should identify and take into account the "public interest." These questions have been examined in the organizational, social, political and economic literature.[1] In the economic literature the interest in corporation-society relationships have been examined by both the institutionals, the radicals, and the social economists, who have put economic reality into its social and cultural context rather than reducing it to a study of maximizing behavior as advocated by conventional economics. This chapter examines the contribution of the institutionals, the radicals, and the social economists to an understanding of the corporate-society relationship and suggests and economic paradigm based on that contribution.

Institutionalism
INSTITUTIONALISM VERSUS CONVENTIONAL ECONOMICS

    In recent years conventional economics increasingly has been considered irrelevant to an understanding of the major problems of the real economic world. First, the "firm" of economic theory is no way comparable to the large corporation. R. M. Cyert and C. L. Hedrick go so far as to state that the firm of economic theory is "a nonexistent entity . . . None of the problems of real firms can find a home within this special construct."[2] Second, conventional economics as the "science of choice" or "science of efficiency" has too narrow a scope to deal with the pressing social and economic problems resulting from the interactions between real firms and their host environments. Gruchy describes the situation as follows:

While conventional economics has much to say about the economics of decision making in both the private and the public sectors, they have given much less attention to problems of greater concern to the public such as the technological and organizational revolutions and their impacts on the structure and functioning of the industrial system, the exercise of economic power by organized business and organized labor, the role of the large industrial corporation in the determination of deterioration and other social costs of continuous economic growth, and the growling gap between rich and poor nations.[3]

    As a result, conventional economics became the object of criticism for various economists, known as the institutionalists, who view conventional economics as irrelevant to the major issues of the times and as largely limited to the study of maximizing behavior. In the pre-

1935 period these institutionalists included Thorstein Veblen, J. R. Commons, W. C. Mitchell, J. R. Clark, A. G. Tugwell, and Gardiner C. Means. In the years since the close of World War II, they have included John Kenneth Galbraith, C. E. Ayres, Gunnar Myrdal, and Gerhard Cohn as the "neo-institutionalists" and Paul. A. Baran, Paul M. Sweezy, Harry Braverman, H. J. Sherman and A. G. Papandreou as the "radical insitutionalists."

NATURE OF INSTITUTIONALISM
In the pre-1939 period the institutionalism of Thorstein Veblen and others was basically a rejection of the Orthodox Marshallian economics that had dominated economic thought up to 1929. The institutionalists viewed economics as the study of the evolving complex of institutions concerned with meeting the material needs of mankind, and they relied on various social disciplines to interpret economic behavior. To justify this reliance, one of these institutionalists asserted that "unless they have been finally and authoritatively established in some writing which has escaped my notice, I feel free to contend that it is less important to keep inside any traditional limits than to follow our natural questionings wherever they may lead, and do whatever work we are especially fitted for and find undone."[4] The neo-institutionalists approached economic reality by putting it its social and cultural context. They extended the scope of economics as viewed by conventional economics by developing a theory of the industrial system that also included the market system rather than being restricted to the market system. In fact, they merely attempted to adapt and adjust conventional economics to the new economic and institutional realities faced by the modern world. With regard to society-corporation relationships, both old and neo-institutionalists analyze these relationships on the basis of historical or legal-political approaches and regard the corporate sector as one of the institutional categories to be included in the analysis. Preston clearly states their position as follows:
The distinguishing characteristic of the Institutionals is their attempt to deal with society and social processes on an aggregative or holistic basis and in terms of major historical and institutional categories, among which the corporate sector is an important, but not the single, object of interest. To repeat, the Institutionals begin at the *society* end of the corporation-society spectrum.[5]

While old and neo-institutionalists agree on the merit of some form of capitalist system, the radical institutionalists or Marxist economists reject all forms of capitalism as irrational or exploitative. They also criticize conventional or orthodox economics along the same lines used by the other institutionalists and differ from them by advocating a "whole new order." Orthodox economics is criticized because it is alleged to be too narrow to account for the artificial scarcity created by large firms and because of its concern for marginal analysis. Conventional economics is criticized because it takes consumer wants as given and disregards the contribution of the other social sciences.[6]

Institutionalism Prior to 1939
The period preceding World War II was a crucial period in the United States, marked by the new industrialization of the American economy, the movement of the frontier to the West Coast, and the resulting intense economic, political, and social strife. This atmosphere led to the emergence of academics bent on criticizing orthodox economics and developing an economics of dissent to be known as "institutional economics." This movement was inspired y the work of Thortstein Veblen and later institutionalists such as John R. Commons, Wesley C. Mitchell, and John M. Clark. In what follows the main contributions of these authors will be presented with an emphasis on corporation-society relationships.

THORSTEIN VEBLEN: EVOLUTIONARY ECONOMICS

Veblen is known as a moralist for his critiques of society and as a sociologist for his theories of socially induced motivations, of the social determinants of knowledge, and of social change, but above all he is known as an economist whose "institutional economics and meticulous anatomy of American high finance and business enterprise have earned him several generations of distinguished followers and a permanent niche among the greats of political economy."[7]

Veblen began by criticizing the doctrine of classic economics, replacing it by what he described as "evolutionary" or cultural" economics. Classic economics, by deriving economic behavior from utilitarian and hedonistic propensities, was seen by Veblen as abstract and unrealistic and only applicable to special historical and restricted contexts. He wrote derisively: "A gang of Aleutian Islanders, slashing about in the trade wind and surf with sails and magical incantations for the capture of shell-fish are held, in point of economic reality, to be engaged in a feat of hedonistic equilibration in rent, wages, and interest."[8]

In Veblen's opinion, the individual is not only rational, as advocated by classic economists of the times,[9] but, most importantly, driven by customs, something. . . . He is not simply a bundle of desires that are to be satiated . . . but rather a coherent structure of propensities and habits which seek realization and expression in an unfolding activity."[10] These activities of man give rise to institutions that develop over time to be used to organize and control individual and social behavior. "Evolutionary economics must be the theory of a cumulative sequence of economic institutions stated in terms of the process itself."[11] As a unit, the evolution of human society is seen by Veblen as "a process of natural selections of institutions."[12] " Institutions are not only themselves the result of a selective and adaptive process which shapes the prevailing and dominant types of spiritual attitudes and aptitudes; they are at the same time special methods of life and human relations."[13] Veblen divides these institutions into "serviceable" and "disserviceable" institutions. A good definition and implication of this dichotomy is this: "Serviceable institutions reflect workmanship and parental instincts or drives which leads to action that contributes to race survival. . . . Disserviceable institutions reflect man's predatory or acquisitive drive which, if uncontrolled by cultural arrangements, will elevate the individual over the community and undermine the life process."[14]

The idea of "serviceability" was pursued by Veblen to introduce concepts such as "trained incapacity," "business sabotage," "blameless cupidity," "conscientious withholding of efficiency," "collusive sobriety," or "sagacious restriction of output."[15]

With respect to the economic system, Veblen's objective is to bring about some form of "industrial democracy" geared toward the production of "economic values" and the enhancement of "human life on the whole."

JOHN R. COMMONS: COLLECTIVE ECONOMICS

Like Veblen, Commons criticized conventional economics and argued for evolutionary economics. Unlike Veblen, he gave organized sale and organized farms the role of countervailing groups to challenge the power of the large industrial corporations. In his *Institutional Economics* he argued for a "rounded-out theory of political economy" to replace conventional economics.[16] He then labeled his views "collective economics," which went beyond the production and technical economics of conventional economists to include cultural relations. To achieve a managed, harmonious equilibrium in the nation's economic activities,

Commons advocated the search for new institutions to eliminate aspects of "banker capitalism" and convert it to "reasonable capitalism." He argued that the most aggravating problem of the capitalist system of the day was the inability to secure full employment. He advocated a system of administrative sovereignty in the form of administrative agencies whose purpose is to supplement the private market system and intervene to ensure the safety of the public interest and assure the public that reasonable practices and values would prevail.[17] Commons' concept of collective economics also stresses the need to use the collective efforts of the nation for a best use of scarce resources. To accomplish this objective he argued for a considerable modification of the institutional framework of the private system that was favorably received in the years of the New Deal and led to the creation of various regulatory agencies aimed at resolving economic conflicts.

WESLEY C. MITCHELL: QUANTITATIVE ECONOMICS

Wesley C. Mitchell as a student of Veblen was also critical of the "analytical" or "marginalist" approaches of conventional economics and believed in a new form of evolutionary economics. Convinced that economics is a "science of human behavior," Mitchell argued for a sound and realistic theory of human behavior rather than the rationalistic and hedonistic psychological theory used by conventional economics.[18] He looked at human behavior as being influenced by social values and the various social and economic institutions.

Mitchell believed that economics has to be based on objective quantitative and statistical analysis of data to be considered a valid science. He was convinced, moreover, that the data should not be accumulated with a theory in mind but accumulated, analyzed, and made to produce conclusions as they themselves contained. In concluding a summary of the existing theories of business cycles in his 1913 *Business Cycles*, Mitchell wrote:

One seeking to understand the current ebb and flow of economic activity characteristic of the present day finds these numerous explanations suggestive and perplexing. All are plausible, but which is valid? None necessarily excludes all the others, but which is the most important? Each may account for certain phenomena; does any one account for all the phenomena? Or can these rival explanations be combined in such a fashion as to make a consistent theory which is wholly adequate? . . . It is by study of the facts which they purport to interpret that the theories must be tested.[19]

This led him to a quantitative study of business cycles and the conviction that some form of national planning was needed to prevent these business fluctuations and preserve the private enterprise system. He was, however, reluctant to determine the content of economic welfare that would be maximized by a planning program and preferred to leave such a task to the people. Mitchell was merely advocating some form of "planned capitalism."

JOHN MAURICE CLARK: SOCIAL ECONOMICS

John Maurice Clark was one of the great contributors to the theory of social cost. Contrary to the new economics of the times, as discussed in Alfred Marshall's *Principles of Economics* (1890) and John Bates Clark's *Essentials of Economic Theory* (1907),[20] Clark dismissed their views of social organization as essentially static and pointed out the existence of a wide discrepancy between social and business efficiency. In fact, Clark viewed economics as a theory of efficiency wherein social efficiency is concerned with the production of social values and private efficiency deals with the production of marketable values. Private efficiency elevates market values over social values, however. As a result, conflict rather than harmony prevails among social groups. Clark viewed social harmony as an important goal, which could be achieved only by the use of social intelligence and collaboration on the part of society's major economic interest groups. In Clark's view, this social harmony necessitates a new social responsibility:

> We have inherited an economics of irresponsibility. We are in an economy of control with which our intellectual inheritance fits but awkwardly. To make control really tolerable we need something more; something which is still in its infancy. We need an economics of responsibility, developed and embodied in our working business ethics.[21]

This concern for social harmony is most evident in J. M. Clark's interest in overhead costs, social costs, and social values. He urged that business assume responsibility for overhead costs, that is, those costs other than the variable costs of direct material and direct labor. In the same book, *Studies in the Economics of Overhead Costs*,[22] he exposed the major dilemma resulting from the conflict between social and private costs and the necessity of using a "social cost keeping" in order to first reveal the full costs of production by adding unpaid social costs to actual costs, and second, to make the "social organism" a reality.[23] Using his words, "this involves the devising of a system of social accounting that will work better than our present system of financial accounting."[24]

In his second work, *Preface to Social Economics*, Clark elaborates on the concept of social value: "the value to society of these utilities consumed by individuals, or the cost to society of these costs that individuals bear."[25] He mainly criticized the classical and neo-classical economic theories for their "assumption of contentment," where supply and demand tend to equalize and resources tend to be fully utilized. To this approach, he maintained that money demands and money expenses are only market phenomena and do not reflect anything of the social wants and social costs of a world "full of unpaid costs and unappropriated services."[26] The solution advocated would be the consideration of the net economic value of a given service as including both potentially exchangeable byproducts in the way of service or damage, valued at the price they would presumably command in exchange, and unmarketables measured by a standard devised from market prices.[27]

This interest in the concept of "social organism" creating social values through a "social cost keeping" led J. M. Clark to elaborate on the appropriate kind of economic systems compatible with his social ideas. For example, in *Economic Institutions and Human Welfare*, Clark saw no possibility for the laissez-faire and collectivist systems and rejected them as unfit for a "humane and democratically conceived society."[28] The total laissez-faire system was unfit because it was up to the market to take charge of what should be the community values, while total collectivism was judged undemocratic because of the possible manipulation by the government for its own end and the reduction of market concepts to accounting devices. In fact, the major reason for rejection of both systems ties in the idea that the balance between social and private cost should not be fixed but "is conceived as an evolutionary process of creative adaptation, operating in the area intermediate between total laissez faire and total collectivism."[29] That area is the so-called balanced economy, or mixed economy, where market forces and socially oriented forces interact for the benefit of social welfare. This system would also include a "social constitution for industry." This social constitution would be the basis of national economic planning geared to "eliminate undesirable fluctuations of industrial activity and to make reasonably free use of our powers of production to support an adequate standard of living, on a sound and enduring basis."[30]

As the above analysis shows, J. M. Clark's contribution to institutional economics and the corporate-society relationship is both original and extensive.[31]

REXFORD G. TUGWELL: EXPERIMENTAL ECONOMICS

Tugwell also disagreed with some of the abstract concepts of orthodox economics and presented economics as a realistic, experimental science. Experimentalism was considered necessary because of the failure of orthodox economics to produce results that count for social welfare and because of the growing popularity of the scientific method. He argues as follows:

The whole conception of science, then-and the modern world has gone over to science-is experimentalism. Scientists have learned to distrust premises and depend upon consequences. And in social science this is bound to involve social facts as they are to be observed in a going society. These facts are the consequences. Theory must have reference to them if it is to be useful.[32]

Because economics is a science, its growth and prestige lies then with experimentalism. In his *Industry's Coming of Age* (1927) Tugwell saw industry as mature and business in an adolescent stage, with conflict the result. The conflict was basically due to the drive on one side by industry for mass production, low unit costs of production, low prices, mass sales, and mass consumption and on the other side by business toward restricted output, high unit cost of production, high prices leading to surplus profits, restricted sales, and limited consumption. Tugwell attributed the conflict to the failure of "corporate coordination," the few hundred large corporations that dominated the economy. He maintained that these corporations protected themselves from economic instability by plowing profits back and using these surpluses to expand in an uncontrollable way. To eliminate this unfair situation, Tugwell called for some type of social control or social management program, to be accomplished by a fourth directive branch of government that would be independent of the executive, judicial, and legislative branches.[33] This branch would act as an advisory unit, setting a national economic policy for industry and agriculture to serve as a guide for economic reform.

GARDINER C. MEANS: ADMINISTRATIVE ECONOMICS

Gardiner C. Means, like most post-Veblenian institutionalists, centered his attention on the large industrial corporation. He observed the rise of corporate capitalism in which fewer and fewer nonfinancial firms received a greater portion of the profit of all nonfinancial firms and which changed the structure and functioning of the industrial system. These changes included the separation of ownership and control of corporate wealth, the distortion of the profit system since corporation profits went in large part not to the corporate managers but to the stockholders, the narrowing of the free market system as administered prices replaced free competitive prices, and the reduction of consumer control of the production process as large corporations came to manipulate demand by means of forceful advertising and salesmanship activities.[34] Faced with this corporate capitalism, Means argued that the large industrial corporation restricts production to maximize surplus profit rather than output or social utility. He maintained that these corporations stop producing when marginal unit cost equals marginal unit revenue, which creates a discrepancy between the industrial system's potential output and its actual total output.

To eliminate this situation and render the corporate absolutism and restriction of output innocuous so that corporate capitalism could serve the interests of the general public, Means pressed for overall national planning to provide economic coordination and guidance, supplementing the market mechanism by administrative governmental action. More specifically, he called for a national program planning to develop production-consumption patterns or a national economic budget. Interestingly, he viewed the action of the program to be directed solely at the large industrial corporations in the core sector and not to interfere with the plans of the smaller firms in the periphery of the economy, the rationale being that the smaller firms have no choice but to follow the path and the directions set by the large firms. The purpose of this national planning endeavor was to ensure optimal use of the nation's resources, which would be reached when "there would be no unemployment of men or machines. . . . The resources going into different uses would be in balance with each other and in relation to consumers' wants . . . and, finally, in doing any particular job, the minimum amount of resources could be used or consumed consistent with the job to be done."[35] Means also viewed national planning as a possible way of reconciling the points of view of all interest groups because it calls for a reconsideration of the relations between government and the major economic interest groups.[36]

Neo-Institutionalism
CLARENCE E. AYRES: INSTRUMENTAL ECONOMICS

Ayres wanted to replace orthodox or conventional economics with the institutional view. His main contribution to the field of economics was the technological or instrumental theory of value. He viewed economics from the point of view of a philosopher and replaced the idealism of orthodox economics by pragmatism or instrumentalism as a new philosophical foundation. Economics at the time was dominated by the assumed dualism between a disorderly actual economic system and a hypothetical, rational and orderly economic order. Instead, Ayres, inspired by the philosophy of John Dewey, viewed the life process of mankind as composed of two main features, the institutional and the technological, the institutional being concerned with the preservation of inherited beliefs, class distinctions, and status arrangements and the technological with tools, scientific knowledge, and experimentation.[37] Following Dewey, Ayres started by considering the life process of mankind. He states, "Doing-and-knowing, science-and-technology is the real life process of mankind. This is the process from which modern industrial civilization has resulted, and it is the process in terms of which en have always judged things good and bad, and actions right and wrong."[38]

This led Ayres to view economics as a cultural process shaped by forces independent of individuals (mainly technology). American capitalism as part of Western culture is then a part of a cultural process going through phases. It is perceived by Ayres as a combination of two economies, a "price economy" and an "industrial economy" concerned with science and and the tools and skills necessary for the production of goods and services. Ayres viewed the industrial economy as more important and the true creative force in the economy.[39] The two economies result in two concepts of value: price and technological values. The price value is a measure of exchange established by the market price. Ayres judged price values as "unreal," "ceremonial," "fancied," or "pseudo-values." He explains as follows: "Prices do not measure real values but only quantify the judgments of people made antecedent to their price transactions. Whether the judgments are wise or foolish is determined not only by the pricing mechanism but by their relation to the technological life stream."[40]

Technological values, on the other and, are determined by science and technology and contribute to the general welfare. He explains, "For every individual and for the community the criterion of value is the continuation of the life process-keeping the machines running."[41] Technological values include economic abundance, equality, freedom, security, and excellence. Ayres proposed to substitute technological values for price values.

Ayres saw a lot of deficiencies in the American economic system.[42] The worst deficiency was the maldistribution of income creating "the paradox of industry potency and social impotence."[43] Were this maldistribution of income eliminated, Ayres predicted the creation of economic abundance and the establishment of a society of excellence.[44] To accomplish this goal, Ayres, like most other institutional economists, advocated economic planning, especially as a way of dealing with the problems of institutional maladjustments:

It is this kind of problem-problems resulting from institutional obstruction-that gives rise to economic planning. The overall problem of economic planning is one of institutional adjustment.
The progress of science and the industrial arts is continually altering the physical patterns of social life as to produce situations contrary to the institutional [ceremonial] practices of the community.[45]

With economic planning, Ayres also advocated a form of guaranteed minimum income plan to be financed by the progressive, personal, and corporate income taxes: "We favor the Welfare State because it tends to give the whole community what the whole community creates, and in doing so gives the community the greatest possible encouragement to create more, so that all of us taken together will be better off than anybody has ever been before." Beyond this Welfare State, Ayres promises a Creative State with its "happy, healthy, . . . well informed . . . [and] superbly productive community."[46]

JOHN KENNETH GALBRAITH: ECONOMICS OF AFFLUENCE

Galbraith, like most other institutionalists, views the economic world as a dynamic evolving process, constantly changing. The change is motivated by technology, which has "an initiative of its own." Technology determines the type of institution and economic and social evolution, forcing man to make necessary adjustments. For example, he states:
It is part of the vanity of the modern man that he can decide the character of his economic system. His area of decision is, in fact, exceedingly small. He could, conceivably, decide whether or not he wishes to have a high level of industrialization. Thereafter the imperatives of organization, technology, and planning operate similarly, and we have seen to a broadly similar result, on all societies. Given the decision to have modern industry, much of what happens is inevitable and the same [in all advanced societies].[47]

Galbraith also views man as a creature of habit, resistant to change and open only to the "conventional wisdom" of the times. While the circumstances of the economic world are changing, man resists as a victim of a cultural lag and by a "system of illusions." Galbraith states that "circumstance has marched far beyond the conventional wisdom,"[48] and urges the creation of an "unconventional wisdom" more in line with the changing technology.

Galbraith interpreted the course of American capitalism going from a "market economy of the 1900s" to an "organized economy" or "direct" or "guided" capitalism of the 1970s, after flirting with welfare capitalism in the 1930s. Galbraith views the guided capitalism as the era of the large corporations, which shift the allocation of resources from the public to the private sector. Basically, the large industrial corporations in the era of guided capitalism see to it that economic resources are poured abundantly into the private sector and only sparsely into the public sector.[49]

These large corporations, comprising the core of the modern economy, are managed by men of diverse talents and background, whom Galbraith labeled the "technostructure." He elaborates:
It extends from the leadership of the modern industrial enterprise down to just short of the labor force and embraces a large number of people and a large variety of talent. It is on the effectiveness of this organization . . . that the success of the modern enterprise now depends.[50]

Galbraith maintained that these large corporations are not controlled by the market. They set prices through informal price arrangements, such as price leadership. They generate consumer demand for their products through various sales methods. They keep stockholders satisfied through the distribution of an adequate dividend. They secured industrial cooperation with the union using the threat of substituting white collar workers and machines for blue collar workers. They also have through industrial planning replaced the free market mechanism.[51]

A first consequence of the rise of the large mature corporations and the shift of economic power to the technostructure is that the consumers became "the mentally indentured servants of the industrial system."[52]

A second consequence is the lack of balance between private goods and public goods: "an atmosphere of private opulence and public squalor."[53] Consequently, "the family which takes it mauve and cerise, air-conditioned, power-steered, and power-braked automobile out for a tour passes through cities that are badly paved, made hideous by litter, blighted buildings, billboards, and posts for wires that should have long since been put underground. They pass on into a countryside that has been rendered largely invisible commercial art."[54]

To correct this situation, Galbraith advocates a *countervailing power* to protect the public from the described exploitation.[55] This countervailing power is only possible, however, in periods of slack demand, when the holders of the "original market power" are willing to share monopoly gains. It is therefore necessary for the state to intervene through social control and social planning to provide a "framework of order." Such intervention, through planning, would secure a balance between private and public goods and achieve a "society of excellence."

GERHARD COHN: ECONOMICS OF NATIONAL PROGRAMMING

Cohn's main thesis is that the American economic concept is too complex and should be complemented by a clear identification of economic national priorities and their achievement with the aid of national economic budget projections.

Cohn had a pluralistic view of the American economy. As he put it, "The United States now seems to be approaching a situation in which neither business, labor, farmers, nor government has disproportionate influence. Each sector is vigorous, dynamic, and powerful, but each recognizes that it will be curbed if its actions adversely affect the general welfare."[56] This pluralistic view is used to support the monitoring of the economy with the aid of national economic programming. Cohn also used the Employment Act of 1946 to argue for planning since the act calls for setting up national goals and determining how to achieve them.[57]

The implementation of Cohn's national programming is through the national economic budget, defined as "a tool of quantitative theoretical analysis" used to express economic policies.[58] Cohn was in favor of some form of indicative planning similar to the one in France, Japan, and some of the Scandinavian countries. He claimed that it would eventually correct the two main imbalances: the imbalance between the public and private sectors; and the imbalance within the private sector between private consumption and business investment. As he put it, the government must have "the strength and skills to deal with any dangerous imbalances in the domestic economy that cannot be corrected without government action."[59] Cohn's objective is still the success of the free enterprise system, made possible by the government's intervention through national economic programming as a supplement to the private market economy. National economic planning is seen as a culmination of goal setting and priority analysis, which may lead to a shift of the scope of economics from an "economics of private priorities" to an "economics of national priorities."

Radical Economics

Radical economics is geared to the critique of contemporary capitalism and to the establishment of a whole new order is assumed to be devoid of the exploitation and internal contradictions of capitalism. Radical economists perceive the existing economic system as hopelessly infected with a number of evils, "to such an extent that no part of it can be extracted which is not contaminated."[60] These evils are generally perceived to be the following:

A. Unequal distribution of income, wealth, and power within individual countries-too much to the wealthy minority, too little to the poor majority. . . .
B. Maldistribution of resources within individual countries- too much to private gods consumed by the upper and middle classes, and to military goods required by the war machine, too little to public goods and services, usable by the poor as routes to equalization of income and wealth. . . .
C. As another aspect of misallocation, the ignoring of the set of social costs (externalities) involved in the term "quality of life" –pollution, alienation, over-population, and resource exhaustion. . . .
D. Failure to eliminate or greatly mollify militarism or racial discrimination.
E. On the international scene, maintenance of prosperity for favored industrial, agricultural, and labor blocs in the advanced countries by measures which forestall desirable development- or slow down any development at all in the less advanced countries.
F. Regarding establishment economics and the other social sciences the charge is obscuring the five issues immediately above.
G. As for economics specifically, the charge is fostering an erroneous "one-dimensional" view of human nature as producing, consuming and making more. In other words, it obscures the most important aspects of "what man is all about."[61]

Radical economics rejects conventional economics and takes most of its material from Marxism. Most of its concern is the problems of inequality and maldistribution and a criticism of contemporary analysis. The most noticeable and important critiques are presented by Braverman, Baran and Sweezy, and Papandreou.[62] In what follows, their works are presented with an emphasis on the corporate society relationships.

PAUL A. BARAN AND PAUL N. SWEEZY: MONOPOLY CAPITAL

Monopoly Capital is an attempt to extend Marx's model of competitive capitalism to the new conditions of monopoly capitalism. In fact, Lenin also based his theory of imperialism on the predominance of monopoly in the developed countries. *Monopoly Capital* is organized and centered around a central theme: *the generation and absorption of surplus under conditions of monopoly capitalism*. The model presented maintains that first the growth of monopoly generates a strong tendency for surplus to rise without a the same time providing adequate mechanisms of surplus absorption and second the surplus that is not absorbed is also a surplus that is not produced, with the consequence that "it is merely potential surplus, and it leaves its statistical trace not in the figures of profits and investment but rather in the figures of unemployment and unutilized productive capacity."[63] This economic surplus is defined as the difference between what a society provides and the cost of producing it.[64]

Baran and Sweezy examine first the giant corporations as the central element of monopoly capitalism. These corporations are shown as profit maximizers and capital accumulators, managed by company men whose fortunes are tied to the corporation's success or failure. They are also perceived as price makers, establishing prices such as to maximize the profits of the group of sellers as a whole. And where a major branch of the economy is experiencing abnormally low profits, it is the state's responsibility under monopoly capitalism to ensure that the deviant industries are brought to the level of the giant corporations.[65] Baran and Sweezy accept the thesis that the monopoly capitalist economy generates impulses to innovation and a downward trend of production costs. This reduction of costs leads to widening profit margins, which lead to an absolute and relative rise of the economy surplus. They conclude, however, that monopoly capitalism is a self-contradictory system: it tends to generate ever more surplus, yet fails to provide the consumption and investment outlets required for its absorption.

One way to absorb this surplus, directly or indirectly, is to use the "sales effort." They maintain that advertising became a vital tool of the corporate world, leading to an ensuring of profit maximization and a protection of monopolistic positions. On equal footing with the sales effort, the absorption of surplus is assumed to take place in the diversion of resources into what is labeled in the national economic accounts as finance, insurance and real estate. This form of surplus absorption is considered characteristic of capitalism in general, and a monopoly capitalism in particular.

Marx alluded to the creation of this new class: "It produces a new financial aristocracy, a new variety of parasites in the shape of promoters, speculators, and merely nominal directors; a whole new system of swindling and cheating by means of corporation promotion, stock issuance, and stock speculation."[66] Baran and Sweezy, for their part, alluded to the social costs created for the maintenance of such a system:

> Just as advertising, production differentiation, artificial obsolescense, model changing, and all the other devices of the sales effort do in fact promote and increase sales, and thus act as indispensable props to the level of income and employment, so that the entire apparatus of "finance, insurance, and real estate" is essential to the normal functioning of the corporate system and another no less indispensable prop to the level of income and employment. The prodigious volume of resources absorbed in all these activities does in fact constitute necessary costs of capitalist production. What should be crystal clear is that an economic system in which *such* costs are socially necessary has long ceased to be a socially necessary economic system.[67]

HARRY BRAVERMAN: LABOR AND MONOPOLY CAPITAL

Braverman's analysis covers the degradation of work in the twentieth century. It was one of the first attempts to rewrite volume one of Marx's *Capital* in the light of a century of development in both Marxism and capitalism. Braverman offers a description of monopoly capitalism through an examination of the labor process. He states that, in the process of studying occupational shifts, he discovered a contradiction between a thesis that maintained that modern work required higher levels of education, training, mental effort, and so forth . . . and another thesis that maintained that work was subdivided into petty tasks, petty operations that are mundane, alienating, and so on. Incapable of reconciling the two theses, he studied the evolution of the labor processes within occupations as well as between them, and this led him to stress the evolution of management and technology and of the modern corporation as well as of social structure. The analysis resulted in a thesis of the degradation of work and the commodification of life in general in the twentieth century, which he attributes to the domination of capital. This view evolved along the following main themes.

1. Having being forced to sell their labor powers to another, the workers also abandon their interest in the labor process, which has become alienating.[68]
2. Monopoly capitalism rests on the manufacturing division of labor, which has also remained the fundamental principle of industrial organization. This division of is carried to a step where the operations not only are separated from each other but also are assigned to different workers.[69]
3. As a result of the extreme division of labor, work under monopoly capitalism becomes fractionalized into meaningless tasks, and, moreover, market forces invade all areas of life turning relations among people into relations among things. As a consequence labor is cheapened.[70]
4. Skill is expropriated from the craft worker and transferred to the owners of capital. As a result, not only are mental and manual labor systematically divided but there is also a systematic separation of conception and execution.[71]
5. The workers are *habituated* to the situation and their natural resistance intensified by a swift changing of technology, antagonistic social relations, and the succession of generations become the subject of

study by scholars of industrial psychology and industrial physiology aimed at finding perfect methods of selecting, training, and motivating workers. These schools are viewed as indifferent to the crucial problem of the degradation of men and women. Braverman states:

The cardinal feature of these various schools and the currents within these is that, unlike the scientific management movement, they do not by and large concern themselves with the organization of work, but rather with the conditions under which the worker may best be brought to cooperate in the scheme of work organized by the industrial engineer. The evolving work processes of capitalist society are taken by these schools as inexorably given, and are accepted as "necessary and inevitable" in any form of "industrial society." The problems addressed are the problems of management: dissatisfaction as expressed in high turnover rates, absenteeism, resistance to the prescribed work space, indifference, neglect, cooperative group restriction on output, and overt hostility to management. As it presents itself to most of the sociologists and psychologists concerned with a study of work and workers, the problem is not that of degradation of men and women, but the difficulties raised by the reactions, conscious or unconscious, to that of degradation.[72]

6. The labor process is transformed by the scientific technical revolution by being displaced to other occupations and industries or adapted to the machinery of production in the form of standardized motion patterns. Mechanization becomes dictated by the effort to increase the productivity of labor or to eliminate it.

Social Economics

Social economics may be characterized by an active concern for current socio-economic problems, namely inflation, unemployment, and the inequitable distribution of income identified with the private sector of the economy. In fact, social economists would reject outright the marketplace role as arbiter of social values and seek to help define and develop those social values. R. P. Cochran states the role of social economics as follows:

A reconstructed social economics would then have as its guiding principle the belief that economic theory is concentrated thought and analysis directed toward ameliorating contemporary social economic problems. It is not merely the deduction of inevitable conclusions from given premises, but the finding of acceptable and meaningful alternatives to contemporary conditions.[73]

Social economics is the study of the social causes and consequences of economic activity. Its technique rests on an integration of social and economic values to ensure that economic decision making is more responsive to, and integrated with, social aims and humanitarian values.[74] Its focus is upon the underlying historical and institutional process governing an aspect of economic behavior. J. A. Stanfield emphasized this point: "The philosophical bent of social economics is to seek out the meaning and purpose of human behavior and to throw in sharp evaluative relief the current pattern of that behavior."[75] Social economics attempt to integrate economic criteria and social values into policy making.[76] This is evident in the two objectives assigned to it: "(1) maximizing human satisfaction, while (2) minimizing the disturbance to the earth and to humanity."[77]

As a result, social economists seek to set their theories within the existing social and economic context. Their methodological approach tends to be "holistic, ameliorative, and value directed."[78] Their subject matter consists of most of the social areas social economics purports to address, which may include anything of concern to society. R. J. Stephens identifies some of these areas as follows:

(i) The determinants of social value within a community, their formation and aggregation, both from individual values and the component parts of the social welfare function;
(ii) The evolution of the existing social and economic institutions within each society, the basis of their formation and change;
(iii) The determination of equity in income and wealth distribution as well as equity in economic and social access to opportunity and rights;

(iv) Concern for the disadvantaged; the causes and cures of poverty and hardship resulting from either short-term changes in income and expenditure or the poverty cycle;

(vi) Matters of environmental policy such as pollution controls, preservation of environmental standards and the use of nonrenewable resources.[79]

Conclusion

Corporation-society relationships are governed by the economic principles espoused by the government and the nation. These same principles determine the role of the corporation in society and define the scope and nature of its activities. The continuum of economic principles ranges from one extreme known as libertarianism to another extreme known as the new left or radical economics. In between views include both the institutionals and the social economists.

Libertarianism is more of a philosophy than a system of economic thought. To libertarians the market rather than any regulatory body is the ultimate judge and guarantee of freedom; they are basically advocates of a total economic laissez faire. Consider the following comments by one outspoken libertarian:

The central idea of libertarianism is that people should be permitted to run their own lives as they wish. We totally reject the idea that people must be forcibly protected from themselves. A libertarian society would have no laws against drugs, gambling, pornography-and no compulsory seat belts in cars. We also reject the idea that people have an enforceable claim on others, for anything more than being left alone.[80]

Needless to say, the provision of some necessary public goods, the presence of externalities, and various instances of market failure make the libertarian philosophy either impractical and/or unfair.

On the other extreme of the continuum, the radical economists are highly critical of contemporary capitalism and the role of the market as arbiter of social values. To use their rhetoric, the radical economists are for a total expropriation of the capitalist class and turning over the ownership of capital goods and land to all people. Unlike the Marxists, however, they advocate a decentralized and participatory system in which workers have a say in the running or corporations. Like the libertarians, the radical economists' positions call for an extreme stance which has been proven to hinder individual initiative.

In between the libertarians and the radical economists we find the institutionalists and the social economists. The social economists may be identified by their deep commitment to human welfare and social justice. The institutionalists may be identified by their commitment to pragmatism and reliance on empirical observation and inductive logic as a way of analyzing economic problems. Both the social economists and the institutionalists show an interest and concern for the social organization and its environment. They work at the social level of generalization to analyze social organization and processes and avoid the use to atomistic analytical units compatible with conventional micro-economics.

Lewis E. Hill called for a synthesis of social and institutional economics:

On the one hand, the main strength of social economics lies in a unique set of metaphysically based and welfare oriented objectives and goals. On the other hand, the main strength of institutional economics lies in a creative pragmatic philosophy and methodology for the economic science. It follows that both schools of economic thought could be strengthened by a synthesis which would merge the goals and objectives of social economics with the pragmatics and methodology of institutional economics.[81]

Such a synthesis would serve to improve corporation-society relationships in a manner beneficial to both. *The economic paradigm governing the relationships of corporation and society need not be the role or importance of the market and/or the state as in libertarianism or radical economics but a clear statement of national and social goals based on commitment to human welfare and social justice and experimentation with institutional arrangements to solve economic and social problems*. This synthesis of social and institutional economics is as the heart and within the spirit of socio-economics and public policy as defined in this book.

Notes
1. Lee E. Preston, "Corporation and Society: The Search for a Paradigm," *Journal of Economic Literature* (June 1975): 434-453.
2. R. M. Cyert and C. L. Hendrick, "Theory of the Firm: Past, Present, and Future: An Interpretation," *Journal of Economic Literature* (June 1972): 398.
3. Allan G. Gruchy, *Contemporary Economic Thought* (Clifton, N. J.: Augustus M. Kelley, 1972), p. v.
4. John M. Clark, "Toward a Concept of Social Value," *Preface to Social Economics* (New York: Farrar and Rinehart, 1936), p. 65.
5. Preston, "Corporation and Society," p. 438.
6. Gruchy, *Contemporary Economic Thought*, p. viii.
7. Lewis A. Coser, *Masters of Sociological Thought* (New York: Harcourt Brace Jovanovich, 1977), p. 263.
8. Max Lerner, ed., *The Portable Veblen* (New York: Viking Press, 1948), p. 20.
9. Alfred Marshall, *Principles of Economics* (1890), (Publisher and city are not available.)
10. Lerner, *Portable Veblen*, p. 233.
11. Ibid., p. 236.
12. Thorstein Veblen, *The Theory of the Leisure Class* (New York: Modern Library, 1934), p. 188.
13. Ibid.
14. Gruchy, *Contemporary Economic Thought*, p. 20.
15. Veblen introduced other interesting words; for example, "the instinct of workmanship," "the parental bent," and "the instinct of idle curiosity" are some of the concepts used to explain the concern for a job well done, the solicitude for one's offspring, and the motive force for scientific curiosity.
16. John R. Commons, *Institutional Economics* (New York: Macmillan, 1919), p. 6.
17. Gruchy, *Contemporary Economic Thought*, pp. 38-39.
18. Wesley C. Mitchell, "The Prospects of Economics," in R. G. Tugwell, ed., *The Trend of Economics* (New York: Knopf, 1924), p. 25.
19. Wesley C. Mitchell, *Business Cycles* (Berkeley: University of California Press, 1913), p. 19.
20. John Bates Clark is J. M. Clark's father.
21. J. M. Clark, *Preface to Social Economics* (New York: Farrar and Rinehart, 1967), p. 67.
22. J. M. Clark, *Studies in the Economics of Overhead Costs* (Chicago: University of Chicago Press, 1923).
23. Ibid., p. 403.
24. Ibid., p. 31.
25. Clark, *Preface to Social Economics*, p. 49.
26. Ibid., p. 45.
27. Ibid., p. 49.
28. J. M. Clark, *Economic Institutions and Human Welfare* (New York: Knopf, 1957), p. 6.
29. Ibid.
30. J. M. Clark, "Economics and the National Recovery Administration," *The American Economic Review* (March 1939): 23.

31. Gruchy, *Contemporary Economic Thought*, pp. 62-63.
32. Rexford G. Tugwell, "Experimental Economics," in R. G. Tugwell, ed., *The Trend of Economics* (New York: Knopf, 1924), p. 395.
33. Rexford G. Tugwell, "The Fourth Power," *Planning and Civic Comment,*, pt. 2 (April-June 1939): 10.
34. Gruchy, *Contemporary Economic Thought*, p. 71.
35. National Resources Planning Board, "Towards Full Use of Resources," *The Structure of the American Economy*, pt. 2. (June 1940): 5.
36. Gruchy, *Contemporary Economic Thought*, p. 76.
37. John Dewey, *Reconstruction in Philosophy* (New York: Henry Holt, 1920), p. 26.
38. C. E. Ayres, *Toward a Reasonable Society* (Austin: University of Texas Press, 1961), p. 15.
39. C. E. Ayres, *The Industrial Economy: Its Technological Basis and Institutional Destiny* (Boston: Houghton Mifflin, 1952), p. 1.
40. C. E. Ayres, *The Theory of Economic Progress* (Chapel Hill: University of North Carolina Press, 1944), p. 227.
41. Ibid., p. 230.
42. C. E. Ayres, *The Problem of Economic Order* (New York: Farrar and Rinehart, 1938).
43. Ibid., p. 81.
44. C. E. Ayres, *The Divine Right of Capital* (Boston: Houghton Mifflin, 1946), p. 30.
45. Ayres, *The Industrial Economy*, p. 192.
46. C. E. Ayres, "Ideological Responsibility," *Journal of Economic Issues* 1 (June 1967), p. 396.
47. John K. Galbraith, *The New Industrial State* (Boston: Houghton Mifflin, 1967), p. 396.
48. John K. Galbraith, *The Affluent Society* (Boston: Houghton Mifflin, 1958), p. 268.
49. Gruchy, *Contemporary Economic Thought*, p. 140.
50. Galbraith, *The New Industrial State*, p. 59.
51. Ibid.
52. Galbraith, *The New Industrial State*, p. 67.
53. Galbraith, *The Affluent Society*, p. 199.
54. Ibid.
55. John K. Galbraith, *American Capitalism: The Concept or Countervailing Power*, 2d ed. (Boston: Houghton Mifflin, 1956), p. 137.
56. G. Cohn and T. Geiger, with the assistance of Manuel Helzner, *The Economy of the American People*, Planning Pamphlet no. 102 (Washington, D. C.: National Planning Association, 1958), p. 106.
57. Gerhard Cohn, "Economic Planning in the United States," *Zeitschrift des Instituts fur Weltwirtschaft* (Hamburg: Weltwirtschaftliches, 1964), p. 40.
58. G. Cohn, "The Nation's Economic Budget: A Tool of Full Employment Policy," in *Studies in Income and Wealth, Conference on Research in Income and Wealth*, vol. 10 (New York: National Bureau of Economic Research, 1947), p. 247.
59. National Planning Association, *Long-Range Projections for Economic Growth: The American Economy in 1970,* Planning Pamphlet no. 107 (Washington, D.C.: NPA, October 1959), p. 11.
60. David Braybooke, "Marcuse's Merits," *Trans-Action* (October 1969): 53.
61. Martin Bronfenbrenner, "Radical Economics in America: A 1970 Survey," *Journal of Economic Literature* (September 1970): 749-750.

62. Harry Braverman, *Labor and Monopoly Capital* (New York: Monthly Review Press, 1974). Paul A. Baran and Paul M. Sweezy, *Monopoly Capital* (New York: Modern Reader Paperbacks, 1966). A. G. Papandreou, *Paternalistic Competition* (Minneapolis: University of Minnesota Press, 1972).
63. Baran and Sweezy, *Monopoly Capital*, p. 218.
64. Ibid., pp. 10-11.
65. Ibid., p. 66.
66. Karl Marx, *Capital*, vol. 3, ch. 27.
67. Baran and Sweezy, *Monopoly Capital*, p. 141.
68. Braverman, *Labor and Monopoly Capital*, p. 58.
69. Ibid., p. 77.
70. Ibid., p. 77.
71. Ibid., p. 118.
72. Ibid., p. 141.
73. Kendall P. Cochran, "Why a Social Economics?" *Review of Social Economy* 3 (1981): 131.
74. Brian Showler, "Social Economics: A Branch or New Roots?" *International Journal of Social Economics* 1, no. 1 (1974): 11.
75. J. Ron Stanfield, "Social Economics: A Place in the Sun," *International Journal of Social Economics* 5, no. 2 (1978): 117.
76. Brian Showler, "The Need for Social Economics," in B. Pettman, ed., *Social Economics: Concepts and Perspectives* (New York: Bradford MCB Books, 1977), p. 40.
77. A. Bendaird-Val, " Social Economics: An Innovative Practical Approach," in Pettman, *Social Economics*, p. 65.
78. W. M. Dugger, "Social Economics: One Perspective," *Review of social Economy* 35, no. 3 (December 1977): 299.
79. R. J. Stephens, "Socio-Economics: A Budding Research Programme?" *International Journal of Social Economics* 8, no. 3 (1978).
80. David Friedman, *Te Machinery of Freedom* (New York: Harper & Row, 1973), p. xiii.
81. Lewis E. Hill, "Social and Institutional Economics: Toward a Creative Synthesis," *Review for Social Economy* 3 (1981): 321-322.

Bibliography
INSTITUTIONALISM PRIOR TO 1939
Burns, Arthur F., *Wesley C. Mitchell: The Economic Scientist*. New York: National Bureau of Economic Research, 1952.
Clark, John M. *Preface to Social Economics*. New York: Farrar and Rinehart, 1936.
---. *Studies in the Economics of Overhead Costs*. Chicago: University of Chicago Press, 1923.
---. "Toward a Concept of Workable Competition." *American Economic Review* 30 (June 1940).
Commons, John R. *Institutional Economics*. New York: Macmillan, 1919.
Friedman, Milton. "Wesley C. Mitchell as an Economic Theorist." *Journal of Political Economy* (December 1950).
Kuznets, Simon. *Institutional Economics: Veblen, Commons and Mitchell Reconsidered*. Berkeley: University of California Press, 1963.
Preston, Lee E. "Corporation and Society: The Search for a Paradigm." *Journal of Economic Literature* (June 1975): 434-453.
Tugwell, Rexford G., ed. *The Trend of Economics*. New York: Knopf, 1924.

Veblen, Thorstein. *The Theory of the Leisure Class*. New York: Macmillan, 1912.
Watkins, Myron W. "Veblen View of Cultural Evolution." In Douglas F. Dowd, ed., *Thorstein Veblen: A Critical Appraisal*. Ithaca: Cornell University Press. 1958.

NEO-INSTITUTIONALISM
Ayres, Clarence E. *The Divine Right of Capital*. Boston: Houghton Mifflin, 1946.
---. "Ideological Responsibility." *Journal of Economic Issues* 1 (June 1967).
---. *Toward a Reasonable Society*. Austin: University of Texas Press, 1961.
Cohn, Gerhard. "Economic Planning in the United States." In *Zeitschrift des Instituts fur Weltwirtshaft*. Hamburg: Weltwirtschaftliches, 1964.
---. *Essays in Public Finance and Fiscal Policy*. New York: Oxford University Press, 1955.
Galbraith, John K. *The Affluent Society*. Boston: Houghton Mifflin, 1958.
---. *American Capitalism: The Concept of Countervailing Power*. 2d ed. Boston: Houghton Mifflin, 1956.
---. *The Liberal Hour*. Boston: Houghton Mifflin, 1960.
---. *The New Industrial State*. Boston: Houghton Mifflin, 1967.
Gottlieb, Manuel. "Clarence E. Ayres and a Larger Economic Theory," *South-western Social Science Quarterly* 41, (June 1960).
Gruchy, Allan G. "Neo-Institutionalism and the Economics of Dissent." *Journal of Economic Issues* 1 (March 1969).
Knapp, K. William. "In Defense of Institutional Economics." *Swedish Journal of Economics* 70 (1968).

RADICAL ECONOMICS
Baran, Paul A. *Political Economy of Growth*. New York: Monthly Review Press, 1957.
---. And P. M. Sweezy. *Monopoly Capital*. New York: Modern Reader Paperbacks, 1966.
Bronfenbrenner, Martin. "Radical Economics in America: A 1970 Survey." *Journal of Economic Literature* (September 1970): 747-766.
Horowitz, David, ed. *Marx and Modern Economics*. New York: Monthly Review Press, 1968.
Huberman, Leo, and P. M. Sweezy, *Introduction to Socialism*. New York: Monthly Review Press, 1968.
Mintz, M., and J. S. Cohen. *America Incorporated*. New York: Dial, 1971.
Papandreou, A. G. *Paternalistic Competition*. Minneapolis: University of Minnesota Press, 1972.
Tanzer, M. *The Sick Society*. New York: Holt, Rinehart and Winston, 1971.

SOCIAL ECONOMICS
Bendaird-Val, A. "Social Economics: An Innovative Practical Approach." *International Journal of Social Economics* 2, no. 3 (1975): 146-171. Reprinted in *Social Economics*.
Davison, R. B. "Social Economics Further Considered." *International Journal of Social Economics* 1, no. 3 (1974): 204-212.
Dugger, W. M. "Social Economics: One Perspective." *Review of Social Economy* 35, no. 3. (December 1977).
Pettman, B. *Social Economics: Concepts and Perspective*. New York: Bradford MCB Books, 1977.
Rohrlich, George F. *Social Economics: Concepts and Perspectives*. Monograph, no. 2. Pratington, United Kingdom: Emmasglen, 1974.

Showler, Brian. "Social Economics: A Branch or New Roots?" *International Journal of Social Economics* 1, no. 1 (1974): 4-12.
Stanfield, J. Ron. "Social Economics: A Place in the Sun," *International Journal of Social Economics* 5, no. 2 (1978): 112-123.
Stephens, R. J., "Socio-Economics: A Budding Research Programme?" *International Journal of Social Economics* 8, no. 3 (1978): 3-25.
Wieser, Von, F. *Social Economics*. Translated by A. Ford Henrich, Fairfield, J.J.: Augustus M. Kelly, 1967.

Appendix 2.A.
Welfare Economics and the Economic Paradigm

Welfare economics aims to evaluate the desirability of alternative economic states with the objective of ascertaining where markets perform well and where they fail. With Adam and Eve had different allocations of apples and fig leaves, the allocation which makes one of them better off without making the other worse off is known as PARETO EFFICIENT. The curve linking all the pareto efficient points is the contract curve. Welfare economics implies that a) under certain conditions pareto efficient outcomes can result from competitive market mechanisms, and b) the same pareto efficient outcomes can result from people freely trading with each other once a mutable assignment of initial enclosements is made.

However, in defense of our economic paradigm, it can be stated that a) an inefficient allocation on the basis of equity or some other criterion may be desired calling for some form of government intervention, and b) market failure, occurring in the presence of market power or nonexistence of markets is another incentive for government intervention.

Appendix 2.B.
Externalities and the Economic Paradigm

The activities in the market place affect the welfare of others. No market failure is obtained if prices are used for the transmission of the effects. A market failure and economic efficiency is created when the effects are outside the market mechanism and are labeled as EXTERNALITIES. The externality is generally the result of the absence of property rights in the resources used, or in the case where the resources are owned in common. Government intervention may be required. However, 16 COASE Theorem implies that once property rights are established, the government intervention is not necessary. Given the difficulties of assigning property rights to common resources the following solutions have been proposed as a way of "INTERNALIZING" the externality:

1¶ Individuals involved in the externality (like for example a polluter and a pollutee) are asked to merge.
2¶ A PIGOUVIAN base may be levied on pollution equal to the marginal social damage at the efficient level, giving the producer a private incentive to pollute the efficient amount.
3¶ A subsidy is offered to polluter to pollute at the efficient level, even though it looks as less of an ethical way of dealing with the problem.
4¶ The government can create a market for pollution rights
5¶ The government can correct the problem through regulation. Environment legislation is a good example as in the US Clean Air Act.

Thus in conformity with the economic paradigm espoused in this chapter a condition of market and government intervention are required to deal with the negative externality problem. Positive externalities can also be encouraged by government intervention in such forms as subsidies, loans, and grants.

3
THE CORPORATE-SOCIETY RELATIONSHIP: TOWARD A RECTIFICATION PARADIGM

We live in a time when there are increasing tensions about the nature of the social contract, the inadequate provision of public goods, economic inequality, and social injustice. Because the corporation is an active market and social agent, its activities can either worsen or correct some of these problems. Thus the relationships of the corporation with society are by definition affected by its role in dealing with the sources of those tensions. The potions open to the corporation are on a continuum ranging from complete indifference to taking an active role in rectifying some of these social problems. Complete indifference would definitely be harmful to the long-term interests of the firm. Involvement in some forms of rectification is a way of ensuring mutual acceptance by society and a role in securing social order and affluence.

Accordingly, the purpose of this chapter is to suggest a rectification paradigm to motivate and/or explain the corporation's role in reducing social tensions. Before introducing the paradigm, the various views on the social contract, general welfare, social equality, and social justice will be presented to clarify some of the alternative options presented in the related literature, integrating political, moral, economic, and legal philosophy.

Historical and Philosophical Concepts of Social Welfare
THE SOCIAL CONTRACT

The theory of the social contract rests on two fundamental ideas, or values, "the value of liberty, or the idea that will, not force is the basis of government, and the value of justice, or the idea that right, not might, is the basis of all political society and of every system of political order."[1] It started mainly in the Middle Ages, an age of religious struggles, and was used by a minority to justify their resistance to any groups imposing the religion of the majority. It prospered and found its best expression with the publication of Hobbes' *Leviathan* in 1651 and of Rousseau's *Du contrat social* in 1762 and is basically an unwritten agreement among the members of a society to act with reciprocal responsibility in their relationships under the governance of the state. It assumes a societal consensus on what is or is not desirable, i.e., an interest in social welfare. Major exponents of the idea of the social contract and the philosophical concept of social welfare include mainly Plato, John Locke, and Jean Jacques Rousseau. In what follows the main ideas of these authors on the social contract are presented as illustrations of the historical and philosophical concepts of social welfare and followed by a discussion of contemporary views of social welfare.

PLATO

Our concern in this book is with Plato's philosophy of the political community. These ideas were mainly shaped by the events of the time and the teaching so Socrates. Plato witnessed a revolution in Athens turning government to arbitrary rules and to the execution of his teacher and friend, Socrates.

The result was that I, who had at first been full of eagerness for a public career, as I gazed upon the whirlpool of public life and saw the incessant movement of shifting currents, at last felt dizzy, and, while I did not cease to consider means of improving this particular situation and indeed of reforming the whole constitution, yet, in regard to action, I kept waiting for favorable moments, and finally saw clearly in regard to all states now existing that without exception their system of government is bad. Their constitutions are almost beyond redemption except through some miraculous plan accompanied by good luck. Hence, I was forced to say in praise of the correct philosophy that it affords a vantage point from which we can discern in all cases what is just for communities and individuals; and that accordingly the human race will not see better days until either the stock of those who rightly and genuinely follow philosophy acquire political authority, or else the class who have political control be led by some dispensation of providence to become philosophers.[2]

In the *Republic*, Plato presents the plan of a three-class state. At the top come the *philosopher-kings*; then come the *administrators*; and below them both are all the *civilians*, who are not capable of ruling themselves. He summarized his whole political program as follows: "The city-state can only be saved if the kinds become philosophers or the philosophers become kings." These philosophers, constituting the elite of society, must be given a moral training so strict and so sever that nothing can divert them from their mission to the state. They are to be the highest example of citizenship, adhering to the following high principles of the political community: asceticism, communism, monolithic power structure, and mysticism. Nisbet explains as follows:

It is in the celebrated guardian class that many see Plato's ideal both of citizenship and community best represented. The guardians are those, selected at birth on eugenic grounds for the arduous and demanding discipline of education in statecraft, who are, so to speak, the very exemplars of what Plato means by citizenship. That their own function within the division of labor in the political community is to guide and govern is of less importance than that they are the embodiments, the avatars, or citizenship in its highest expression. What Plato demands of his guardians in the political community may safely be taken as his supreme vision of all that is required in the total political community.[3]

Needless to say, these theories and ideas have led us to regard Plato as an elitist, an absolutist, and a utopian.[4] This view is eloquently expressed by Popper:

What a monument of human smallness is this idea of the philosopher-king. What a contrast between it and the simplicity and humanness of Socrates, who warned the statesman against the danger of being dazzled by his own power, excellence, and wisdom, and who tried to teach him what matters most-that we are frail human beings. What a decline from this world of irony and reason and truthfulness down to Plato's kingdom of the sage whose magical powers raise him high above ordinary men; although not quite high enough to forgo the use of lies, or to neglect the sorry trade of every shaman-the selling of taboos, of breeding taboos, in exchange for power over his fellow-men.[5]

Given these criticisms, it may be suggested that Plato's political program was intended to be an *ideal* program, the outline of a goal or standard to be used as a guide of action.

JOHN LOCKE

Locke is considered one of the principal exponents of the social contract theory. Phrases by Locke such as "life, liberty, and property," "consent of the governed," and "the majority have the right to act and conclude the rest" are generally accepted and often quoted ideas.

His account of civil society begins with the state of nature: a state of freedom and equality but also a state of real obligations: "The state of nature has a law of nature to govern it, which obliges everyone, and reason, which is that law, teaches all mankind . . . that being equal and independent, no one ought to harm another in his life, health, liberty and possessions."[6]

Men, however, cannot live alone and a change from a state of nature to a civil society takes place by consent, where each men or woman agrees to join and unite in a community. This creates a social compact, which involves the consent of everyone to submit to the determination of the majority and whereby men exchange the liberty of the state of nature for obedience to the laws of civil society. Of the natural rights that man is allowed to keep is the right of property. For reasons of expediency, Locke advocated that the decisions of the society, resulting from the social contract, be taken by a majority vote rather than by unanimous agreement. Arguing for the majority rule, he states:

For that which acts any community, being only the consent of the individuals of it, and it being one body, must move one way, it is necessary the body should move that way whither the greater force carries it, which is the consent of the majority, or else it is impossible it should act or continue one body, one community.[7]

Following the decision to form a civil society, the next step is to establish the legislative power. Locke suggests that it be kept separate and distinguished from the executive. Its creation is the first common act resulting from the social contract. People as trustor create the legislature as trustee on their own behalf.

There are naturally some defects to Locke's contract theory, namely, "its artificially, its neglect of the deeper psychological factors underlying the cohesion of society, the logical inconsistencies involved in trying to reconcile individual consent with obedience to government by majority rule."[8]

JEAN JACQUES ROUSSEAU

The social contract is popularly connected with the name of Rousseau, most likely because the title of his most famous work is *The Social Contract*. His view of the state of nature was different from the Lockean abode of peace and good will. Rousseau viewed the original men as being much stronger than they are today. They moved from the state of family to a tribe, from the nomadic existence to a fixed residence and the acquisition of property. "The first man," says Rousseau, "who, having enclosed a piece of ground, bethought himself of saying, *This is mine*, and found people simple enough to believe him, was the real founder of civil society."[9] States and civil governments followed, mainly created by the rich to safeguard their possessions, leading to tyranny and unavoidable abuses. While this exposé from the discourse seems to suggest that insurrection and revolution is the only remedy, Rousseau in *The Social Contract* proceeds to advocate not revolution but a form of political organization to make government legitimate.

In *The Social Contract*, Rousseau starts from a view of man bound to provide for his own preservation to a view of man changing to a civil state where justice is substituted for instinct and duty replacing "physical impulses and the right of appetite." He then argues for a social contract to end this state of nature and to form "an association which all will defend and protect with the whole common force the person and goods of each associate, and in which each, while uniting himself with all, may still obey himself alone, and remain as free as before." This social contract reduces itself to the following terms:

Each of us put his person and all his power in common under the supreme direction of the general will, and, in one corporate capacity, we receive each member as an indivisible part of the whole.
At once, in place of the individual personality of each contracting party, this act of association creates a moral and collective body, composed of as many members as the assembly contains votes, and receiving from this act its unity, its common identity, its life and its will.[10]

The general emphasis in *The Social Contract* is on the superiority and desirability of social life over the state of nature. Man loses his natural liberty to gain civil liberty instead, with the right of property guaranteed by the law instead of mere violent possession.

Rousseau viewed the general will as the sole source of legitimate power in society. There is a strongly authoritarian, even totalitarian, character to Rousseau's political community, even if the objective is to liberate the individual from the toils and traps of society. He states: "Each citizen would then be completely independent of all his fellow men, and absolutely dependent upon the state: which operation is always brought by the same means; for it is only by force of the state that the liberty of its members can be secured."[11]

What Rousseau intended is an independence from other members of society but not from the state. The state is important to man's potential being and growth, and for that to be possible there must be "an absolute surrender of the individual, with all its right and all its power, to the community as a whole."[12] Rousseau's advance of the general will arise from his dislike of traditional society and the need to emancipate the individual from it. In the general will lies "liberation from social tyranny, emancipation from self and its egotistical demands, the achievement of a form of spiritual communion that had previously been reserved for heaven, the attainment of virtue, and withal a conception of power as absolute as it is sealing and providential."[13]

Views of General Welfare

General welfare is secured by an efficient production of all the goods necessary for society to maintain an adequate quality of life. It depends on the working of the economy and particularly the public and private sectors. In what follows both systems are examined in terms of their contribution to the public interest.

THE PUBLIC AND PRIVATE SECTOR

The economy of most nations is very complex. The of the United States is a huge phenomenon producing in 1982 over $1 trillion as a result of hundreds of millions of transactions taking place each day among individuals, the corporations, and the state. The production of goods and services is shared by both the public and private sectors. The output of the public sector includes products such as education, national defense, and police and fire protection. The output of the private sector includes commodities such as food, medical care, housing, and investment goods such as residences, business structures, and producer's equipments and inventories. This type of economy, which combines outputs produced by both the public and private sectors, is referred to as a mixed economy. The nature of of the mixed economy in terms of the public and private sectors' contribution to the GNP has been changing over the years. While the trend seems toward a steady increase of the public sector's contribution, there is a lack of public consensus on which sector should be dominating.

One school of thought argues forcefully for a major role of the private sector, while another argues for a more important role for the public sector and for government intervention. The private sector argument is well represented by the following quote from Professor Milton Friedman, an ardent advocate of private sector dominance:

Every act of government intervention limits the area of individual freedom directly and threatens the preservation of freedom indirectly. . . . The widespread use of the market reduces the strain on the social fabric by rendering conformity unnecessary with respect to any activities it encompasses. The wider the range of activities covered by the market, the fewer are the issues on which explicitly political decisions are required and hence on which it is necessary to achieve agreement. In turn, the fewer the issues on which agreement is necessary, the greater is the likelihood of getting agreement while maintaining a free society. . . . A government which maintained law and order, defined property rights, served as a means whereby we could modify property rights and other rules of the economic game, adjudicated disputes about the interpretation of the rules, enforced contracts, promoted competition, provided a monetary framework, engaged in activities to counter technical monopolies and to overcome neighborhood effects widely regarded as sufficiently important to justify government intervention, and which supplemented private charity and the private family in protecting the irresponsible, whether madman or child-such a government would clearly have important functions to perform. The consistent liberal is not an anarchist.[14]

The public sector is also well represented by Professor John Galbraith, an ardent advocate of public sector dominance:

This disparity between our flow of private and public goods and services is no matter of subjective judgment. On the contrary, it is the source of the most extensive comment which only stops short of the direct contrast being made here. In the years following World War II, the papers of any major city-those of New York were an excellent example-told daily of the shortages and shortcomings in the elementary municipal and metropolitan services. The schools were old and overcrowded. The police force was under strength and underpaid. The parks and playgrounds were insufficient. Streets and empty lots were filthy, and the sanitation staff was underequipped and in need of men. Access to the city by those who work there was uncertain and painful and becoming more so. Internal transportation was overcrowded, unhealthful, and dirty. So was the air. Parking on the streets had to be prohibited, and there was no space elsewhere. These deficiencies were not in new and novel services but in the old and established ones. Cities have long swept their streets, helped their people move around, educated them, kept order, and provided horse rails for vehicles which sought to pause. That their residents should have a nontoxic supply of air suggests no revolutionary dalliance with socialism.[15]

The debate centers on the merits and/or deficiencies of the market system. An examination of the structure and the performance of the market system followed by a discussion of the economic effectiveness of public sector decisions will clarify the arguments in the debate.

THE WORKING OF THE MARKET SYSTEM

The private market economy consists of two primary actors, households and businesses, and two markets, the product market and the factor market. Households buy and businesses sell products in the product market, while households sell and businesses buy factor services in the factor market. The prices of either products or factors of production are set in the two markets in an automatic process referred to as the law of supply and demand. For these two markets to function efficiently the following conditions must be met:

1. *Perfect competition in all markets*: Enough buyers and sellers exist in the market that no one has control over the price of goods or services exchanged.
2. *Increasing costs in all industries*: Each industry experiences increasing costs, to where the costs are either constant or decreasing corresponds to a natural monopoly.
3. *Exclusion principle*: Each good, service, or factor of production is exclusive in the sense that they provide satisfaction only to the buyer of the good, service, or factor. Goods, services, or factors of production that are not consistent with the exclusion principle possess *spillover effects*.
4. *Absence of Public Goods*: This assumption eliminates all goods that possess spillover effects.
5. *Complete Knowledge*: All buyers and sellers have full knowledge of all the options in the market.
6. *Complete Mobility*: All resources are mobile in response to changes in prices.

If all these assumptions are met, the private market system will work efficiently and in the public interest: it will produce what is desired by people; it will produce it most efficiently; and it will distribute it according to the individual's contribution to the total social output.

MARKET FAILURE AND THE NEED FOR COLLECTIVE ACTION

The markets are in general not perfectly competitive because of failure to meet one or several of the above assumptions. The market failure requires that some economic goals be attained with collective action. As a first example, some firms are experiencing decreasing costs leading to a situation of natural monopoly. A situation where only a few firms can function efficiently leads to natural oligopolies. In both cases competition is decreased, requiring correction of various forms of regulation-antitrust legislation, public regulation, public ownership. As a second example, the complicity of society leads to the creation of pillover cost or benefit in violation of the exclusion principle. They arise whenever one individual's action benefits or harms someone else with or without his or her consent. These spillovers create inefficiencies in the market because they are not internalized in the decision making of the individual creating them or consuming them. In the case of spillover benefits, as in the case of education, the free market produces a smaller output than the socially optimum output. In the case of spillover costs, as in the case of pollution, the free market produces a greater output than the socially optimum output taking into account social costs and benefits. In both cases, collective action is required to correct the economic inefficiency and misallocation of resources. The collective action may take the form of government production of the good as a public good, the levying of a special tax and the granting of inducements to correct for a spillover cost or to reward for a spillover benefit, the use of administrative regulation, or the use of persuasive power. This collective action is generally initiated and implemented by the public sector to compensate for the failure of the market system to produce the optimal social output. Haveman states the problem as follows: "Because the private economy sometimes fails to operate in the public interest, sometimes fails to achieve an efficient allocation of society's resources, and sometimes generates an income distribution which violates ethical sensibilities, collective action through a public sector is required."[16]

Accordingly, in what follows, the working of the public sector is examined.

The Working of the Public Sector

Public and nonprofit organizations go beyond the efficiency objective sought by profit-oriented firms to include various goals such as achieving an "equitable" distribution of income, maintaining economic stability and full employment, and controlling the balance of payments. The range of problems addressed by the public sector include those relating to the provision of public and private education; transportation services; health care services for the poor, the military, and the aged; recreational facilities; and national defense. In addition, the public sector is heavily involved in managing hospitals, natural resources, income maintenance and income transfer programs, research support programs, the production of energy, and the provision of public and fire protection.

Various alternative ways are used by the public sector to engage in these activities. The commonly used alternative is direct action, whereby the government (local or federal) takes an active role in providing such goods as national defense, highways, low income housing, recreational facilities, postal services, police and fire services, and sewage treatment facilities. Direct action may take the form or either explicit expenditures to provide these services or cash and/or tax subsidies to encourage private initiative to deal with these problems. In addition, the government is involved in various income transfer and maintenance programs, such as social security, welfare and unemployment compensation, and transfer in-kind programs in the form of food, health care, education, and housing redistribution.

It is generally accepted to divide the economic activities of the government into three branches: *allocative, distributional,* and *stabilization*, each pursuing a single objective and producing one type of public good.[17] The allocative branch pursues the efficiency objective, which is the efficient allocation of resources. The stabilization branch is concerned with the formulation and execution of macro-economic policies to effect full employment. The distribution branch is concerned with the equity objective, which is to promote a desirable distribution of income. Since this chapter is not concerned with the macro-economic policy, only the allocative and distributional branches are examined.

INCOME DISTRIBUTION

The market system rewards people for their output performance and not for their efforts. Consequently, people who are not endowed with the necessary skills required by the market system, such as education, training, or capital endowment, may earn little. These skills may also change in response to changes in consumer preferences and demands, leading to changes in the rewards received by people. Finally, social problems and particularly racial tension and discrimination may create inequitable and "inefficient" income distribution. For these and other reasons, the government is justified in undertaking some forms of income redistribution.

Weisbrod suggests a number of alternative approaches to be used by a government that desires to alter the distribution of income, which involve programs to transfer money, to transfer income in kind, or to enhance earning power for the group to be aided.[18] He also suggested six standards for judging the desirability of any alternative means for redistributing income, namely, the administrative cost, the target efficiency, the allocative efficiency, the nondemeaning benefits, consumer versus taxpayer sovereignty, and flexibility over time.[19]

First, the administrative cost is judged relevant to program selection. Target efficiency is the second standard for ensuring that the "deserving" and only the deserving are aided. The degree to which a program benefits only the "target" group is termed the program's *vertical target efficiency*. The degree to which the program benefits all the members of the "target" group is termed its *horizontal target efficiency*. Third, allocative efficiency refers to the need to minimize the negative effects of the redistributional scheme on the incentives of those who benefit from the redistribution and of those who are made worse off by it. Fourth, nondemeaning benefits refers to the need to ensure that the benefits are not provided in a manner that tends to stigmatize or to destroy self-respect. Fifth, consumer versus taxpayer sovereignty reflects a choice regarding who ought to determine the pattern of consumption by beneficiaries of a public program. The conflict between the two criteria reflects two distinct views of society.[20] Sixth and last, flexibility over time refers to the need to evaluate the desirability of the program over time and to verify whether it will remain satisfactory as conditions change.[21]

ALLOCATIVE FUNCTION

The allocative function of government is concerned with an efficient allocation of resources for the benefit of the public interest. The definition of the public interest involves making a distinction between collective action and individual action and between public action and private action. Collective action or public action arises any time a group desires provision of goods or services that it cannot have through individual or private action. These goods or services are produced for the public interest and are known as pure public goods and quasi-public goods.

Pure private goods and services are divisible and excludable, divisible in the sense that they may be divided into finite units of consumption and excludable in the sense that nonbuyers may be excluded from the benefits of consumption. In addition, to be efficiently produced by the private market system, private goods must be produced under nonmonopoly conditions, be unassociated with significant production or consumption externalities, and assorted with low cost information concerning the quality of competing products.

At the extreme opposite pole to pure private goods are pure public goods. Unlike the pure private goods, pure public goods are indivisible and imperfectly excludable, may be associated with significant production or consumption externalities, are often produced under conditions of decreasing costs of production, and may not be assorted with accurate and inexpensive market information.

A general definition of public good is that of the perfect collective consumption good:

There are certain goods that have the peculiarity that once they are available no on can be precluded from enjoying them whether he contributed to their provision or not. These are the public goods. Law and order is an example, and there are many others too familiar to make further exemplification worthwhile. Their essential characteristic is that they are enjoyed but not consumed [and that their benefits are derived] without any act of appropriation.[22]

This definition is restricted, however, to a collective consumption good that does not embrace much of what public expenditure policy concerns. As a result, Steiner defined a public good as any publicly induced or provided collective good.[23] He also distinguished between three types of public goods: public goods arising from nonmarketable services of particular goods; public goods arising from market imperfections; and public goods arising because of concern with the quality of the environment.[24]

The first type of public good arises when collective concern and public action are needed to allocate resources in accord with "true valuations." They are particularly needed when the production of a good or service creates side effects whose value is not reflected in the prices of the outputs sold or the resources used, which is the case when external economies or diseconomies are produced. Familiar examples are discharges of noxious wastes into water or air, downstream navigational or flood control consequences of a private power dam, and civic beautification or uglification incident upon the building of private golf courses, factories, or slaughterhouses.[25]

The second type of public good arises when public collective action is needed to correct market failure caused by market imperfections. Imperfections that may hinder the efficiency of the market include inadequate information, monopoly power, time lags, and high transaction costs.

The third type of public good arises when even with existing perfectly functioning markets people choose collective action rather than market solutions to allocative problems with respect to the distribution of income, the nature or quality of goods produced, or the patterns of consumption that markets produce.

A pure public good is characterized by indivisibilities in production or jointness in supply and the impossibility or inefficiency of excluding a person from the enjoyment of a particular commodity once it has been made available to other individuals in society. For these goods a collective *voice* process or nonmarket decision making is necessary to reveal individual preferences and achieve Pareto efficiencty.[26] For the private goods the preferences are expressed by the purchases (*entry* or *exit*) of buyers. There are, however, some goods, labeled either quasi-public goods or mixed goods, that fall between the two extremes of public and private goods and that may require a mixture of exit and voice processes.

Dennis C. Mueller, in a seminal article later expanded into a book, identified four strategies for deciding the quantities of quasi-public goods, namely: voting with the feet, the theory of clubs, voting with the feet in the presence of jointness of supply, and the theory of revolution.[27]

If the joint supply property is relaxed and a limited degree of exclusion is assumed, people can reveal their preference by moving into the community providing the most desirable fraction of the public good. This strategy, voting with the feet, allows people to group themselves into groups of like tastes.[28]

If exclusion is possible and economies of scale exists (join supply property), people can reveal their preference by forming clubs where members have identical taste for the public good.[29] Any effort to discriminate against an individual will induce him to exit and join another club or create a new one. This is the theory of clubs.

When the public goods are produced with economies of scale, people can reveal their preference with a combination of voting with the feet and the ballot. People moving from one community to another may be offered a subsidy or asked to pay a tax depending upon whether they impose an external economy or diseconomy on the new community. A central authority may be asked to levy the taxes and offer subsidies. The solution based on a central authority "vests the entire population with a property right in both communities and achieves allocational efficiency by taxing *all* members of the favored community to subsidize the disfavored community."[30] This is Mueller's "voting with the feet in the presence of jointness of supply."

The theory of revolution strategy is eloquently stated by Mueller as follows: "When neither the ballot, nor the feet constitute adequate models of expression, there is still Chairman Mao's barrel of the gun."[31] The strategy calls for the creation of a new polity by revolution. Gordon Tullock proposed a model to explain a revolutionary's behavior as follows:

$R = BP + D - C$

Where
R = potential revolutionary's action
B = new government's public good benefits
P = probability that the individual's participation brings about success
D = private gains from participation in the revolution
C = private costs

A positive R induces the individual to participate in a revolution while a negative R creates the opposite attitude.[32]

THE PUBLIC INTEREST

The creation of the public goods for the public interest identified earlier requires a conceptualization of the notion of the public interest. Steiner has identified three views of the public interest: the point of view of individual utility; the point of view of willingness to pay; and the point of view of an aggregate social welfare function.[33]

The point of view of individual utility considers the public interest of a society as simply an aggregate of the private interests of the individuals comprising that society. The individuals are assumed to desire both private and public goods, which legitimizes the dual role of private markets and the government. This point of view assumes that unanimity prevails and that individual utilities can be measured and compared. This point of view is not, however, without its criticisms. Consider the following:

The major objection to a utility consensus view of social welfare functions is that it is nonoperational and does not seem to provide guidance to the decisions of real societies. Certainly we *do* take decisions with less than unanimous consent. Certainly, too, many public goods provide benefits in excess of their contributions only to very small minorities of the society, but with the evident acquiescence of sizeable majorities. One can argue that, *ex post*, individuals are thus revealed to value the benefits which accrue primarily to other. But this rationalization leads us back to a *de facto* definition: whatever the government does is revealed to be desired by people.[34]

The point of view of willingness to pay asks not how much an individual values a given public good but how much he is willing to be taxed to provide it. Placed in the context of the pure theory of public expenditure,[35] this view implies that a good is worth producing if the aggregate sum of the willingness to pay of different individuals exceeds the cost.

One limitation of this point of view is the distributional question. More explicitly, some of the taxpayers may end up receiving more than they are willing to pay for and being coerced to provide what others want. Consider the following:

Citizens have social values about appropriate tax policies, too. Suppose we are building a public playground to be used by underprivileged children. If A is a rich misanthrope and B a poor Samaritan, there is no compelling reason why B should carry more of the tax burden, even though he may be willing to do so.[36]

The point of view of an aggregate social welfare function assumes that individuals voluntarily yield certain coercive powers to a government which determines social priorities by an aggregation process. In this view the political process articulates the public interest by determining the aggregate social values. In doing so, competing objectives are reconciled by a process of implicit or explicit "weighting." Harsanyi proved that individuals and social preferences satisfy the von Neumann and Morgenstern-Marschak postulates and if each individual is indifferent between two states of the world implies social indifference between the states, then social welfare is a weighted sum of individual utilities:[37]

$$W = \sum_{i=1}^{n} a_i U_i$$

An example is the Bergson-Samuelson social welfare function:[38]
$W = W (Z_1, Z_2, \ldots)$
Where W is a real value function of all variables (Z_1's) that might affect social welfare. The Z_1's and W are assumed to represent the ethical values of a society or of individuals in it. Needless to say, this social welfare function is difficult to determine and may require the introduction of value judgments or ethical postulates.

Kenneth Arrow introduced five axioms that he argued every social welfare function should meet because they may be considered as the basic value judgments of the community contained in the social contract or constitution.[38] These five axioms may be stated briefly as follows:
1. *Unlimited domain*: All possible orderings of individual preferences are possible.
2. *The Pareto postulate*.
3. *Transitivity*: The social welfare function gives a consistent ordering of all feasible alternatives.
4. *Nondictatorship*: No individual can impose his preferences.
5. *Independence of irrelevant alternatives*: The Social choice between any two alternatives is independent of preferences over any other alternatives.

Arrow showed that no social welfare function satisfies these five postulates. To get rid of the paradox, researchers relied on a relaxation of each of the assumptions and found that such a procedure raises more difficult questions of choices.[40] Consider the following statement:

From a public choice perspective, relaxation of either the independence or unrestricted domain axioms appears to be the most appealing way out of the paradox. Each in turn raises questions as to what issues are to be decided, who is to decide, and of those who decide, which preferences shall be weighted. Such choices directly or indirectly involve interpersonal utility comparisons and must rest on some additional value postulates, which if explicitly introduced would imply specific interpersonal utility comparisons. The latter cannot be avoided.[41]

Given a choice of any view of the public interest, it is left to the political process to implement it. Two views of the nature of the political process may be identified: *majority principle* and *pluralism*.

Majority principle derives from a theory of leadership motivation put down by Anthony Downs.[42] In *An Economic Theory of Democracy* he hypothesizes that "parties in democratic politics are analogous to entrepreneurs in a profit-seeking company. So as to attain their private ends, they formulate whatever policies they believe will gain the most votes, just as entrepreneurs produce whatever products will gain the most profits."[43] In brief, they will attempt to maximize political support. To do so they will rely on the *majority principle* in their policy decisions, which basically correspond to the level of support at which the marginal gains of those supporting the policy equals the marginal loss of those rejecting the policy.

The pluralistic nature of the political process assumes that decisions are the result of the interaction of various important special interest groups. The general view is that pluralism generates a socially desirable outcome given that it represents and equilibrium and consensus among competing groups. This view has, however, been challenged by various authors. The most effective objection was advanced by Olson, who argued that there is a systematic bias in a pluralistic society that causes only special interest groups to exercise political power.[44] An expression of the special interest groups is evident in their lobbying effort.

View of Social Equality

The idea of social equality is as old as Plato and Aristotle. Aristotle equated equality with justice: In the popular mind the description "unjust" is held to apply both to the man who takes more than his due and to the man who breaks the law. It follows that the man who does not break the law and the man who does not take more than he is entitled to will be "just." "Just" therefore means (a) lawful and (b) what is "equal," that is, fair.[45]

In fact, Aristotle distinguished between distributive and corrective justice. Corrective justice is accomplished by the judge settling disputes and correcting any unfairness arising from transactions. Distributive justice deals with "the distribution of honor or money or such other possessions of the community as can be divided among its members."[46] It allocates shares to persons in proportion to their relative equality or inequality. If the persons are not equal, they would not receive equal parts. This shows Aristotle's belief that there is no equality among men, either in nature or society. For injustice or inequality may arise from treating unequals equally as from treating equals unequally.[47]

The idea of equality blossomed in the eighteenth century, and it was Rousseau's statement in *The Social Contract*, "Man is born free; and everywhere he is in chaings,"[48] that led the authors of the American Declaration of Independence to the proclamation, "All men are created equal." - This concept of social equality was introduced to ensure people of equality before the law and not necessarily equality in social life.

Inequality continues to be, however, a fact of life in modern society. Two positions emerge on the question of inequality. One position stresses that inequality is equitable, inevitable, and due to differences in the efforts and competences of individuals. The other position stresses that inequality is "not natural" and that the resulting social classes lead to conflict and instability in society.[49] Inequality is generally used to refer to the differences in the distribution of such factors as income, wealth, and social status. It is usually associated with such concepts as social stratification and social class. Social classes have been defined as individuals or families occupying similar positions in a hierarchy of income, wealth, or occupations, or in a Marxist sense as individuals' relationships to the system of production. Stratification refers to "the set of rules governing access to the different social positions and to incumbency in the different social roles."[50] Social class and stratification are two different dimensions of the ways inequality operates in a society: stratification by assigning individuals to social roles; and classes' by designating the presence or absence of ownership of the means of production. An important question arises at this point: Is inequality justified? Various views exist in sociology as an answer to the question: the functionalist view of inequality, the IQ view; and the Marxist view.

The functionalist view of inequality maintains that inequality is functional and necessary to the survival of society. Davis and Moore, in defense of the functionalist view, argued that, first, every society must allocate its members to various jobs within the division of labor and motivate them to perform adequately and, second, every society must offer rewards as incentives to acquire the skills needed to perform important jobs. "Inevitably, then," Davis and Moore assert, "a society must have, first, some kind of rewards that it can use as inducements, and, second, some way of distributing these rewards differentially according to positions."[51] In brief, social inequality is viewed as the device used by society to ensure that the most important positions are conscientiously filled by the more qualified people.

The IQ ideology is similar to the functionalist view and maintains that inequality is due to differences in scarce intellectual abilities leading to differential social rewards.[52] Both Jensen and Herrnstein argue that genetic differences lead to different IQs and different social positions, making inequality in social rewards inevitable. The IQ ideology has been challenged by Bowles and Gintis to show that other factors such as social class background and schooling may explain the inequality.[53]

The Marxist view of inequality maintains that inequality results from the differences in the relationships of men to the productive processes of a society due to the differences in allocation of the rewards to those owning the means of production and those providing labor to these owners. Marx refers to it as follows:

It is always the direct relationship of the owners of the conditions of production to the direct producers-a relation always naturally corresponding to a definite stage in the development of the methods of labor and thereby its social productivity- which reveals the innermost secret, the hidden basis of the entire social structure, and with it the political form of the relation of sovereignty and dependence, in short, the corresponding specific form of the state.[54]

In brief, the specific relations of production dictate the existing economic inequalities. Thus, Marx viewed private property as the source of economic equality. It is a fact, however, that abolition of private ownership of the means of production in the socialist countries has not eliminated social inequalities. As Shkaratan states, "When socialism liquidates private property, it eliminates the consequences of private property-antagonistic classes-but it does not eliminate the original cause of social inequality: the division of labor into socially heterogeneous types."[55]

From this brief discussion on the various views of inequality, it appears that neither the functionalist view nor the IQ view nor the Marxist view provides an adequate explanation and/or justification of economic inequalities in both capitalist and socialist societies. The question of economic inequality remains a matter of important debate in today's society.

Inequality is then a fact in today's society. In Western societies, inequality faces the tradition of individualism and egalitarianism. One way out of the conflict between inequality and the spirit of egalitarianism is the idea of equality of opportunity in general and equality of educational opportunity in particular. The generally accepted view is that equality of educational opportunity will result in greater social mobility and economic equality.

Views of Social Justice

Two theories of justice, John Rawls' theory of justice, as presented in his book *A Theory of Justice*, and Robert Nozick's "entitlement theory," as presented in his book *Anarchy, State, and Utopia*, contain principles for evaluating laws and institution from a moral standpoint.[56] In what follows both theories and their implications for economic equality are presented.

RAWLS' THEORY OF JUSTICE

The goal of Rawls' work is to develop a moral theory about justice in the form of principles to apply to the development of "the basic structure of society." Rawls starts by comparing life to a game of chance where nature bestows on each individual a generation, a culture, a social system, a family, and a set of personal attributes that determines his or her happiness. Accepting this random allocation is viewed as unjust and a set of just institutions is required. To establish just such institutions Rawls suggests that individuals step behind a "veil of ignorance" that eliminates any knowledge about potential positions and benefits under a given set of principles. Then, to reach a social contract, they must choose from this original position principles of justice leading to the just society. From this original position and under the veil of ignorance, individuals will choose two principles of justice as follows:

First: each person is to have an equal right to the most extensive basic liberty compatible with a similar liberty for others. Second: social and economic inequalities are to be arranged so that they are both (a) reasonably expected to be to everyone's advantage, and (b) attached to positions and offices open to all.[57]

Rawls maintains that the two principles are lexicographically ordered, the first over the second. He states:

Now it is possible, at least theoretically, that by giving up some of their fundamental liberties men are sufficiently compensated by the resulting social and economic gains. The general conception of justice implies no restrictions on what sort of inequalities are permissible; it only requires that everyone's position be improved. . . . Imagine . . . that men forgo certain political rights when the economic returns are significant and their capacity to influence the course of policy by the exercise of these rights would be marginal in any case. It is this kind of exchange which the two principles as stated rule out; being arranged in serial order they do not permit exchanges between basic liberties and economic and social gains.[58]

The first principle shows the emphasis placed by Rawls on liberty and the precedence of liberty over the second principle of justice. Liberty can only be restricted when it infringes on other people's liberty. Labeled as the priority rule, it was formulated as follows: "The principles of justice are to be ranked in lexical order and therefore liberty can be restricted only for the sake of liberty. There are two cases: (a) a less extensive liberty shared by all, and (b) a less than equal liberty must be acceptable to those citizens with the lesser liberty."[59]

The second principle of justice, which Rawls labeled the difference principle, contains a lexicographic ordering of the welfare of the individuals from lowest to highest, where the welfare of the worst-off individual is to be maximized first before proceeding to higher levels. In its most general form, the difference principle states:

In a basic structure with n relevant representatives, first maximize the welfare of the worst-off representative, minimize the welfare of the second worst-off man, and so on until the last case which is, for equal welfare of all the preceding n-1 representatives, maximize the welfare of the best-off representative man. We think of this as the lexical difference principle.[60]

The two principles show a "democratic" conception that eliminates "those aspects of the social world that seem arbitrary from a moral point of view."[61] This does not necessarily eliminate economic inequality. Rawls justifies some differences in income first: as incentives to attract people to certain positions and motivate them to perform; and as to guarantee that certain public interest positions will be filled.[62]

To implement Rawls' theory, the idea "basic structure" of society may be a "constitutional democracy," which preserves equal basic liberties, with a government that promotes equality of opportunity and guarantees a social minimum and an economic system based on the market. Who are the "individuals" likely to espouse Rawls' conception of justice? Steven Lukes argues that it applies to the modern, Western, liberal, individualistic man:

They are "committed to different conceptions of the good," they "put forward competing claims" and are "not prepared to abandon their interest," they "tend to love, cherish and support whatever affirms their own good," they demand equality of opportunity, but regard unequal rewards as necessary incentives, and their rationality consists in acquiring the means to further their ends and, importantly, in a safety-first policy of planning for the worse possible outcome. They allegedly "understand political affairs and the principles of economic theory; they know the basic of social organization and the laws of human psychology."[63]

Rawls' concept is equally applicable to any liberal man from the developing countries. It calls for the creation of background institutions for distributive justice and divided into four branches concerned with allocation, stabilization, transfer, and distribution.[64] The allocation branch is to maintain the price system workably competitive. It is charged with "identifying and correcting, say, by suitable taxes and subsidies and by changes in the definition of property rights, the more obvious departures from efficiency caused by the failure to measure accurately social benefits and costs."[65] The stabilization branch strives to maintain full employment. The transfer branch is to assure a "social minimum," guarantee a certain level of well-being, and honor in the claim of need.[66] Rawls suggests that this social minimum be established before allowing the rest of the total income to be settled by the price system. Finally, the distribution branch has the task of preserving a just distribution by means of taxation and necessary adjustments in the rights of property. Two aspects of this branch are distinguished. First, it imposes a number of inheritance and gift taxes and creates restrictions on the rights of bequest. The rationale behind this first aspect is "not to raise revenue (release resources to government) but gradually and continually to correct the distribution of wealth and to prevent concentrations of power detrimental to the fair value of political liberty and fair equality of opportunity."[67] Second, it raises the revenue that justice requires. The rationale behind this second aspect is that "social resources must be released to the government so that it can provide for the public goods and make the transfer payments necessary to satisfy the difference principle."[68]

NOZICK'S THEORY OF JUSTICE

While Rawls was interested in the justice of one or another pattern of distribution, Nozick was interested in the processes whereby distribution comes out. He first argued that Rawls' theory of justice violates people's rights and, consequently, cannot be morally justified, that it ignores people's entitlements and is, like most other theories of justice, patterned. Patterned theories of justice imply that "a distribution is to vary along some natural dimension, weighted sum of natural dimensions, or lexicographic ordering of natural dimensions."[69] Examples of such distributions include those based on need, merit or work. Nozick maintains, "To think that the task of a theory distributive justice is to fill in the blank in 'each according to his _____' is to be predisposed to search for a patter; and the separate treatment of 'from each according to his _____' treats production and distribution as two separate and independent issues."[70]

Nozick argues that such theories of justice, based on the patterned and end-state principles, violate people's rights and exclude recognition of an entitlement principle of distributive justice, whereby individuals are entitled to their possessions as long as they got them by legitimate means, including voluntary transfers, exchanges, and cooperative productive activity.[71] He justifies this theory as follows:

1. A person who acquires a holding in accordance with the principle of justice in acquisition is entitled to that holding.
2. A person who acquires a holding in accordance with the principle of justice in transfer, from someone else entitled to the holding, is entitled to the holding.
3. No one is entitled to a holding except by (repeated) applications of 1. and 2.[72]

The principles involve, respectively, the question of original acquisition of holdings, the transfer of holdings, and the rectification of injustices in holdings. Nozick introduced a proviso, however, to ensure that an individual's entitlements do not result in a net loss in what remains for

other persons to use. Nozick's theory is then a *theory of justice in holdings*. It is a very special kind of theory of distributive justice, as emphasized by Nozick:
The term "distributive justice" is not a neutral one. Hearing the term "distribution," most people presume that some thing or mechanism uses some principle or criterion to give out a supply of things. . . . However, we are not in the position of children who have been given proportions of pie by someone who now makes last-minute adjustments to rectify careless cutting. There is *no* central distribution, no person or group entitled to control all the resources, jointly deciding how they are to be doled out. What each person gets, he gets from others who give to him in exchange for something, or as a gift. In a free society, diverse persons control different resources, and new holdings arise out of the voluntary exchanges and actions of persons. There is no more a distributing or distribution of shares than there is a distribution of mates in a society in which persons choose whom they shall marry. The total result is the product of many individual decisions which the different individuals involved are entitled to make.[73]

Corporate Society: Toward a Rectification Paradigm
We have so far covered the various views on the social contract, general welfare, social equality, and social justice as portrayed in the literature on political, moral, economic, and legal philosophy. These views point to various social problems in need of correction and/or rectification and of relevance to the role of the corporation in society. The rectification may be needed to create social order and influence and motivate full participation of individuals in the promotion of the national identity and national goals. The active role of the corporation in helping and securing this rectification effort may be needed to protect the long-term interests of the firm as a profitable, going concern in a stable and prosperous society. The rectification effort may be outlined as follows:
1. A social contract must arise from a societal consensus of what is or is not desirable to ensure social welfare. It is an unwritten agreement between the members of society (including corporations) to act with reciprocal responsibility under the governance of the state.
2. The general welfare of society, the public interest, must arise from a societal consensus of what sorts of public goods should be produced. As Olson points out, an ideal society would be one in which individuals had rather different tastes for private goods and rather similar tastes for public goods.[74] Such a society would benefit from the role of the corporations in providing different goods for different tastes efficiently and in participating in securing those public goods agreed on by the public.
3. Economic inequality cannot be explained by the functionalist view, the IQ ideology, or the Marxist view. It does, however, affect people's well-being, their chances of realizing various opportunities and goals, and such crucial aims as their health, happiness, and life expectancy. There is an absolute reason or justification for some form of rectification to correct, reduce, and/or abolish economic inequality. The rectification must take place in the form of a socially accepted theory of justice in distribution based on a combination of need, merit, contribution, and desert. The corporation's role in correcting economic inequality may be expressed in its employment, investment, production, research, and development policies. They should be aimed at meeting both objectives of securing an adequate return to the firm and of reducing economic inequalities.
4. Social justice implies an equal right to liberty, a concern for the welfare of the worst-off individual in society, and a right of people to control holdings acquired through means sanctioned by the principles of justice in acquisition and in transfer. It calls for rectification to those who have been the subject of social or economic injustice. The rectification of past injustices cannot be denied. The corporation's role in rectifying past injustices may go from the injustices to possible compensation of people.

Notes
1. Ernest Barker, *Social Contract* (New York: Oxford University Press, 1948).

2. Plato, *Epistle 7*, in *Thirteen Epistles of Plato*, trans. L. A. Post (Oxford: Claredon Press, 1925), pp. 64-65.
3. Robert Nisbet, *The Social Philosophers* (New York: Crowell, 1973), p. 115.
4. J. Ly Thorston, *Plato: Totalitarian or Democrat* (Englewood Cliffs, N.J.: Prentice-Hall, 1963).
5. Karl R. Popper, "Plato as Enemy of the Open Society," in Thorston, p. 102.
6. J. Locke, *Second Treatise on Civil Government*, in Barker, *Social Contract*, p. 6.
7. Locke, *Second Treatise on Civil Government*, ch. 8, sect. 96, in Barker, *Social Contract*, p. 81.
8. J. W. Gough, *The Social Contract* (Oxford: Claredon Press, 1957), pp. 145-146.
9. J. J. Rousseau, *Discourse on the Origin of Inequality Among Men* (1755), p. ii.
10. J. J. Rousseau, *The Social Contract*, p. 16.
11. Ibid., p. 52.
12. Ibid., p. 114
13. Nisbet, *The Social Philosophers*, p. 153.
14. Milton Friedman, *Capitalism and Freedom* (Chicago: University of Chicago Press, 1962), p. 15.
15. John Kenneth Galbraith, *The Affluent Society* (Boston: Houghton Mifflin, 1958), pp. 251-253.
16. Robert H. Haveman, *The Economics of the Public Sector* (New York: Wiley, 1976), p. 49.
17. R. Musgrave, *The Theory of Public Finance* (New York: McGraw-Hill, 1959), pp. 3-27.
18. Burton A. Weisbrod, "Collective Action and the Distribution of Income: A Conceptual Approach," in R. H. Haveman and Julius Margolis, eds., *Public Expenditures and Policy Analysis*. 2d ed. (Chicago: Rand McNally, 1977), p. 105.
19. Ibid., p. 113.
20. Ibid., p. 114-123.
21. Ibid., pp. 129-130.
22. Rober Dorfman, "General Equilibrium with Public Goods" (Paper presented to International Economics Association Conference on Public Economics, September 1966), p. 4.
23. Peter O. Steiner, "The Public Sector and the Public Interest," in Haveman and Margolis, *Public Expenditures and Policy Analysis*, p. 31.
24. Ibid., p. 33.
25. Ibid.
26. Albert O. Hirschman, *Exit, Voice and Loyalty* (Cambridge: Harvard University Press, 1970). In this book, Hirschman introduced two options for expressing individual preferences: either through an *entry* or *exit* option, or through a *voice* option.
27. Dennis C. Mueller, "Public Choice: A Survey," *Journal of Economic Literature* (June 1976): 412-415; and Dennis C. Mueller, *Public Choice* (Cambridge: Cambridge University Press, 1979), pp. 125-147.
28. This strategy was first noted by Charles M. Tiebout, "A Pure Theory of Local Expenditures," *Journal of Political Economy* (October 1965): 416-424. The strategy rests on important and questionable assumptions, namely, the full mobility of all citizens.
29. J. H. Buchanan, "An Economic Theory of Clubs," *Economia* (February, 1965), pp. 1-14.
30. Mueller, "Public Choice," p. 414.
31. Ibid.
32. Tullock, Gordon, "The Paradox of Revolution," *Public Choice* (Fall 1971), pp. 88-99.

33. Steiner, "The Public Sector and the Public Interest," p. 41.
34. Ibid., p. 45.
35. H. R. Bowles, "The Interpretation of Voting in the Allocation of Economic Resources," *Quarterly Journal of Economics* 58 (November 1943): 350-356.
36. Steiner, "The Public Sector and the Public Interest," p. 46.
37. J. C. Harsanyi, "Cardinal Wefare, Individualistic Ethics, and Interpersonal Comparisons of Utility," *Journal of Political Economy* 63 (August 1955): 309-321.
38. A. Bergson, "A Reformulation of Certain Aspects of Welfare Economics," *Quarterly Journal of Economics* 52 (February 1938): 310-334; P. A. Samuelson, 1947), p. 221.
39. K. Arrow, *Social Choice and Individual Values* (New York: Wiley, 1951; rev. ed., New York: Yale University Press, 1963), pp. 104-105.
40. Bergson, "A Reformulation of Certain Aspects of Welfare Economics," pp. 310-340; A. Bergson, "On the Concept of Social Welfare," *Quarterly Journal of Economics* 68 (May 1954): 233-252; C. Hildreth, "Alternative Conditions for Social Orderings," *Econometrica* 21 (January 1953): 81-94; M. C. Kemp and A. Asimakopulos, "A Note of 'Social Welfare Functions' and Cardinal Utility," *Canadian Journal of Economics and Political Science* 18 (May 1952): 195-200; A. K. Sen, *Collective Choice and Social Welfare* (San Francisco: Holden-Day, 1970), pp. 123-125.
41. Mueller, "Public Choice," pp. 421-422.
42. A. Downs, *An Economic Theory of Democracy* (New York: Harper & Row, 1957).
43. Ibid., p. 295.
44. M. Olson, *the Logic of Collective Action* (Cambridge: Harvard University Press, 1965, chs. 5 and 6.
45. Aristotle, *Ethics* (Harmondsworth: Penguin Books, 1955), p. 140.
46. Ibid., pp. 144-145.
47. Ibid., pp. 145-147.
48. J. J. Rousseau, *The Social Contract and Discourses* (London: Everyman's Library, 1947), p. 3.
49. Stanislaw Ossowski, *Class Structure in the Social Consciousness* (New York: Free Press, 1963); Gerhard E. Lenski, *Power and Privilege* (New York: McGrawHill, 1966).
50. Judah Matras, *Social Inequality, Stratification and Mobility* (Englewood Cliffs, N. J.: Prentice-Hall, 1975), p. 9.
51. Kingsley Davis and Wilbert E. Moore, "Some Principles of Stratification." *American Sociological Review* 10 (1945): 246.
52. R. Herstein, "IQ," *Atlantic Monthly* (September 1971): 43-64: Arthur R. Jensen, "How Much Can We Boost IQ and Scholastic Achievement?" *Harvard Educational Review* Reprint Series, no. 2 (1969): 126-134.
53. Samuel Bowles and Herbert Gintis, "IQ in the United States Class Structure," pp. 7-84. In Alan Gartner, Colin Greer, and Frank Riessman, eds., *The Assault on Equality* (New York: Harper & Row, 1974); and Samuel Bowles and Herbert Gintis, *Schooling in Capitalist America* (New York: Basic Books, 1976), pp. 121-122.
54. Karl Marx, *Capital: A Critique of Political Economy*, vol.3 (Moscow: Foreign Language Publishing House, 1962), p. 772.
55. O. I. Shkaratan, "Sources of Social Differentiation of the Working Class in Soviet Society," *International Journal of Sociology* (Spring-Summer 1973): 11.

56. J. A. Rawls, *A Theory of Justice* (Cambridge: Harvard University Press, 1971); R. Nozick, *Anarchy, State, and Utopia* (New York: Basic Books, 1974).
57. Rawls, *A Theory of Justice*.
58. Ibid., pp. 62-63.
59. Ibid., p. 250.
60. Ibid., p. 83.
61. Ibid., p. 15.
62. Ibid., p. 315.
63. Steven Lukes, *Essays in Social Theory* (New York: Columbia University Press, 1977), p. 189.
64. Rawls, *A Theory of Justice*, p. 275.
65. Ibid., p. 276.
66. Ibid.
67. Ibid., p. 277.
68. Ibid.
69. Nozick, *Anarchy, State and Utopia*, p. 156.
70. Ibid., pp. 159-160.
71. Ibid., pp. 150-231.
72. Ibid., p. 151.
73. Ibid., pp. 149-150.
74. M. Olson, "Economics, Sociology, and the Best of All Possible Worlds," *The Public Interest*, no. 12 (Summer 1968): 96-118.

Bibliography
BOOKS
Barker, Ernest. *Social Contract*. New York: Oxford University Press, 1948.
Bowles, Samuel, and Herbert Gintis. *Schooling and Capitalist America*. New York: Basic Books, 1976.
Clarke, Edward H. *Demand Revelation and the Provision of Public Goods*. Cambridge, Mass.: Ballinger, 1980.
Downs, A. *An Economic Theory of Democracy*. New York: Harper & Row, 1957.
Haveman, Robert H. *The Economics of the Public Sector*. New York: Wiley, 1976.
___. And Julius Margolis, eds. *Public Expenditures and Policy Analysis*, 2d ed. Chicago: Rand McNally, 1977.
Hirschman, Albert O. *Exit, Voice and Loyalty*. Cambridge: Harvard University Press. 1970.
Mueller, Dennis C. *Public Choice*. Cambridge: Cambridge University Press, 1979.
Nisbet, Robert. *The Social Philosophers: Community and Conflict in Western Thought*. New York: Crowell, 1973.
Nozick, R. *Anarchy, State and Utopia*. New York: Basic Books, 1974.
Olson, M. *The Logic of Collective Action*. Cambridge: Harvard University Press, 1965.
Phillips, Derek L. *Equality, Justice, and Rectification*. New York: Academic Press, 1979.
Rawls, J. A. *A Theory of Justice*. Cambridge: Harvard University Press, 1971.

ARTICLES

Bowles, Samuel, and Herbert Gintis. "IQ in the United States Class Structure," pp. 7-84. In Alan Gartner, Colin Greer, and Frank Riessman, eds., *The New Assault on Equality*. New York: Harper & Row, 1974.
Buchanan, J. H. "An Economic Theory of Clubs." *Economica* (February 1965): 1-14.
Davis, Kingsley, and Wilbert E. Moore. "Some Principles of Stratification." *American Sociological Review* 10 (1945).
Herstein, R. "IQ." *Atlantic Monthly* (September 1971): 43-64.
Jensen, Arthur R. "How Much Can We Boost IQ and Scholastic Achievement?" *Harvard Educational Review*, Reprint Series, no. 2 (1969): 126-134.
Mueller, Dennis C. "Public Choice: A Survey." *Journal of Economic Literature* (June 1976).
Tiebout, Charles M. "A Pure Theory of Local Expenditures." *Journal of Political Economy* (October 1965): 416-424.

Appendix 3.A.
Rectification Paradigm and Income Redistribution

The rectification paradigm implies the search for the "right" income distribution. Ethical judgments may be needed for the task. To start there is a need, in assessing the income distribution, to determine the number of people below the poverty line, defined as a fixed level of real income considered to be enough to provide a minimally adequate standard of living. Judgments differ when it comes to determining the poverty line and the best income distribution policy. In general, the maximum criterion stipulates that the best income distribution strategy is the one that maximizes the entity of the person who has the lowest utility. Advising Pareto efficient redistribution assumes that no one is made worse off as a result of the income transfer. So determining the income distribution strategy is a way of defining what a good society should be like.

Expenditures programs for the poor are a way of implementing some form of income redistribution. Examples of cash transfer program include up to 1966 the AFDC (Aid to Families with Dependent Children) and since 1966 the TANF (Temporary Assistance for Needy Families). Another worth while program is the EITC (Earned Income Tax Credit), which is really a subsidy to the earnings of low income families. It is a tax credit that lower tax liability. Other programs include a) the supplemental security income (a basic monthly benefit for the aged, blind or disabled), b) Medicaid, c) food stamps and child nutrition programs, d) housing assistance subsidies, and e) other federal programs aimed at enhancing earnings, generally involving education (like the Head Start program) or employment and job training.

Other forms of income redistribution programs include a) social security, b) Unemployment insurance and c) health care programs.

Social insurance is generally justified by the following arguments:

a. Adverse selection: In a private insurance system, the firms face the problem of information asymmetry as the buyer knows more about their health. As a result, the insurance companies end up insuring buyers that are averse to their interests- a phenomena known as adverse selection. In addition, as a way of insuring against living to long people buy from insurance companies amenities that pay a fixed amount for life. Therefore, a social insurance for all will take come of the problems of information asymmetry, adverse selection and amenities' limitations.
b. Lack of funds as most people fail to accumulate enough funds for retirement making social insurance a viable and useful alternative
c. Moral hazard as people opt out of insurance because they know that once in a desperate situation government will step in to the rescue. So a compulsory social insurance is in order.

Let's examine each of the social insurance programs:

A. Social Security: Officially OASDI-Old Age, Survivors, and Disability Insurance, is a result of the employers' contribution via a base on payrolls. It is a redistribution program benefiting all those covered by the program, is giving them an actuarially form return. Limitations of the social security system involve 1) a wealth substitution effect as people will fail to save sufficiently as they perceive social security boxes as sufficient savings and, 2) a retirement effect as the system may motivate people to retire early. A problem facing the social security system is up to 2016 the social security payroll taxes exceed the benefits paid out. Solutions may include raising taxes, cutting benefits or public borrowing.

Privatizing the system is also considered:

B. Unemployment Insurance: The program intends to replace income due to unemployment. Private markets are inadequate to provide much insurance because of 1) adverse selection whereby those most likely to become unemployed are those most in demand of the unemployment insurance, and 2) a hazard when those employees obtaining insurance face a high level of unemployment rate. Basically the government unemployment insurance avoids the adverse selection but does not eliminate the moral hazard problem. The payroll tax used in unemployment insurance is experience rated which is generally described as imperfect.

C. The Health Care Situation: The case for government intervention in the health care system rests on reasons of 1) information asymmetry, 2) adverse selection, and 3) moral hazard. It can be explained as follows:
   1. Information asymmetry in the sense that the patient does not know much about the needed medical solutions; giving the doctor flexibility in selling whatever he/she wants.
   2. Adverse selection in the sense that those most likely to have a high risk are those seeking insurance policies, leading the insurers to set high premiums.
   3. A moral hazard results from those insured taking higher risks and over consuming health care.

The US health care system is huge taking almost 20% of the GDP. It includes a) private insurance and b) government programs. Let's examine each:
1. Private insurance: most of it provided by through employers. With the Kennedy-Kassenbraum act-the Health Insurance Portability and Accountability Act- an employer has to include a new employee (who previously had insurance) in the company's group insurance plan within 12 months.
2. Government insurance programs include Medicare (a health insurance for people age 65 and older and the disabled) with inducements since 1997 for Medicare beneficiaries to enroll in managed care arrangements. New proposals for the role of government in the health care system includes a) single layer system which will be funded by taxes and provide all citizens, regardless of health and income status, with free care services, b) a prescription drug benefit, and c) OBAMACARE as a combination of public and private role in the health care of the citizens.

4
CORPORATION AND SOCIETY:
TOWARD AN ETHICAL PARADIGM

None of our institutions exists by itself and is an end in itself. Every one is an organ of our society and exists for the sake of society. Business is no exception. Free enterprise cannot be justified as being good for business. It can be justified only as being good for society.[1]

This is the attitude that is beginning to dominate the public view of business organization: first, business is a corporate citizen; and second, it should be a good corporate citizen. This attitude arose from the need to control the overwhelming effects of large corporate entities on society and to involve businessmen in correcting some of society's ills. This point of view, however, is not accepted by everyone concerned with corporate-society relationships. Sometimes labeled the strict constructionists, they criticize the social responsibility advocates and argue mainly that profit maximization is the only acceptable objective of business corporations. The debate has generated a huge literature arguing both viewpoints. This chapter will set forth the main points in the debate and argue for an ethical paradigm of the corporate-society relationship more favorable to and supportive of corporate social involement.

Corporate Social Involvement in Three Enterprise Models
THE CLASSICAL VIEW

The classical view of firm behavior as formulated in the nineteenth century argued for perfect competition where (1) the economic behavior is separate and distinct from other types of behavior; (2) the objective function is to maximize profits; and (3) the criterion of business performance is economic efficiency and progress. So motivated by these principles, the business firm was considered to have discharged its responsibilities to society if it efficiently met the market demands for its product. This view evolved to become known as the fundamentalist position. Fundamentalism rests on the market contract model for a description and a prescription of corporate-society relationships. As Preston and Post describes the situation,

According to the market contract model, each unit (firm or individual) in society makes an implicit market contract model with the other members of society, providing them with goods and services they desire on terms more favorable than they can obtain elsewhere and obtaining its own requirements and rewards from them in return.[2]

This description implies that the responsibility of individuals and firms is to identify and respond to market stimuli and to make profits for the share-holders. Any corporate action on social issues is considered to violate management's responsibility to shareholders. As the most outspoken supporter of the fundamentalist position, Milton Friedman refutes the notion that the responsibility of corporate officials goes beyond serving the interests of their stockholders or their members. In a free economy, Friedman maintains that "there is one and only one social responsibility of business-to use its resources and engage in activities designed to increase its profits so long as it stays within the rules of the game, which is to say, engages in open and free competition, without deception or fraud."[3]

Friedman's view derives first from a general view holding that an individual should be allowed to pursue his or her own interest. Because, to quote Adam Smith "by pursuing his own interest, he frequently promotes that of the society more effectually than when he really intends to promote it."[4] It derives also from a question of knowledge and propriety. Corporate officials may not know what the social interest is and are not appointed to serve the social interests. The corporation is a creation of the stockholders, who own it and decide on its conduct. Friedman asks a relevant question: "Is it tolerable that these public functions of taxation, expenditure, and control be exercised by the people who happen at the time to be in charge of particular enterprises, chosen for those posts by strictly private groups?"[5]

This view is reflected in most textbooks in the field of corporate finance and accounting, where authors operate on the assumption that management's primary goal is to maximize the wealth of its stockholders and is generally referred to as the shareholder wealth maximization (SWM) model. According to the SWM model, the firm accepts all projects yielding more than the cost of capital and in equity financing prefers retaining earnings to issuing new stocks. Management is assumed to use decision rules and techniques that are in the best interests of the stockholders in terms of maximizing their wealth.

The classical, fundamentalist, or SWM view is generally defended on two grounds, one positive and one legal.[6] The positive case argues that role specialization and the market contract define the nature of corporate society relationships and allow the achievement of a social optimum. Therefore management cannot expand its role without affecting the performance of those tasks defined by the market contract, possibly leading to decreased efficiency and misallocation of resources. The legal case argues that the corporate charter acts as a limitation on the nature and scope of business activities and on the legal responsibilities of managers. Basically, it limits their authority to consider or modify the nonmarket aspects of their activities.

THE MANAGERIAL VIEW

The managerial view arose in the 1930s as a result of the gap existing between the classical view and the new nature of corporation business. Berle and Means were the first to point to the effects of the widespread separation of ownership from the management of the large business corporations and the greater decision-making powers held by these managers.[7] From these criticisms emerged a managerial view focusing on the central role of professional managers. The corporation is viewed now as a permanent *institution* with a life and a purpose of its own. The managers/trustees run these corporations in the interests not only of the shareholders but also of the employees, customers, suppliers, and other parties having rights in the organization that are not merely contractual claims.[8] According to an accepted manifesto of the managerial view: "The modern professional manager also regards himself, not as an owner disposing of personal property as he sees fit, but as a trustee balancing the interests of many diverse participants and constituents in the enterprise, whose interests sometimes conflict with those of others."[9]

What all this implies is that the managers have enough discretionary control of corporate resources to consider adding social responsibility considerations in setting the objectives of the corporation. The extent of the involvement in social responsibility is defined mainly by the humanitarian predispositions of its management and is controlled by fears of stockholder dissatisfaction, of losing competitive power, and of adverse effects on earnings. The managerial view is not, however, indifferent to profit maximization. It merely adds an additional consideration in the resource allocation procedure, which is to recognize responsibility for other things besides profit maximization.[10]

THE SOCIAL ENVIRONMENT VIEW

The social environment model views the large corporation as a repository of huge economic and political power with concomitantly important social responsibilities. The large corporation is believed to have a keen interest in the total societal environment and not merely its markets. It recognizes explicitly the impact not only of economic forces but also of political and social forces. Consequently it responds to social demands for active participation in correcting some of society's ills, such as "inadequate educational systems, hard-core unemployment, hazardous pollution of natural resources, antiquated transportation, shameful housing, insufficient and ineffective public facilities, lack of equal opportunity for all, and a highly dangerous failure of communication between young and old, black and white."[11]

In adopting this more socially responsible attitude and responding to the pressures of new dimensions-social, human, and environmental-business organizations may have to alter their main objective, whether stockholder wealth maximization or management welfare maximization, to include as an additional constraint the welfare of society at large. This view is referred to as the social welfare maximization model."[12] Under this model, the firm undertakes all projects that, in addition to the usual profitability objective, minimize the social costs and maximize the social benefits created by the productive operations of the firm. Consider, for example, the following assertions:

Business decision-making today is a mixture of altruism, self-interest, and good citizenship. Managers do take actions which are in the social interest even though there is a cost involved and the connection with long range profits is quite remote. . . .

The kind of managers we are discussing can be called social responsive managers. In their decision making they give substantial weight to social inputs along with economic and technical inputs, and they seek to provide social outputs for a wide variety of claimants. The change toward this type of role will take years, but the trend is clear. . . .

In order to perform their new socio-economic role effectively, business leaders need to develop value systems that recognize responsibilities to claimants other than stockholders. There is strong evidence that managers already have this kind of value system.[13]

Social Responsibility

Various definitions of social responsibility have been presented in the literature and in practice encompassing a continuum going from limited or no involvement to total involvement with and concern for the social environment. These definitions fall into five categories: restricted to profit maximization, enlightened self-interest; going beyond profit maximization; ever widening concentric circles; and toward social responsiveness.

RESTRICTED TO PROFIT MAXIMIZATION

This definition, espoused by the classical view and strongly advocated by Friedman, restricts the responsibility of management of profit maximization. Friedman expresses it eloquently:

Few trends could so thoroughly undermine the very foundations of our free society as the acceptance by corporate officials of social responsibility other than to make as much money for their stockholders as possible. This is a fundamental subversice doctrine. If businessmen do have a social responsibility other than making maximum profits for stockholders, how are they to know what is?[14]

In fact, Friedman goes further by arguing that if businessmen continue to engage in forms of social responsibilities and act as guardians of the public life, then the state may require that they, like public officials, be elected or appointed.[15] And business will cease to be a private institution, followed by the downfall of pluralism and its replacement by a monolithic business society.[16] This view of the social responsibility question calls for a choice between social responsibilities and profits or between a monolithic and pluralistic society.

ENLIGHTENED SELF-INTEREST

This model, especially developed by Wallich and McGowan under the auspices of the Committee for Economic Development, attempts to rationalize corporate social investment.[17] Under this model, Wallich and McGowan maintain that, because shareholders hold diversified portfolios, they would encourage firms to invest in any activity for which the return to the entire sector of publicly owned corporations exceeds the cost. Thus, investment decision criteria are expanded to include consideration of a social or group rate of return in addition to a private return. Consequently, the types of behavior that bring returns to the corporate sector as a whole actually operate to the benefit of the holder of a a diversified portfolio. Shareholders' interest is expanded to include interest in the corporate sector as a whole- in the form of improved environmental conditions, a better labor force, and strong public approval of private business.[18] Wallich and McGowan conclude their proposition as follows:

The conclusion of this analysis is that the proposition that corporate involvement in social policy is contrary to the stockholders' interest is both misleading and irrelevant. Involvement in social policy is tantamount to the adoption of a policy of evaluation investment opportunities by including returns other than those directly accruing to the investing corporation in the form of increased profit. Once it is recognized that corporations are not usually owned by a group of investors who owns shares in only one corporation but by individuals who as a group typically own shares in a very large number of corporations, the whole concept of stockholder interest becomes extremely fuzzy. Nevertheless, it can be said that the adoption of a policy of including all returns appropriable through the market system will enable investors to reach higher welfare levels than they would if corporations adhered to a narrower approach to evaluation of returns.[19]

This statement implies that stockholder' interest is better served by corporate policies that consider improving the kind of society in which business can grow and prosper.

GOING BEYOND PROFIT MAXIMIZATION

This view advises going beyond profit maximization to broadening the scope of management responsibility. J. Backman suggests that "social responsibility usually refers to the objectives or motives that should be given weight by business in addition to those dealing with economic performance."[20] The question becomes to determine the activities that go beyond profit maximization.

One definition of social responsibility suggests going beyond the economic and legal motives. McGuire, for example, makes the following suggestion:

The idea of social responsibilities supposes that the corporation has not only economic and legal obligations, but also certain responsibilities to society which extend beyond these obligations. The corporation today must take an interest in politics, in the welfare of the community, in education, in the "happiness" of its employees- in fact, in the whole social world about it. In a sense, therefore, it must act "justly" as a proper citizen should.[21]

One other definition goes a step further to include voluntary activities.[22] This definition is more compatible with the managerial view presented earlier, which may suggest that corporate social action take the form of corporate giving. In fact the managerial theory clearly suggests that, as companies grow larger, corporate giving will comprise a rising fraction of corporate income and will be determined by the extensiveness of local public contracts, which generate social pressures.[23]

EVER WIDENING CONCENTRIC CIRCLES

This definition of social responsibilities intends to cover the continuum of economic and non economic concerns. As advocated by the Committee of Economic Development, it covers three concentric circles. The inner circle "includes the clear-cut basic responsibilities for the efficient execution of the economic function- products, jobs, and economic growth." The intermediate circle "encompasses a responsibility to exercise this economic function with a sensitive awareness of changing social values and priorities: for example, with respect to environmental conservation, living, and relations with employees." The outer circle "outlines newly emerging and still amorphous responsibilities that business should assume to become more broadly involved in actively improving the social environment."[25]

Davis and Blomstrom also favor this "widening circle" approach to a definition of social responsibility.[26] The inner circle "represents the traditional responsibility of business for its basic economic functions." The intermediate circle "represents the widening area of responsibility that arises directly from performance of the basic economic functions." The outer circle "represents an area that is still not well defined, but there is a rising public expectation for business to modify its singular pursuit of economic goals and help society with some of its unsolved general social problems."[27]

A similar representation is proposed by Steiner, for whom responsibilities rang from "traditional economic production" to "government dictated" to "a voluntary area" and finally to "expectations beyond realities."[28]

TOWARD SOCIAL RESPONSIVENESS

This definition expands social responsibility beyond mere accountability or obligation to cover fully the total social effort and performance of business. R. Ackerman and R. Bauer criticize the concept of social responsibility as assuming an obligation and placing emphasis on motivation rather than performance and propose instead a concept of "social responsiveness."[29] S. Prakash Sethi proposes a conceptual framework to classify corporate responses along three dimensions: corporate behavior or social obligation; social responsibility; and social responsiveness.[30] Social obligation refers to corporate behavior in response to market forces or legal constraints. Social responsibility *"implies bringing corporate behavior up to a level where it is in congruence with currently prevailing social norms, values, and performance expectations. . . . While the concept of social obligation is proscriptive in nature, the concept of social responsibility is prescriptive."*[31] Social responsiveness is the adaptation of corporate behavior to social needs. The difference between social responsibility and social responsiveness is presented as follows: "While social responsibility related activities are prescriptive in nature, activities related to social responsiveness are proactive, i.e., anticipatory and preventive in nature."[32]

Social responsiveness represents, then, the corporate response to social responsibility and to actual and future social issues. Accordingly, William Frederick termed the responsiveness of a firm as CSR, which he defined as follows:

Corporate social responsiveness refers to the capacity of a corporation to respond to social pressures. The literal act of responding, or of achieving a generally responsive posture, to society is the focus. . . . One searches the organization for mechanisms, procedures, arrangements, and behavioral patterns that, taken collectively, would mark the organization as more or less capable of responding to social pressures.[33]

Thus, corporate social responsiveness goes beyond the moral and ethical connotation of social responsibility to the managerial process of response. The managerial processes proposed in the literature include (1) planning and social forecasting;[34] (2) organizing for social response;[35] (3) controlling social activities;[36] and (4) social decision making and corporate social policy.[37]

Dimensions of Corporate Social Responsibilities

The areas of social responsibility include various activities and are expanding from one firm to another and from one industry to another. Various attempts have been made in the literature to list the possible areas of social involvement. Most of the empirical research focuses on the annual reports of corporations as a source of social involvement data.[38] The most exhaustive survey of social responsibility has been conducted yearly since 1971 by the firm of Ernst & Ernst.[39] It includes an evaluation of the extent and nature of social responsibility disclosure in the annual reports of the Fortune 500 industrials, the Fortune 50 Life Insurance Companies and fifty commercial banks. The seven general categories constitute an exhaustive list of the possible dimensions of corporate responsibility disclosed in annual reports. They are as follows:

ENVIRONMENT
Pollution control in the conduct of business operations
Prevention or repair of damage to the environment resulting from processing of natural resources
Conservation of natural resources
Other disclosures relating to the environment

ENERGY
Conservation of energy in the conduct of business operations
Energy efficiency of products
Other energy-related disclosures

FAIR BUSINESS PRACTICES
Employment of minorities
Advancement of minorities
Employment of women
Advancement of women
Employment of other special interest groups
Support for minority businesses in the United States
Socially responsible business abroad
Other statements on fair business practices

HUMAN RESOURCES
Employee health and safety
Employee training
Other human resource disclosures

COMMUNITY INVOLVEMENT
Community activities
Health-related activities
Education and the arts
Other community activity disclosures

PRODUCTS
Safety
Reducing pollution arising from use of a product
Other product-related disclosures

OTHER SOCIAL RESPONSIBILITY DISCLOSURES
Other disclosures

Additional information

Proposed areas and dimensions of corporate social responsibility, however, go beyond what is disclosed in annual reports. Business is being asked to engage in an expanding list of social activities that serve a wide area of social needs. Two comprehensive lists of areas of social involvement may serve as an illustrative example of the spectrum of activities to improve society.
The first list, proposed by K. Davis and R. L. Blomstrom, includes the following:

ECOLOGY AND ENVIRONMENTAL QUALITY
Clean-up of existing pollution
Design of processes to prevent pollution
Aesthetic improvements
Noise control
Dispersion of industry
Control of land use
Required recycling

CONSUMERISM
Truth in lending, in advertising, and in all business activities
Product warranty and service
Control of harmful products

COMMUNITY NEEDS
Use of business expertise and community problems
Reduction of business's role in community power structure
Aid with health care facilities
Aid with urban renewal

GOVERNMENTAL RELATIONS
Restrictions on lobbying
Control of business political action
Extensive new regulation of business
Restrictions on international operations

BUSINESS GIVING
Financial support for artistic activities
Gifts to education
Financial support for assorted charities

MINORITIES AND DISADVANTAGED PERSONS
Training of hard-core unemployed
Equal employment opportunity and quotas for minority employment
Operation of programs for alcoholics and drug addicts
Employment of persons with prison records
Building of plants and offices in minority areas

Purchasing from minority businessmen
Retraining of workers displaced by technology

LABOR RELATIONS
Improvement of occupational health and safety
Prohibition of "exports of jobs" through operations in nations with low labor costs
Provision of day-care centers for children of working mothers
Expansion of employee rights
Control of pensions, especially vesting of pension rights
Impatience with authoritarian structures; demand for participation

STOCKHOLDER RELATIONS
Opening of boards or directors to public members representing various interest groups
Prohibition of operations in nations with "racist" or "colonial" governments
Improvement of financial disclosure
Disclosure of activities affecting the environment and social issues

ECONOMIC ACTIVITIES
Control of conglomerates
Breakup of giant industry
Restriction of patent use[40]

The second list, proposed by the Research and Policy Committee of the Committee for Economic Development, includes the following:

ECONOMIC GROWTH AND EFFICIENCY
Increasing productivity in the private sector of the economy
Improving the innovativeness and performance of business management
Enhancing competition
Cooperation with government in developing more effective measures to control inflation and achieve high levels of employment
Supporting fiscal and monetary policies for steady economic growth
Helping with the post-Vietnam conversion of the economy

EDUCATION
Direct financial aid to schools, including scholarships, grants, and tuition refunds
Support for increases in school budgets
Donation of equipment and skilled personnel
Assistance in curriculum development
Aid in counseling and remedial education
Establishment of new schools, running schools and school systems
Assistance in the management and financing of colleges

EMPLOYMENT AND TRAINING
Active recruitment of the disadvantaged
Special functional training, remedial education, and counseling

Provision of day-care centers for children of working mothers
Improvement of work/career opportunities
Retraining of workers affected by automation or other causes of joblessness
Establishment of company programs to remove the hazards of old age and sickness unemployment, health, and retirement systems

CIVIL RIGHTS AND EQUAL OPPORTUNITY
Ensuring employment and advancement opportunities for minorities
Facilitating equality of results by continuing training and other special programs
Supporting and aiding the improvement of black educational facilities, and special programs for blacks and other minorities in integrated institutions
Encouraging adoption of open-housing ordinances
Building plants and sales offices in the ghettos
Providing financing and managerial assistance to minority enterprises and participating with minorities in joint ventures

URBAN RENEWAL AND DEVELOPMENT
Leadership and financial support for city and regional planning and development
Building or improving low-income housing
Building shopping centers, new communities, new cities
Improving transportation systems

POLLUTION ABATEMENT
Installing of modern equipment
Engineering new facilities for minimum environmental effects
Research and technological development
Cooperating with municipalities in joint treatment facilities
Cooperating with local, state, regional, and federal agencies in developing improved systems of environmental management
Developing more effective programs for recycling and reusing disposable materials

CONSERVATION AND RECREATION
Augmenting the supply of replenishable resources, such as trees, with more productive species
Preserving animal life and the ecology of forests and comparable areas
Providing recreational and aesthetic facilities for public use
Restoring aesthetically depleted properties such as strip mines
Improving the yield of scarce materials and recycling to conserve the supply

CULTURE AND THE ARTS
Direct financial support to art institutions and the performing arts
Development of indirect support as a business expense through gifts in kind, sponsoring artistic talent, and advertising
Participation on boards to give advice on legal, labor, and financial management problems
Helping secure government financial support for local or state arts councils and the National Endowments for the Arts

MEDICAL CARE
Helping plan community health activities
Designing and operating low-cost medical care programs
Designing and running new hospitals, clinics, and extended care facilities
Improving the administration and effectiveness of medical care
Developing better systems for medical education, nurses' training
Developing and supporting a better national system of health care

GOVERNMENT
Helping improve management performance at all levels of government
Supporting adequate compensation and development programs for government executives and employees
Working for the modernization of the nation's governmental structure
Facilitating the reorganization of government to improve its responsiveness and performance
Advocating and supporting reforms in the election system and the legislative process
Designing programs to enhance the effectiveness of the civil services promoting reforms in the public welfare system, law enforcement, and other major governmental operations[41]

Arguments About Social Responsibility

The question of whether business has a responsibility to society has generated a continuous debate and various articles in the literature replete with arguments for and against the assumption of such activity.

ARGUMENTS FOR SOCIAL RESPONSIBILITY

Paul A. Samuelson, a distinguished economist, argued that "a large corporation these days not only may engage in social responsibility, it had damn well better try to do so."[42] What may lead a firm to engage in social responsibility are the advantages and benefits that may result. Numerous advantages are cited in the literature.[43] The most noteworthy are the following:

1. The acceptance of social responsibility may be an intelligent and prudent response to society's new activism and new expectations of business. This has been stated as the Iron Law of Responsibility, which is that "in the long run, those who do not use power in a manner which society considers responsible will tend to lose it."[44]
2. Involvement in social responsibility may serve the long-run self-interest of business by creating a better environment, community, and society, which may also be conducive to low-cost production.
3. Social responsibility may create a more favorable public image, which may generate better customers, better employees, and better investors, to cite only a few benefits.
4. Involvement in social responsibility may prevent the government from enacting more regulations to protect society and hence may prevent the creation of more restrictions on the normal conduct of business operations.
5. Involvement in social responsibility may show that business may be adapting its attitudes and behavior to society's new norms, which are more and more norms favoring social responsiveness.
6. It may be in the best interest of the stockholder for business to engage in activities aimed at improving the social environment.
7. Social responsibility may be a way of acknowledging the complex web of social interdependence. One negative action by business is perceived to have serious repercussions on various groups and interests.
8. Social responsibility may ensure conservation of national wealth and culture and prevent irresponsible acts. As Davis and Blomstrom argue, "Too much is at stake to risk irresponsibility, so

responsible business action becomes necessary in order to maintain a viable institution and a favorable public image."[45] On the same issue, Joseph McGuire rightfully comments that the "men who adhere to the doctrine of social responsibilities, who recognize that they are men first and businessmen second, are more representative of businessmen in general than are those who have produced the harmful scandals of recent years."[46]

9. Social responsibility may reduce the "social tension" of a society. N. H. Jacoby refers to the "social tension" of a society as the "sum of the expectation-reality gaps of all the social problems within the range of public consciousness."[47] Hence the people have high expectations about the role of business in the betterment of society but face generally a different reality when business performance falls short of expectations. The expectations can only be met by more involvement by business in solving some social problems and correcting some injustices and inequities.

ARGUMENTS AGAINST SOCIAL RESPONSIBILITY

Milton, Friedman, a distinguished economist, arguing against the idea of social responsibility, stated that "few trends could so thoroughly undermine the very foundations of our free society as the acceptance by corporate officials of a social responsibility other than to make as much money for their stockholders as possible."[48]

What may lead firms and individuals to refuse to engage in or encourage social responsibility are the disadvantages that may result. Numerous disadvantages are cited in the literature.[49] The most noteworthy are the following:

1. Social responsibility diverts management from their main objective, which is to maximize profit. Again, Friedman, the major proponent of the profit maximization view, explains:

    In a free enterprise, private property system, a corporate executive is an employee of the owners of the business. He has direct responsibility to his employers. That responsibility is to conduct the business in accordance with their desires, which generally will be to make as much money as possible while conforming to the basic rules of the society. . . . Insofar as his actions in accord with his "social responsibility" reduce returns to stockholders, he is spending their money. Insofar as his actions raise the price to customers, he is spending the customers' money. Insofar as his actions lower the wages of some employees, he is spending their money.[50]

2. Social responsibility is an attempt to promote business power and give business an excessive concentration of power. As Ben W. Lewis has written, "If we are to have rulers, let them be men of good will; but above all, let us join in choosing our rulers- and in ruling them."[51] Friedman joins his debate by arguing that the state may require that businessmen, like public officials, be elected or appointed.[52]

3. Social responsibility may create a monolithic business society to replace the actual pluralistic one. The strongest support of this view comes from Theodore Levitt:

    But at the rate we are going there is more than a contingent probability that, with all its resounding good intentions, business statesmanship may create the corporate equivalent of the unitary state. Its proliferating employee welfare programs, its serpentine involvement in community, government, charitable, and educational affairs, its prodigious currying of political and public favor through hundreds of peripheral preoccupations, all these well-intended but insidious contrivances are greasing the rails for our collective descent into a social order that would be as repugnant to the corporations themselves as to their critics. The danger is that all these things will turn the corporation into a twentieth-century equivalent of the medieval Church. The corporation would eventually invest itself with all-embracing duties, obligations, and finally powers- ministering to the whole man and molding him and society in the image of the corporation's narrow ambitions and its essentially unsocial needs.[53]

4. Social responsibility requires heavy outlays of money and efforts, which may be beyond business' limited economic resources. Another consequence may be the bankruptcy of marginal firms in various industries. Friedman again argues,

    The large enterprise can have money to exercise social responsibility only if it has a monopoly position: if it's able to hire its employees at lower wages than they are worth: if it is able to sell its product at a higher price than can otherwise be charged. If it is a monopoly, it ought to be prosecuted under antitrust laws. Any businessman who boasts to the public that he has been using corporate funds to exercise a social responsibility should be regarded as asking for an investigation by the Antitrust Division of the Justice Department.[54]

5. Social responsibility requires social skills, techniques of measurement and verification that businessmen don't know or don't have the time or motivation to learn. This view is claimed to be held not only by free-market believers but also leftists:

> They believe that businessmen are crass and ignoble people who grasp for every dollar they can and who single-mindedly engage in the pursuit of profit. They would not hesitate to take advantage of their neighbors wherever a dollar is concerned. Obviously, men like this are not to be trusted with programs which primarily show concern for one's neighbors. They are philosophically and emotionally unfit for the job.[55]

Conclusion

The "strict constructionists," like Milton Friedman and Henry Manne, argue that business serves society best when it restricts its activities to profit maximization and participates in social activities only to the extent that they are necessary to its own well-being. The social responsibility advocates, on the other hand, argue that business ought to engage in social responsibilities that go beyond compliance with law and include measures to be a good corporate citizen. Basically the two positions depend on how business managers answer the following question: Is the basis of business maximization of profit to the point of greed and avarice or is it to be a good corporate citizen and adopt the view that spiritual, ethical, and moral considerations should play an important role in profit making?

The latter choice implies the existence of a societal value system upon which the public generally agrees. An explicit societal value system is generally considered to be lacking. As McGuire explains:

Unfortunately, in our modern world, societal value systems are not clearly set forth in all their detail, and in some respects it is difficult to find out exactly what constitutes the public agreement. In many instances the value "norms" of society consist of wide bands rather than narrow lines, and the difference between behavior that is just barely tolerated and that which is intolerable is difficult to distinguish. Thus, in some cases where business practices are unethical it may be that such behavior results from the confusion or the fuzziness with which societal values and norms are transmitted to the individual and in the way in which they are interpreted by him.[56]

There is, however, an increasing interest in business values and ethical guidelines to reassess and improve business's social conduct. Various surveys reveal that business people, governmental officials, and public opinion are very concerned with questions of business ethics and morality and are ready to translate that concern into action.[57] There is an acceptance of the idea that social responsiveness requires that business decisions be made against ethical as well as legal and monetary benchmarks. For example, J. W. Clark, S. J., proposed a tentative statement of ethical guides:

The Guide of Social Institutions. Ethical action is based upon the support of the social institutions which are generally accepted by a given society. . . .

The Guide of Individual Integrity. A proper support of social institutions supposes a personal commitment to individual integrity. . . .

The Guide of Official Legislation. Ethical conduct by executives requires observance of legislation imposed by legitimate civil authority. . . .

The Guide of Representative Authority. Ethically responsible executives recognize their power and authority as representative, i.e., held in the interest of others. . . .

The Guide of Parity Between Authority and Moral Responsibility. Moral responsibility is coextensive with authority; that is, in his decision-making capacity, an executive is morally responsible for all the effects of his decisions within his control.

The Guide of the Private Enterprise. Support of social institutions in the United States includes support of private enterprise as a legitimate and essential system of economic organization.[58]

Similarly, Alvar O. Elbing, Jr., looking at the value issue in a social rather than a narrowly economic framework, proposes the following:
1. Business activity cannot be viewed as amoral. . . .
2. Since business activity is in the moral realm the value issue cannot be considered a peripheral issue. .
3. The marketplace is inadequate as an arbiter of business values since it cannot adequately arbitrate business as a social system. . . .
4. Economic considerations cannot be carried on in isolation from social considerations, or in isolation from a value framework without endangering social values. . . .
5. With recognition of the network of social consequences of business activity we can no longer measure the influence of business solely in terms of economic wellbeing and national wealth.[59]

Along the same lines, Keith Davis proposes the following five guidelines for the conduct of business in a responsible manner:
One basic proposition is that *social responsibility arises from social power.* . . .
A second basic proposition is that *business shall operate as a two-way open system with open receipt of inputs from society and open disclosure of its operation to the public.* . . .
A third basic proposition is that *social costs as well as benefits of an activity, product, or service shall be thoroughly calculated and considered in order to decide whether to proceed with it.* . . .
A fourth basic proposition is that the *social costs of each activity, product, or service shall be priced into it so that the consumer (user) pays for the effects of his consumption on society.*
A fifth basic proposition is that *beyond social costs business institutions as a citizens have responsibilities for social involvement in areas of their competence where major social needs exist.*[60]

As a final example, Thomas J. Zenisek suggested the following characteristics of a "societal-type" firm:
1. A firm must cooperate to the best of its ability with the federal government.
2. A firm must not degrade the environment.
3. A firm must do all that is possible to provide minority groups with an opportunity to become active and important members of the free enterprise system.
4. A firm (like a citizen) is a free participant in society with all the responsibilities which are associated with that citizenship.
5. A firm must actively and openly participate in politics.
6. A corporation's existence depends on its public charter; therefore, it must yield to societal demands.
7. A firm must actively work to promote social justice.
8. A firm is as much a social institution as it is an economic one.[61]

Large corporations are the dominant carriers of the social values held by most members of American society. These values are known to center on material advancement, individual autonomy, equal opportunity, and competitive achievement. But should the ethical values governing personal conduct also govern institutional conduct? For example, should the ethic of individualism, encompassing private enterprise and competition, be used to justify acts such as the closing down of a community plant, which, while making a profit, is comparatively inefficient; the degrading of air or water but within legal limits; economizing on the quality of a product but in ways that do not jeopardize sales; converting work into jobs that are more productive but devoid of inherent interest; encouraging economic growth, expansion of consumption and output, regardless of the impact on society?[62]

The answer is obviously in favor of a new set of business values and ethics to justify business interest of a better social order and environment. If business continues to be trapped by its own vision and values and reluctant to adopt a new set of ethical values compatible with the social change, then the unfortunate consequences may be a forced solution. Neil W. Chamberlain warns about such consequences:

If more radical change does not come from an insurgent group within the dominant class itself, it is likely to come from some new thrusting group outside that class, riding on a new social vision, asserting changed social values. If this occurs, we may be confident that in due course there will develop a quite separate ethic, not applicable to society at large but only to the new institution which presides over the new order. It will be based on that institution's survival needs, but rationalized as necessary to the preservation of the social order. It is this institutional imperative which embodies- as in corporate society today- the true limits of any institution's social responsibility.[63]

Thus, a new set of business values and ethics is required for business to deal with the new environmental conditions. It may be described as the *"ethos" to designate the all-embracing field within which different types of values (religious, ethical, socio-economic, and cultural) are found.*"[64] Following a proposal made by W. Bernthal,[65] we may visualize the value hierarchy as follows:

1. If the decision criterion is the individual, the objective of corporate action should be the betterment of individual welfare in terms of freedom, opportunity, self-realization, human dignity, respect, etc.
2. If the decision criterion is the society, the objective of corporate action should be the betterment of social welfare, in terms of quality of life, culture, civilization, order, justice, concern for social issues, etc.
3. If the decision criterion is the economic system, the objective of corporate action should be the promotion of consumer welfare, in terms of allocation of resources, production and distribution of goods and services, economy and quality of production, etc.
4. If the decision criterion is the business firm, the objective of corporate action should be the promotion of ownership welfare in terms of profits, survival, growth, image, etc.

Notes

1. Peter F. Drucker, *Management: Tasks, Responsibilities, Practices* (New York: Harper & Row, 1973), p. 41.
2. Lee E. Preston and James E. Post, *Private Management and Public Policy: The Principle of Public Responsibility* (Englewood Cliffs, N.J.: Prentice-Hall, 1975), p. 30.
3. Milton Friedman, *Capitalism and Freedom* (Chicago: University of Chicago Press, 1962), p. 133.
4. Adam Smith, *The Wealth of Nations* (1776; London: Cannan, 1930), p. 421.
5. Friedman, *Capitalism and Freedom*, p. 134.
6. Preston and Post, *Private Management and Public Policy*, pp. 31-34.
7. Adolf Berle and Gardiner Means, *The Modern Corporation and Private Property* (New York: Macmillan, 1932).
8. Frank X. Sutton et al., *The American Business Creed* (Cambridge: Harvard University press, 1956), pp. 5-58.
9. Committee for Economic Development, *Social Responsibilities of Business Corporations* (New York: CED, 1971), p. 22.
10. Committee for Economic Development, *Social Responsibilities of Business Corporations*, pp. 27, 29.
11. *Business Week* (May 15, 1971): 63.
12. A Belkaoui, *Conceptual Foundations of Management Accounting* (Reading, Mass.: Addison-Wesley, 1980), p. 61.
13. G. Steiner, *Business and Society* (New York: Random House, 1975), pp. 168, 169.
14. Friedman, *Capitalism and Freedom*, p. 133.

15. M. Friedman, as reported in the Social Science Reporters, *Eighth Social Science Seminar on "Three Major Factors in Business Management: Leadership, Decision-Making and Social Responsibility"* (San Francisco: March 19, 1958): 4-5.

16. Theodore Levitt, "The Dangers of Social Responsibility," *Harvard Business Review* (September-October 1958): 44.

17. H. Wallich and J. J. McGowan, "*Stockholder Interest and the Corporation's Role in Social Policy*," pp. 39-59, in Community for Economic Development, *A New Rationale for Corporate Social Policy* (new York:CED, 1970).

18. Committee for Economic Development, *Social Responsibilities of Business Corporations* (New York: CED, 1971), p. 30.

19. Wallich and McGowan, "Stockholder Interest and the Corporation's Role in Social Policy," p. 55.

20. J. Backman, *Social Responsibility and Accountability* (New York: New York University Press, 1975), p. 2.

21. Joseph W. McGuire, *Business and Society* (New York: McGraw Hil, 1963), p. 144.

22. H. G. Manne and H. C. Wallich, *The Modern Corporation and Social Responsibility* (Washington, D. C.: American Enterprise Institute, 1972), p. 5.

23. Neil H. Jacoby, *Corporate Power and Social Responsibility: A Blueprint for the Future* (New York: Macmillan, 1973), pp. 198-199.

24. Archie B. Carroll, "A Three-Dimensional Conceptual Model of Corporate Performance," *Academy of Management Review* 4, no. 4 (1979): 500.

25. Jacoby, *Corporate Power and Social Responsibility*, pp. 198-199.

26. Committee for Economic Development, *Social Responsibilities of Business Corporations*, p. 15.

27. K. Davis and R. L. Blomstrom, *Business and Society: Environment and Responsibility* (New York: McGraw-Hill, 1975), pp. 8-9.

28. G. A. Steiner, *Business and Society*, 2nd ed. (New York: Random House, 1975), p. 169.

29. Robert W. Ackerman and Raymond a. Bauer, *Corporate Social Responsiveness: The Modern Dilemma* (Reston, Va.: Reston Publishing, 1976), p. 6.

30. S. Prakash Sethi, "A Conceptual Framework for Environmental Analysis of Social Issues and Evaluation of Business Response Patterns," *Academy of Management Review* 17, no. 3 (1979): 63-74.

31. Ibid., p. 66. Emphasis mine.

32. Ibid.

33. William C. Frederick, "From CSR_1 to CSR_2: The Maturing of Business-and-Society Thought," Graduate School of Business, Working Paper, no. 279, University of Pittsburgh, 1978.

34. K. Newgren, "Social Forecasting: An Overview of Current Business Practices," in A. B. Carroll, ed., *Managing Corporate Responsibility* (Boston: Little, Brown, 1977).

35. T. W. McAdam, "How to Put Corporate Responsibility Into Practice," *Business and Society/Innovation* 6 (1973): 8-16.

36. A. B. Carroll and G. W. Belier, "Landmarks in the Evolution of the Social Audit," *Academy of Management Journal* (1975): 589-599.

37. E. H. Bowman and M. Haire, " A Strategic Posture Toward Corporate Social Responsibility," *California Management Review* 18 (1975): 49-58; Carrol, *Managing Corporate Social Responsibility*; H. Gordon Fitch, "Achieving Corporate Social Responsibility," *Academy of Management Review* (January 1976): 38-46; J. E. Post and M. Mellis, "Corporate

Responsiveness and Organizational Learning," *California Management Review* 20 (1978): 57-63; Lee E. Preston and James E. Post, *Private Management and Public Policy: The Principle of Public Responsibility* (Englewood Cliffs, N. J.: Prentice-Hall, 1975); and G. A. Steiner, "Social Policies for Business," *California Management Review* 15 (1972): 17-24.

38. W. F. Abbott and R. J. Monsen, "On the Measurement of Corporate Social Responsibility: Self-Reported Disclosures as a Method of Measuring Corporate Social Involvement," *Academy of Management Journal* 22, no. 3 (1979): 501-515; D. R. Beresford, "How Companies Are Reporting Social Performance," *Management Accounting* 56, no. 2 (1974): 41-44; Sandra L. Holmes, "Corporate Social Performance: Past and Present Areas of Commitment," *Academy of Management Journal* 20, no. 3 (1977): 434-438; N. Elias and M. Epstein "Dimensions of Corporate Social Reporting," *Management Accounting* (March 1975): 36-40; and J. Chan, "Corporate Disclosure in Occupational Safety and Health: Some Empirical Evidence," *Accounting, Organizations and Society* 4, no. 4 (1979): 273-281.

39. Ernst and Ernst, *Social Responsibility Disclosure* (New York: Ernst & Ernst, 1978).

40. Davis and Blomstrom, *Business and Society*, pp. 8-10.

41. Committee for Economic Development, *Social Responsibilities of Business Corporations*, pp. 37-40.

42. Paul A. Samuelson, "Love That Corporation," *Mountain Bell Magazine* (Spring 1971): 24.

43. Keith Davis, "The Case for and Against Business Assumption of Social Responsibilities," *Academy of Management Journal* (June 1973): 312-322.

44. K. Davis and R. L. Blomstrom, *Business, Society, and Environment: Social Power and Social Response*, 2nd ed. (New York: McGraw-Hill, 1971), p. 95.

45. Davis and Blomstrom, *Business, Society, and Environment*, p. 90.

46. Joseph W. McGuire, *Business and Society* (New York: McGraw-Hill, 1963), p. 147.

47. Neil H. Jacoby, "The Corporation as a Social Activist," in S. P. Sethi, ed., *The Unstable Ground: Corporate Social Policy in a Dynamic Society* (Los Angeles: Melville, 1975), p. 227.

48. Friedman, *Capitalism and Freedom*, p. 133.

49. Levitt, "The Dangers of Social Responsibility," pp. 41-49.

50. Milton Friedman, "Does Business Have a Social Responsibility?" *Baule Administration* (April 1971): 13-14.

51. American Economic Association, "Economics by Admonition," *American Economic Review*, Supplement (May 1959): 395.

52. Milton Friedman, as reported in Social Science Reporters, *Eighth Social Science Seminar*, pp. 4-5.

53. Levitt, "The Dangers of Social Responsibility," p. 44.

54. Milton Friedman, "Milton Friedman Responds," *Business and Society Review* (Spring 1972): 6-7.

55. Davis, *The Case for and Against Business Assumption of Social Responsibilities*, p. 319.

56. McGuire, *Business and Society* p. 282.

57. James S. Bowman, "Managerial Ethics in Business and Government," *Business Horizons* (October 1976): 48-54; Sandra L. Holmes, "Executive Perceptions of Corporate Social Responsibility," *Business Horizons* (June 1976): 34-40; Alister K. Mason and S. R. Maxwell, "The Changing Attitude to Corporate Social Responsibility," *Business Quarterly* (Winter 1975): 42-50; James E. Grunig, "A New Measure of Public Opinions on Corporate Social Responsibility," *Academy of Management Journal* (December 1979): 738-764.

58. John W. Clark, "A Tentative Statement of Ethical Guides," *Social Environment of Managing* (February 1979).
59. Alvar O. Elbing, Jr., "The Value Issue of Business: The Responsibility of the Businessman," *Academy of Management Journal* (March 1970): 75.
60. Keith Davis, "Five Propositions for Social Responsibility," *Business Horizons* (June 1975): 19-24. Emphasis in the original.
61. Ibid.
62. N. W. Chamberlain, *The Limits of Corporate Responsibility* (New York: Basic Books, 1973), p. 206.
63. Ibid., p. 209.
64. Clarence C. Walton, *Ethics and the Executive: Values in Managerial Decision Making* (Englewood Cliffs, N.J.: Prentice-Hall, 1969), p. 24. Emphasis in the original.
65. W. F. Bernthal, "Value Perspectives in Management Decisions," *Journal of the Academy of Management* (December 1962): 195.

Bibliography
BOOKS
Ackerman, Robert W. *The Social Challenge to Business.* Cambridge: Harvard University Press, 1975.
___, and Raymond A. Bauer. *Corporate Social Responsiveness: The Modern Dilemma*. Reston, Va.: Reston Publishing, 1976.
Anshen, Melvin, ed. *Managing the Socially Responsible Corporation*. New York: Macmillan, 1974.
Chamberlain, N. W. *The Limits of Corporate Responsibility*. New York: Basic Books, 1973.
Committee for Economic Development. *A New Rationale for Corporate Social Policy*. Lexington, Mass.: Heath, 1970.
___. *Social Responsibilities of Business Corporations*. New York: Committee for Economic Development, 1971.
Jacoby, Neil H. *Corporate Power and Social Responsibility: A Blueprint for the Future*. New York: Macmillan, 1973.
Kolasa, Blair J. *Responsibility in Business: Issues and Problems*. Englewood Cliffs, N.J.: Prentice-Hall, 1972.
Manne, H. G., and H. C. Wallich. *The Modern Corporation and Social Responsibility*, Washington, D.C.: American Enterprise Institute, 1972.
McGuire, Joseph W. *Business and Society*. New York: McGraw-Hill, 1963.
McKie, James W. *Social Responsibility and the Business Predicament*. Washington, D.C.: Brookings Institution, 1974.
Preston, Lee E., ed. *Research in Corporate Social Performance and Policy*. Greenwich, Conn.: JAI Press, 1981.
Preston, Lee E., and James E. Post. *Private Management and Public Policy: The Principle of Public Responsibility*. Englewood Cliffs, N.J.: Prentice-Hall, 1975.
Sawyer, George C. *Business and Society: Managing Corporate Social Impact*. Boston: Houghton Mifflin, 1979.
Sethi, S. P., ed. *The Unstable Ground: Corporate Social Policy in a Dynamic Society*. Los Angeles: Meville, 1975.
Walton, Clarence C. *Corporate Social Responsibilities*. Belmont, Cal.: Wadsworth, 1967.

___. *Ethics and the Executive: Values in Managerial Decision Making.* Englewood Cliffs, N.J.: Prentice-Hall, 1969.

Williamson, Oliver E. *Corporate Control and Business Behavior: An Inquiry Into the Effects of Organization Form on Enterprise Behavior*, Englewood Cliffs, N.J.: Prentice-Hall, 1970.

ARTICLES

Abbott, Walter F. "On the Measurement of Corporate Social Responsibility: Self-Reported Disclosures as a Method of Measuring Corporate Social Involvement." *Academy of Management Journal* 22, no. 3)1979): 501-515.

Ackerman, Robert W. "How Companies Respond to Social Demands." *Harvard Business Review* (July-August 1973): 88-98.

Aldag, Ramon J., and Donald W. Jackson, "Assessment of Attitudes Toward Social Responsibilities." *Journal of Business Administration* (Spring 1977): 65-80.

Alexander, Gordon, and Rogene A. Bucholz, "Corporate Social Responsibility and Stock Market Performance." *Academy of Management Journal* 21, no. 3 (1978): 479-486.

Anderson, R. H. "Social Responsibility Performance: Measurement and How!" *Cost and Management* (September-October 1979): 12-16.

Armstrong, J. Scott. "Social Irresponsibility in Management." *Journal of Business Research* (September 1977): 185-213.

Baker, Donald G., and Neil H. Jacoby. "Corporate Power and Social Responsibility." *Wall Street Review of Books* (March 1974): 73-80.

Banks, Louis. "The Mission of Our Business Society." *Harvard Business Review* (May-June 1975): 57-65.

Bennett, Roy F. "Business and Social Responsibility." *Cost and Management* (September-October 1976): 14-16.

___. "Business and Social Responsibility." *Cost and Management* (October 1979): 14-16.

Bowman, James S. "Managerial Ethics in Business and Government." *Business Horizons* (October 1976): 48-54.

Burck, Gilbert. "The Hazards of Corporate Responsibility." *Fortune* (June 1973): 114-217.

Cadbury, Sir Adrian. "The Social Responsibility of Business: An Issue That Will Not Go Away." *AMA International Forum* (February 1978): 32-38.

Capon, Frank S. "The Place of Business in Society." *Financial Executive* 38, no. 10 (October 1970): 34-46.

Carroll, Archie B. "Corporate and Social Responsibility: Its Managerial Impact and Implications." *Journal of Business Research* 2, no. 1 (January 1974): 75-88.

___. "A Three-Dimensional Conceptual Model of Corporate Performance." *Academy of Management Review* 4, no. 4: (1979): 497-505.

Cheit, Earl F. "Why Managers Cultivate Social Responsibility." *California Management Review* (Fall 1964): 3-22.

Clark, John W. "A Tentative Statement of Ethical Guides." *Social Environment of Managing* (February 1979): 60-72.

Conlan, James E. "The Public's Negative Attitude Towards business Won't Change Until You Work to Change It." *Rotarian* (February 1978): 35-36.

Corson, John J., and George A. Steiner. "Social Responsibility: A New Dimension of Corporate Accountability," pp. 1-20. In Committee for Economic Development, *Measuring Business's*

Social Performance: The Corporate Social Audit. New York: Committee for Economic Development, 1974.

Crawford, Ronald L., and Harold A. gram. "Social Responsibility as Interorganizational Transaction." *Academy of Management Review* (October 1978): 880-888.

Davis, Keith. "The Case for and Against Business Assumption of Social Responsibilities." *Academy of Management Journal* (June 1973): 312-322.

___. "Five Propositions for Social Responsibility." *Business Horizons* (June 1975): 19-24.

Elbing, Alvar O., Jr. "The Value Issue of Business: The Responsibility of the Businessman." *Academy of Management Journal* (March 1970): 79-89.

Fitch, H. Gordon. "Achieving Corporate Responsibility." *Academy of Management Review* (January 1976): 38-46.

French, James P. "What Does Business Owe Society?" *Society* (1976): pp. 50-54.

Friedman, M. "The Social Responsibility of Business Is to Increase the Profits." *New York Times Magazine* (September 13, 1970): 1-6.

Grunig, James E. "A New Measure of Public Opinions on Corporate Social Responsibility." *Academy of Management Journal* 22, No. 4 (1979): 738-764.

Henderson, Hazel. "Redefining the Rights and the Responsibilities of Capital." *Management Review* (October 1977): 9-20.

Holmes, Sandra L. "Corporate Social Performance: Past and Present Areas of Commitment." *Academy of Management Journal* 20, no. 3 (1977): 433-438.

___. Executive Perceptions of Corporate Social Responsibility." *Business Horizons* (June 1976): 34-40.

___. "Structural Responses of Large Corporations to a Social Responsibility Ethic." Unpublished.

Humble, John. "A Practical Approach to a Social Responsibility." *Management Review* (May 1978): 18-22.

Katz, Wilber J. "Responsibility and the Modern Corporation." *Journal of Law and Economics* (1979): 75-85.

Keim, Gerald D. "Corporate Social Responsibility: An Assessment of the Enlightened Self-Interest Model." *Academy of Management Review* (January 1978): pp. 53-64.

___. "Managerial Behavior and the Social Responsibility Debate: Goals Versus Constraints." *Academy of Management Journal* (March 1978): 57-68.

Keim, Gerald D., James J. Benjamin, and Robert H. Strawser. "Rationales for Changes in Corporate Behavior." *Atlanta Economic Review* (May-June 1977): 9-14.

Kotz, Eugene, and Rick Shriner. "Model of Social Responsibility Development." Unpublished.

Lipson, Harry A. "Current Efforts to Measure Corporate Social Performance." *Atlanta Economic Review* (March-April 1975): 15-19.

Lodge, George Cabot. "Ethics and the New Ideology: Can Business Adjust?" *Management Review* (July 1977): 10-19.

Mason, Alister K., and S. R. Maxwell. "The Changing Attitude to Corporate Responsibility." *Business Quarterly* (Winter 1975): 42-50.

Nadeau, Pierre. "La Responsabilité sociale de l'entreprise," *Commerce* (October 1979): 102-108.

Nader, Ralph, Mark Green, and Joel Seligman. "Who Rules the Corporation?" *McGraw-Hill Management Awareness Program* (March-April 1977): 5-21.

Pledger, Rosemary, and Richard E. Vaden. "Traditional American Ideals and Corporate Responsibility." *Marquette Business Review* (Summer 1976): 69-71.

Shanklin, William L. "Corporate Social Responsibility: Another View." *Journal of Business Research* 4, no. 1 (February 1976): 75-84.

Zenisek, Thomas J. "Corporate Social Responsibility: A Conceptualization Based on Organizational Literature." *Academy of Management Review* 4, no. 3 (1979): 359-368.

Appendix 4.A.
Ethical Paradigm and Political Economy

Government as a mechanism for maximizing individuals' self interest is assumed by political economy. The procedures used to determine the public expenditures dictated by the ethical paradigm and direct democracy are either the "unamnity rules" or the "majority voting rules."

The unanimity rules assume agreement of all people in democracies dictatorship and juries in a given situation, equating "unanimous consent" with "silent consent." It assumes an informed public with facts published with transparency and freedom of information laws, an open and balanced democracy with competing political parties. The failure of unaminity roles in the determination of an efficient level of public goods is due mainly to the difficulty of obtaining an honest revelation of preference.

The majority rule allows for a majority to decide in the selection of alternatives. Ray's theorem dictates that the majority rule needs to be fair and respect the following properties.
1. Fairness with a) anonymity in the sense that each vote counts, and b) neutrality in the sense that each alternative is treated equally.
2. Decisiveness in the sense that there is only one winner
3. Ronotonicity in the sense that the alternative preferred will be chosen.

Various limitations need to be mentioned:
a. The majority rule can be viewed as a "tyranny of the majority," that can be connected by guaranteeing certain inalienable rights. As Anthony McGawn, "One man's right to be property in the antebellum south was another man's slavery."
b. Another limitation is the EPE (Erroneus Priorities Effect) when groups act on what they think is important and not what is influential to make a change. As the 6th law of the science of structural dialogic design by Dye stated that: learning occurs in a dialogue as the observers search for influence relationships among the members of a set of observations.
c. The majority can lead to poor deliberation and an aggressive culture and conflict. "The voters who are casually interested in doing something can defect one voter who has dire opposition to the proposed of the two.
d. Related to the argument above the pair voting can go on for ever leading to the "CYCLING" phenomenon, which has been shown to lead to debilitating instability.
e. In the case of majority rules, people preferences are not single peaked the median voter theorem will lead to an outcome of majority voting as a reflection of the preferences of the median voter. The resulting problem is logrolling or vote trading as a way of leading to an efficient provision of public goods. Special interests tend to win at the logrolling game, with the costs borne mainly by the minority. Given all the limitations of the unanimity, simple majority and logrolling the problem becomes to find an ethically accepted method for translating individual preferences into collective preferences.

The addition to the limitations of both the unanimity and majority rates, Arrow's Impossibility Theorem comes to the conclusion that in general it is impossible to find a rule that satisfies all of this criterion, casting doubts on the very ability of democracies to function.

What is heeded is a virtual uniformity of tastes to make a democracy work. This discussion has an important implication and conclusion to the ethical paradigm that all public and private institutions should have the express purpose of molding people's tastes to make some that uniformity emerge as far as the need to control the overwhelming effects of large corporate entities on society and involve business in correcting some of society's ills.

Appendix 4.B
Ideology and the Ethical Paradigm

When it comes to the relationship between the individual and the state there are two major approaches: a) the organic view of government and b) the mechanistic view of government. They can be identified as follows:
1. In the organic view of government, society is viewed as a national organism with individuals as parts of the organism and the government as its heart. It follows then that the state sets the goals for society and society has to act and realize them. The goals differ from a heart's perfect nationality, to racial purity lest for the nazis or a socialist objective to name only a few.
2. In the mechanistic view of government, government is just a creation by individuals to include their individual goals, with the power to insure the benefit of the people and avoid anamoly where as noted by Thomas Hobbes, "the life of man (becomes) solitary, poor, nasty, brutish, and short. The goals differ depending on ideology, with libertarians arguing for a limited government and social democrats more in favor of government intervention.

The approach taken in the ethical paradigm to socio-economics is for mechanistic view of government and an active role of government in ensuring an ethical paradigm in the social contract and the functioning of society.

It calls for a government capable of having through its activities a substantial effect on resource allocations then a budget on the expenditures and revenues. The major categories of federal expenditures include:
a. National diffuse
b. Social security
c. Medicare
d. Public welfare activities
e. Payment of interest on debt

The major categories of federal revenues include:
a. Individual income taxes
b. Corporate tax
c. Social insurance which are payroll tax collections used to finance social security and medicare.

5
Economics of Social Issues

The market mechanism is Adam Smith's "invisible hand," which allocates resources efficiently and equitably without any government interference. In most market economics this mechanism has worked well, as evidenced by the achievement of very high levels of output, productive efficiency, a variety of consumer goods, and general prosperity. In short, the market mechanism has worked well in providing consumer goods. It has, however, worked less than perfectly in dealing with some of the social problems facing modern societies. The market failure to correct and/or eradicate some of the social ills has been attributed to various sources, including short-run business fluctuations, income inequality, presence of monopolies, inadequate provision of public goods, deteriorating quality and rising costs of services, misallocation of resources between present and future, imperfect information, moral hazard , and beneficial and detrimental externalities. The most important source of market failure remains, however, the failure to reflect or internalize externalities that consist of the unaccounted interactions among economic agents. The price of a product does not include all the marginal social cost or the marginal social benefit generated by the production or consumption activities. As a result the market mechanism will yield an inefficient allocation of resources and a failure to correct some of the social ills.

This chapter examines the nature of externalities and the economics of social issues and compares the solutions to each of theses issues by both the market and nonmarket solutions. The comparison between the two approaches is accomplished on the basis of society's objective, namely, social efficiency and equity.

Externalities
SOURCES OF EXTERNALITIES

Most economists agree that perfect competition in all markets will lead to a position of maximum social welfare given the assumptions that underlie the analysis. If markets are highly competitive and consumers and producers are rationally attempting to reach a maximum level of satisfaction, then the available resources will be allocated in a way that maximizes social welfare.

In such economic situations, first of all, producers will value the marginal product of a variable productive service as equal to its marginal product multiplied by the market price of the commodity in question. Hence, in the case of labor, a profit-maximizing firm would hire additional laborers until the wage aid to the last worker employed just equals the dollar value of the extra product he produces. Secondly, consumers who wish to maximize satisfaction subject to a limited money income will allocate their expenditures so that the last dollar spent on any particular item will yield an amount of satisfaction equal to the last dollar spent on any other item. Lastly, if, in addition, the purchasing power distribution conforms to the ethical standards of the society and if consumer control over resource allocation is accepted as ethically correct, then the prices of goods and factors of production represent their accurate contributions to social welfare.

Thus, prices provide automatic valid guidelines for investments and production provided the private valuation corresponds to the social valuation. The private valuation of a given process of production rests on the difference between private costs and private benefits, which is the net private benefits. The private costs and private benefits measure, respectively, the value of the best alternative uses of the resources available to a producer and the benefits according to the producer. The social valuation of the same process of production rests on the difference between social cost and social benefits, which is the net social benefit. The social costs and social benefits measure, respectively, the value of the best alternative uses of the resources available to society and the benefits accruing to society.

Again, when the marginal net private benefits are equal to the marginal net social benefit, the private market system will lead to an allocation of the resource in the ways that are efficient and in the interest of society. But in the cases where the marginal net private benefits differ from the marginal net social benefits, the market system will fail to achieve maximum social welfare.

Indirect effects of such nature, causing the market failure under various labels such as "third party" effects, "spillover effects," and, more clearly, "external diseconomies," are the social costs not considered by the private marginal cost pricing rule.

The immediate result is that an apparently efficiently working economy, one in which outputs are quickly adjusted so that prices everywhere tend to equate private marginal cost, must lead the economy very far from the optimal social welfare solution. In short, "Optimal solutions by macroeconomic units will not give rise to social optima; on the contrary, they may and will coincide with a disrupting of the natural and social environment."[1]

Externalities are difficult to measure because of their complex nature. Although generated either in the process of production of certain goods, or in their final use by the public, the private marginal cost pricing rule does not attach any value to these damages. As a direct result the social value of a good, i.e., the market value of the good minus the estimated value of the diseconomy, will not only be inferior to its market price but even negative. When the private marginal cost pricing rule is changed to a social marginal cost pricing rule, a social optimum will be reached through the internalization of the externality. Hence Scitovsky maintains, "It is generally true that one can always enhance economic efficiency by commercializing any noncommercial situation or activity and by internalizing any external economy."[2] Mishan distinguishes between two ways of internalization:

1. Either the firm reduces output until the social value of a good is raised to reach its marginal cost of production; or
2. We may leave the market price unchanged and instead transform the private marginal cost into social marginal cost by adding to the private marginal cost the value of any externality generated through production or use of the good in question.[3]

TYPES OF EXTERNALITIES

Consumption externalities arise whenever the utility of one individual is affected by the consumption of another individual. If the action taken by one individual results in uncompensated advantages to other consumers, the result is an external economy of consumption. If an individual replaces his old, noisy, and polluting car with a new, quiet, and energy-efficient model, benefits accrue to all his neighbors resulting in external economies of consumption. Similarly, if the action taken by one individual results in uncompensated disadvantages to other consumers, the result is an external diseconomy of consumption. If individual X builds a fence that casts a shadow on another individual's vegetable garden, he or she imposes a burden on Y. In brief, consumption externalities result from the interdependence of consumers' satisfactions: an individual's satisfaction is dependent upon other people's satisfaction.

Production externalities arise when an increase in one firm's production creates benefits to other firms that may not be accounted for by the producing firms using the conventional market mechanism. As an example, the production increase of GM cars may result in an increase in steel production and therefore create an external economy of production for the steel industry. Similarly, when the increase in one firm's production creates uncompensated costs to others, it creates an external diseconomy of production. As an example, the increased production of one firm may result in a higher number of trucks on the road, increased traffic congestion, and more waste materials in the environment, creating, therefore, an external diseconomy of production. In brief, production externalities result from the direct interdependence among producers: one firm's output enters as an input in another firm's production function. Because most firms use materials produced by other firms to produce their own output, a distinction has to be made between pecuniary and technological externalities.

A pecuniary externality arises when the rise in output by one firm causes a rise in the price of its inputs. The other firms using the output of that firm as an input are subject to pecuniary external diseconomies. Pecuniary external economies are less common than pecuniary external diseconomies. Pecuniary externalities are not to be confused with the true externalities, consumption or production externalities identified earlier, which are directly conveyed to others through the market system. Pecuniary externalities are basically secondary price effects that are indirectly conveyed to others through the market system. If consumers shift from beef to fish, the price of beef will decrease and that of fish will increase. Similarly, the beef producers will be worse off. All of these changes took place indirectly through the marketplace, and no true externalities were created.

Technological externalities occur whenever a firm cannot realize all the gains or is not forced to incur all the costs that accrue to other firms or individuals in society as a result of its actions. An external diseconomy is said to exist when the marginal social cost is greater than the marginal social benefit. It is a technological external diseconomy when it is caused by a physical or technical process and is borne by economic decision units independent from the one who caused it. The usual example of a pure technological externality is the case of honey and apple production, where the cost of honey is affected by the level of apple production. For the individual producing the honey there is no difference between the private and social marginal product. However, for the apple producer the private marginal product is less than the social marginal product of labor. Two solutions exist, either the apple producer gets subsidized or the production of apple and honey is accomplished by the same individual, which will internalize the externality.

MEASUREMENT ISSUES

Economists' attempts to ascertain the monetary value of externalities and thereby to bring them within the scope of economic analysis to date have not been very successful. In the first place, some categories of external diseconomies, manifestly important ones, do not lend themselves easily to measurement. Also, the chain of casualty might be very complex. As an example: "Air pollution is not only the result of, and not proportionate to the volume of production and the emissions of residual waste products, they are also governed by the interactions of a whole series of variables which may react upon one another."[4] Also, it is difficult to attribute to a specific sector of the economy the consequences of some external diseconomies which depend upon complementary economic activities. As Kapp explains, "Environmental and social costs must be looked upon as the outcome of an interaction of several complex systems (economic, physical, meteorological, biological, etc. . . . in which a plurality of factors interplay through a 'feedback' process)."[5]

Furthermore, external diseconomies and social costs depend for their measurement on the magnitude of the perception and awareness of the issue in a particular society. It is "a matter of social evaluation, i.e., the magnitude of the social costs upon the importance which organized society attributes to both tangible and the intangible values involved."[6] Moreover, some of the consequences of externalities are intangibles; Ridker speaks of psychic costs, and, as such, "even if the available monetary estimates of social costs were complete, they would have to be considered as fragmentary, because some of the social losses are intangible in character and have to be evaluated in other than monetary terms."[7]

A distinction has been made between separable and non-separable externalities in an article by Otto A. Davis and A. H. Whinston.[8] In the case of separable externalities, only the total costs are affected, not the marginal (incremental) costs. For example, if firm A builds installations that reduce the natural ventilation so that the management of a neighboring hotel must install a central air conditioner, the total cost function of the hotel would be increased by a fixed outlay while its marginal cost would stay constant. In the case of non-separable externalities, the marginal cost would be affected. As the authors state: "The difference between the separable and non-separable cases lies in the fact that externality enters the cost function in a multiplicative manner rather than in a strictly additive way."[9] This distinction between separable and non-separable externalities adds to the difficulties of measurement and of computation of the appropriate charges to be levied.

Davis and Whinston discussed also the complex problem of assessing the value of reciprocal externalities. A reciprocal externality occurs if firm A imposes an externality that raises the costs of firm B, when firm B carries on a production process that creates another externality that raises the costs of firm A. Non-separable reciprocal externalities are likely to lead a merger of the firms, neither one being able to reach maximum profit without dependence on the other.

In conclusion, then, the existence of externalities can pose difficult problems for measurement and social policy. With respect to social policy, the question of dealing with technological externalities calls for some governmental intervention and a form of mixed economy to correct the misallocation caused by these externalities. In what follows, some of the corrective actions are examined in general before presenting the main social issues and problems affected by externalities and the market and nonmarket solutions advocated to resolve them.

CORRECTIVE ACTIONS

The market mechanism generally fails to achieve an efficient allocation of resources when externalities are present. Intervention may be necessary to correct the problems caused by externalities. The numerous solutions proposed in the literature and in practice are witness to the fact that no correct solution has been derived yet. These solutions include mainly: prohibition, directive, voluntary payment, merger, taxes and subsidies, sale of pollution rights, negotiation, and regulation. Let us briefly examine each of them now and explore their merits later when the economics of social issues are examined.

1. *Prohibition.* This solution consists of prohibiting the activity generating the externality. In most cases this solution is neither feasible nor practical given that the productive activity and the resulting consumer good may be either vital or just needed by a segment of society.
2. *Directive.* This solution consists of deciding the right amount of externality to be borne by society rather than completely prohibiting the productive activity. The right amount may be the level of production where the marginal cost of controlling the externality is equal to the marginal benefit of control.
3. *Payment.* This solution suggests that private parties take the initiative and pay the responsible party to eliminate the externality.

4. *Merger.* As suggested earlier, non-separable reciprocal externalities are likely to lead to a merger of the responsible firms, neither one being able to reach maximum profit without dependence on the other.
5. *Taxes and Subsidies.* This solution consists of imposing a suitable excise tax on those firms whose activities create external costs and providing subsidies to those firms whose activities generate external benefits. This solution is the classic remedy to the externality problem put forward in the 1920s by A. C. Pigou.[10]
6. *Sale of Pollution Rights.* This solution consists of selling licenses giving the owner the right to pollute up to some specified level and for a specified period of time. The level would correspond to some acceptable emission standard determined by governmental units. This method allows the producers to internalize the social cost of pollution into their cost accounting as an additional cost of production.
7. *Regulation.* This solution consists of regulating the use of specific devices intended to reduce the external costs imposed by the externality. An example of such regulation is to require the addition of auto safety equipment to reduce the harmful effects of auto accidents.
8. *Negotiation.* This solution assumes that if bargaining is costless, the externality problem may be resolved by negotiation between the concerned parties. This solution is another classic remedy to the externality problem put forward by R. Coase.[11]

The Economics of Social Issues

Besides externalities, other sources of market failures are known to contribute to the difficult correction of some of the social ills affecting modern societies. In what follows, a selected list of social issues will be examined in terms of their economic and social aspects and the contribution of both market and nonmarket analysis. The social issues to be examined include health care, education, housing, pollution, crime, energy, poverty, inequality, and discrimination. Before presenting the economics of these issues, it is important to define society's objectives for resource allocation. These criteria will then be used to compare the contribution of market and nonmarket mechanisms to the solving of these social issues.

The criteria used by society in resource allocation are defined in terms of the need to reach the highest attainable level of economic welfare, generally termed the "socially efficient level of output," and the best equitable distribution of that output to all the members of society. Thus, the social criteria used for resource allocation are the achievement of efficiency and equity.[12]

The socially efficient level of output corresponds to the level of output where the marginal social cost is equal to the marginal social benefit. When this output is reached, social efficiency is generally achieved. This rationale applies as well to the production of economic goods like butter as to the production of social goods like health care, education, and housing.

Social equity is difficult to define because it rests on the personal value judgments of how resources should be distributed among members of the society. In fact, both social efficiency and social equity rests on the type of economic organization used by the particular society, which can be easily reduced to either a market solution or a nonmarket solution.

To recapitulate, the problem is to allocate resources, whether economic or social goods, in a way that both social efficiency and equity are achieved, and through a type of economic organization, either a market solution or a non-market solution.

Thus, in what follows each of the areas of social concerns will be examined with the social criteria for resource allocation as the main guide and the choice of the best economic solution as the main objective. The areas examined will be health, education, housing, pollution, crime, energy, and poverty, inequality, and discrimination.

ECONOMICS OF HEALTH CARE

Health is vital to individual and collective welfare. It must be allocated in such a way as to ensure social efficiency and social equity. To ensure an efficient health care system, a socially efficient number of hospitals is necessary. Such a number is where the marginal social costs of hospital buildings is equal to the social benefits of hospital buildings. There are, however, measurement issues associated with these social costs and benefits. The social costs are those associated with the costs of educating and training physicians, nurses, and other hospital employees and other hospital employees and the costs of building hospitals may be easy to measure. The social benefits of health care are the elimination or reduction of the costs of being ill. They are composed of the costs resulting from the suffering and the loss of earnings during and after illness.

To ensure an equitable health care system, it should be distributed to all those who need it. Again, both social efficiency and equity may be produced either with a market or a nonmarket approach.

The market approach to the health care system is generally argued to be efficient, to which critics of the market approach claim that the health care market possesses a few characteristics that may make it inefficient, namely, uncertainty of demand and consumer ignorance leading to monopoly and externalities.[13] Uncertainty of demand results from the unpredictability of health problems. Consumer ignorance results from the difference in knowledge between the doctor and the patient, which confers a monopoly power on the suppliers of medical services. Externalities in health care exist because the treatment of some communicable diseases create external benefits for those living in the patient's environment, which creates a divergence between the private and the social benefits.

The market approach to the health care system is also generally argued to be equitable. However, that argument may easily be proven wrong because those with higher incomes are able to get better health treatment. Given that health care is a necessity, a generally held belief is that health should not be left to the market system and should be provided to all members of the society in need of medical attention. An operational expression of this point of view is to refer health care to government policies. Three types of policy are suggested by LeGrand and Robinson: national health insurance; market improvement policies; and cost controls, which may promote efficiency and equity.[14]

Existing national health insurance includes two policies: Medicare (for the elderly), and Medicaid (for the poor). Proposals such as the Kennedy Plan aim to extend it to the whole population. The merits of national health insurance are (1) ensuring everyone access to "adequate" health care; (2) eliminating the financial cost connected with the acquisition of health services; and (3) controlling and limiting rising health care costs.[15]

Market improvement policies are intended to promote competition and encourage health maintenance organizations (HMOs), which offer subscribers medical care in return for a fixed annual fee. The oldest HMO in existence, the Ross-Loos Health Plan, traces its origin to 1929, when it was organized to provide health care for employees of the Los Angeles Water Department. In addition to protecting workers from unexpected medical costs, HMOs were shown to reduce health care costs drastically. In fact, a 1973 federal law mandated most firms with more than twenty-five workers to offer HMO coverage along with conventional health insurance if contacted by a federally qualified HMO. There are two types of HMOs, "staff model" and "group model." The staff model HMO employs doctors directly and provides them with a central office facility and administrative support. A "group model" HMO contracts either with existing multispecialty medical group practices or, while under an "independent practice association," contracts with individual members to serve HMO members. HMOs are growing and even attracting the interest of investors.[16]

Finally, cost controls are intended to set a ceiling to what physicians can charge in the form of specific administrative regulations.

ECONOMICS OF EDUCATION

Education is essential to human promotion and continuous economic growth. Education is also a social good in need of an efficient and equitable allocation. The social efficiency of education requires a maximization of the net benefits of education. While the costs of education may be relatively easy to identify and measure, the benefits are less obvious. Two benefits may be distinguished, namely, production benefits and social benefits. Production benefits are the return on human capital resulting from investment in education. Social benefits are the benefits resulting from the socialization function of education.

The social equity of education dictates that the equality of opportunity in education becomes a right. This equality may be interpreted in a strong sense of equality of access or in a weaker sense as the right to a certain minimum of education.

The market approach to education is also generally argued to be efficient and equitable, to which critics of the market approach argue that, first, inefficiency may result from capital market imperfections, lack of information, external costs and benefits, and monopoly and, second, inequity may result from income inequality.[17]

Capital market imperfections result from the failure and reluctance of financial institutions to lend to low-income households with little collateral. Lack of information results from the complexity of the choice of an educational institution and the lack of expertise of those making the choice. External costs and benefits result from education. The benefits are either employment benefits or benefits to society in general. Blaug identified the following externalities of education: income gains to other than those receiving the education in question; income gains to subsequent generations from a more educated present generation; provision of an effective mechanism for identifying talent, assisting economic occupational mobility of the labor force; provision of an environment that stimulates research and invention; encouragement of "socially responsible" behavior; encouragement of political stability through a more informed electorate and better-educated political leaders; transmission and nurturing of a cultural heritage; and widening of intellectual and cultural horizons to enhance the value of leisure time.[18] Finally, monopoly, or exactly spatial monopoly, results when there is only one school in a town with a low population.

Given these deficiencies in the market approach, there is a need for government to play an active role in education, especially in the form of financial assistance to students, research support, and so on. Those not satisfied with the government's role and performance in the domain of education generally suggest the introduction of education vouchers, whereby vouchers are allocated families to buy education in the school of their choice. The voucher system is designed to guarantee a minimum of education to low-income families. Advocates of the voucher system suggest that it would create a greater variety of education institutions, increase school responsiveness to parental values and concerns, stimulate competition among schools and hence quality, promote innovation, encourage parental initiative and involvement in education, and, finally, increase total resources for education.[19] The voucher system may create strong diversity in the school system, however, and may lead to segregation and different standards of schooling.

An alternative plan suggested by Howard R. Bowen proposes a grant-loan to students combined with grants to educational institutions.[20] The grant-loan is designed to help students from low-income families, while the grants to institutions are intended to help institutions meet rising costs of education. This last plan is intended to provide more equity in access to education.

ECONOMICS OF HOUSING

The major goal on the mind of every American is to secure adequate housing. It is also a national goal, as evidenced by the following statement from the Housing Act of 1949: "The Congress hereby declares that the general welfare and security of the Nation and the health and living standards of its people require . . . the realization as soon as feasible of the goal of a decent home and a suitable living environment for every American family."

This goal is far from realized, as evidenced by the deteriorating inner areas of many of the nation's cities. To society, equity considerations dictate that housing is a necessity of life and that a minimum standard of accommodation is required. However, given the substandard housing predominating in the inner areas of the cities, there is ample evidence that the market system has failed to meet the efficiency and equity considerations in housing. There are several reasons for the market failure, namely, income limitations, capital market imperfections, lack of information, discrimination, supply inelasticities and externalities.[21]

It is intuitively evident that income limitations act as a barrier to entry into the market of good-quality homes, which may result in an equitable housing situation. Second, capital market imperfections may result from the redlining practiced by financing companies, which may define certain areas as bad risks, thereby restricting the amount and number of long-term mortgages to the targeted area. Third, lack of information and discrimination may exist in the housing market, which may confine certain income groups and ethnics to certain neighborhoods. Fourth, inefficiency in the housing market may result from short-run supply inelasticity, whereby, there is a time lag before the housing market adjusts to an increase in demand. The inelasticity of supply in the housing market results in a higher housing price rather than a higher number of houses as a result of an increase in demand. Finally, externalities exist in the housing market depending on the type of housing conditions practiced by the owner. Improvement in the condition of a house results in a social benefit, while neglect results in social cost.

Given all these problems leading to failure in the housing market, government intervention has taken various forms, namely, rent control, public housing, and price and income subsidies. The basic motivation for government intervention in the housing market is:
A desire to increase the consumption of housing services by households beyond what they choose or can afford in an unregulated market; the desire to ensure that the financial burden of renting or buying accommodations is not "too" high; and the desire, which is commonly found in many developed countries, to foster home ownership by the occupiers of the dwellings.[22]

Public housing is another governmental policy aimed at providing housing of an acceptable minimum standard. It has generally failed due to high land cost, lack of maintenance and operating funds, and generally inhuman, high-density environments.

Income and price subsidies are another form of assistance aimed a providing housing. Price subsidies take place in the form of leased housing programs, rent supplement programs, and housing voucher programs. The general belief is that the nation's poor would be better served by receiving direct housing subsidies rather than living in public housing projects or federally subsidized apartments. A voucher idea would have housing payments made directly to low-income families, who would be responsible for the conditions of their apartments. Under a voucher program, there would be no restrictions on where households could spend the subsidy. They could be renters or homeowners having trouble meeting their mortgage payments. The only requirement would be that they live in adequate housing, as determined by inspections when they apply for vouchers and once a year thereafter.

ECONOMICS OF POLLUTION
Pollution contributes to the destruction of the environment- the air, water, and land around us- and has recently reached monstrous proportions. The environment's use by both producers and consumers as a dumping ground for wastes that are not biodegradable or that are not recycled creates the pollution problem. Pollution, then, may be air pollution, water pollution, or land pollution.

Air pollution results from the dumping into the atmosphere of wastes such as carbon monoxide, sulfur oxides, nitrogen oxides, hydrocarbons, and particulates. These emissions are creating dangerous situations. First, carbon monoxide may be creating a "greenhouse effect" that could cause the earth to warm up. Second, sulfur and nitrogen combine with water vapor tin the atmosphere to form sulfuric acid and nitric acid, which fall to earth as acid rain, killing lakes, dissolving buildings, corroding metals, damaging other materials, and creating a health hazard. Third, hydrocarbons coming from car exhausts create ozone in the atmosphere, which is highly toxic to vegetation and may be the cause for crop reductions. Fourth, toxic metals are poisonous to many life forms and are a possible threat to aquatic life. Finally, fluorocarbons can waft high into the stratosphere, where they can destroy part of the ozone shield, thus increasing the incidence of skin cancers.[23]

Water pollution results from the dumping of material into the water, endangering aquatic life. The level of dissolved oxygen necessary to support aquatic life is built up by aeration and the photosynthetic processes of plant life and is reduced by the biochemical oxygen demand (BOD) needed to decompose organic matter dumped into the water.

Land pollution results from the dumping of various types of wastes on land and from strip mining.

Pollution results from one or both of the following basic factors: "(1) the fact that no one has property rights or enforces them in the environment being polluted, and (2) the collectively consumed characteristics of the environment being polluted."[24] The absence of property rights on the air, some streams, and some lands and the public goods nature of the environment make it possible for people to use the environment as they wish. In doing so, they impose spillover costs on others. Given the harmful effects of pollution, nonpolluters may tend to underuse the environment, while given its nature as a public good, polluters may be motivated to overuse it. What results is a misallocation of environmental services.

From society's point of view, it may be efficient and equitable to engage in some form of pollution control. Efficiency requires determining the level of pollution control at which the marginal cost of pollution control equals the marginal benefit of controlling pollution. This requires a definition of the costs and benefits of pollution control. The costs of pollution control are those costs necessary to keep the environment clean, while the benefits of pollution control are those increases in the well-being of the members of the society that results from the control process. Equity in pollution control requires determining a fair method of allocating the cost of control.

Does the market system allow efficiency and equity to be reached in pollution control? The answer is, unfortunately, no, because operating firms and individuals in the market system base their decisions on private costs and benefits. Two of these solutions will be examined next, namely, the expansion of property rights and government policies aimed at curbing or controlling pollution.

A proposal put forward by E. J. Mishan suggests that property rights be extended to cover amenity rights.[25] In the case of pollution, the property owners may ask for compensation, forcing the polluters to internalize the costs of pollution and to reach an efficient level of pollution control. Another scheme proposed by J. H. Dales is to set a board that would sell to polluters a number of "pollution rights," to be defined by the level of air and water quality deemed desirable for a given area.[26]

Government policies are aimed at reaching an efficient level of pollution control. Two policies are generally recommended: direct controls or indirect controls. Direct controls consist of regulations eliminating certain types of pollution by passing laws defining the acceptable emission standards. Direct controls will be efficient if the regulatory body is able to determine the desirable level of pollution and if the standards are enforceable. Indirect control consist of either placing a tax on each unit of discharge or granting subsidies to polluters as a way of inducing the polluter to reduce the amount of pollution that is discharged.

A comprehensive approach to pollution control emanates from the "material balance approach" first proposed by Ayres and Kneese.[27] Basically, the approach recognizes the environment as a large shell surrounding the economic system. The raw materials are the inputs flowing from the environment to be transformed into consumer goods. In both the production and consumption of these goods residuals are thrown back to the environment unless they are recyclable and recycled. Because these residuals cannot be destroyed but can only be converted, a comprehensive approach requires that they be converted into their least damaging form.

ECONOMICS OF CRIME

Crime is one of the major inconveniences of living in the big cities and a serious social problem in the United States. It affects all aspects of life when security becomes individuals' overriding concern. Crime includes all activities deemed either immoral or illegal. Criminal acts include violent crimes such as murder, rape, aggravated assault, and armed robbery; crimes against property such as fraud, burglary, theft, embezzlement, forgery, arson, vandalism; traffic in illegal goods and services such as gambling, narcotics, loan sharking, prostitution, and alcohol; and other crimes including everything from nonpayment of alimony to speeding.[28] These crimes impose a direct cost on society in terms of the loss of earnings of the victims and indirect cost in terms of costs of prevention, apprehension, protection, and correction. In facing crime problems society's objectives include efficiency equity, and civil liberties.

Ideal efficiency would be zero crime. Given the cost of crime control, which could be prohibitive if the level to be reached was zero, the most efficient level of crime control becomes one at which marginal costs of crime control are equal to the marginal benefits of crime control. Equity involves ensuring adequate distribution of resources to combat crime throughout the city. Finally, the drive to combat crime should not infringe on the civil liberties of people. The idea is to avoid transforming the country into a police state.

The market approach to crime control may consist of private police patrols. Given the free rider possibility, the private police patrol may not be efficient. This is evident since police patrols have the characteristics of public goods, namely, nonrivalry and nonsecludability.

Everyone benefits from their services and nobody can be excluded from using them. Both characteristics lead to a market failure for crime control.

Government intervenes in the process of crime control by providing police, court, and prison protection. However, increasing social expenditures for police, courts, and prisons is not necessarily the best deterrent for crime given the irrationality of crime. A more humane approach to crime reduction is to improve the conditions of the poor.

ECONOMICS OF ENERGY

Energy is an important commodity for the technological and economic progress of a nation and the quality of life of its citizens. Disruptions of its continuous supply can create social havoc. There is, however, a growing scarcity of various sources of energy, as evidenced by the price of resources. It may be alarming given that the increasing scarcity of oil is taking the form of exhaustion of the most accessible and cheapest source of energy. At present, most energy comes from three nonrenewable fossil fuels- oil, coal, and natural gas. Given the increasing rate of consumption of these fuels and their increasing scarcity, the energy problem is in need of solutions.

Society's main objectives in matters of energy are to ensure a continuous and adequate supply of energy and to divide on its use over time. Assuming a given supply of energy is available, the second objective translates into determining the efficient allocation of the energy supply over time. This second objective, however, requires making a decision on the actual consumption rate affecting us and the future consumption rate affecting generations not present at the time the decision is taken. The question of future generations' needs creates a problem of fairness and equity. Given these objectives and problems, can the market system be used to provide solutions? If demand and supply expectations are reasonably accurate, the market system in general and the price mechanism in particular may be relied upon to generate an efficient allocation of energy use over time. However, not only may the expectations not be accurately determined due to imperfect information, there are also other sources of market failure similar to those encountered earlier with health care, education, and housing, namely, externalities and monopoly.[29]

First, imperfect information results from the uncertainty surrounding predictions of demand or supply of energy. Second, externalities arise mainly from the social costs of pollution related to energy extraction, protection, and distribution. Finally, monopoly results mainly from the limited supply and the existence of catels likely to restrict output and raise the price of energy. A good example of an emerging energy monopoly is the Organization of Petroleum Exporting Countries (OPEC).

Given these sources of market failure, government has intervened several times and in different ways. Of the various ways used by government, we may include price controls, taxes, subsidies, regulation, research and development and conservation.

First, government may intervene to restrict prices below the market level to protect consumers. Price controls, however, may act as a disincentive for producers to increase output and may lead to shortages. Second, the externalities generated by energy producers identified earlier may be controlled and/or eliminated by taxes or subsidies and by regulatory policies. Finally, government may plan for the future by encouraging research and development and energy conservation. Most of these government policies were proposed by the Carter administration. In fact, the 1977 Carter program centered on four points:
1. The creation of an Energy Department

2. The imposition of conservation measures including additional taxes on gasoline, taxes on gas-guzzling cars, and a fifty-five-mile-per-hour federal speed limit.
3. The imposition of mandatory switching of industry from fuel oil and natural gas to coal as an energy source.
4. The continuation of price controls on domestic crude oil and its products and on natural gas.[30]

Congress was reluctant to pass the program. Carter proposed another program in 1979 emphasizing the following points:
1. A reduction of U.S. dependence on foreign oil.
2. The development of alternative energy sources-synthetic fuels, nuclear power, and others.
3. A windfall profits tax on all oil produced and sold by domestic producers.
4. The continuation of conservation measures.

Other suggested measures that could be taken by the government include imposing tariffs on imported oil, fuel rationing, and subsidies for alternative energy sources such as oil shale conversion, wind energy, and nuclear fusion.

ECONOMICS OF POVERTY, INEQUALITY, AND DISCRIMINATION

Poverty has always existed in the United States. It became a concern after Michael Harrington published in 1962 a little book called *The Other America*. Poverty became defined in terms of a poverty line separating the poor from the nonpoor. In 1980, for example, the poverty line for a typical family of four was about $8,400, which placed 10 percent of all American families in the poverty category. Being poor implies that others are rich, which leads the issue from the particular case of poverty to the more general level of inequality. As measured by the Lorenz curve, inequality in the United States has been found to be higher than in most other developed countries. Which brings to mind the question, What are the reasons for inequalities?

In general poverty and inequalities stem from differences in innate ability, in skills, in willingness to work or earnings capacity,[31] in inheritance, in luck, in risk taking, and in wages to compensate for more demanding jobs. These sources of inequality are generally considered as just by most people. The list does not include, however, one source generally considered unjust, which is discrimination on grounds of either disability, age, race, or sex. Unfortunately, the costs of discrimination in the working place are both high and subtle and ultimately destructive for all involved. Society's objectives are to correct for the costs of poverty, inequality, and discrimination.

The market rewards people for the amount of resources they are willing to use, whether these resources are labor, capital, or even good will. The sources of inequality identified above, however, allow the market to reward certain people more than others, resulting in both an inefficient and inequitable distribution.

The government's response to poverty is motivated by the need to find a trade-off between equality and efficiency. It is generally shown that measures intended to restrain economic equality may lead to reduced economic efficiency and harm the nation's productivity. In any case, government policies to combat poverty take various forms including, income supplementation policies, including cash income assistance (such as Aid for Families with Dependent Children, Supplemental Security Income, General Assistance, and Old Age, Survivors Disability, and Health Insurance) and in-kind assistance (such as food stamps, Medicaid, Medicare, and public housing); negative income tax intended to guarantee an adequate income; minimum wage; and social policies favoring the acquisition of skills, the removal of monopoly practices and discrimination, the existence of generous benefits for the long-term unemployed, handicapped, sick, and others.

Needless to say, these programs generate a heated debate between those arguing their necessity for keeping the social order and those proposing reduction and/or elimination of these programs on the grounds that they may be destroying work incentives or that they are being abused. It is, however, reassuring to notice that most people are in agreement with policies to combat discrimination. In fact, the Civil Rights Act of 1964 outlawed various forms of discrimination and established the Equal Employment Opportunities Commission (EEOC). Affirmative action became a national goal. Those arguing that affirmative action is leading to "reverse discrimination" were upset by two landmark decisions by the U.S. Supreme Court, the Bakke decision for affirmative action in the schools and the Weber decision for affirmative action in the work place.

The Search for an Economic Remedy
For the market to produce an efficient level of output, the private marginal benefit must equal the social marginal benefit and the private marginal cost must equal the social marginal cost. With respect to the first condition, sources of market failure such as imperfect information, consumer ignorance, and external economies render the market allocation unlikely to result in an efficient level of output. With respect to the second condition, sources of market failure, such as monopoly, and external diseconomies again render the market allocation unlikely to result in efficient level of output.

Similarly, the market fails to provide an equitable distribution of the level of output given the presence of poverty, inequality, and discrimination. The failure of the market to provide an efficient and equitable level of output for most of the social issues requires some form of government intervention either by directly providing the good or service, by regulating the market, and/or by imposing a system of taxation/subsidization. Government intervention has not necessarily met the criteria of efficiency and/or equity in most of the social issues. Experimentation may be needed before finding the type of economic organizations most adequate to deal with each of the social issues. For example, the voucher programs in education and in housing, the negative income tax proposals for inequality, and the HMOs in health care are indicative of the type of experiments needed. *The issue of market versus nonmarket solutions seems to obscure the real issue, which is to correct some of the social and unfair ills of society.* Experimentation in various forms of economic organizations coupled with measurement and audit of their social costs and benefits is the key. Accordingly, applied socioeconomics, with its emphasis on measurement and audit of costs and benefits, may help in the choice of the type of economic organization needed to deal with each of the social issues.

Notes
1. K. William Kapp, "Environmental Disruptions and Social Cost: A Challenge to Economics," *Kylos* (December 1970): 844.
2. Tibor Scitovsky, *Welfare Competition* (Homewood, Ill: Richard D. Irvin, 1971), p. 268.
3. G. Mishan, *The Cost of Economic Growth* (New York: Praeger, 1967), p. 54.
4. Kapp, "Environmental Disruptions and Social Costs," p. 836.
5. Ibid., p. 834.
6. K. William Kapp, *The Social Costs of Private Enterprises* (Cambridge: Harvard University Press, 1950), p. 21.
7. R. G. Ridker, *Economic Costs of Air Pollution* (New York: Praeger, 1968).

8. Otto A. Davis and A. H. Whinston, "Externalities, Welfare and the Theory of Games," *Journal of Political Economy* (June 1962): 120.
9. Ibid.
10. A. C. Pigou, *The Economics of Welfare*, 4th ed. (London: Macmillan, 1946).
11. Ronald Coase, "The Problem of Social Cost," *Journal of Law and Economics* (October 1960): 1-44.
12. Julian LeGrand and Ray Robinson, *The Economics of Social Problems* (New York: Harcourt Brace Jovanovich, 1980), p. 1.
13. Ibid., p. 30.
14. Ibid., p. 38.
15. Karen Davis, *National Health Insurance: Benefits, Costs, and Consequences* (Washington, D.C.: Brookings Institution, 1975), pp. 2-5.
16. Michael L. Millenson, "Investors eye HMOs as a Way to Remain Financially Healthy," *Chicago Tribune*, May 18, 1982, sec. 3, p. 1.
17. Ibid., p. 49.
18. M. Blaug, *An Introduction to the Economics of Education* (Harmondsworth, England: Penguin, 1979).
19. A. T. Peacock and J. Wiseman, *Education for Democrats* (London: Institute of Economic Affairs, 1964).
20. Howard R. Bowen, "Who Pays the Higher Education Bill?" in M. D. Orwig, ed., *Financing Higher Education: Alternatives for the Federal Government* (Iowa City, Ia.: American College Testing Program, 1971).
21. LeGrand and Robinson, *The Economics of Social Problems*, pp. 65-80.
22. A. J. Culyer, *The Political Economy of Social Policy* (New York: St. Martin's Press, 1980), p. 261.
23. Ronald Kotulak, "We Are Living in a Garbage Can," *Chicago Tribune* March 21, 1982, p. 14.
24. R. H. Leftwich and Ansel M. Sharp, *Economics of Social Issues* (Plano, Tex.: Business Publications, 1982), p. 149.
25. E. J. Mishan, *Technology and Growth: The Price We Pay* (New York: Praeger, 1970).
26. J. H. Dales, *Pollution, Property and Prices* (Toronto: University of Toronto Press, 1968).
27. R. Ayers and A. V. Kneese, "Production, Consumption and Externalities," *American Economic Review* (June 1969): 282-297.
28. Leftwich and Sharp, *Economics of Social Issues*, p. 125.
29. LeGrand and Robinson, *The Economics of Social Problems*, p. 125.
30. Leftwich and Sharp, *Economics of Social Issues*, p. 197.
31. Irwin Garfinkel and R. H. Haveman, *Earnings Capacity, Poverty and Inequality* (New York: Academic Press, 1977), p. 39.

Bibliography

Aaron, H. *Why is Welfare So Hard to Reform?* Washington, D.C.: Brookings Institution, 1973.
Anderson, F. R., et al. *Environmental Improvement Through Economic Incentives*. Baltimore: John Hopkins University Press, 1977.
Anderson, R. *The Economics of Crime*. London: Macmillan, 1976.
Baumol, William J. *Welfare Economics and the Theory of the State*. 2nd ed. Cambridge: Harvard University Press, 1965.

Becker, G. "Crime and Punishment: An Economic Approach." *Journal of Political Economy* 76 (1968): 169-217.
Carnegie Commission on Higher Education. *Higher Education: Who Pays? Who Benefits? Who Should Pay?* New York: McGraw-Hill, 1973.
Coase, Ronald. "The Problem of Social Cost." *Journal of Law and Economics* (October 1960): 1-44.
Cooper, M. H., and A. J. Rogers, III. *Environmental Economics*. Hinsdale, Ill.: Dryden Press, 1971.
Cullis, J. G., and P. A. West. *The Economics of Health*. New York: New York University Press, 1979.
Culyer, A. J. *The Political Economy of Social Policy*. New York: St. Martin's Press, 1980.
Dales, J. H. *Pollution, Property and Prices*. Toronto: University of Toronto Press, 1968.
Davis, Otta A., and I. Kamien Morton. "Externalities, Information and Alternative Collective Action." pp. 74-95. In Robert Haveman and Julius Margolis, eds., *Public Expenditures and Policy Analysis*. Chicago: Markham, 1971.
Demsetz, H. "Toward a Theory of Property Rights." *American Economic Review* (May 1967); 347-359.
Dorfman, R., and N Dorfman, eds. *Economics of the Environment: Selected Readings*. 2nd ed. New York: Norton, 1978.
Edwards, R. C., et al. *The Capitalist System*. End ed. Englewood Cliffs, N. J.: Prentice-Hall, 1978.
Freeman, C., and M. Jahoda. *World Futures: The Great Debate*. New York: Universe Books, 1978.
Freh, H. E., III, and P. B. Ginsburg. *Public Insurance in Private Medical Markets*. Washington, D.C.: American Enterprise Institute, 1978.
Fuchs, V. R., *Who Shall Live? Health, Economics and Social Choice*. New York: Basic Books, 1974.
Fuerst, J. S. *Public Housing in Europe and America*. New York: Halstead Press, 1974.
Garfinkel, Irwin, and R. H. Haveman. *Earnings Capacity, Poverty and Inequality*. New York: Academic Press, 1977.
Goldman, Marshall I. *Controlling Pollution: The Economics of a Cleaner America*. Englewood Cliffs, N. J.: Prentice-Hall, 1967.
Green, C. *Negative Taxes and the Poverty Problem*. Washington, D.C.: Brookings Institution, 1967.
Havighurst, C. "Controlling Health Care Costs." *Journal of Health Politics, Policy and the Law* 1 (1977): 471-498.
Jencks, C. *Education Vouchers: A Report on the Financing of Elementary Education by Grants to Parents.* Cambridge, Mass.: Center for the Study of Public Policy, 1970.
Kapp, K. William. "Environmental Disruptions and Social Cost: A Challenge to Economics." *Kylos* (December 1970).
___. *The Social Costs of Private Enterprise*. Cambridge: Harvard University Press, 1950.
Kelly, Donald R., Kenneth R. Stunkel, and Richard R. Wescott. *The Economic Superpowers and the Environment; The United States, the Soviet Union and Japan*. San Francisco: Freeman, 1976.
Kneese A. *Economics and the Environment*. New York: Penguin, 1977.

___, and Charles L. Schultze. *Pollution, Prices and Public Policy.* Washington, D.C.: Brookings Institution, 1975.
Lecomber, R. *Economics of Natural Resources.* New York: Halsted Press, 1979.
Leftwich, R. H., and Ansel M. Sharp. *Economics of Social Issues.* Plano, Tex.: Business Publications, 192.
LeGrand, Julian, and Ray Robinson. *The Economics of Social Problems.* New York: Harcourt Brace Jovanovich, 1980.
Magaziner, Ira C., and Robert B. Reich. *Minding America's Business: The Decline and Rise of the American Economy.* New York: Harcourt Brace Jovanovich, 1982.
McClure, W. "The Medical Care System Under National Health Insurance: Four Models." *Journal of Health, Politics, Policy and the Law* 1 (1976): 22-68.
Meade, J. "External Economies and Diseconomies in a Competitive Situation." *Economic Journal* (March 1952): 54-67.
Mishan, E. J., "The Postwar Literature on Externalities: An Interpretive Essay." *Journal of Economic Literature* 9 March 1971): 1-28.
Mishan, G. *The Cost of Economic Growth.* New York: Praeger, 1967.
Mitchell, E. J. *U.S. Energy Policy: A Primer.* Washington, D.C.: American Enterprise Institute, 1974.
Okun, A. *Equality and Efficiency: The Big Trade Off* (Washington, D.C.: Brookings Institution, 1975).
Perlman, R. *The Economics of Poverty.* New York: Basic Books, 1974.
Phelps, E. *Economic Justice.* New York: Penguin, 1973.
Pigou, A. C. *The Economics of Welfare.* 4th ed. London: Macmillan, 1946.
Ridker, R. G. *Economic Costs of Air Pollution.* New York: Praeger, 1968.
Schiller, B. *The Economics of Poverty and Discrimination.* Englewood Cliffs, N.J.: Prentice-Hall, 1976.
Schultz, T. W. *The Economic Value of Education.* New York: Columbia University Press, 1963.
Scitovsky, Tibor. *Welfare Competition.* Homewood, Ill: Richard D. Irwin, 1971.
Seneca, J. J., and M. K. Taussig. *Environmental Economics.* 2nd ed. Englewood Cliffs, N.J.: prentice-Hall, 1979.
Smith, W. F. *Housing: The Social and Economic Elements.* Berkeley: University of California Press, 1970.
Thurow, Lester C. *Poverty and Discrimination.* Washington, D.C.: Brookings Institution, 1969.
Tobin, J. "On Limiting the Domain of Inequality." *Journal of Law and Economics* 13 (1970): 263-277.
Wenner, Lettie McSpadden. *One Environment Under Law: A Public-Policy Dilemma.* Pacific Palisades, Cal.: Goodyear, 1976.
Windham, D. M. "The Economics of Education: A Survey." In N. W. Chamberlain, ed., *Contemporary Economic Problems.* Homewood, Ill: Richard D. Irwin, 1973.
Wolozin, Harold, ed. *The Economics of Air Pollution.* New York: Norton, 1966.
Worchester, D. A., "Pecuniary and Technological Externality, Factor Rents, and Social Costs." *American Economic Review* (December 1969): 873-885.

Appendix 5.A.
The Economic Remedy and Public Goods

The economic remedy, advanced in this book, rests in a mixed economy that combines the best in market and nonmarket solutions to the social issues facing each country in general, and a particular emphasis in handling efficiency the public goods. Public goods and private goods differ on two dimensions:

a. While the consumption of a private good, like a piece of pizza, is rival, the consumption of a public good, like national defense, is nonrival, in the sense that once it is provided, the additional resource cost of another person consuming national defense is zero.
b. While the consumption so a private good like pizza, is excludable, the consumption of a public good, like national defense, is nonexcludable, in the sense that to prevent anyone from consuming national defense is either very expensive or impossible.

Because of the difficulties associated with getting everybody to reveal their true preferences for a public good, market forces may not be able to provide the efficient level of public goods. In addition the free rider phenomenon works against market forces sustability. So, efficiency calls for a government provision of a public good.

Some have called for a privatization of the government functions, arguing that it is more efficient to have a mix of private and public good provision. The choice may depend on the following considerations:

1. The choice may depend on who will provide for lower relative wages and material costs.
2. The allocation of fixed administrative costs to a higher base, results in lower fixed administrative costs.
3. A diversity of tastes may argue for privatization even if public provision lead to lower administrative costs.
4. Commodity egalitarianism, making a public good available to everyone, argues for a public provision of the public good.
5. For privatization to be efficient, the government needs to write a contract with the private provider that can COMPLETELY define the quality of the service songlet by the government. The evidence shows the prevailing existence of incomplete contracts.

6
MICRO SOCIO-ECONOMICS: PROPOSED APPROACHES

Micro Socio-Economics is that part of social accounting interested in the evaluation, measurement, and disclosure of the social performance of firms. The word *micro* is used to differentiate it from macro social economics, which is more oriented toward the evaluation, measurement, and disclosure, of national performance. Micro social economics represents, in fact, the approach used by practitioners and academic accountants interested in the measurement and disclosure of the environmental effects of organizational behavior. This chapter will present the results of the institutional efforts in the proposed approaches and the demand for micro social economics. The diversity of these efforts, approaches, and demand is witness to the growing interest and importance of micro social economics and also to the confusion over what should be done to deal adequately with the issue.

The National Association of Accountants
REPORT OF THE COMMITTEE ON ACCOUNTING FOR CORPORATE SOCIAL PERFORMANCE

The stated objective of this committee was to develop systems of accounting for corporate social performance.[1] Four major areas of social performance were identified: community involvement; human resources; physical resources and environmental contributions; and product or service contributions. Community involvement includes all socially oriented activities intended to benefit the employees. Product and service contributions include activities intended to benefit the customers. Finally, physical resources and environmental contributions include activities intended to benefit the total environment of the firm.

The committee also provided a list of items under each of the four major areas identifying typical examples of social performance. The list includes the following examples of corporate social performance:

A. COMMUNITY INVOLVEMENT
　1. General philanthropy- Corporate support of educational institutions, cultural activities, recreational programs, health and community welfare agencies and a similar eleemosynary organizations.
　2. Public and private transportation- Alleviating or preventing urban transportation problems, including the provision of mass transportation of employees
　3. Health services-providing health care facilities and services and the support of programs to reduce disease and illness
　4. Housing- Improving the standard of dwellings, the construction of needed dwellings and the financing of housing renovation and construction
　5. Aid in personal and business problems-Alleviation of problems related to the physically handicapped, child care, minority businesses, disadvantaged persons, etc.
　6. Community planning and improvement-Programs of urban planning and renewal, crime prevention, etc.
　7. Volunteer activities- Encouraging and providing time for employees to be active as volunteers in community activities
　8. Specialized food programs- The provision of meals to meet the dietary needs of the aged, the infirm, the disadvantaged child and other groups
　9. Education- The development and implementation of educational programs to supplement those of the public or private schools such as work study programs; and employee service on school boards, school authorities and college university trustee and advisory boards

B. HUMAN RESOURCES
　1. Employment practices- Providing equal job opportunities for all persons, creation of summer job
　2. Training programs- Providing programs for all employees to increase their skills, earning potential and job satisfaction

3. Promotion policies- Recognizing the abilities of all employees and providing equal opportunities for promotion
4. Employment continuity- Scheduling production so as to minimize lay-offs and recalls, maintaining facilities in efficient operating condition so that they will not have to be abandoned because of deterioration, and exploring all feasible alternatives to closing a facility
5. Remuneration- Maintaining a level of total salaries and wages plus benefits which is in line with others in either the industry or community
6. Working conditions- Providing safe, healthful and pleasant working environment
7. Drugs and alcohol- Providing education and counseling for employees to prevent or alleviate problems in these and similar areas
8. Job enrichment- Providing the most meaningful work experiences practical for all employees
9. Communications- Establishing and maintaining two-way communication between all levels of employees to secure suggestions, to provide information as to what the company is actually doing and how each department's activities relate to the total corporate activity, and to inform employees' families and friends of corporate activities

C. PHYSICAL RESOURCES AND ENVIRONMENTAL CONTRIBUTIONS
1. Air- Timely meeting of the law and going beyond the law in avoiding the creation of, alleviating, or eliminating pollutants in these areas
2. Water- Timely meeting of the law and going beyond the law in avoiding the creation of, alleviating, or eliminating pollutants in these areas
3. Sound- Timely meeting of the law and going beyond the law in avoiding the creation of, alleviating, or eliminating pollutants in these areas
4. Solid waste- Disposal of solid waste in such a manner as to minimize contamination, reduce its bulk, etc., and the design of processes and products which will minimize the creation of solid waste
5. Use of scarce resources- The conservation of existing energy sources, the development of new energy sources, and the conservation of scarce materials
6. Aesthetics- The design and location of facilities in conformance with surroundings and with pleasing architecture and landscaping

D. PRODUCT OR SERVICE CONTRIBUTIONS
1. Completeness and clarity of labeling, packaging, and marketing representation- Assurance that labeling and representation as to methods of use, limitations on use, hazards of use, shelf-life, quantity of contents, and quality *cannot be misunderstood*
2. Warranty provisions- Adherence to all stated or implied warranties of a product with implementation through timely recalls, repairs or replacements
3. Responsiveness to consumer complaints- Prompt and complete responses to all complaints received
4. Consumer education- Literature and media programs to keep consumers informed of product or service characteristics, methods and areas of use of products, and of planned product changes or discontinuances
5. Product quality- Assurance through adequate control- "quality assurance"- that quality is at least equal to what customers may reasonably expect on the basis of company representations
6. Product safety- Design or formulation and packaging of products to minimize possibilities of harm or injury in product use
7. Content and frequency of advertising- Giving full consideration to the omission of any media material which may be adverse or offensive; and the avoidance of repetition to the extent that it becomes repugnant
8. Constructive research- Orienting technical and market research to meet defined social needs and to avoid creating social and environmental problems or to minimize such problems; e.g., energy consumption

EPSTEIN, FLAMHOLTZ, AND McDONOUGH

Corporate Social Performance dealt with one aspect of accounting for corporate social performance, namely, accounting for corporate product and service contributions. A survey of the current state of accounting for the social contributions of product and/or services was conducted on a sample of eight hundred of the largest U.S. corporations. The two primary objectives of the survey were to identify the types of measures currently used to account for product and service contributions and to ascertain the levels of interest, involvement, and sophistication in accounting for product and service contributions.[2]

A framework composed of seven measurement categories was offered to the respondents to indicate their degree of involvement in the monitoring/measuring activities:

1. *Descriptions*: periodic reports made on the effects of product or service contributions on customers and/or society.
2. *Inventories*: records or classification of a firm's product or service contributions.
3. *Time records*: records of the amount of time spent by personnel in product and service contributions.
4. *Cost allocations*: costs that have been allocated by some criterion to product or service contributions.
5. *Cost tracing*: costs that have been traced directly to product or service contributions.
6. *Nonmonetary benefits* (costs): assessments of benefits or costs of product or service contributions in nonmonetary, quantitative terms.
7. *Monetary benefits* (costs): assessments of benefits or costs of product or service contributions in monetary terms.[3]

The principal findings of the survey were as follows: First, product and service contributions are first among the four areas of social performance. Second, corporations do not, in most cases, account for the costs and benefits of those activities dealing with social responsibilities. Third, corporations do not attempt to account for their involvement with product and service contributions. Fourth, measurements of benefits in monetary terms are most common, followed in order of use by descriptions and inventories. Fifth, banks and retail corporations are most involved in accounting for product and service contributions. Sixth, product and service contributions for customers showed the highest level of involvement; product and service contributions for society were reported fourth. And seventh, there are differences in the relative importance of product and service contributions to customers and product and service contributions to society in various industries.[4]

Needless to say, the authors recognized the limited development of corporate social accounting systems in practice, given that the survey revealed "neither the existence of additional pioneering efforts nor any significant level of adoption of existing approaches."[5]

NIKOLAI, BAZLEY, AND BRUMMET

The Measurement of Corporate Environmental Activity dealt with one aspect of corporate social performance, namely, accounting for corporate environmental activity.[6] The study relied on three stages: a questionnaire; an interview-case study; and an integration stage.

The purpose of the questionnaire was to ascertain the "state of the art" concerning the measurement techniques used to evaluate costs and benefits of corporate environmental activity and the resulting effect upon corporate decision making. The main findings of this stage show, first, that the responding companies were much more involved in the monetary measurement of the costs of environmental factors than of the benefits that accrue to them and, second, that the measurement activity was focused in areas where conventional measurement techniques may be used, such as equipment costs and research and development costs, as opposed to aesthetic and image-promotion costs.[7]

The purpose of the interview-case study was to determine how "companies are organized to make environmental decisions, how they measure the specific costs and benefits associated with these decisions, and how they incorporate such measurements into their planning and control processes."[8] The findings show mainly that the involvement in corporate environmental activity is generally the result of a strong commitment and direction of top management and techniques used tend to be rather traditional.

Unlike the previous two stages, the integrative stage was a prescriptive stage designed to "review, synthesize, and integrate the existing organizational structures, environmental definitions, and measurement techniques along with the modifications of the information systems, as ascertained from the interview-case study stage in order to develop recommendations for measurement and decision making concerning environmental activity."[9] The findings proposed definition and suggestions on environmental costs, environmental benefits, environmental investment planning, operational planning, and environmental organizational structure.

With respect to environmental cost, the authors examined four possible definitions:
1. The incremental traceable cost incurred for the environmental aspects of a project.
2. The total cost incurred for the environmental aspects of a project.
3. The incremental traceable cost incurred for a total project for which the primary motivation is to produce environmental benefits.
4. The total cost incurred for the total project for which the primary motivation is to produce environmental benefits.[10]

They concluded that the first definition is the most acceptable. They also concluded that these initial costs should be categorized as land costs, equipment costs, engineering costs, research and development costs, and miscellaneous costs, operating costs as equipment operating costs, additional production costs, maintenance costs, disposal costs, monitoring costs, depreciation, and miscellaneous costs, and, finally, exit costs as restoration costs.

With respect to environmental benefits, they defined them as the benefits to the environment that result from an expenditure of an environmental cost. These benefits were categorized further as internal and external:

Internal environmental benefits are those environmental benefits which directly benefit the company while indirectly benefiting society. External environmental benefits are those environmental benefits which directly benefit society while indirectly benefiting the company.[11]

Examples of internal environment benefits included recyclable raw materials, energy production, by-product sales, development of salable processes, and improved working conditions in terms of reduced turnover, ability to attract new employees, reduced absenteeism, improved employee efficiency, and public acceptance. Examples of external water environment benefits included improvements in public water supply, swimming and other sports, fish and wildlife support, agricultural and industrial water supply, navigation, health, aesthetics, and overall impact. Examples of air environment benefits included improvements in health, agricultural vegetation, wild vegetation, property damage, wildlife support, aesthetics, and overall impact.

With respect to environmental investments policy, an environmental capital investment request form is recommended. With respect to operational planning, the authors suggested the extending of corporate responsibility beyond the traditional objectives to include social objectives, via an "environmental responsibility accounting." With respect to control, the authors suggested a comparison of actual and standard costs incurred and benefits obtained from environmental investments. As an example, three "environmental activity" variances are proposed for each department:

Environmental Discharge Variance = Standard level of Pollutant Discharge – Actual Pollutant Discharge
Environmental Effectiveness Variance = Desired level of Environmental Benefits – Actual level of Environmental Benefits
Environmental Efficiency Variance = Standard Cost for Actual Discharge level – Actual Cost for Actual Discharge level.[12]

The environmental capital investment request is as follows:

1.	Description:			
2.	**Nonmonetary Benefits**		Quantitative	Nonquantitative
	Internal			
	Development of salable process			
	Reduced turnover			
	Ability to attract new employees			
	Reduced absenteeism			
	Improved employee efficiency			
			Quantitative	Nonquantitative
	External (*water*)			
	Public water supply			
	Recreational facilities			
	Fish and wildlife support			
	Aesthetics			
	Health			
	Overall impact			
	External (*air*)			
	Health			
	Agricultural vegetation			
	Wild vegetation			
	Property damage			
	Wildlife support			
	Aesthetics			
	Overall impact			
3.	**Annual Monetary Benefits and Costs:**		Year	
		1	2	n
	A. Monetary Benefits:			
	Recyclable raw materials			
	Energy production			
	Byproduct sales			
	Other			
	Total Monetary Benefits			
	B. Monetary Costs: (*from cost scorecard*)			
	Total Monetary Costs			
	Net Cash Flows Before Taxes (A-B)			
	Depreciation (for CPCF amortization)			
	Net Income Before Taxes			
	Income Taxes			
	Net Income After Taxes			
	+Depreciation (or CPCF amortization)			
	Net Cash Flow After Taxes			
4.	**Initial Costs** (*cash outflows*):			
	Costs:			
	Life of Project			
5.	**Methods**			
	Net Present Value			
	Internal Rate of Return			
	Accounting Rate of Return			
	Payback			

The American Accounting Association
REPORT OF THE COMMITTEE ON MEASURES OF EFFECTIVENESS FOR SOCIAL PROGRAMS

The charge of the committee was to prepare a report on the implications for accounting of integrating into the formal accounting and reporting process various nonfinancial statistics and measures that are essential to the evaluation of efficiency and effectiveness in social programs.[13] The committee relied on a definition of a social program as a plan of action, an experiment introduced into society for the purpose of producing a change in the status of the society or some of its members.[14]

It is first noted that uniform principles or guidelines to facilitate comparisons of different social programs are lacking. To compensate for the weaknesses of the annual report- The Economic Report of the President- various individuals and organizations called for a concept of a "social report," and attempts were made to introduce a Senate bill known as the Full Opportunity and Social Accounting Act. This indicates the growing interest and concern with the evaluation of social programs. There are, however, difficulties, and sometimes impossibilities, of measuring effectiveness of social programs.

The committee identified mainly the following problems associated with obtaining social measures:

1. Often, there is inconsistency between a societal concept as theoretically formulated and the operational definition by which it is empirically measured. *Fractional Measurement*, accordingly appears since it is difficult to construct an operational definition that covers a concept in all its attributes.
2. A social accounting system relies often on *indirect* measurement, e.g., measuring societal concepts by using data originally collected for other purposes.
3. Social systems used *formalistic-aggregative measurement* of collective attributes.
4. Social systems are fluid, nonstationary systems where *over time* various indicators relevant at some point become outmoded and new problems emerge which require new indicators.[15]

These problems had implications for the evaluation of social programs. They were discussed as follows:

1. With respect to the fractional measurement problem, it is recommended that the evaluation of social programs rely on more indicators of different dimensions, do not ignore the qualitative dimensions, avoid substituting the measurement of means for the measurement of goals and focus on a social unit's success in terms of a system model versus a goal model. The difference between the two approaches is that "the goals model expects organizational effectiveness to increase with the increase of more means (resources) to the organization (or social unit). The system model, on the other hand, perceives that these may be in balance in allocating a social unit's resources to the goal activities and indirect non-goal activities that have to be met first in order to attain the goals set for a social unit.[16]
2. With respect to the *indirect measurement* problem, it is recommended to develop various indices for the different dimensions of a concept.
3. With respect to the problem of the *measurement of collective attributes*, it is recommended to focus on the relevant social unit rather than the formal social unit and on global measures (data characterizing the collectivity itself, apart from its members) rather than on aggregated measures (data based on the statistical manipulation of attributes of the members or attributes of their relationship).
4. With respect to the problem of nonstationary, it is recommended that measurement of effectiveness be adaptive over time in order to be relevant in dynamic systems.

The committee found also through a questionnaire survey that the public accounting profession is either involved in or favoring involvement in the effectiveness of social programs. In a final section, the committee examined the role of three central financial agencies- the

Department of Management and Budget (OMB)- in respect to providing information for planning and evaluating federal social programs and gave several examples of account-auditor development of evaluation data and effectiveness measures. The examples covered the following social issues: controlling industrial water pollution; preservation of wilderness areas; program for aiding educationally deprived children; effectiveness of the Economic Opportunity program; and job opportunity in the business sector. To help these federal and other endeavors, the committee suggested potential involvement for the accounting profession. The suggestions include the following by order of importance:
1. Participation of the accounting profession in the determination of society's goals and objectives.
2. Involvement of the accounting profession at the "criteria setting" or "surrogate development" level.
3. Involvement of the accounting profession as a data manipulation and data verification expert.
4. Involvement of the accounting profession at auditing the disbursement of public funds.

Based on these types of involvement, the committee identified the following potential implications for the accounting profession:
1. Development of a theoretical base for social accounting.
2. More specialization within the profession.
3. More interaction (formal or informal) with other professions, particularly statisticians and social scientists.
4. More education and "professional schools."
5. More clearly defined ethical standards.
6. Greater separation between the audit and management services staff.
7. More legal problems.
8. More government intervention.
9. Research and development by accounting firms and governmental accountants.
10. Greater exposure to the public.
11. Growth in management services.
12. A control function over the statistics generated and disseminated by social programs and government agencies.[17]

REPORT OF THE COMMITTEE ON ENVIRONMENTAL EFFECTS OR ORGANIZATIONAL BEHAVIOR

The charge of this committee was to develop measurement and reporting methods useful in communicating to internal and external users the effects of an organization's behavior on the physical environment, with attention to measuring and reporting the environment effects of alternative modes of operation.[18]

The committee focused on the pollution problem, its economic, international, and accounting aspects. From an economic point of view, pollution creates externalities or social costs that are not internalized and hence inflicted on individuals in society and upon society in general. From an international point of view, the extent of internalization of social costs in a given country may create cost differentials and give producers from other countries not active in pollution abatement a competitive edge. This may cause a shifting of trade patterns with corresponding impact on individual firms, on balances of payments, and on the international political scene. From an accounting point of view, the pollution issue creates a host of new problems with regard to financial reporting, internal reporting, the attest function and decision making.

Given these problems, the committee explores the following related issues: internal reporting of environmental effects; external reporting of environmental effects; and the implications for accountants.

With respect to internal reporting, the committee called for the use of both financial and nonfinancial information, a multidisciplinary approach to the gathering of information and to new models to deal with the uncertainties associated with environmental effects.

With respect to the external reporting effects, the committee agreed to the importance of the pollution problem but was unable to discover reasonably accurate techniques for measuring the social costs of pollution. The committee suggested, however, the following reporting alternatives: (1) display environmental control expenses on a separate line in the income statement; (2) disclose separately total environmental control expenditures in the statement source and applications of funds; (3) classify separately environmental control facilities (and related depreciation) in the balance sheet; (4) environmental controls resulting in extraordinary losses (e.g., plant shutdowns) or corrections of prior years (e.g., restoration of prior-year site damages) presently call for separate disclosure under generally accepted accounting principles, estimate then whenever they are material in amount; and (5) use actual accounting for environmental liabilities, disclosing material future pollution control outlays when they arise out of past transactions (in lieu of the current practice of footnote disclosure)."[19] The committee also recommended that every firm be required to report and its auditors attest to a verbal statement.

With respect to the implications for accountants, the committee suggested eight challenging and important research problems.[20]

REPORT OF THE COMMITTEE ON THE MEASUREMENT OF SOCIAL COSTS

The charge of this committee was to identify one or more of the most critical accounting issues that currently face those who are teaching and/or doing research in the area of social costs and prepare (or commission) brief statements setting forth the alternative positions with respect to those issues.[21]

The committee first presented an overview of the changing climate in which businesses operate as exemplified by eight corporate purposes adopted by one corporate group: profit; sensitivity to the natural and human environment; growth; responsiveness to consumer needs; equitable distribution of benefits; dynamic business structure; fair treatment of employees; and legal and ethical behavior. As a response, the committee suggested the development of new measurement concepts "to enable management to identify issues, recognize implications of current and planned actions, set priorities and select specific activities."[22] Two opposing views of the role accountants should play vis-à-vis the changing business climate were then presented.

The first view calls for a total involvement of the accountant in the design and installation, administration and operation, and finally verification and attestation of detection and measurement systems in the social sphere. As a beginning, a taxonomy for measurement of social performance, including both social costs and social benefits, is needed. This performance should be a more inclusive measurement of organizational performance than is provided by conventional accounting. This total performance is viewed as including the five "outputs":

1. Net income, which benefits stockholders and provides resources for further business growth.
2. Human resource contribution, which assists the individual in the organization to develop new knowledge or skills.
3. Public contribution, which helps the organization's "community" to function and provide services for its constituency.
4. Environmental contribution (closely allied with public contribution), which affects "quality of life" for society.
5. Product or service contribution, which affects customer well-being and satisfaction.[23]

This classification requires extending performance measurement to transactions not normally considered business transactions, which will include:
1. Human resource contributions such as employee training programs, changes in quality of life and attitudes of people who comprise the organization, employee recruiting programs, or safety programs.
2. Public contributions such as contributions to educational and cultural programs, support for urban housing or transportation programs or volunteer community affairs.
3. Environmental contribution aspects of production operations, use of resources, or recycling operations.
4. Product safety, product durability, product utility, or consumer satisfaction.[24]

The second view calls for no involvement by the accountant in the area of social accounting. Accountants should be concerned only with "those costs which are imposed on the corporate (accounting) entity by law, public pressure, or by choice of the corporation itself."[25] A second argument for this view is that accountants may not have the necessary measurement technology for social accounting. The committee, then addressed three facts of social reporting: internal social reporting; external social reporting; and social attestation.

First, internal social reporting is viewed as necessary to provide relevant information for making compliance decisions (minimum vs. maximum) in response to social premises and legal requirements. Second, external social reporting may lead to special disclosure to each of the major constituents: stockholders, employees, customers, and society at large. Third, attestation of social reports would add a desirable degree of credibility.

REPORT OF THE COMMITTEE ON SOCIAL COSTS

The charge of this committee was to identify one or more of the most critical issues that currently face those who are teaching and/or doing research in the social accounting area and prepare (or commission) brief statements setting forth the alternative positions with respect to those issues.[26]

The issues examined include social audits, types of measurement of socially relevant corporate activities, and cost concepts of social accounting.

With respect to social audits, the committee identified three measurement levels of the activities evaluated in a social audit:

Measurement Level I- Identified and described (or "inventoried");
Measurement Level II- Measured in terms of *nonfinancial* measures of cost/benefit to the firm's owners; measured in terms of *nonfinancial* measures of cost/benefits to constituents other than the owners of the firm (employees, customers, local and regional inhabitants, etc. . . .);
Measurement Level III- Measured in terms of *financial* cost/benefit to the firm's owners; measured in terms of *financial* cost/benefit to constituents other than the owners of the firm (employees, customers, local and regional inhabitants, etc.).[27]

With respect to the types of measurement of socially relevant corporate activities, the committee identified four possible levels of measurement:
1. The first level identifies the set of activities that have social relevance. This is also labeled taking an inventory.
2. The second, or input, level consists of determining the extent of the efforts being expended in each of the identified socially relevant activities.
3. The third level of measurement counts the immediate outputs of a social action or process.
4. The fourth level of measurement evaluates the worth of the output in spite of the lack and difficulty of measurement values in most cases.

With respect to cost concepts of social accounting, the committee classified the distinction between the ways economists and social accountants use the concept of social cost.

To economists social costs are the total cost to society of the production of a good or service, which is basically a concept of economic cost and opportunity cost. A more limited definition equates social costs with externalities. In the area of social accounting the cost measurement includes:
(a) Those costs of business activities that are paid or borne by the firm and provide benefits to other entities (such as employment of a work force, affirmative action programs, the portion of a firm's pollution control program that provides spill-over benefits to other entities, philanthropy, taxes, etc.) and also (b) those costs that arise from business activity that are paid or borne by entities other than the entity giving rise to the social impact (such as damages to the environment, health and mortality effects from production and consumption of goods and services produced by the entity, use of public streets and property by the entity, etc.).[28]

The costs identified in the first group are relevant in social accounting as surrogates of social benefits, while those identified in the second group are considered social costs, "in the sense of external diseconomies which arise from the activities of a business entity, e.g., environment pollution."[29] Given this definition of social cost, the committee examined selected problems in social measurement, namely, measuring the social costs of air pollution, affirmative action programs, community impact of plant closings, and human resource accounting.

REPORT OF THE COMMITTEE ON ACCOUNTING FOR SOCIAL PERFORMANCE
The charge of this committee[30] was (1) to review current efforts in accounting for corporate social performance and provide an update of the previous committee's work in this area; (2) to review and develop a critical evaluation of the state of the art of social performance measurement; (3) to identify high potential areas for research in social measurement and, if feasible, study in depth one or more of these identified areas; and (4) to cooperate with the Committee on Education and the director of education in exploring the possibilities for social measurement subject matter input to accounting curricula and the AAA continuing education program.[31]

Of the three areas examined the most interesting development is the suggestion of the twenty-two areas for research in accounting for social performance.[32] Although these suggestions may not be exhaustive, as the content of this book shows, they constitute important areas in need of urgent answers.

The American Institute of Certified Public Accountants
The AICPA's first attempt in social accounting was to organize a seminar where the participants showed an interest in the development of more useful and reliable methods of measuring the effectiveness of social programs. The proceedings, published under the title *Social Measurement*, set out the various views of the participants on the need for social measurement.[33]

The second attempt by the Committee on Social Measurement of the AICPA resulted in a more comprehensive, three-part treatment of the various aspects of the measurement corporate social performance, under the title *The Measurement of Corporate Social Performance*.[34]

The first part covered an introduction to corporate social measurement before examining the major characteristics of an ideal system of social measurement. The ideal system for measuring corporate social measurement was deemed unattainable in the near future, leading the committee to conclude that much can be achieved by developing and initial system. The best characteristics of such initial systems are "(1) that it is practical, (2) that it can be developed and implemented in stages, and (3) that almost from the outset, it can be useful."[35] The initial system is intended to measure the impacts on social conditions affecting significantly the quality of life.

The approach will be opportunistic and eclectic given the absence of a conceptual framework to guide the choice of techniques and measures.

The second part shows how the initial system might be used in a number of areas of significant social concern- the environment, nonrenewable resources, human resources, suppliers of purchased goods and services, products, services and customers, and the community. For each of the areas of social concern the committee identified first the major constituencies of publics affected and the major impact and actions that affect these constituencies and social conditions having a major effect on the quality of life. Then it dealt with measurement methodologies for each of the areas and suggested social measures appropriate for each area. The suggested social measures appropriate for the areas of the environment, nonrenewable resources, human resources, suppliers of purchased goods and services, products, services and customers, and the community are shown, respectively, in Exhibits 6.1, 6.2, 6.3, 6.4, 6.5, and 6.6. The coverage of each of these areas was followed with a description of certain activities and experiences of the government in developing and using social information.

The third part covers the reporting and use of social information by both internal and external users, problems of credibility and assurance, and suggestions for making the initial system operational.

Propose Approaches to Micro Social Accounting
NARRATIVE DISCLOSURE
The narrative disclosure approach would consist of verbal statements depicting the environmental effects of organizational behavior. In fact, the Committee on Environmental Effects of Organizational Behavior called for verbal descriptions of the following: (1) identification of environmental problems- specific organizational problems with regard to control, imposed control standards, compliance deadlines, penalties for noncompliance, environmental considerations contained in executory contracts, and other contingent aspects; (2) abatement goals of the organization- detailed description of plans for abatement, projection of time schedules, estimates of cost and/or budgeted expenditures; (3) progress of the organization- description of tangible progress, cost to date, expected future costs, and pertinent nonmonetary information relative to the organization's attainment of environmental goals; and (4) disclosure of material environmental effects on financial position, earnings, and business activities of the organization.[36]

The nature of the narrative disclosure is by definition nonquantitative. It is a necessary first step to allow firms to learn more about the best ways of measuring and disclosing the environmental effects of organizational behavior.

Exhibit 6.1
The Environment- Suggested Information and Sources

General Area and Specific Attribute	Specific Information	Sources of Information or Evidence
1. Air quality: a. Physical and chemical composition. b. Appearance (effect of color of smoke). c. Odor.	1. a. Emissions of the five items included in ambient air quality standard; significant emissions of toxic materials. Frequency and extent of violation of permitted levels. b. Frequency, intensity, and duration of unpleasant periods. c. Frequency, intensity, and duration of unpleasant periods.	1. a. Measurements obtained by the use of measurement instruments, frequently carried out under procedures specified by governmental regulatory bodies; special technical studies. b. Citizen perceptions; measurements using photographic and other methods of scaling. c. Citizen surveys; intermittent observations and measurements.
2. Water quality: a. Physical and chemical composition. b. Appearance. c. Quality of use.	2. a. Discharges of metals, chemicals, pesticides, heat, radionuclides, oxygen dissolving and decomposing materials, microbiological contaminants and other effluents, particularly toxic effluents, affecting water quality. b. Discharges affecting appearance, smell, and similar qualities. c. Types of use (highest) permitted by quality of water.	2. a. Measurements obtained by the use of measurement instruments, frequently carried out under procedures specified by governmental regulatory bodies; special comparisons with practical and available technologies. b. Intermittent observations and measurements; citizen perception surveys. c. Special study.
3. Noise and vibrations. 4. Solid waste disposal.	3. Noise and vibrations noticeable outside facility. 4. Quantities and waste disposal practices, including ultimate disposal of sludge.	3. Intermittent tests; citizen perception surveys. 4. Special studies; internally developed quantitative data.
5. Land: a. Surface characteristics.	5. a. Impact on terrain—on the quantity and quality of soil, erosion, water drainage, dust conditions, land cover, etc.	5. a. Engineering studies; studies of results of operating practices (as in farming and timber management).

General Area and Specific Attribute	Specific Information	Sources of Information or Evidence
b. Land use. 6. Ecology, flora, and fauna.	b. Impact of types and amount of land use by facility on surrounding areas. 6. Effects on the ability of an ecological area or system to support flora and fauna—with particular reference to diversity, endangered species, displacement of the more desirable by the less desirable, etc.	b. Special studies. 6. Special studies.
7. Aesthetics: a. Aesthetic quality of corporate facility as a free-standing unit. b. Harmony, composition with surroundings.	7. a. Attractiveness of exterior of building, grounds, etc. b. Suitability and attractiveness in terms of natural surroundings, other uses of land area, etc.	7. a. Citizen perceptions; opinions of expert b. Citizen perceptions; opinions of expert

SOURCE: American Institute of Certified Public Accountants, The Measurement of Corporate Social Performance (New York: AICPA, 1977), pp. 89-90. Copyright © 1977 by the American Institute of Certified Public Accountants, Inc. Reprinted with permission.

NOTES: The information that will be of most interest and value will be that which concerns the following:
1. Absolute quantities; comparisons with regulatory standards or known danger points; comparisons with performance in prior periods; relationship to best practical and/or available technology; comparison with others in the industry.
2. Share of total regional pollution.
3. Effects of major new facilities and activities (including construction).
4. "Irreversible" land uses.
5. Citizen perceptions and experts' views.
6. Corporate policies with respect to environmental matters and procedures.
7. Efforts made and planned to enhance the environment or reduce damaging effects; the results achieved or expected; capital costs; operating expenses, and cost recoveries.
8. Research and development efforts.

Exhibit 6.2
Nonrenewable Resources- Suggested Information and Sources

General Area and Specific Attribute	Specific Information	Sources of Information or Evidence
1. Materials used in manufacture of product and related packaging material.		
a. Source, quantity, and relative availability.	a. Analysis of material consumption (including rough breakdown of purchased semifinished products) showing quantities used and relative availability or scarcity. Sources of materials used, broken down among new, internally generated scrap and recycled materials. Major changes in the foregoing, with an attribution to various causes set forth in 1.b.	a. Straightforward analyses of internal data, with appropriate assumptions and estimates.
b. Causes of change.	b. Description of significant actions taken and their consequences (see 1.a.), e.g., • changes in product concept • changes in design specifications to reduce overall consumption, permit use of more abundant and scrapped or recycled materials, renewable resources, etc. • improvements in yield and reduction of rejects • changes in manufacturing techniques and procedures • support of recycling activities	b. Descriptions of policies, procedures, and organizational arrangements; analysis of results achieved.
c. Research and development and other future-oriented activities.	c. Nature of projects and their objectives or expected impacts; results of recent research and development efforts.	c. Appropriate descriptions of projects, scale of efforts, analyses of results of recent projects, etc.
2. a. Actions to bring consumer-required useful life and material-related physical life into greater harmony.	2. a. Product life of principal products in hands of customers; customer requirements and performance vs. physical condition of product at time of discard; determination of reasons for pending discard. Relative emphasis on durability and serviceability; on service utility vs. style; on speed of introduction of innovations and technological obsolescence.	2. a. Customer surveys; analysis of causes of customer discards and physical condition of products; review of corporate product policies and strategies.
b. Marketing related programs.	b. Relative emphasis on service utility vs. other product characteristics tending to obsolete the product.	b. Same as 2.a.
c. Customer education.	c. Efforts to extend product life by appropriate education of the customer in the care and proper use of the product.	c. Same as 2.a.; customer surveys of adequacy of these efforts.
d. Service and repair.	d. Steps taken to minimize need for servicing requirements, to simplify home maintenance and provide commercial servicing facilities.	d. Same as 2.a.
3. Conservation of energy.		
a. Arising out of operations—e.g., manufacturing, distributing, administration, etc.	a. Extent of reductions in light, heat, power, transportation, etc., with some indication of major cause/effect relationships.	a. Straightforward internal analyses by major areas. Policies, procedures, and organizational arrangements to achieve reductions.
b. Arising out of product use in hands of customers.	b. Reductions or replacements for energy of major products and improvements brought about by various methods, such as design changes and customer education in care and use.	b. Laboratory tests. Field analyses of products under actual conditions of use.

General Area and Specific Attribute	Specific Information	Sources of Information or Evidence
4. Creation of "new" materials of commercial value.	4. Creation of materials out of renewable resources or out of substances not previously used as materials. Discovery of important new and different deposits or sources of existing materials. Development of scientific and technological knowledge and techniques for increasing the recovery of materials from existing or submarginal sources or for increasing the conversion of the material into energy or other uses. Improvements in materials arising from modifying their characteristics so that they will be useful longer.	4. Internal information as to efforts and results achieved through research and development and exploration (for minerals, petroleum etc.).
5. Renewable but limited resources.	5. Appropriate items selected from 1 to 4 above, relating especially to conservation, efficient production and conversion to useful products, efficient use, renewal, development of new sources and qualities, etc.	5. Same as above.

SOURCE: American Institute of Certified Public Accountants, *The Measurement of Corporate Social Performance* (New York: AICPA, 1977), pp. 98-100. Copyright © 1977 by the American Institute of Certified Public Accountants, Inc. Reprinted with permission.

Exhibit 6.3
Human Resources- Suggested Information and Sources

General Area and Specific Attribute	Specific Information	Sources of Information or Evidence
Income, Security and Stability		
1. Income		
a. Current income	a. Direct compensation (such as wages, salaries, commissions, bonuses, profit-sharing) • in total • per capita compensation by deciles or quartiles • per capita compensation for meaningful classifications of employees	a. Payroll and personnel records
	• comparisons with industry and community averages and with own data for prior years (and with changes in Consumer Price Index) • comparisons with U.S. government data on "income requirements," "poverty level cut-off," etc., especially for lower deciles	Industry or community surveys, governmentally provided statistical data
	Fringe benefits of essentially short-term nature (e.g., health insurance)	Internal policy and practice statements, brochures
b. Future income	b. Pension plans • essential elements • rights of employees, trusteeship, etc. • current cost, prior service liabilities • treatment of present retirees	b. Description of plans; corporate accounting and personnel records; survey of present retirees
	Social Security • current costs of corporate contributions	Accounting records

General Area and Specific Attribute	Specific Information	Sources of Information or Evidence
c. Income protection	c. Unemployment insurance payments to government and union plans	c. Accounting records
	Practices in terms of illness, long-term disability, death, etc.	Policies and practice statements
	Re-employment assistance	Policies and practice statements
2. Security and stability		
a. Overall situation	a. Statistical information as to • turnover and longevity of employment • involuntary turnover • days of employment per employee for year • re-engagement/retention policies for whatever classifications of employees are most meaningful	a. Personnel records
b. Relationship to causes • schedule-related instability	b. Attribution of instability to major causes	b. Analysis of internal data
• obsolescence of skills and facilities	Nature, extent, and success of efforts to produce greater security and stability, including training efforts to prevent or compensate for technological obsolescence, transfer policies (relocations), peak/valley smoothing, etc.	Special studies.* policy/practice statements, analysis of training course content, etc.
• other, such as product discontinuance • uncontrollable variations, e.g., • supplier strike • customer demand • seasonability		

Physical Work Environment

General Area and Specific Attribute	Specific Information	Sources of Information or Evidence
3. Health and safety		
a. Severity and frequency of industrial accidents and illnesses (fatal and nonfatal)	a. Statistical information on frequency and severity, with identification of causes; additional information on good or bad situations	a. Internal records; OSHA reports, special studies and analyses
b. Protection provided against exposure	b. Existing and increased efforts to provide protection against physical, chemical and other risks attributable to materials, processes, equipment, etc. Fatigue relief, and similar practices	b. Internal proposals, authorizations, departmental reports of safety programs, process changes, etc., and analyses of results; results of OSHA audits and similiar reviews by inside and outside experts. Work practices; policy statements
4. Work place conditions		
a. Avoidance of essentially negative conditions	a. Situation with respect to such matters as work space (crowding); heat, light, ventilation; noise	a. Special studies and analyses;* comparisons with "good" practice as evidenced by government regulations, industry practice, etc.; surveys of employee perceptions and attitudes
b. Positive attractiveness	b. Aesthetics, cleanliness, and orderliness of plant, rest and restroom areas, food facilities, etc.	b. Special studies and analyses; surveys of employee attitudes and perceptions
c. Adequacy of resources to perform job	c. Adequacy of equipment, support facilities, organizational procedures and supervisory assistance to carry out work in time and manner expected	c. Surveys of workers and supervisors; special studies and analyses of indicated problem areas
5. Individual and public transportation (to and from the job)	Safety and availability of private and public transportation and parking	Surveys of employees; special studies and analyses

Psychological Work Environment

General Area and Specific Attribute	Specific Information	Sources of Information or Evidence
6. Job content	6. Psychological satisfactions derived from work—current status, improvements, etc. Efforts made to increase work satisfaction through changes in work scope (usually via enlargement, greater challenges, and increases in responsibility), increases in variety, etc.	6. Special studies and analyses; surveys of employees
7. Coworker relationships	7. Positive aspects (e.g., cooperation, human interchange, etc.) Negative aspects (e.g., isolation, antagonism, tension, etc.)	7. Special studies and analyses; surveys of employees
8. Management-worker relationships	8. Basic management style • openness, communication, democracy/autocracy • tension and competition vs. cooperation • work pace, handling of operational changes	8. Special studies and analyses; surveys of employees
9. Nonwork opportunities	9. Opportunities for personal and family leisure and recreation (vacation, holiday, out-of-town travel arrangements, etc.) Company-sponsored opportunities for employee participation in social, cultural, recreational activities as an extension of work relationships	9. Policies and practices; surveys of employees Practices; survey of employees; data on participation
10. Personal assistance	10. Nature and extent of counseling on personal problems	10. Survey of employees; data on utilization

Opportunity and Equity

General Area and Specific Attribute	Specific Information	Sources of Information or Evidence
11. Employment distribution	11. Distribution of employment by groups, especially such disadvantaged groups as racial minorities, women, youth and aged, physically and mentally handicapped, the inadequately educated. Such information would include data on work force representation in total, by position classes, by stability of employment, etc. Efforts to improve distribution	11. Personnel department records; EEO reports; comparable external data Personnel policies and practices; data on activities and their effectiveness

12. Employment opportunity facilitation	12. Actions to facilitate the employment of those with a personal disadvantage by such means as day care centers, special transportation arrangements, special pre-job training and initial orientation work rearrangements, and suitable hiring/testing/recruiting policies and practices; the results achieved	12. Personnel practices; information on nature and extent of activities undertaken and employee utilization; survey of employees and of potential or former employees
13. Upward mobility	13. Actions to increase the promotability of employees, both directly on the job and by means of training opportunities, personality and health improvements; results achieved	13. Personnel policies and practices; activities undertaken as indicated by training and personnel department records; surveys of employees; personnel department records of upward mobility
14. Job creation	14. Increases and decreases in job opportunities through corporate growth or contraction—in total and by major position classes	14. Personnel department records
Overall		
15. Overall relationship	15. Evidences of company's overall relationship with its employees in relation to— • voluntary resignations • absenteeism and tardiness • grievances and complaints • work stoppages • below-standard output • tension-related psychosomatic illness • alcoholism and drug addiction • suicides	15. Personnel department records; surveys of present and former employees

SOURCE: American Institute of Certified Public Accountants, *The Measurement of Corporate Social Performance* (New York: AICPA, 1977), pp. 115–119. Copyright © 1977 by the American Institute of Certified Public Accountants, Inc. Reprinted with permission.

* It is assumed throughout that special studies and analyses would be made by insiders and/or outsiders with appropriate kinds and degrees of skill and appropriate degrees of independence.

Exhibit 6.4
Suggested Information on Suppliers

General Area and Specific Attribute	Specific Information	Sources of Information or Evidence
1. Supplier selection	1. Description of major social criteria and their relative importance Changes in suppliers selected; reasons and volume of purchases involved Changes made by continuing suppliers in order to comply with company criteria; nature and magnitude of changes brought about Percentage of purchases meeting all criteria satisfactorily	1. Statements of policy and procedures; supplier profiles; internal analyses of changes, volumes of purchases, etc.
2. Contract specifications	2. Nature of socially significant contract terms specified Areas of use, volume of purchases affected, and magnitude of impact	2. Statements of policy and procedures; internal analyses of changes, volumes of purchases, etc.
3. Utilization	3. Procedures used to identify and evaluate social impacts associated with specific goods and services Efforts made to maximize the "good" and minimize the "bad" by reduction in use, substitution, recycling or reuse, product redesign, etc.; extent of resultant change	3. Statements of policy and procedures; results of studies; records of changes
4. General treatment	4. Policy Actions taken and results achieved Supplier satisfactions and dissatisfactions	4. Statements of policies and procedures; analysis of impacts of changes; surveys of suppliers

SOURCE: American Institute of Certified Public Accountants, *The Measurement of Corporate Social Performance* (New York, AICPA, 1977), p. 127. Copyright © 1977 by the American Institute of Certified Public Accountants, Inc. Reprinted with permission.

Exhibit 6.5
Suggested Information for Products, Customers, and Services

General Area and Specific Attribute	Specific Information	Sources of Information or Evidence*
1. Nature of products and services (corporate mission) Intrinsic worth of products and services (optional)	Purposes served and relationship to quality of life conditions, social values, and goals	1
2. Market coverage		
a. Extent to which products, particularly essentials, meet the needs of all customers—particularly those of minorities and lower income groups	a. Existence of product differentiation based upon needs and ability to pay	1, 3, 5, 6
	Sales and analyses showing extent of purchases by various social groups	5
b. Assumption of responsibility for continuity of essential products and services (e.g., utilities, fuel, food, transportation) in contrast to a purely profit-maximizing philosophy	b. Policy statement; practical evidences of preparations or of actual actions	1, 6
c. Extent to which company attempts to serve all markets with essentials by means of marketing and distribution policies and facilities	c. Existence of policies, procedures, and facilities	1, 3, 5, 6
	Sales analyses showing extent of purchases by various social groups	5
3. Characteristics of products and services		
a. Effectiveness and efficiency with which stated functions or purposes are fulfilled	a. Comparative performance data, under conditions of normal use, related to key determinants of utility	1, 2, 3, 5
	Nature of improvements made or in the offing; research and development activities	6
b. Diversity of choice based on significant differentiation, related to important aspects of product use	b. Bases of differentiation in physical, price, and other terms; and indication of ranges offered	1, 5
	Differentiation to meet social requirements (see item 2)	1, 3, 5, 6
c. Customer-use characteristics	c. Safety record in hands of customers	3, 4, 5
Safety	Hazards and safety features	1-6
	Improvement efforts	1, 5, 6
	Record in hands of customers	3, 4, 5
Sanitary aspects (noncontamination)	Design features and procedures	1, 2, 4, 6
	Quality control	1, 5, 6
	Record in hands of customers	3, 4, 5
Durability and reliability	Design features	1-6
	Quality control	1, 5, 6
	Physical life vs. obsolescence	1, 3, 5
	Customer experience	3, 4, 5
Installability and serviceability	Design features	1, 3, 5, 6
Reusability	Design features permitting or facilitating reuse where nonrenewable resources are involved	1, 3, 5
	Existence of policy/procedures	1, 6
Consideration of life-cycle costs (especially those for repairs, energy, and disposal) as well as initial costs	Typical results based on experience in customer use and laboratory tests	3, 4, 5
Aesthetic appearance	Nature of policy/procedure	1
	Typical reactions	3, 4, 5, 6
Noise, odor, and other nuisance abatement	Policies and procedures	1
	Design features	1-6
	Customer experience	3
d. Product improvement and productivity improvement	d. Nature and extent of major changes	5
	Interrelationship of the social and the economic	1
4. Marketing practices		
a. Advertising and promotion full and fair disclosure; avoidance of manipulation of customers and prospective customers	a. Policy and procedures with respect to key aspects	1
	Reactions to specific advertising and promotion	2-6
	Specific efforts to avoid manipulation of children, the aged, the less educated, foreign, and similar groups	1, 3, 6

b. Avoidance of undesirable side effects and efforts to obtain desirable side effects from advertising and promotion

b. Actions with respect to—
- Nature of TV programming — 1, 3, 4, 6
- Creation or perpetuation of undesirable stereotypes — 1, 3, 4, 6
- Sensitivities of special groups — 1, 3, 4, 6
- Support of social values and goals — 1, 3, 4, 6
- Aural and visual intrusion on privacy, enjoyment of nature, etc. — 1, 3, 4, 6

c. On-site marketing

c. Adequacy of information about product function, characteristics, and performance — 1, 3, 6
- Packaging design and representations — 1–6
- Grading and labeling — 1, 2, 6
- Unit pricing — 1, 2, 6
- Open dating — 1, 2, 6
- Display techniques — 1, 3, 4, 6
- Warranty or other remedy in case of dissatisfaction — 1–6
- Nature of personal selling — 1, 3, 6

d. Practices in restraint of trade

d. Policy and procedures aimed at avoidance Performance — 1

e. Supplier relations—suppliers include advertising agencies, distributors, warehouses, transportation agencies, and others involved in the marketing and distribution process

5. Customer financing
   a. Extent of coverage

a. Equality of availability, subject to reasonable credit risks — 1, 4
Terms which fairly distinguish between various conditions of payment — 1, 5

b. "Truth in lending"

b. Nature of disclosure of costs; repossession conditions and other credit terms — 1, 3, 4, 6

c. Collection and repossession

c. Policies, practices, and methods of handling delinquencies and repossessions — 1, 3, 4, 5, 6
Personal counseling practices — 1, 3, 6

6. Post-sale activities
   a. Customer education in the effective, efficient, and safe use of the product and service in a manner appropriate to the products' or services' characteristics
   b. Product warranties and other recourse in case of claimed misrepresentation, malfunction, or other dissatisfaction
   c. Service

a. General public education (as for food, energy, and liquor) — 1, 3, 5, 6
Availability of user manuals and other user aids — 1, 3, 5, 6
b. Policy and procedures — 1, 2, 4, 5, 6
Customer experience — 1, 3, 4
c. Policy — 1, 3
Distribution of facilities — 3, 4, 5, 6
Quality of service — 3, 5, 6
Speed of service — 3, 4, 6
Honesty — 3, 4, 5, 6
Cost — 3, 4, 5, 6

7. Responsiveness to public and customer reactions and requirements

7. Availability (and encouragement) of open channels of communication — 1, 3, 5, 6
Active attempts to obtain reactions and ideas from customers and noncustomers
Handling of complaints and claims — 1, 3, 5, 6
Utilization of public and customer information — 1, 3, 5, 6

8. Impact of use of products and services
   a. Impact on actual user

a. By-products of use, particularly those which affect the user's ability to be a desirable and/or effective member of society to a major extent (mental and physical health and well-being would be very important in this context) — 1, 3, 4, 5, 6

b. Impacts on others indirectly affected by user's use and/or subsequent waste disposal, primarily as a result of affecting the various environments of others: the physical environment the cultural and aesthetic environment the political, social, and government environment the behavioral environment	b. Nature and extent of impacts Attempts to enhance the good and to minimize or compensate for the bad	1, 3, 4 6
c. Impact on current and future availability of scarce or nonrenewable resources	c. Nature and extent of impacts Attempts to reduce use through such efforts as product redesign, material substitution, and recycling	1 5, 6

SOURCE: American Institute of Certified Public Accountants, *The Measurement of Corporate Social Performance* (New York: AICPA, 1977), p. 127. Copyright © 1977 by the American Institute of Certified Public Accountants, Inc. Reprinted with permission.

*KEY TO SOURCES OF INFORMATION AND EVIDENCE:
1. Policy statements and procedures, responsibilities set forth in position descriptions and studies of actions and results.
2. Special studies comparing company's product specifications with those recommended by trade associations and similar organizations, the requirements of governmental regulations, and authenticating testing laboratories.
3. Surveys of customers and noncustomers with regard to marketing and use of products.
4. Nature of organized reactions to company's products, marketing practices, services, etc., as evidenced by legal actions and complaints; studies and reports of consumer groups, public interest organizations, and governmental agencies.
5. Analyses of internal data as to specifications, quality and performance, market distribution and similar matters.
6. Actions taken to improve performance with actual or expected consequences.

Exhibit 6.6
Suggested Information on the Community

General Area and Specific Attribute	Specific Information	Sources of Information or Evidence
1. Corporate citizenship a. Character espousal	a. Statement of goals for community and of corporate policy with respect to them. Activities in support of these goals	a. Corporate policy statements; internal and external statements of key officials in support of community goals; actions and activities taken; community survey
b. Participation in community service and quality of life activities	b. Contributions in cash, in kind, and in time—amounts and purposes Leadership roles; other assistance	b. Normal records of corporation or its foundation Survey of management and key employees; personnel and community relations department records; officer/board membership in major community organizations; community survey
c. Organizational example	c. Performance with respect to such matters as the following: • Law abidingness and concern for the rights of others • Aesthetics • Concern for operational impacts • Respect for government and governmental processes • Participation in public debate; behavior in the face of opposition	c. Statements of corporate policy; evidences in the form of actions taken with respect to corporate interfaces with the community; community survey; expert opinions
d. Participation in social mini-programs	d. Extent of participation in or management of major programs, of a type often carried out or sponsored by the government, as part of	d. Records and reports relating to the specific activities prepared by project or program management

SOURCE: American Institute of Certified Public Accountants, *The Measurement of Corporate Social Performance* (New York: AICPA, 1977), pp. 162–163. Copyright © 1977 by the American Institute of Certified Public Accountants, Inc. Reprinted with permission.

FOOTNOTE DISCLOSURE

While the narrative disclosure consists of verbal statements, essentially nonquantitative, to be included in the descriptive, nonaccounting section of the annual report, the footnote treatment consists of quantitative measurements on the social involvement of the firms to be included as an additional footnote in the financial statements section of the annual report. An example of the footnote treatment in social reporting is shown in Exhibit 6.7. It is an excerpt from the Ansul Company 1974 annual report, which describes a waste disposal reserve anticipated for future pollution costs. The footnote treatment is a practical way of introducing financial statement readers to the voluntary expenditures and contingent liabilities facing a socially responsible firm. The footnote disclosure may have more merit than the narrative disclosure given that it would be covered by the auditor's report and opinion. It is, however, limited to the voluntary "social awareness expenditures" and does not include the remaining social costs and benefits. The footnote disclosure may be used to accommodate the Beams and Fertig proposal that resource impairment resulting from the environmental pollution be recognized and reported on an accrual basis.[37] More explicitly, their proposal includes a disclosure of expected future outlays for environmental damages resulting from past and current production activities, legal liabilities that result from a firm's violation of existing laws, contingent liabilities from probable actions where firms are in violation, liabilities for those expected future outlays that will not create asset values for the firm, and liabilities for eventual land restoration during the stripping operations by mining companies.[38]

Other interesting examples of footnote disclosures found in annual reports include the following footnotes on extraordinary items and on pollution facilities:

A reserve of $78 million before taxes ($39.6 million after tax effect) was provided in 1970 for estimated extraordinary losses to be incurred in connection with the anticipated abandonment of facilities which are unprofitable, obsolete, or unusable and which cannot, in the opinion of management, be made profitable by economically justifiable expenditures, and of facilities which do not meet environmental standards and which, in the opinion of management, cannot be brought into compliance for similar economic reasons. In 1970, the . . . Water Department Authority sold $2 million of 7.5 percent Water Development Revenue Bonds (principal maturing $200,000 annually) to provide funds for the purchase and expansion of an existing stream pollution control facility of the company at. . . . Of this amount $1,552,781 was paid to the company for the existing facility, and the remaining $447,219 is held by the trustee to be used for the expansion of the facility. The company leases the facility for an annual amount sufficient to pay principal and interest on the bonds. The cost of the existing facility is included with property, plant, and equipment in the accompanying balance sheet. Property, plant, and equipment and long-term debt will be increased as funds held by the trustee are expended. The company has treated this transaction as a loan for both accounting and tax purposes.[39]

ADDITIONAL ACCOUNTS

The pollution-generating activities of some firms may lead to site deterioration if an efficient disposal of industrial waste is lacking. Furthermore, failure to account for these site deteriorations can lead to misstatements in the financial reports of the of the major polluters. To correct for this situation, Floyd A. Beams proposed accounting procedures to deal with industrial site deterioration caused by pollution.[40]

Exhibit 6.7
Excerpt From the Ansul Company 1974 Annual Report: Notes to Consolidated Financial Statements

Note 7—Stock Option Plan. Under the 1966 Management Employee Qualified Stock Option Plan, options have been granted to certain officers and key employees to purchase shares of common stock at 100 percent of fair market value on the date of grant. Options become exercisable as to 50 percent of the optioned shares during the second year after grant and the balance during the third year. All options terminate five years after grant.

STOCK OPTION TRANSACTIONS	NUMBER OF SHARES	AVERAGE PRICE PER SHARE (DOLLARS)
Outstanding January 1, 1973	83,033	9.57
Changes during 1973		
Granted	7,946	11.28
Terminated	(7,831)	14.21
Exercised	(1,523)	8.98
Outstanding December 31, 1973	81,625	9.31
Changes during 1974		
Granted	8,072	14.20
Terminated	(600)	12.13
Exercised	(12,175)	9.22
Outstanding December 31, 1974	76,922	9.82

(1973 adjusted for 4 percent stock dividend in 1974.)

At December 31, 1974, 66,229 shares (50,216 at December 31, 1973) under option were exercisable and 10,147 shares (17,678 at December 31, 1973) were available for grant.

Note 8—Deferred Items.

DEFERRED ITEMS AT DECEMBER 31, 1974, & 1973	1974 (DOLLARS)	1973 (DOLLARS)
Deferred currency exchange gains	740,369	1,137,595
Waste disposal reserve	1,915,000	1,000,000
Total	2,655,369	2,137,595

The waste disposal reserve has been provided for anticipated costs that may be associated with the recycling or disposal of a salt waste byproduct of our domestic agricultural chemical production. During 1974, we determined that any recycling or disposal program probably will be completed over a period of time exceeding one year. As a result we have classified the waste disposal reserve and related future tax benefits as noncurrent items. The December 31, 1973, balance sheet and statement of changes in financial position have been restated to conform with the 1974 classifications.

SOURCE: Steven C. Dilley, "External Reporting of Social Responsibility," MSU Business Topics (Autumn 1975): 18. Reprinted by permission of the publisher, Division of Research, Graduate School of Business Administration, Michigan State University.

Beams suggested first that the charge for delayed site maintenance of prior years would seem to qualify as a prior-period adjustment to retained earnings in accordance with the criteria outlined in APB Opinion no. 9 and the corresponding credit made to a new account called allowance for industrial site deterioration. Second, two new expense accounts would be recognized: *industrial site maintenance* expense for outlays made to to re-establish a deteriorated plant site; and *industrial site deterioration* expense for charges stemming either from air or water pollution or from industrial waste accumulation. Both expenses are offset by a credit to the allowance for industrial site deterioration.

In the area of auditing, Beams notes that the existing legal requirements on pollution prevention and the increased responsibility of the auditor may lead the auditor to ensure that contingent liabilities, where firms are in violation of antipollution laws, were not omitted. In fact, the AICPA's Statement of Auditing Standards suggests the qualification of an opinion, when uncertainty prevails, as follows:

In our opinion, subject to any future assessments and charges, presently undeterminable, that may result from past and current environmental damage, the accompanying financial statements fairly present the financial position of XYZ Company at December 31, 19___, and the results of its operations and the changes in its financial position for the year then ended, in conformity with generally accepted accounting principles applied on a basis consistent with that of the preceding year.

In the area of taxation, Beams notes that the charges for industrial site and for prior-period adjustments are currently nondeductible and urges congress to relax the present laws to allow these deductions as an incentive for better social concern from corporations.

Beams; proposal of additional accounts for environmental disclosures did not fall on deaf ears. As reported earlier, the AAA Committee on Environmental Effects of Organizational Behavior recommended recognition of environmental expenses in the income statement, environmental expenditures in the statement of changes in the financial position, environmental control facilities as assets in the balance sheet, and environmental liabilities as liabilities in the balance sheet. In fact the committee suggested three types of liabilities: (1) the liability for assessed but unpaid penalties or pollution taxes for noncompliance with standards; (2) the liability for estimated penalty or tax (not assessed) for noncompliance with standards or deadlines; and (3) the liability for the estimated cost of voluntary "restorations: of the environment for past or current damages.[41]

Both Beams; and the committee's proposals constitute a step forward toward a more comprehensive financial statement. Beams' proposal is, however, applicable for firms engaged in strip mining, agribusiness, resort development and management, and other industries where the condition of the soil, land surface, and still bodies of water is an important factor and may have limited applicability for accounting for the effects of air pollution and water pollution of *flowing* waterways.[42]

POLLUTION REPORTS

At one time most social reporting in annual reports was limited to a disclosure of total pollution control expenses and compliance with environmental laws and regulations. John Tepper Marlin observed that such disclosures do not by themselves tell the story and proposed two standards of reporting on a company's pollution.[43]

The first report would compare the company's pollution controls with the state-of-the-art standards to be produced jointly by the Ecology and social Measurement committees of the AICPA and an Industry Institute Committee. An example of such a pollution report given in Exhibit 6.8, which shows the adequacy of the pollution controls of a company's five pulp and paper mills based on an internal audit conducted by accountants and engineers. This report may also be accompanied by an auditor's opinion, to read as follows:

In addition to the financial statements, we have examined to the extent considered necessary in the circumstances all assertions in this report regarding the company's compliance with environmental regulations and the adequacy of its existing and planned pollution control equipment. In our opinion these assertions are consistent with independent inquiries made with regulatory authorities, equipment suppliers and outside scientific consultants; with inspection of company records of equipment purchased and periodic efficiency ratings; and with state-of-the-art standards developed by the AICPA committees on environmental accounting and social measurement and the committee on pollution control of the American Paper Institute.[44]

The second report would present the actual net pollution emissions and the federal standards by type of pollutant. An example of such pollution performance report is shown in Exhibit 6.9. It shows the pollution performance of three paper companies in New York State in terms of oxygen demand, solid emissions, and eight other forms of pollution, along with the corresponding federal standards. This report may also be accompanied by the following (hypothetical) auditor's opinion:

In addition to Company B's financial statements, we have examined to the extent considered necessary in the circumstances its assertions regarding the amount of pollution caused by its mills. In our opinion, based on consultation with plant staff and governmental authorities, and on an independent sampling of emissions by a private environmental consulting firm, the reported emissions fairly reflect the pollution caused by the mills at the time of our investigation, and the company has budgeted adequate operating expenses to maintain this level of control.[45]

The two pollution reports proposed by Marlin present a practical way to deal with the performance evaluation of a firm's polluting activities. In fact, these reports may be extended to all the social areas where state-of-the-art standards may be produced and firms' performance may be measured. The proposal rests, however, on the existence and/or production of federal standards for each area of significant social concern and on the possibility of achieving a consensus on these standards.

SOCIAL RESPONSIBILITY ANNUAL REPORT

Steven Dilley and Jerry Weygandt rightfully note that arguments such as the companies will never permit disclosures of social data, the information will be too difficult to develop, or the collection of data will cause internal hassle are practical objections that should not restrain progress in social measurement.[46] Accordingly, they have presented a social responsibility annual report (SRAR) based on a cost outlay approach. This report includes various unrelated reports covering the performance of an actual Midwestern gas and electric company in the pollution, health and safety, and minority recruitment and promotion areas.

The first statement shown in Exhibit 6.10 describes the industry of which the audited company is part, the purpose and scope of the social audit, and the organizations conducting the audit and paying for it. Notice that in this case the social audit is both performed and financed by other than the reporting company.

The next two statements shown in Exhibits 6.11 and 6.12 provide neutral information on the company and its community. Both exhibits are included to help the reader develop an insight into the nature of the company and its community and the possible issues of social concern on the company.

The next two statements shown in Exhibits 6.13 and 6.14 provide information on air pollution, thermal pollution, and water consumption. Most of the data used were found in Federal Power Commission Form no. 67, "Steam-Electric Plant Air and Water Quality Control Data."

Exhibit 6.8
State-of-the-Art Pollution Control Report for Ideal Paper Co.: Production, Water Use, and Pollution Control of Mill

LOCATION	PRODUCTION (tons per day)		WATER USE (millions gallons per day)	POLLUTION CONTROL ADEQUACY				
				Water			Air	
	Pulp	Other		Primary	Secondary	Tertiary	Gas and Odor	Part
Mill A	1600	1750	89	✓	✓	X	✓	X
Mill B	1200	970	95	✓	1973	X	✓	X
Mill C	1200	1100	82	✓	1973	1973	1974	✓
Mill D	610	840	40	1974	1975	X	X	✓
Mill E	0	1395	61	✓	—	—	—	✓
Total*	4610	6055	367	80%	25%	0%	50%	60%
				80.8%	34.7%	0%	60.7%	39.3%

SOURCE: John Tepper Marlin, "Accounting for Pollution," *Journal of Accountancy* (February 1973):43. Copyright © 1973 by the American Institute of Certified Public Accountants, Inc. Used by permission.

NOTE: Presently adequate state-of-the-art pollution controls are indicated by a check mark; inadequate controls by an X. A dash means equipment not needed. Where adequate equipment is being installed, the expected year of completion is indicated.

* Two total figures are given. The first line is the percentage of plants that now have adequate controls. The second line is the proportion of pulp production that is adequately controlled. It is obtained by adding up pulp capacity of adequately controlled plants and dividing this by the total production of all plants requiring controls.

Exhibit 6.9
Sample Net Pollution Emissions and Federal Standards, By Type of Pollutant

	COMPANY A (NSSC Pulp)	COMPANY B (Kraft Pulp)	COMPANY C (Tissue Manufacturer)			Federal Drinking Water Standards	
			No. 1 White Water Tank	No. 1 Sewer	Pulping Area Floor Drain	Desirable	Permissable
Production (tons per day)	70	550	170	170	170	—	—
Flow (thousands of gallons per day)	5,000	1,900	127	410	23	—	—
A. Biochemical oxygen demand	344	18	93	156	234	(8)	(14)
Chemical oxygen demand	1,742	110	46	254	573	?	?
Solids, dissolved	1,454	478	3	114	28	200	500
Solids, suspended	264	21	16	170	399	(6)	(10)
B. Color	40	220	0	12	7	10	75
Coliform bacteria	760,000	20	0	0	1,900	100	10,000
Phenols	45	0	2	5	4	0	0.001
Sulfate	9	186	−0.8	0.2	3	50	250
Chloride	15	388	0.7	0.5	3	25	250
Copper	15	0	35	30	25	0	1
Lead	0	0	−12	−9	2	0	0.05
Zinc	−50	0.02	1498	20	22	0	5

SOURCE: John Tepper Marlin, "Accounting for Pollution," *Journal of Accountancy* (February 1973): 45. Copyright © 1973 by the American Institute of Certified Public Accountants, Inc. Used by permission.

NOTE: Question mark indicates missing source figures. Dash means not applicable.

Exhibit 6.10
Introductory Statement

Utility Company is a gas and electric firm operating in the Midwestern United States. Its rates and return on investment are regulated by a state utility commission. The company operates exclusively within a single state, although it receives natural gas and coal from outside the state's borders.

This SRAR has been prepared to measure Utility Company's response to current social concerns. The data contained in this report are true and accurate within the current limits of scientific measurement techniques available for research of this type. Each of the elements attempts to convey to the reader information that may be useful in his social evaluation of the company.

The data were developed as a result of a social audit of the Utility Company. X-Y-Z Associates, an independent research organization, conducted the audit and prepared the following SRAR. Financing for this research project was provided by a Midwestern university.

X-Y-Z Associates, Inc.

SOURCE: Steven C. Dilley and Jerry J. Weygandt, "Measuring Social Responsibility: An Empirical Test," *Journal of Accountancy* (September 1973): 64. Copyright © 1973 by the American Institute of Certified Public Accountants, Inc. Used by permission.

Exhibit 6.11
Company Information

Type of company	Gas-electric public utility			
1971 operating revenues	$40,000,000			
1971 operating income	$ 5,500,000			

	RESIDENTIAL	INDUSTRIAL AND COMMERCIAL	GOVERNMENT AND INSTITUTIONAL	MISC.
Electric sales revenue (%)	40.0	46.5	8.5	5.0
Number of electric customers	66,000	10,000	40.0	2
Gas sales revenue (%)	48.0	50.0	—	2.0
Number of gas customers	41,000	6,500	—	5

Number of employees				
	Subject to union agreements			340
	Supervisors and professional staff			140
	Total			500
	Percent of community population			17%
Age of company	60 years			
Average salary of employees				
	Subject to union agreements			$10,650
	Supervisors and professional staff			$13,500
Community ownership			TOTAL	COMMUNITY*
	Common stockholders		9,000	5,000
	Number of stockholders holding greater than 5 percent of outstanding shares		None	None
Subsidiary companies owned	None			
Stock investments in nonsubsidiary companies	None			

SOURCE: Steven C. Dilley and Jerry J. Weygandt, "Measuring Social Responsibility: An Empirical Test," *Journal of Accountancy* (September 1973): 65. Copyright © 1973 by the American Institute of Certified Public Accountants, Inc. Used by permission.

NOTE: Asterisk indicates state in which company is located. Dash indicates not applicable.

Exhibit 6.12
Descriptive Characteristics of the Company Social Impact on the Community

Area in square miles:	700
Population:	300,000
Minority group (blacks), % of population:	1.1
Type:	Urban-suburban, some rural
Location:	Midwestern U.S.
Economic base:	Industrial, government services
Physical characteristics:	Rolling plains
Weather characteristics:	Large seasonal variations in temperature; substantial yearly precipitation
Number of government units:	50
Median family income:	$11,000
Population	
Earning less than poverty level (%):	5.4
Earning more than $15,000 (%):	27.2

SOURCE: Steven C. Dilley and Jerry J. Weygandt, "Measuring Social Responsibility: An Empirical Test," *Journal of Accountancy* (September 1973):66. Copyright © 1973 by the American Institute of Certified Public Accountants, Inc. Used by permission.

Exhibit 6.13
Utility Company Emissions of Air Pollutants (In Millions of Dollars), 1971

YEAR	PARTICULATE MATTER		
	Coal	Oil	Gas
1971	3.3717	0.003	0.111
1970	4.3920	0.001	0.095

	SULFUR OXIDES		
	Coal	Oil	Gas
1971	17.71	0.046	0.005
1970	22.22	0.027	0.004

	NITROGEN OXIDES		
	Coal	Oil	Gas
1971	2.69	NA	NA
1970	3.58	NA	NA

SOURCE: Steven C. Dilley and Jerry J. Weygandt, "Measuring Social Responsibility: An Empirical Test," *Journal of Accountancy* (September 1973):66. Copyright © 1973 by the American Institute of Certified Public Accountants, Inc. Used by permission.

NOTE: The company was in compliance with all state and federal laws in regard to air pollution during 1971. Federal air pollution emission standards generally apply to new power plants. No new coal-fired boilers were put in service during 1971. State regulations require compliance with stringent air pollution standards by 1973. To meet those more stringent standards, the company will have to reduce its pollution emissions by 1973. To accomplish this goal, the company is installing electrostatic precipitators to trap 99.5 percent of the particulate matter, using as much natural gas as is available, and using low-sulfur coal when it can be obtained. The pollutants emitted during 1971 can impose social costs upon the community that the company serves. These social costs are composed of increased soiling costs, increased incidence of respiratory disease, and decreases in property values. NA indicates not applicable.

Exhibit 6.14
Utility Company Water Resource Demands for Electric Power Generation, 1971

Type of cooling system:	Once-through		
Source of cooling water:	Freshwater lake, area 5.4 sq. mi.		
Cooling water data:	TEMPERATURE AS RECEIVED	TEMPERATURE AS DISCHARGED	DIFFERENCE
Winter maximum	40°F	69°F	29°F
Summer maximum	70°F	105°F	26°F
Average rate of water consumption during 1971	1 cu. ft./sec.		
Average rate of water withdrawal from water body	352 cu. ft./sec.		
Average rate of water discharge to water body	351 cu. ft./sec.		
Depth of water withdrawal	37 ft.		
Depth of water discharge	surface		

SOURCE: Steven C. Dilley and Jerry J. Weygandt, "Measuring Social Responsibility: An Empirical Test," *Journal of Accountancy* September 1973:67. Copyright © 1973 by the American Institute of Certified Public Accountants, Inc. Used by permission.

The next two statements shown in Exhibits 6.15 and 6.16 provide information, respectively, on occupational health and safety and minority recruitment and promotion. The occupational health and safety statement is a simple adaptation of the report that must be filed on occupational injuries and illnesses under the Occupational Safety and Health Act of 1970. The minorities recruitment and promotion statement includes information found on Form EEO-1 used by the Equal Employment Opportunity Commission lists company's efforts in the area of minority employment.

The final statement shown in Exhibit 6.17 is a statement of funds flow for socially relevant activities. It is broken down into two categories- environmental expenditures and other social expenditures- because environmental problems are the most significant social problems facing gas and electric utilities.

The SRAR proposal is again a practical one given the availability of the information disclosed. It can be extended to most areas of social concern where federal standards of performance exist.

ENVIRONMENTAL EXCHANGE REPORT

Wayne Corcoran and Wayne E. Leininger, Jr., offered a conceptual framework for reporting exchanges between a firm and its environment, an "environmental exchange report."[47] Interaction between a firm and its environment involves the exchange of human, physical, and financial resources. The environmental exchange report recognizes the exchange of human and physical resources and selected financial data or relevance to areas of social concern. Most of the exchanges of the finance resources are already internalized in the statement of changes in the financial position.

The environmental exchange report shown in Exhibit 6.18 divides the exchanges into input and output. The input and output include both human and physical resources. They are defined as follows:

Human resource input consists of all the human effort expended in the organization and includes, therefore, information such as number of employees, educational level, tenure with the firm; number of man hours used by the firm; and number of hours of paid vacations and sick leave. Other possibilities are measures of wage and productivity increases, promotions, and the profiles of new employees. Human resource outputs consist of such items as wages paid to employees as well as information about employee terminations.

Physical resource input includes all physical resources used (air, water, raw materials, and the physical output of other firms), and descriptive information should indicate the source, future availability, and amount of each resource employed in the production process. . . .

Physical output into the environment should describe the physical products marketed, the waste and residue resulting from the productive process, and the resources, such as water, that are returned to the environment.[48]

The environmental exchange report proposal is also a practical and easy approach to micro social accounting. It fails to include the performance of the company on other areas of social concerns, and as such it is a rather restrictive report.

SOCIAL INCOME STATEMENT

Lee Seidler has suggested the preparation of socially oriented financial statements and other accounting analyses in dollar terms.[49] He has proposed two social income statement formats, one for a profit-oriented company and one for a not-for-profit company.

Exhibit 6.15
Utility Company Occupational Health and Safety Statement for the Period July 1, 1971 to December 31, 1971

Average number of employees during the period	500
Total hours worked by all employees	403,000
On-the-job fatalities during the period	0
Number of workdays lost due to on-the-job injuries	35
Number of employees affected	6
% of total employees	1.2
Number of workdays lost due to occupational illness	0
Number of employees affected	0
% of total employees	0

SOURCE: Steven C. Dilley and Jerry J. Weygandt, "Measuring Social Responsibility," *Journal of Accountancy* (September 1973):68. Copyright © by the American Institute of Certified Public Accountants, Inc. Used by permission.

NOTE: The data for this statement were derived from OSHA Form No. 103. The information contained on that report is required by the Williams-Steiger Occupational Health and Safety Act. The mutual reporting period ran from July 1, 1971, to December 31, 1971. Subsequent reporting periods will run from January 1 to December 31 of each year.

Exhibit 6.16
Utility Company Minorities Recruitment and Promotions Statement, 1971

Total population of community	300,000
% minorities	1.1
Total number of employees	500
Total number of minority Negro and Spanish-surnamed employees	9
Subject to union contracts	8
% of all employees subject to union contracts	2.2
% of all employees	1.6
Supervisory and professional staff	1
% of all supervisory and professional staff	0.7
% of all employees	0.2
Total number of female employees	83
Subject to union contracts	71
% of all employees subject to union contracts	19.9
% of all employees	14.2
Supervisory and professional staff	12
% of all supervisory and professional staff	8.6
% of all employees	2.4
Special minority recruitment and advancement programs	
Negroes and Spanish-surnamed employees	0
Dollars spent	0
Females	0
Dollars spent	0

SOURCE: Steven C. Dilley and Jerry J. Weygandt, "Measuring Social Responsibility," *Journal of Accountancy* (September 1973):68. Copyright © 1973 by the American Institute of Certified Public Accountants, Inc. Used by permission.

Exhibit 6.17
Utility Company Statement of Funds Slow for Socially Relevant Activities, 1971

Environmental			
Installation of electrostatic precipitators (Note 1)		$ 26,000	
Construction of power plants (Note 2)		2,089,000	
Construction of transmission lines (Note 3)		35,000	
Electrical substation beautification (Note 4)		142,000	
Incremental cost of low-sulfur coal (Note 5)		33,670	
Conversion of service vehicles to use of propane gas (Note 6)		3,700	
Incremental cost of underground electric installations (Note 7)		737,000	
Incremental cost of silent jackhammers (Note 8)		100	
Environmental research			
Thermal	$17,000		
Nuclear	1,955		
Other	38,575		
Subtotal		57,530	
Total environmental funds flow			$3,124,000
Other benefits			
Charitable contributions		$ 26,940	
Employee educational and recreational expenditures (Note 9)		6,000	
Total other benefits			32,940
Total 1971 funds flow for socially relevant activities			$3,156,940
As a percentage of 1971 operating revenues			7.9
As a percentage of 1971 advertising expenses			8,500

SOURCE: Stephen C. Dilley and Jerry J. Weygandt, "Measuring Social Responsibility," *Journal of Accountancy* (September 1973):69. Copyright 1973 by the American Institute of Certified Public Accountants, Inc. Used by permission.

Exhibit 6.18
XYZ Company, Environmental Exchange Report for Year Ending December 31, 1970

INPUT

HUMAN RESOURCES:

Time—During the year, 100 individuals were hired, bringing total employment to 1,000. Employees made available 2,000,000 man-hours to the firm, and there were no layoffs during the year. 75,000 man-hours were lost because of sickness or other personal reasons, and employees earned 100,000 man-hours of paid vacation.

TIME WITH FIRM (years)	PERCENTAGE OF EMPLOYEES	EDUCATION LEVEL*	PERCENTAGE OF EMPLOYEES	AGE OF EMPLOYEES (years)	PERCENTAGE OF EMPLOYEES
under 1	10	under 12 yrs.	20	18–25	20
1–3	15	12 yrs.	40	26–30	23
3–5	42	13–14 yrs.	10	31–40	27
5–10	30	college degree	30	41–50	19
over 10	3			51–65	11

*The firm invested $50,000 in assisting employees further their education.

PHYSICAL RESOURCES:

Direct Materials—

(A) 500 tons of cast iron (35% of which is recycled scrap metal)
(B) 10,000 tons of steel (30% of which is recycled scrap metal)

The firm pursues a policy of purchasing from manufacturers who not only produce quality products but are also leaders in the area of pollution control.

(C) 200,000 board feet of lumber

The supplier of the lumber estimates that it took 35 years to grow this lumber. This lumber is used in the end product and for packaging and is not recoverable.

Indirect Materials—

(A) 500 tons of oil and related products
(B) 5,000,000 gallons of water
(C) 60 tons of paper and related products (20% of which is recycled scrap)

OUTPUT

HUMAN RESOURCES:

10 employees were dismissed, 25 terminated voluntarily, and 13 retired with annual pensions ranging from $3,500 to $20,400 with a mean of $5,200.

ANNUAL EARNINGS (dollars)	MEAN (dollars)	AVERAGE INCREASE (dollars)	PERCENTAGE OF EMPLOYEES	PERCENTAGE HOLDING OTHER EMPLOYMENT	MEAN UNEMPLOYED DEPENDENTS	MEAN YEARS WITH FIRM
under 5,000	4,780	500	15	75	2.1	2
5,000–7,499	7,200	600	20	42	4.1	5
7,500–9,999	8,900	600	40	20	4.3	8
10,000–14,999	11,700	720	20	5	4.6	11
over 15,000	18,000	840	5	0	3.8	15

PHYSICAL RESOURCES:

End Product—500,000 widgets with two-year guarantees and estimated life of five years. It is thought that the bounty offered for recovery of widgets will result in the return of 75% of the widgets and that 80% of raw materials contained in the recovered widgets will be reprocessed for future use. 100,000 board feet of lumber are not recoverable.

Water—5,000,000 gallons were removed from the Blue River, and 4,000,000 gallons were returned. The installation of several cooling pounds eliminated appreciable thermal pollution to the river. The Massachusetts Department of Natural Resources has certified that the water returned to the river was in all aspects purer than the water removed. The remaining 1,000,000 gallons were dissipated into the atmosphere in the form of steam.

Air—5 tons of solid material in the form of dust were unavoidably emitted into the atmosphere. During the month of June, the firm was fined $3,000 for excessive emissions into the air caused by the breakdown of our air pollution control system. Management decided against suspending production during the breakdown period.

Waste—Packaging of product resulted in 50 tons of paper and plastic waste and 100,000 board feet of lumber that are not recoverable. 15 tons of solid waste resulted from the production process and are not recoverable in any form.

Financial—

TAXES PAID	BY FIRM	BY EMPLOYEES
Federal	$1,000,000	$1,200,000
State	500,000	200,000
Local	450,000	800,000
CONTRIBUTIONS		
Colleges and Universities	40,000	20,000
United Fund	10,000	20,000
Massachusetts Social Action Board	10,000	unknown

SOURCE: Wayne Corcoran and Wayne E. Leininger, Jr., "Financial Statements—Who Needs Them?" *Financial Executive* (August 1970), 40-47. Used by permission.

The social income statement format proposed for a profit-oriented company is shown in Exhibit 6.19. To the value added by production of the enterprise are added the socially desirable outputs not sold and are subtracted the socially undesirable effects not paid for. In essence, the format calls for an internalization of the social costs (external diseconomies) and the social benefits (external economies). The net result is a net social profit or loss of the company.

The social income statement format proposed for a not-for-profit company is shown in Exhibit 6.20. It is a social income statement for a university compared with a conventional income statement. Notice that the revenues in the conventional statement represent the costs to society in terms of the payments paid by society to the university in exchange for educational services. The costs in the conventional statement represent the benefits to society in terms of the cost of services it has performed for society.

The two income statement formats provide a practical framework for social accounting experimentation. A more detailed list of social benefits and costs would make the two formats more exhaustive and more informative.

COMPREHENSIVE SOCIAL BENEFIT-COST MODEL

Ralph Estes proposes "an accounting model that systematically reflects the worth of all resources consumed, including those resources or values which are free to the consuming entity (noninternalized costs of external diseconomies), and the worth of all benefits produced, including those that provide no compensation to the producing entity (external economies)."[50] Estes notices that the conventional accounting model excludes certain external economies and diseconomies and generally reflects the view of the entity looking out, toward society. He proposed a different point of view, that of society looking at the entity with the social benefits equal to the values or utilities actually received of society and social costs equal to the full detriments to society, paid and unpaid. This more rational resource allocation is to be based on a model having the following structure:

$$SS = \sum_{i=1}^{n} \sum_{t=1}^{\infty} \frac{B_i}{(1+r)^t} - \sum_{j=1}^{m} \sum_{t=1}^{\infty} \frac{C_j}{(1+r)^t}$$

where
SS = social surplus or deficit
B_i = the ith social benefit
C_j = the jth social cost
r = an appropriate discount rate
t = time period in which benefit or cost is expected to occur.[51]

The comprehensive social report based on this model reflects the direct effects of a single entity on society. The indirect effects are reported in the footnotes. It could be used to report the indirect effects if the following conditions were met: "(a) *each* element of society accurately measured and reported all social benefits and costs created, (b) each element was periodically assessed or rewarded an amount equal to its net social surplus or deficit, and (c) each element adjusted the prices of its goods and services upward in response to assessments or downward for rewards."[52]

The model takes the society's point of view by reporting social costs and benefits (benefits and costs to society). It represents a comprehensive format for companies experimenting with micro social accounting.

Exhibit 6.19
Social Income Statement of a Profit-Seeking Organization

Value added by production of the enterprise

+ Socially desirable outputs not sold (social benefits)
   a. Job training
   b. Health improvement of workers
   c. Employment of disadvantaged minorities
   d. Others

− Socially desirable effects not paid for (social costs)
   a. Air pollution
   b. Water pollution
   c. Health problems caused by company's products
   d. Others

Net Social Profit (or loss)

SOURCE: Adapted with suggested modifications from Lee J. Seidler, "Dollar Values in the Social Income Statement," *World* (Peat, Marwick, Mitchell and Co.) (Spring 1973):21. Copyright © 1973 Peat, Marwick, Mitchell, & Co. Used by permission.

Exhibit 6.20
Income Statement of a University

CONVENTIONAL INCOME STATEMENT	SOCIAL INCOME STATEMENT
Revenues: (private benefits)	Revenues: (social benefits)
Tuition paid to university	Value of instruction to society
Research grants*	Value of research to society
State aid	
Less Costs: (private costs)	Less Costs: (social costs)
Instructional	Tuition paid to university
Research costs*	Cost of research
Student aid	State aid
Overheads	Other—lost production, etc.
Result:	Result:
(Deficit) to the university	Profit to society

SOURCE: Adapted with minor modifications from Lee J. Seidler, "Dollar Values in the Social Income Statement," *World* (Peat, Marwick, Mitchell, & Co.) (Spring 1973):18. Copyright © 1973 Peat, Marwick, Mitchell, & Co. Used by permission.

*Research is shown as the same figure in both parts of the conventional statement, at the amount received and expended.

MULTIDIMENSIONAL INCOME STATEMENT

Colantoni, Cooper, and Deitzer have suggested two types of income statements aimed at extending ordinary accounting and auditing in the private sector to social reporting.[53]

The first report presents the conventional income statement items classified first in the customary way of conventional accounting and second connected to other dimensions (social and physical environment) to pinpoint various aspects of social performance. Hence, the net income per ton of output of $9.43 before the environmental programs is reduced to $6.40 with such programs. An example of environmental programs is OSHA index < 75 on a scale in which 100 represents an acceptable level of employee safety. To reach this level the exhibit shows that dollar costs per ton of output required are $1.25 and $0.20 of employee wages and benefits, $0.30 in consumption of materials and supplies, and so on, and that a reduction in taxes of $1.25 and in profit of $1.50 resulted from the program. Needless to say, these data need to be accompanied by related verbal narratives and explanatory notes.

The second report shows a multidimensional extension highlighting the social performance of the company in areas of interest to selected constituencies of employees, suppliers, stockholders, and government. For example, the column "External Payment" represents payments by the firm to various components of society comprising $1,440 million as a wage payment to labor, $360 million as a benefit payment on behalf of labor to insurance companies, FICA taxes, and so on.

A STOCHASTIC FLOW FORMAT

Most of the techniques examined thus far have required some form of "balance sheet" type of disclosure. This form of disclosure applies also to the EEO-1 report required by the U.S. Equal Employment Opportunity Commission (EEOC) to keep a record of the percent of minorities and women employed in nine overall job categories. An example of an EEO-1 report is shown in Exhibit 6.21. Churchill and Shank objected to this "stock" or balance sheet approach to affirmative action measurement and proposed a "flow" measure to monitor the rate of progression of employees within the management ranks.[54] Using information available in current personnel files from an actual corporation, they developed matrices of employee transition probabilities, as shown in Exhibits 6.22 and 6.23. These matrices show the probability of being separated or promoted from any of the eight job categories to any of the other categories. They may be used to observe and assess management succession processes for men and women. Five generalizations may be suggested as the kind of analysis to which such data can be subjected:

1. The Diagonal Drag: The diagonal in each matrix represents employees who stay in the same job category from one year to the next.
2. Separations: Column 1 of both exhibits (when zero stands for separation) represents employees who left the firm from all categories.
3. Backsliding: Entries below the main diagonal represent employees who were demoted.
4. Leapfrogging: Entries above the main diagonal represent employees who were promoted.
5. Promotions: Entries one level above the main diagonal represent normal, one-step promotions.

Once these generalizations are made, the next step suggested is a statistical test (x^2 test) to see if there were any significant overall differences among the various matrices.

This approach is intended to provide more relevant information to users for evaluating the efficiency of affirmative action programs by providing insights as to comparative retention rates, promotion rates, and demotion rates at various management levels.

Exhibit 6.21
The Anonymous Corporation (1973 EEO-1 Report)

EEOC REPORTING GROUPS	MINORITIES (percent)	WOMEN (percent)	TOTAL*
Group I—Professionals	3.0	61.7	280
Group II—Technicians	2.0	30.8	200
Group III—Sales	5.4	86.8	9,597
Group IV—Office and clerical	10.5	89.7	3,494
Group V—Craftsmen	6.0	15.1	381
Group VI—Operations	7.9	37.3	579
Group VII—Laborers	7.0	28.8	828
Group VIII—Service	18.4	68.5	3,005
Group IX—Officials and managers	3.8	43.1	1,634
Total (all groups)	8.2	75.0	20,000

SOURCE: Neil C. Churchill and John K. Shank, "Accounting for Affirmative Action Programs: A Stochastic Flow Approach," *Accounting Review* (October 1975): 649. Reprinted by permission.

*In response to a desire for anonymity, the totals in this EEOC report were multiplied by a constant that forced the totals to 20,000 but did not change the proportions. All other data in this and the other tables are those actually found in the corporation.

Exhibit 6.22
Transition Probabilities Matrix for Promotion of Male Employees, for a Selected Multilocation Retail Enterprise

JOB CATEGORY AT BEGINNING OF YEAR	JOB CATEGORY AT THE END OF THE YEAR								
	0	1	2	3	4	5	6	7	8
0	1.000	0.000	0.000	0.000	0.000	0.000	0.000	0.000	0.000
1	.200	.450	.200	.100	.050	.000	.000	.000	.000
2	.207	.010	.556	.101	.086	.040	.000	.000	.000
3	.115	.000	.033	.713	.102	.020	.012	.000	.004
4	.145	.000	.005	.023	.626	.150	.028	.023	.000
5	.140	.000	.014	.000	.021	.650	.091	.049	.035
6	.185	.000	.015	.000	.000	.031	.662	.092	.015
7	.147	.000	.000	.000	.000	.007	.042	.748	.056
8	.131	.000	.000	.000	.000	.000	.000	.024	.845

SOURCE: Neil C. Churchill and John K. Shank, "Accounting for Affirmative Action Programs: A Stochastic Flow Approach," *Accounting Review* (October 1975): 649. Reprinted by permission.

Exhibit 6.23
Transition Probabilities Matrix for Promotion of Female Employees, for a Selected Multilocation Retail Enterprise

JOB CATEGORY AT BEGINNING OF YEAR	JOB CATEGORY AT THE END OF THE YEAR								
	0	1	2	3	4	5	6	7	8
0	1.000	0.000	0.000	0.000	0.000	0.000	0.000	0.000	0.000
1	.218	.595	.139	.044	.004	.000	.000	.000	.000
2	.152	.004	.750	.053	.024	.015	.000	.000	.000
3	.137	.000	.024	.742	.048	.048	.000	.000	.000
4	.113	.000	.028	.014	.676	.155	.014	.000	.000
5	.141	.000	.026	.000	.038	.692	.026	.051	.026
6	.000	.000	.000	.000	.000	.000	.786	.214	.000
7	.152	.000	.030	.000	.030	.000	.091	.667	.030
8	.009	.000	.000	.000	.000	.000	.000	.000	.091

SOURCE: Neil C. Churchill and John K. Shank, "Accounting for Affirmative Action Programs: A Stochastic Flow Approach," *Accounting Review* (October 1975):649. Reprinted by permission.

The Demand for Micro Social Economics
MARKET REACTION

The disclosure of social information is essential if investors are going to consider properly the negative effects of social awareness expenditures on earnings per share along with any compensating positive effects that reduce risk or create greater interest from a particular investment clientele.

Some argue that risk-reducing effects will more than compensate for social awareness expenditures: "Between firms competing in the capital markets those perceived to have the highest expected future earnings in combination with the lowest expected risk from environmental and other factors will be most successful at attracting long term funds."[55] Others believe that "ethical investors" form a clientele that responds to demonstrations of corporate social concern.[56] Investors of this type would like to avoid particular investments entirely for ethical reasons, as the 1966-68 Committee on External Reporting of the American Accounting Association points out,[57] and would prefer to favor socially responsible corporations in their portfolios. The United Church of Christ, for example, has issued a sixty-one page booklet, *Investing Church Funds for Maximum Social Impact*, which advises investment in socially responsible firms. A different view is summed up in the Beams-Fertig thesis, which holds that corporations that report the least activity in avoiding social cost will appear more successful to investors and will be favored by the market.[58]

Given these two hypotheses in general and the nature of the market reaction to the disclosure of social information in particular, various empirical studies examined the market reaction issue. Market-based studies were conducted by Belkaoui, Spicer, Ingram, Anderson and Frankle, Ingram and Frazier, Bikki and Freedman, and Chugh, Haneman, and Mahapatra.[59]

Belkaoui examined the impact of the disclosure of pollution control expenditures in the market. His investigation of fifty companies' pollution control expenditures showed a significant change centered on the date of disclosure, and the resulting expectations had a substantial and temporary effect on the stock market performance. This result follows the efficient market hypothesis in its semi-strong form. Under the naïve investor hypothesis, it verifies the existence of an "ethical investor." In general, the findings refute the suggestion that the worst offenders in the reporting of social costs will be rewarded more in the capital market.

Spicer concentrated on acertaining the extent to which investor perceptions of a moderate to strong association between the investment worth of a corporation's securities and its social performance on key social issues appeared warranted. He tested for associations between a number of economic and financial indicators of investment worth (profitability, size, total and systematic risk, price-earning ratio) and corporate performance on the issue of pollution control in a sample of company drawn from the pulp and paper industry. A significant association was found, which shows that firms in the pulp and paper industry with better pollution control records tend to have higher profitability, larger size, lower total risk, and higher price-earnings ratios than companies with poorer pollution control records. In short, pollution controls in the sample of firms from the pulp and paper industry are useful for assessing firms' total and systematic risks.[60] These results are similar to those of Bragdon and Marlin, who found that pollution control and profitability are compatible.[61]

Ingram examined the information content of the firms' voluntary social responsibility disclosures. In a first test, he investigated investor reaction to the total sample and did not find significant stock price movement around the disclosure date. In a second test, he found that the information content of firms' social responsibility disclosures is conditional upon the market segment with which the firm is identified, where the market segment is identified by the type of social disclosure, the industry to which the firm belonged, the sign of the firm's excess earnings in the year of disclosure, and the year of disclosures.

Anderson and Frankle investigated the impact of voluntary social reporting on the stock market by using an iso-beta portfolio analysis. The returns to portfolios composed of securities of socially disclosing firms were compared with returns to portfolios of equivalent (systematic) risk composed of securities of nondisclosing firms. They concluded that the information content of social disclosure was valued positively by the market.

Ingram and Frazier investigated the lack of disclosure quality of social reporting by examining the relationships between measures of firms' environmental performances and the environmental disclosures contained in the firm's annual reports. The results of the study indicated only a weak association between quantitative measures of disclosures content and independent measures of social performance (consisting of the indices of firms' performances desired by the Council on Economic Priorities). This weak association was attributed to the lack of external monitoring of firms social disclosures and possible biasing by poor performers to appear like the better performers.

Bikki and Freedman focused on the investor reacting to pollution disclosures particularly by firms belonging to highly polluting industries (chemical, pulp and paper, oil refining, and steel) which will be materially affected by the pollution-related regulations. Their results in general indicated that investor reaction to firms disclosing pollution information was different from that to nondisclosing firms. The implication of their results is that disclosure of pollution information by firms from highly polluting industries is positively associated with investor reaction, and therefore the information will aid investors to adjust their expectations.

Chugh, Haneman, and Mahapatra examined the effects of the water and pollution control legislation in the United States upon the market risk of the firms in the most directly affected industries, such as chemicals, electric utilities, iron and steel, petroleum, nonferrous metals, and textiles, during the period of 1953-1975. Their results suggest that the market risk of "polluter" firms had gone up during the 1970s, which lend some support to the statement of businessmen about the general uncertainty associated with pollution control legislation.

In a following paper Mahapatra investigated the long-term response of investors to corporate social responsibility response.[62] The study failed to reject the hypothesis that pollution control expenditures are negatively associated with systematic risk and rejected the hypothesis that pollution control expenditures are positively associated with profitability. These results were interpreted as consistent with the "rational economic investor" concept and efficient market hypothesis and not the "ethical investor" concept.

Trotman and Bradley investigated some of the characteristics of Australian companies that may be associated with their disclosures of social responsibility information.[63] They found that companies which provide social information are on average larger in size, have a higher systematic risk, and place a stronger emphasis on the long term than do companies that do not disclose the information.

Wiseman evaluated the quality and accuracy of environmental disclosures made in corporate annual reports.[64] His results indicate that corporate environmental disclosures are incomplete and are not related to the firm's actual environmental performance.

POTENTIAL USERS AND USES

When it comes to users, some interest groups or "publics" may be intuitively included as possible users of social information. Each of the users which may be identified should be able to incorporate social information in their evaluation of corporate performance. There is, however, a lack of normative and/or descriptive models on the users; needs in terms of social information. One exception, shown in Exhibit 6.24 identifies principal users, their major objectives, and the nature of useful information. While the list of uses appears intuitive and justifiable, there is a need for empirical research to evaluate the desirability of social information for various users and uses and the demand for corporate social information for various users and uses and the demand for corporate social responsibility reporting. Again, the evidence in the literature is mixed.

A survey of ten possible interested groups performed by Opinion Research Corporation showed a lack of agreement concerning the desirability of social responsibility reporting.[65] In fact, the answers to the question, What is the proper role of the accounting profession in terms of advocacy and encouragement of corporate social auditing? Led the researchers to conclude:

There is much wider agreement among key publics on the issue of what the proper role of the accounting profession should be with respect to the advocacy and encouragement of corporate social accounting. The findings suggest that having the accounting profession play an active role in this area is an idea which is popular only in academic circles and among corporate social activists.[66]

The same conclusion was reached by Duff and Phelps, Inc., in a report prepared for Arthur Andersen and Company.[67] They concluded:

The question for the corporate reporting system is whether these matters are relevant to investors' needs. If not, are they unfairly burdening the system with unnecessary information? . . . It is our observation, however, that much of the information disclosed is disregarded by investors as immaterial to investment decisions.[68]

Buzby and Falk attempted to assess the demand for and importance of nine social items of information to universities as investors.[69] Based on their results they concluded that universities, as investors, may not represent a strong source of the demand for many of the topics that might be covered by external corporate social responsibility reporting.

Schreuder assessed the reactions of Dutch employees toward the social reports actually published.[70] The social report was perceived to be of medium importance compared with other corporate communication reports. The result was partially attributed to the differences in reading patterns and the importance attached to specific reporting items between the functional levels of employees.

Belkaoui conducted an experiment to investigate the impact of socioeconomic statements on the investment decision.[71] In the experiment, alternative disclosure of socio-economic accounting information, namely, the abatement costs of pollution, were investigated as accounting techniques that may influence the investment decision of potential users. The theoretical rationale stemming from the linguistic relativity paradigm in accounting was that in general the accounting techniques may tend to facilitate or render more difficult various (nonlinguistic) managerial behaviors on the part of the users and that in this particular context the investment decision effects from different professional groups using alternative socio-economic information will be different. The findings attest to the general relevance of socio-economic accounting information for the bankers under any investment strategy focusing on capital gains.

Buzby and Falk reported the results of a survey of 250 mutual fund presidents, which indicates that a majority of the funds had investment policies that considered some, but not all, of the nine social activities.[72] Again, the lack of consensus arising from the empirical research calls for a better and thorough examination of the potential users and uses of social information.

Exhibit 6.24
Users and Their Needs

Principal users	Major objectives	Nature of useful information
1. Sociological and economic theoreticians.	• Examining the utility of present economic theories with respect to such matters as resource allocation, pricing, growth, income, and employment and determining their implications for governmental economic and regulatory policy. • Examining the utility of present sociological, psychological, and political theories about the behavior and impact of business on society as a whole and on specific social groups. • Developing better theories by which to explain and guide society, business, and other groups in their relationships.	• Information about large-scale causes and effects; therefore, information about the country as a whole or major segments of it. The social equivalent of Gross National Product and of matrix-type input-output models would be close to ideal, although they would be difficult or even impossible to implement on a large scale. • Information about a specific company or community would be less helpful, except for use as part of a sample from which generalizations were drawn.
2. Social commentators, activists, and public interest groups (The Council on Economic Priorities, the Nader organizations, the National Resources Defense Council, Inc., etc.).	• Informing and influencing public opinion and corporate action, influencing legislation and regulation, laying the basis for court actions. • Examining whether a social concern has the degree of importance attached to it by society.	• General and specific information about an industry's or a company's performance in specific areas (e.g., employment, pollution, credit, and product safety) with respect to ongoing operations and, at times, major contemplated projects.
3. Legislative and executive branches of federal, state, and local governments and their commissions and regulatory agencies.	• Framing or revising laws. • Making and interpreting detailed rules. • Setting standards in specific terms. • Executing government programs. • Monitoring and regulating the private sector. • Adjudicating disputes.	• Information which covers entire range from (a) information about society in specific areas affecting specific publics, costs and benefits and technology available for different levels of performance to (b) very specific information about specific companies and specific aspects of the operation of those companies.
4. Participants or prospective participants (e.g., present or prospective employees, suppliers, and customers).	• Considering a company's social performance in deciding whether to enter into or maintain an economic relationship.	• An indication of company's overall social performance. • Social performance in area of greatest econom interest (e.g., employment).
5. The immediate neighborhood and the broader communities (extending to the nation and the world).	• Establishing and maintaining a satisfactory relationship (perhaps, an appropriate balance of good and bad impacts) between the company and those affected by its impacts.	• A fairly comprehensive profile of significa impacts on communities most affected, with substantial amount of information about pro lem impacts. • Increasingly general information as communiti become larger or more remote and impacts individual companies become proportionate smaller.
6. Investors/owners.	• Assisting in deciding whether the overall economic and social performance of a company justifies their providing capital for its operations.	• Primarily, the overall profile of social perform ance. • At times, specific information about specif areas considered of particular importance by th individual or organizational investor.
7. Corporate management.	• Being aware of, and prepared for, present or potential reactions of the other principal users. • Meeting governmental and other legally enforceable requirements. • Establishing and achieving management's own set of corporate objectives. • Monitoring and rewarding social performance through the company's own promotion, disciplinary, and compensation systems.	• Company-oriented information—as general c specific in nature as is required. • A considerable amount of information abou industry problems of major importance and o the performance of competitors. • More general knowledge about the performanc of business in general.

SOURCE: American Institute of Certified Public Accountants,

INTERNATIONAL DEVELOPMENTS

The concern for social reporting is not limited to the United States. Attempts are being made in various countries to supplement conventional accounting information by information on the social performance of firms. Various examples may be cited.

In Austria, the effort is limited to narrative disclosure and emphasis on employee information.[73] In Belgium, the emphasis is also on employee information.[74] In Britain, since 1975, some of the largest British companies are publishing a value added statement. The benefits claimed are principally improvement in attitude, motivation, and behavior.[75] An example of a value added statement is shown in Exhibit 6.25. There are also continuous discussions on increased social responsibility disclosure. In the *Future of Company Reports*, published by the Secretary of State in 1977, it was stated:

Social accounting on a comprehensive basis is, however, in an experimental phase, with debate about the underlying concepts and with details of the necessary measurement techniques not yet agreed. For the present the government considers that development in social accounting should take place outside the framework of the legal requirements for disclosure in company reports and accounts.

Egypt is a good example of a country where financial and reporting statements are used to monitor operational activities and to inform the central government of the operations of firms in the countries. They usually rely on uniform systems of accounts and social accounting, where social accounting is defined as "to represent the application of accounting concepts and standards to the collection, compilation, and presentation of aggregate data for a national economy."[76]

In France, active interest in social reporting following the Sudreau Report on the reform of the enterprise.[77] It called for a new role of the firm, as evidenced by the following quotation:

The relationship of man to his work, human relationships within an organization, the exercise of power at the top, the relations of industry with the community, are indissociable aspects of a realistic reform of the enterprise. On each of these points, progress is possible and necessary. It requires changes in both law and practice. Some are apparently minor changes; others are fundamentally important. All are complementary and must be pursued in conjunction with each other by a gradual process, keeping in mind the overall view and the priority to be given to improving working conditions. Each stage should be conceived in the perspective of a step forward for both the enterprise and society.[78]

The Sudreau report recommended the preparation of "an annual social balance sheet at the level of each firm, based on indicators representative of its social situation and working conditions." As a result a law enacted in 1977 required all enterprises employing over 750 employees, including industrial, commercial, professional, civic, and public organizations, to prepare a *bilan social* (social balance sheet) for dissemination to both the shareholders and, through the works council, to the employees. The law was extended in 1982 to enterprises employing more than 300 employees. The information disclosed in the balance sheet covered the following seven sections: the labor force; remuneration and fringe benefits; health and safety conditions; other working conditions; training; the state of industrial relations; and conditions of the life of employees and their families related to employment in the enterprise. Needless to say, the employees are the main constituent group dealt with in the social report.

Social reporting is not new to Germany given its long and outstanding interest in the field of welfare economics. In fact, early attempts presented an integral, welfare-theoretical approach to social reporting. This school of thought is best represented by Eichhorn's work.[79] An example of Eichhorn's societal profit and loss account is shown in Exhibit 6.26. He also advocated a social balance sheet where the net social assets or liabilities are the difference between the sum of the total human and public assets and the total human and public liabilities. Needless to say, this approach may suffer from the difficult problems of operationalization and implementation.[80]

Exhibit 6.25
Deriving The Value Added Statement

A. The conventional income statement of a company for 198A was:

Sales		$1,000,000
Less: Materials used	$100,000	
Wages	200,000	
Services purchased	300,000	
Interest paid	60,000	
Depreciation	40,000	
Profit before tax		$ 300,000
Income Tax (assuming 50% tax rate)		150,000
Profit after tax		150,000
Less divident payable		50,000
Retained earnings for the year		$ 100,000

B. A value added statement for the same year would be:

Sales		$1,000,000
Less: Bought-in materials and services and depreciation		440,000
Value added available for distribution or retention		$ 560,000
Applied as follows:		
To employees:		$ 200,000
To providers of capital		
Interest	$60,000	
Dividends	50,000	110,000
To government		150,000
Retained earnings		100,000
Value added		$ 560,000

Exhibit 6.26
Eichhorn's Societal Profit and Loss Account

Erwerbswirtschaftliche Erfolgsrechnung		Gesellschaftsbezogene Erfolgsrechnung	
Costs	Revenues	Social costs	Social benefits
Profit		Net social benefits	

Gesellschaftsbezogene Erfolgsrechnung

Social costs	Social benefits
I. Producer's surplus for	I. Consumers' surplus for
1. labour performances	1. product A
2. fixed assets	2. product B
3. materials	3. product C
4. capital	4. product D
5. entrepreneurial performances	
6. bought-in performances	
II. Value of negative external effects on:	II. Value of positive external effects on:
1. employees	1. employees
2. population	2. population
3. companies	3. companies
4. public entities	4. public entities
III. Net social benefits	III. Net social costs

SOURCE: Hein Schreuder, "Corporate Social Reporting in the Federal Republic of Germany: An Overview," *Accounting Organizations and Society* 4, nos. 1/2 (1979):110. Reprinted with permission.

Instead, the practice or corporate social reporting is proceeding along the following three different experimental systems: "(1) a broadly based and partially integrated reporting linking companies' expenditures to social benefits; (2) an extension of the traditional reporting of socially relevant information, and, most recently; (3) corporate goal accounting and reporting."[81]

Corporate social accounting in Japan has expanded since 1970 from the study of the application of accounting to national economic and analysis to the application of accounting to social problems. Tokutani and Kawano classify Japanese work in social accounting into three distinct groups:

1. The cost approach to corporate social accounting dealing with the measurement, internalization, and disclosure of social cost information.
2. The responsibility approach to corporate social accounting dealing with the quantification of responsibility, the development of accounting principles and accounting postulates in connection with corporate social responsibility, and the social need for disclosing social responsibility information.
3. The audit approach to corporate social responsibility advocating a social audit or a social responsibility audit.[82]

In other countries, such as New Zealand,[83] Norway,[84] Poland,[85] Sweden,[86] and the Netherlands, various attempts are being made in favor of social accounting. Most of these countries focus on the relations of the firm with its employees.

Conclusions

The efforts, approaches, and demand for social accounting are numerous, diverse, and well intentioned. They point to the growing interest and importance of micro social accounting and also to the confusion over what should be done to deal adequately with the issue. What is evident from this state-of-the-art chapter is the need for a conceptual framework or theory of micro social accounting to guide the development of identification, measurement, and disclosure techniques. An attempt to present a theory of micro social accounting and relevant techniques of identification, measurement, and disclosure is presented in the next chapter.

Notes

1. Wayne Keller, "Accounting for Corporate Social Performance," *Management Accounting* (February 1974): 39-41.
2. Marc J. Epstein, Eric G. Flamholtz, and John J. McDonough, *Corporate Social Performance: The Measurement of Product and Service Contributions* (New York: National Association of Accountants, 1976), p. 14.
3. Ibid., p. 84.
4. Ibid., p. 15.
5. Ibid., p. 67.
6. Loren A. Nikolai, John D. Bazley, and R. Lee Brumment, *The Measurement of Corporate Environmental Activity* (New York: National Association of Accountants, 1976).
7. Ibid., p. 25.
8. Ibid., p. 2.
9. Ibid., p. 3.
10. Ibid., p. 52.
11. Ibid., p. 59.
12. Ibid., 81.
13. American Accounting Association, "Report of the Committee on Measures of Effectiveness for Social Programs," *Accounting Review*, supplement, 47 (1972): 337-396.

14. Mildred Francis, "Thoughts on Some Measures of Effectiveness of Social Programs" (Paper prepared for Robert E. Jensen, College of Business Administration, University of Maine, Orono, March 1971), p, 3.

15. American Accounting Association, "Report of the Committee on Measures of Effectiveness for Social Programs." P. 348.

16. Ibid., p. 349.

17. Ibid.

18. American Accounting Association, "Report of the Committee on Environmental Effects of Organizational Behavior, *Accounting Review*, supplement, 48 (1973): 75-119.

19. Ibid., p. 80.

20. Ibid., pp. 116-117.

21. American Accounting Association, "Report of the Committee on the Measurement of Social Costs," *Accounting Review*, supplement, 49 (1974): 98-113.

22. Ibid., pp. 100-101.

23. Ibid., pp. 101-102.

24. Ibid., p. 102.

25. Ibid.

26. American Accounting Association, "Report of the Committee on Social Costs," *Accounting Review*, supplement, 50 (1975): 53.

27. Ibid., p. 55.

28. Ibid., p. 71.

29. Ibid.

30. American Accounting Association, "Report of the Committee on Accounting for Social Performance," *Accounting Review*, supplement, 51 (1976): 39-69.

31. Ibid., p. 41.

32. Ibid., pp. 66-67.

33. American Institute of Certified Public Accountants, *Social Measurement* (New York: AICPA, 1972).

34. American Institute of Certified Public Accounts, *The Measurement of Corporate Social Performance* (New York: AICPA, 1977).

35. Ibid., p. 23.

36. American Accounting Association, "Report of the Committee on Environmental Effects of Organizational Behavior," p. 110.

37. Floyd A. Beams and Paul e. Fertig, "Pollution Control Through Social Cost Conversion," *Journal of Accountancy* (November 1971): 37-42.

38. Ibid., p. 42.

39. These examples were provided by the editors of the *Journal of Accountancy* (March 1977): 76.

40. Floyd A. Beams, "Accounting for Environmental Pollution," *New York Certified Public Accountant* (August 1970): 657-661.

41. American Accounting Association, "Report of the Committee on Environmental Effects of Organizational Behavior," p. 80.

42. Ralph Estes, *Corporate Social Accounting* (New York: Wiley, 1976).

43. John Tepper Marlin, "Accounting for Pollution," *Journal of Accountancy* (February 1973): 41-46.

44. Ibid., p. 44.

45. Ibid., p. 45.
46. Steven C. Dilley and Jerry J. Weygandt, "Measuring Social Responsibility: An Empirical Test," *Journal of Accountancy* (September 1973): 64.
47. Wayne Corcoran and Wayne E. Leininger, Jr., "Financial Statements- Who Needs Them?" *Financial Executive* (August 1970): 34-38, 45-47.
48. Ibid., p. 45.
49. Lee J. Seidler, "Dollar Values in the Social Income Statement," *World* (Peat Marwick, Mitchell and Co.) (Spring 1973): 14, 16-23.
50. Estes, *Corporate Social Accounting*, p. 91.
51. Ibid., p. 94.
52. Ibid.
53. Claude S. Colantoni, W. W. Cooper, and H. J. Dietzer, "Budgeting Disclosure and Social Accounting," in Meinholf Dierkes and Raymond Bauer, eds., *Corporate Social Accounting* (New York: Praeger, 1973): 376-377.
54. Neil C. Churchill and John K. Shank, "Accounting for Affirmative Action Programs: A Stochastic Flow Approach," *Accounting Review* (October 1975): 643-656.
55. "Pollution Price Tag: 71 Billion Dollars," *U. S. News and World Report* (August 17, 1970): 41.
56. American Accounting Association, "Report of the Committee on External Reporting," *Accounting Review*, supplement, 44 (1969): 118.
57. American Accounting Association, "Report of the Committee on Environmental Effects of Organizational Behavior," p. 88.
58. Beams and Fertig, "Pollution Control Through Social Cost Conversion," pp. 37-42.
59. Ahmed Belkaoui, "The Impact of the Disclosure of the Environmental Effects of Organizational Behavior on the Market," *Financial Management* (Winter 1976): 26-31; B. Spicer, "Investors, Corporate Social Performance and Information Disclosure: An Empirical Study," *Accounting Review* (January 1978): 94-111; Robert W. Ingram, "An Investigation of the Information Content of (Certain) Social Responsibility Disclosures," *Journal of Accounting Research* (Autumn 1978): 270-285; John C. Anderson and Alan W. Frankle, "Voluntary Social Reporting: An Iso-Beta Portfolio Analysis," *Accounting Review* (July 1980): 467-479; Robert W. Ingram and Katherine Beal Frazier, "Environmental Performance and Corporate Disclosure," *Journal of Accounting Research* (Spring 1980): 603-613; Jaggi Bikki and Martin Freedman, "An Analysis of Information Content of Pollution Disclosures," *Financial Review* (in press); and Lal C. Chugh, Michael Haneman, and S. Mahapatra, "Impact of Pollution Control Regulations on the Market Risk of Securities in the U.S.," *Journal of Economic Studies* (May 1978): 64-70.
60. Similar findings were reported in Barry H. Spicer, "Market Risk, Accounting Data and Companies' Pollution Control Records," *Journal of Business Finance and Accounting* (Spring 1978): 67-84.
61. Joseph H. Bragdon and John Marlin, "Is Pollution Profitable?" *Risk Management* (April 1972).
62. S. Mahapatra, "Long Term Response of Investors to a Corporate Social Responsibility Performance," *Journal of Business Finance and Accounting* (in press).
63. K. T. Trotman and G. W. Bradley, "Associations Between Social Responsibility Disclosure and Characteristics of Companies," *Accounting, Organizations and Society* 6, no. 4. (1981): 355-362.

64. J. Wiseman, "An Evaluation of Environmental Disclosures Made in Corporate Annual Reports," *Accounting, Organizations and Society* (February 1932): 53-64.

65. Opinion Research Corporation, *Public Accounting in Transition: American Shareowners and Key Publics View the Role of Independent Accountants and the Corporate Reporting Controversy* (New York: Aurthur Andersen, 1974).

66. Ibid., pp. 53-54.

67. Duff and Phelps, Inc., *A Management Guide to Better Financial Reporting: Ideas for Strengthening Reports to Shareholders and the Financial Analyst's Perspective on Financial Reporting Practices* (New York: Arthur Andersen, 1980).

68. Ibid., p. 49.

69. Stephen l. Buzby and Haim Falk, "Demand for Social Responsibility Information by University Investors," *Accounting Review* (January 1979): 23-27.

70. Hein Schreuder, "Employees and the Corporate Social Report: The Dutch Case," *Accounting Review* (April 1981): 294-308.

71. Ahmed Belkaoui, "The Impact of Socio-Economic Accounting Statements on the Investment Decision: An Empirical Study," *Accounting, Organizations and Society* (September 1980): 263-283.

72. Stephen L. Buzby and Haim Falk, "A Survey of the Interest in Social Responsibility Information by Mutual Funds," *Accounting Organizations and Society* (May 1979): 191-201.

73. Hanns-Martin Schoenfeld, "Social Reporting: Its Present Developments in West Germany, Austria, and Switzerland," in Hanns-Martin Schoenfeld, comp., *The Status of Social Reporting in Selected Countries*, (Urbana, Ill.: Center for International Education and Research in Accounting, 1978), pp. 1-19.

74. David Cooper and Simon Essex, "Accounting Information and Employee Decision Making," *Accounting, Organization and Society* 2, no. 3 (1977): 201.

75. Michael F. Morley, "The Value Added Statement in Britain," *Accounting Review* (July 1979): 629.

76. Dhia D. Alhashim, "Social Accounting in Egypt," *International Journal of Accounting, Education and Research* 12, no. 2 (Spring 1977): 128.

77. P. Sudreau, "The Reform of the Enterprise, *Accounting, Organizations and Society* 1, no. 1 (1976): 97-99.

78. P. Sudreau, *Rapport du Comité d'Etudes pour la Reforme de l'Enterprise* (Paris: La Documentation Francaise, 1975).

79. P Eichhorn, *Gesellschaftsbezogene Unternehmensrechung* (Gottingen: Verlag Otto Schwarz, 1974).

80. Hein Schreuder, "Corporate Social Reporting in the Federal Republic of Germany: An Overview," *Accounting, Organizations and Society* 4, no. ½ (1979): 111.

81. Meinoff Dierkes, "Corporate Social Reporting in Germany: Conceptual Developments and Practical Experience," *Accounting, Organizations and Society* 4, no. ½ (1979): 92.

82. Masao Tokutani and Masao Kawano, "A Note on the Japanese Social Accounting Literature," *Accounting, Organizations and Society* 3, no. 2 (1978): 184.

83. John Robertson, "Corporate Social Reporting by New Zealand Companies," *Journal of Contemporary Business* (Winter 1978): 113-133.

84. Cooper and Essex, "Accounting Information and Employee Decision-Making," pp. 201-217.

85. Ali Ya Jaruga and H. M. Schoenfeld, "Social Reporting at the Enterprise Level in Poland," in Schoenfeld, comp., *The Status of Social Reporting in Selected Countries*.
86. Jan-Erik Grojer and Agneta Stark, "Social Accounting: A Swedish Attempt," *Accounting, Organizations and Society* 2, no. 4 (1977): 349-386.

Bibliography

Alhashim, Dhia D. "Social Accounting in Egypt." *International Journal of Accounting, Education and Research* 12, no. 2 (Spring 1977): 128.

American Accounting Association. "Report of the Committee on Accounting for Social Performance," *Accounting Review*, supplement, 51 (1976): 39-69.

___. "Report of the Committee on Environmental Effects of Organizational Behavior." *Accounting Review*, supplement, 48 (1973): 76-119.

___. "Report of the Committee on External Reporting." *Accounting Review*, supplement, 44 (1969): 118.

___. "Report of the Committee on Measures of Effectiveness for Social Programs." *Accounting Review*, supplement, 47 (1972): 337-396.

___. "Report of the Committee on the Measurement of Social Costs." *Accounting Review*, supplement, 49 (1974): 98-113.

___. "Report of the Committee on Social Costs." *Accounting Review*, supplement, 50 (1975): p. 53.

American Institute of Certified Public Accountants. *The Measurement of Corporate Social Performance*. New York: AICPA, 1977.

___. *Social Measurement*. New York: AICPA, 1972.

Anderson, John C., and Alan W. Frankle. "Voluntary Social Reporting: An Iso-Beta Portfolio Analysis." *Accounting Review* (July 1980): 467-479.

Beams, Floyd A. "Accounting for Environmental Pollution." *New York Certified Public Accountant* (now *CPA Journal*) (August 1970): 657-661.

Belkaoui, Ahmed. "The Impact of Socio-Economic Accounting Statements on the Investment Decision: An Empirical Study." *Accounting, Organizations and Society* (September 1980): 263-283.

___. "The Impact of the Disclosure of the Environmental Effects of Organizational Behavior on the Market." *Financial Management* (Winter 1976): 26-31.

Bikki, Jaggi, and Martin Freedman. "An Analysis of the Information Content of Pollution Disclosures." *Financial Review* (in press).

Bragdon, Joseph H., and John Marlin. "Is Pollution Profitable?" *Risk Management* (April 1978).

Buzby, Stephen L., and Haim Falk. "Demand for Social Responsibility Information by University Investors." *Accounting Review* (January 1979): 23-37.

___. "A Survey of the Interest in Social Responsibility Information by Mutual Funds." *Accounting Organizations and Society* (May 1979) 91-201.

Chugh, Lal C., Michael Haneman, and S. Mahapatra. "Impact of Pollution Control Regulations on the Market Risk of Securities in the U.S." *Journal of Economic Studies* (May 1978): 64-70.

Churchill, Neil C., and John K. Shank. "Accounting for Affirmative Action Programs: A stochastic Flow Approach." *Accounting Review* (October 1975): 643-656.

Colantoni, Claude S., W. W. Cooper, and H. J. Deitzer, "Budgeting Disclosure and Social Accounting." In Meinholf Dierkes and Raymond Bauer, eds., *Corporate Social Accounting*. New York: Praeger, 1973.
Cooper, David, and Simon Essex. "Accounting Information and Employee Decision Making." *Accounting, Organizations and Society* 2, no. 3 (1977): 201.
Corcoran, Wayne, and Wayne E. Leininger, Jr. "Financial Statements- Who Needs Them?" *Financial Executive* (August 1970): 34-38, 45-47.
Dierkes, Meinoff. "Corporate Social Reporting in Germany: Conceptual Developments and Practical Experience." *Accounting, Organizations and Society* 4, no. ½ (1979): 92.
Dilley, Steven C. "External Reporting of Social Responsibility." *MSU Business Topics* (Autumn 1975): 18.
___, and Jerry J. Weygant. "Measuring Social Responsibility: An Empirical Test." *Journal of Accountancy* (September 1973): 64.
Duff and Phelps, Inc. *A Management Guide to Better Financial Reporting: Ideas for Strengthening Reports to Shareholders and the Financial Analyst's Perspective on Financial Reporting Practices*. New York: Arthur Andersen, 1980.
Eichhorn, P. *Gesellschaftsbezogene Unternehmensrechung*. Gottingen: Verlag Otto Schwarz, 1974.
Epstein, Marc J., Eric G. Flamholz, and John J. McDonough. *Corporate Social Performance: The Measurement of Product and Service Contributions*. New York: National Association of Accountants, 1976.
Estes, Ralph. *Corporate Social Accounting*. New York: Wiley, 1976, p. 62.
Francis, Mildred. "Thoughts on Some Measures of Effectiveness of Social Programs." Paper prepared for Robert E. Jensen, College of Business Administration, University of Maine, Orono, March 1971.
Grojer, Jan-Erik, and Agneta Stark. "Social Accounting: A Swedish Attempt." *Accounting, Organizations and Society* 2, no. 4 (1977): 349-386.
Ingram, Robert W. "An Investigation of the Information Content of (Certain) Social Responsibility Disclosures." *Journal of Accounting Research* (Autumn 1978): 270-285.
___, and Katherine Beal Frazier. "Environmental Performance and Corporate Disclosure." *Journal of Accounting Research* (Spring 1980): 603-613.
Keller, Wayne. "Accounting for Corporate Social Performance." *Management Accounting* (February 1974): 39-41.
Mahapatra, S. "Long Term Response of Investors to a Corporate Social Responsibility Performance." *Journal of Business Finance and Accounting* (in press).
Marlin, John Tepper. "Accounting for Pollution." *Journal of Accountancy* (February 1973): 41-46.
Morley, Michael F. "The Value Added Statement in Britain." *Accounting Review* (July 1979): 629.
Nikolai, Loren A., John D. Bazley, and R. Lee Brummet. *The Measurement of Corporate Environmental Activity*. New York: National Association of Accountants, 1976.
Opinion Research Corporation. *Public Accounting in Transition: American Shareowners and Key Publics View the Role of Independent Accountants and the Corporate Reporting Controversy*. New York: Arthur Andersen, 1974.
"Pollution Price Tag: 71 Billion Dollars." *U.S. News and World Report* (August 17, 1970): 41.

Robertson, John. "Corporate Social Reporting by New Zealand Companies." *Journal of Contemporary Business* (Winter 1978): 113-133.
Schoenfeld, Hanns-Martin. *The Status of Social Reporting in Selected Countries*. Urbana, Ill.: Center for International Education and Research in Accounting.
Schreuder, Hein. "Corporate Social Reporting in the Federal Republic of Germany: An Overview." *Accounting, Organizations and Society* 4, no. ½ (1979): 111.
___. "Employees and the Corporate Social Report: The Dutch Case." *Accounting Review* (April 1981): 294-308.
Seidler, Lee J. "Dollar Values in the Social Income Statement." *World* (Peat Marwick, Mitchell and Co.), (Spring 1973): 14, 16-23.
Spicer, B. "Investors, Corporate Social Performance and Information Disclosure: An Empirical Study." *Accounting Review* (January 1978): 94-111.
___. "Market Risk, Accounting Data and Companies' Pollution Control Records." *Journal of Business Finance and Accounting* (Spring 1978): 67-84.
Sudreau, P. *Rapport du Comité d'Etudes pour la Reforme de l'Entreprise*. Paris: La Documentation Francaise, 1975.
___. "The Reform of the Enterprise." *Accounting, Organizations and Society* 1, no. 1 (1976): 97-99.
Tokutani, Masao, and Masao Kawano. "A Note on the Japanese Social Accounting Literature." *Accounting, Organizations and Society* 3, no. 2 (1978): 184.
Trotman, K. T., and G. W. Bradley, "Associations Between Social Responsibility Disclosure and Characteristics of Companies." *Accounting, Organizations and Society* 6, no. 4 (1981): 355-362.
Wiseman, J. "An Evaluation of Environmental Disclosures Made in Corporate Annual Reports." *Accounting, Organizations and Society* (February 1982): 53-64.

7
MICRO APPLIED SOCIO-ECONOMICS CONCEPTS AND MEASUREMENT

The previous chapter presented the results of institutional, academic, and professional efforts in micro social accounting. The diversity of these efforts showed a growing interest and importance of social accounting and also pointed to the confusion over what should be done to deal adequately with the issue. One way of contributing to a solution is to suggest ways of conceptualizing micro social accounting and ways of measuring and evaluating the environmental effects of organizational behavior. The conceptualizing of micro social accounting will provide a conceptual framework to justify and rationalize the new field and guide future developments. The techniques of measurement and evaluation will provide management with tools to incorporate consideration of the social consequences of its actions explicitly into a decision-making process and action and to provide both a corporation's particular constituencies and the general public and a valid, pertinent data other than profit-and-loss statement information on which to base their evaluation of management's performance.[1] Accordingly, this chapter will present an "emerging" conceptual framework for micro social accounting and ways of measuring and evaluating the environmental effects of organizational behavior.

Toward a Conceptual Framework of Micro Socio-Economics

A conceptual framework for micro social economics is equivalent to a constitution; it should be a coherent system of interrelated objectives and fundamentals that can lead to consistent standards and that prescribes the nature, function, and limits of micro social economics. Such a framework would be useful for the development of a coherent set of standards and techniques, for the resolution of new and emerging practical problems, for increasing users' understanding of and confidence in social reporting, and for enhancing comparability among companies' social reports.

A conceptual framework for micro social accounting does not exist for the moment in either the professional or academic literature. However, various attempts have been made in the accounting literature to outline some of the elements of the framework contributing to an "emerging" conceptual framework for micro social accounting. These elements are the objectives, fundamental concepts, and operational guidelines.

PROPOSED OBJECTIVES

The objectives for micro social economics are the first and essential steps to the formulation of a micro social accounting framework. Then the socio-economic-accounting concepts will be true because they will be based on accepted objectives. In spite of the importance of these objectives, there has never been a formal attempt by the profession to accomplish such a task.

Several noticeable exceptions, which may serve as de facto objectives for micro social accounting, were provided in an article by K. V. Ramanathan.[2] Three objectives are (1) to identify and measure the periodic net social contribution of an individual firm, including not only the costs and benefits internalized to the firm but also those arising from externalities affecting different social segments; (2) to help determine whether an individual firm's strategies and practices that directly affect the relative resource and power status of individuals, communities, social segments, and generations are consistent with widely shared social priorities on the one hand and individuals' legitimate aspirations on the other; (3) to make available in an optimal manner to all social constituents relevant information on a firm's goals, policies, programs, performance, and contributions to social goals.[3]

The first two objectives are presented as measurement objectives to social accounting, while the third objective is a reporting objective. The first objective calls for the measurement of a firm's periodic net social contribution, which includes both private and social costs and benefits. The second objective calls for the measurement of the firm's contribution to social goals. The third objective calls for a reporting of the results of the first two objectives.

PROPOSED CONCEPTS

Concepts based on the objectives of micro social accounting would constitute the basic foundation for a micro social accounting theory. In the same article cited earlier, K. V. Ramanathan proposed six concepts for social accounting:[4]

1. A *social transaction* represents a firm's utilization or delivery of a socio-environment resource that affects the absolute or relative interests of a firm's various social constituents and that is not processed through the market place.
2. *Social overheads (returns)* represent the sacrifice (benefit) to society from those resources consumed (added) by a firm as a result of its social transactions.
3. *Social income* represents the periodic net social contribution of a firm. It is computed as the algebraic sum of the firm's traditionally measured net income, its aggregate social overheads, and its aggregate social returns.
4. *Social constituents* are the different distinct social groups (implied in the second objective and expressed in the third objective of social accounting) with whom a firm is presumed to have a social contract.
5. *Social equity* is a measure of the aggregate changes in the claims that each social constituent is presumed to have in the firm.
6. *Net social asset* of a firm is a measure of the aggregate non market contribution to the society's well-being less its nonmarket depletion of the society's resources during the life of the firm.[5]

The first concept, the social transaction, calls for the recognition of all the "transactions" between the firm and society that are not handled presently through the marketplace. These nonmarket transactions are basically positive or negative externalities. The second concept is that of social overheard and social return. The nonmarket transactions resulting from the social transaction generate either a social overhead, which is a social cost imposed on society, or a social return, which is a social cost imposed on society, or a social return, which is a social benefit. The third concept, social income, is a measure of the overall performance of the firm to include the traditional net income, the social overheads, and the social returns. The fourth concept is that of social constituents. To measure adequately, the social overheads, social returns, and the resulting social income, the different social groups likely to be affected by the firm's operational and other activities need to be identified. These groups are the social constituents of the firm, with whom the firm has an explicit or implicit social contract. The fifth concept is that of social equity, that is, the claims that each social constituent has in the firm. The sixth concept, social assets, constitute the firm's nonmarket contribution to society, which are increased by positive externalities and decreased by negative externalities.

PROPOSED QUALITATIVE CHARACTERISTICS

To be useful, a micro social accounting report must meet certain qualitative criteria. These criteria are intended to guide the social accountant to produce the "best," or most useful, information for managers.

The Financial Accounting Standards Board, a standard-setting body for micro social accounting, has proposed certain criteria for selecting and evaluating financial accounting and reporting policies.[6] These criteria, which also apply to micro social accounting, include decision usefulness, benefits over costs, relevance, reliability, neutrality, verifiability, representational faithfulness, comparability, timeliness, understandability, completeness, and consistency. As shown in Exhibit 7.1, these criteria may be organized as a hierarchy of informational qualities.

Most micro social accounting is concerned to some degree with decision making; thus, *decision usefulness* becomes the overriding criterion for choosing among micro social accounting alternatives. The type of information chosen is the one that, subject to any cost considerations, appears the most useful for decision making.

Micro social accounting information, like any other commodity, will be sought if the benefits to be derived from the information exceeds its costs. Thus, before preparing and disseminating the cost accounting information, the benefits and costs of providing the information must be compared.

Relevance has been appropriately defined as follows: "For information to meet the standard of relevance, it must bear upon or be usefully associated with the action it is designed to facilitate or the result it is desired to produce. This requires that either the information or the act of communicating it exert influence . . .on the designated actions."[7] Relevance, therefore, refers to the information's ability to influence managers' decisions by changing or confirming their expectations about the results or consequences of actions or events. There can be degrees of relevance. The relevance of particular information will vary among users and will depend on their needs and the particular contexts in which the decisions are made.

Reliability refers to that "quality which permits users of data to depend upon it with confidence as representative of what it proposes to represent."[8] Thus, the reliability of information depends on its degree of faithfulness in the representation of an event. Reliability will differ among users depending on the extent of their knowledge of the rules used to prepare the information. Similarly, different users may seek information with different degrees of reliability.

The absence of bias in the presentation of accounting reports or information is neutrality. Thus, neutral information is free from bias toward attaining some desired result or inducing a particular mode of behavior. This is not to imply that the preparers of information do not have a purpose in mind when preparing the reports; it only means that the purpose should not influence an predetermined result. Notice that neutrality is in conflict with one of the concepts of social accounting, namely, the feedback concept. It may be argued that social accounting reports are intended to report on managerial performance and influence behavior and hence cannot be neutral.

Verifiability is "that attribute . . . which allows qualified individuals working independently of one another to develop essentially similar measures or conclusions from an examination of the same evidence, data, or records."[9] It implies consensus and absence of measurer bias. Verifiable information can be substantially reproduced by independent measurers using the same measurement methods. Notice that verifiability refers only to the correctness of the resulting information, not to the appropriateness of the measurement method used.

Representational faithfulness and completeness refer to the correspondence between the accounting data and the events those data are supposed to represent. If the measure portrays what it is supposed to represent, it is considered free of measurement and measurer bias.

Comparability describes the use of the same methods by different firms, and consistency describes the use of the same method over time by a given firm. Both qualitative characteristics are more important for financial accounting information than for social accounting information.

Timeliness refers to the availability of data when they are needed or soon enough after the reported events. A trade-off is necessary between timeliness and precision.

EXHIBIT 7.1: A HIERARCHY OF QUALITATIVE CHARACTERISTICS

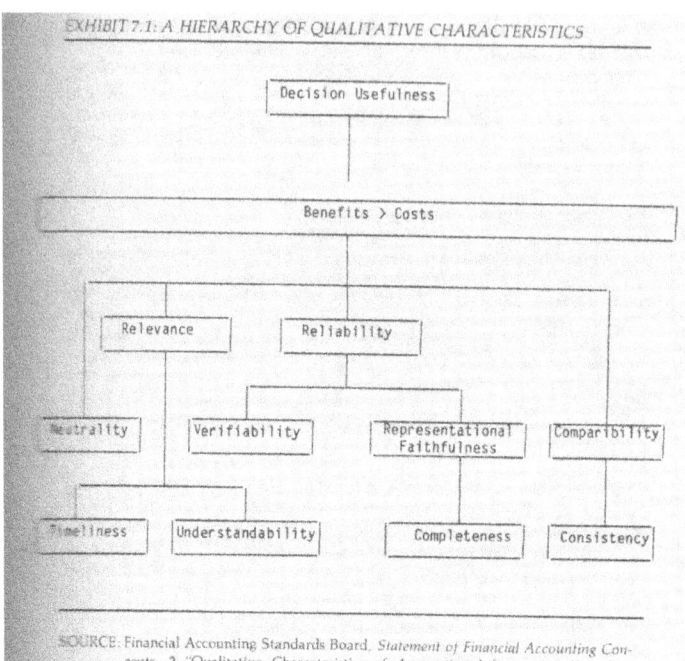

SOURCE: Financial Accounting Standards Board, *Statement of Financial Accounting Concepts,* 2 "Qualitative Characteristics of Accounting Information" (Stamford, Conn: FASB, May 1980).

The clarity of the information and ease of grasp by the users is its understandability. The preparer's level of understanding is generally different from the user's. Thus, efforts should be made by the preparer to increase the understandability of accounting information, in both form and content, to increase its usefulness to the user.

PROPOSED CONCEPTUAL FRAMEWORK
A conceptual framework is a constitution, a coherent set of interrelated *objectives* and *fundamentals* that can lead to consistent standards and that prescribes the nature, function, and limits of financial accounting and financial statements. The objectives identify the goals and purposes of accounting. The *fundamentals* are the underlying concepts of accounting, concepts that guide the selection of events to be accounted for, the measurement of those events, and the means of summarizing and communicating them to interested parties. Concepts of that type are fundamental in the sense that other concepts flow from them and repeated reference to them will be necessary in establishing, interpreting, and applying accounting and reporting standards.[10]

Applied to micro-socio-economic accounting, the conceptual framework is intended to act as a constitution for the process of choosing techniques of measurement, evaluation, and communication of social information. The constitution specifies both objectives and fundamentals. The discussion in the previous sections centered on proposed objectives and fundamentals. The discussion in the previous sections centered on proposed objectives and fundamentals applicable to socio-economic accounting. Therefore, an "emerging" conceptual framework for micro social accounting seems to exist. Exhibit 7.2 provides an overview of the conceptual framework for micro social accounting. At the first level, the proposed objectives identify the goals and purposes of micro social accounting. At the second level are the proposed concepts and qualitative characteristics of micro social accounting. Finally, at the third level, the operational guidelines specifies the techniques of measurement and evaluation will be presented in the rest of the chapter. The conceptual framework for micro social accounting presented in Exhibit 7.2 is only tentative, awaiting formalization by the accounting profession and other concerned groups.

Measurement and Evaluation in Micro Social Accounting
THE CONCEPT OF ENVIRONMENTAL DAMAGE
The environment is a resource that affects the ways things live and develop. It is above all a nonreproducible capital asset offering vital services to man. The most valuable of these services involves "the *dispersing, storing, or assimilating of residuals* which are generated as a byproduct of economic activity."[11] This service is generally portrayed in the materials balance model and its corollary, the principle of materials balance, which portrays the flow of raw materials into consumer goods then into wastes from production and residuals from consumption.[12] The other services provided by the environment involves a support of human life, amenity services, and a source of material inputs. Given these services is altered. The alteration or damage is generally caused by the wastes and residuals that the environment may fail to absorb or assimilate:
In economic terms, this damage is equal to the reduction in the value of environmental quality caused by the disposal of residuals. Hence, whenever residual disposal impairs life, reduces the value of property, or constrains the quality of natural recreation sites, the quality and quantity of nonresidual absorptive environmental services is reduced and environmental damages exist. These damages are measured by the value of the non-waste-receptor environmental services forgone because of the disposal or residuals. As such, environmental damage conforms to the classical economic notion of opportunity costs.[13]

EXHIBIT 7.2: A CONCEPTUAL FRAMEWORK FOR MICRO SOCIAL ACCOUNTING

	Objectives		First Level:
	1. Measurement		Objectives
	2. Reporting		

Qualitative Characteristics	Concepts		Second Level:
1. Decision usefulness	1. Social transaction		Fundamental concepts
2. Benefits over costs	2. Social overhead		
3. Relevance	3. Social income		
4. Reliability	4. Social constituents		
5. Neutrality	5. Social equity		
6. Timeliness			
7. Understandability			
8. Verifiability			
9. Representational faithfulness			
10. Comparability			
11. Consistency			
12. Completeness			

Techniques of Measurement	Techniques of Evaluation	Techniques of Reporting	Third Level: Operational guidelines

Environmental damage is first a consequence of the overuse and abuse of what is in fact a free commodity. Second, it is aggravated by the widely held belief that the use of the residual absorptive services of the environment is limitless and costless. In fact, the damage itself results in the reduction in the other environmental services in addition to a reduction in the residual absorptive services.

OPTIMAL LEVEL OF ENVIRONMENTAL QUALITY

The above discussion implies that environmental quality can be achieved by a reduction in environmental damage. There are two types of costs or damage associated with the use of the waste-absorptive services of the environment: the total damage costs created by the reduction in the on-residual absorptive services of the environment due to residual discharges; and the cost of abatement needed to reduce the residuals released to the environment. The optimal level of environmental quality will be the level that minimizes the sum of these two costs: damage costs and abatement costs. This strategy may be applied to any type of residual.

There are several studies attempting to estimate environmental damage in economic terms. These studies have attempted to measure *direct* damage in monetary terms and disamenities such as recreational and aesthetic losses. They are examined next.

AIR POLLUTION

National estimates of air pollution damages exist for the United States, Canada, and Great Britain.[14] The damage caused by air pollution has also been examined in terms of its impact on human health, materials, vegetation, and property values.

With respect to human health, various studies have tried to assign economic values to the health effects of air pollution.[15] For example, Ridker defines four types of costs: those due to premature death, those associated with mobility, treatment costs, and prevention or avoidance costs. The costs of premature death due to disease are calculated as the sum of an individual's expected earnings discounted for each additional productive year of life had he not died prematurely. The following formula was used:

$$V_a = \sum_{n=a}^{\infty} \frac{Pa^n_1 \cdot Pa^n_2 \cdot Pa^n_3 \cdot Yn}{(1+r)^{n-a}}$$

where
V_a = present value of the future earnings of an individual at age a;
Pa^n_1 = probability that an individual of age a will live to age n;
Pa^n_2 = probability that an individual of age a living at age n will be in the labor force at age n;
Pa^n_3 = probability that an individual of age a living and in the labor force at age n will be employed at age n;
Yn = earnings at age n; and
r = rate of interest.

Similarly, the burial costs associated with premature death are calculated as the difference between the present cost of burial and the present value of the future expected cost of burial. The following formula was used:

$$C_a = C_o[1 - \sum_{n=a}^{\infty} \frac{(Pa^n_1)}{(1+r)^{n-a}}]$$

where
C_o = cost of burial;
C_a = present value of the next expected gain from delaying burial at age a; and
Pa_1^n and r as above.

Ridker computed the costs associated with various diseases and assumed that twenty percent of the costs may be attributed to air pollution. In fact, most other studies adopted the same approach, which is to estimate the costs of specific diseases and attribute a percentage of these costs to air pollution.

With respect to materials, the negative effects of air pollution include corrosion of metals, deterioration of rubber, discoloration of paint, and soiling. Various studies have tried to assign economic values to those consequences.[16] For example, the Midwest Research Institute (MRI) presents the results of a systematic study of all the physical and chemical interactions between materials, pollutants, and environmental parameters needed to computes the economic value of the material and then applies the rate of deterioration to this value to estimate the economic loss from deterioration. The economic value of material exposed to air pollution Q is calculated as follows:

$Q = P \times N \times F \times R$

Where
P = product of the annual dollar production volume;
N = economic life of the material based on usage;
F = weighted average factor for the percentage of material exposed to air pollution;
R = labor factor reflecting the in-place or as-used value of the material.

The rate of deterioration or interaction V is then calculated by estimating the difference between the deterioration rates in polluted and unpolluted environments divided by the average thickness of the material. The MRI study also computes the costs due to soiling by assigning an economic value to aesthetic loss suffered by a material through soiling.[17] The formula used is

$L = Q \times V$

Where
Q = value of the exposed material as defined earlier
V = soiling interaction value per year.
$V_{fibers} = 0.10\Delta f/RW$
$V_{non-fibers} = 0.10\Delta f/RWpt$

Where
W = material price per pound;
R = labor force;
P = density;
t = average thickness;
Δf = increased frequency of cleaning due to pollution.

With respect to vegetation, several studies attempted to estimate damage to vegetation from air pollution.[18] These studies were, however, criticized for the limitations of their methodologies.[19]

With respect to property values, several studies attempted to estimate the effects of air pollution on residential property values. The estimates were based on linear regression models using either a cross-sectional or a time-series approach. The units show negative although not significant effects of pollution on property value, rent, and land use intensity.

NOISE

The effects of noise are generally assembled through its effects on property values, with property values as dependent variables and noise parameters as one of the independent variables.[20] Other studies relied on a survey in which people were asked how much less a certain house in a noise-defined environment would have to be than an ordinary house before one could consider buying it.[21] These studies are far from being conclusive in the damage produced by noise. To that effect Wyzga states:

Theoretically from surveys, litigation, etc., it appears as if there is damage involved, which includes a decrease in property value, but the studies to date have been largely unsuccessful in uncovering any relationship between noise levels and property values. It could be that most of these studies have not properly adjusted for housing supply or the fact that some individuals are more sensitive to noise than others. These and other potential influences need to be investigated, and more realistic models need to be developed if we are to obtain reasonable estimates of the relationship between noise and property values.[22]

WATER POLLUTION

Various studies investigating the damages caused by water pollution focused on the disamenities due to pollution. Most studies concerned themselves with measuring the recreational benefits arising from the use of unpolluted water. Various measurement methods used for estimating recreational benefits are given by Clawson and Knetsch.[23] These are as follows:

1. *Maximum price method*: estimates the total benefit of a recreational resource to be the sum of the maximum prices that various users would pay for the employment of the resource.
2. *Gross expenditure method*: estimates the total amount spent on recreation by the user as a surrogate measure of recreational benefits.
3. *Market value of fish method*: estimates the total amount spent on recreation by the user as a surrogate measure of recreational benefits.
4. *Cost method*: equates the benefits to the costs used to generate them.
5. *Market value method*: uses the prices charged at privately owned recreational areas as a surrogate measure of recreational benefits.
6. *Direct interview method*: assesses directly how much the users are willing to pay for using the resource.

ESTIMATING SOCIAL COSTS

Having identified the nature of the environmental damage and the resulting environmental damage functions, the next step is the economic measurement of the environmental damage. The idea is to attach a monetary value to each type of damage. In general two types of damages are considered: financial losses and amenity losses.[24] Financial losses may be defined as the change in the level of outlays following a change in environmental quality. Examples of financial losses include productivity losses resulting from the environmental damage and increased costs of health care. Amenity losses may be defined as the psychic costs resulting from the suffering, bereavement, and limitation imposed on individuals, families, and society.

The estimation of financial losses generally relies on direct determination of the monetary value of changes in the demand for marketable goods and services due to environmental changes. Four problems may be identified with this approach:
1. The specification of effects, or the problem of identifying the marketable goods and services which are affected by a change in the environment;
2. The relating of effects to a specific level of environmental deterioration;
3. The problem of finding the proper prices, including the interest rate, which should be used in a monetary evaluation;
4. The problem of interpreting the calculated financial values and relating them to the monetary damage in the context of the problem under study.[25]

The estimation of amenity losses differs because of their intangible nature. The methods used tend to be indirect. One method may be use questionnaires in which the affected individuals are asked to specify the amount of money necessary to compensate them for environmental deterioration. A second method is to use the relationship between the loss of a specific amenity and the demand for private goods to estimate the amenity loss. A third method is to use the market reactions in terms of changes in prices. A comparison of land values, for example, may indicate a loss of amenity. Finally, litigation results may be used to estimate amenity losses.

ESTIMATING SOCIAL BENEFITS

Social benefits are the gains associated with a reduction of the externality or nuisance. In the case of pollution, for example, the benefits are measured by a comparison of the existing level of pollution and "acceptable" level of pollution. Thus, benefits result from a "willingness to pay" to reduce the nuisance. It implies the existence of a demand curve for environmental quality.[26] Three techniques have been used to estimate the demand in connection with air and water pollution: measuring benefits from market data; measuring benefits from nonmarket data; and measuring benefits on the basis of property values.

Measuring benefits from market data uses the relationships between private marketed goods and public goods to draw inferences on the demand of public goods. The demand for the public good is inferred from market transactions on the related private good. The level of environmental quality as a public good, however, enters the individual utility functions in the broad categories. First, it is an input in the production of market goods and services. Its demand can be estimated by examining changes in factor incomes "such as land units, costs savings in production, and changes in consumer associated with the private good outputs."[27] Second, if it enters directly in the utility function as a consumption good, its demand can be estimated in terms of shifts in the demand curve for a private complementary good, or in terms of the demand for a perfect substitute.

Measuring benefits from nonmarket data relies on nonmarket means such as surveys, questionnaires, bidding games, and voting. The idea is to induce people to reveal directly or indirectly their preferences for the provision of public goods. Basically, three approaches may be used. The first approach is to ask people about their willingness to pay to obtain a given level of public good.[28] The second approach is to ask individuals how much of the public good they would demand at a given price or under given conditions of taxation.[29] The third approach uses a voting mechanism in which two parties or candidates compete for votes after adopting different positions on the provision of a public good.[30]

Ronald Ridker was the first to use property values as a basis for benefit estimation. He argues as follows:

If the land market were to work perfectly, the price of a plot of land would equal the sum of the present discounted streams of benefits and costs derivable from it. If some of its costs rise (e.g., if additional maintenance and cleaning costs are required), or if some of its benefits fall (e.g., if one cannot see the mountains from the terrace) the property will be discounted in the market to reflect people's evaluation of these changes. Since air pollution is specific to locations and the supply of locations is fixed, there is less likelihood that the negative effects of air pollution can be significantly shifted on to other markets. We would therefore expect to find the majority of effects reflected in this market, and we can measure them by observing associated changes in property values.[31]

Following Ridker's example, the approach adopted was to derive benefit measures from property value differences at a point in time.

Various social programs may be necessary to connect some of the social ills imposed by the environmental effects of organizational behavior. A choice has to be made for the program most suitable and most feasible given the state of the technology and the funds available. This section of the chapter presents two widely accepted techniques for the evaluation of social programs: cost-benefit analysis and cost-effectiveness analysis.

Cost-Benefit Analysis

Cost-benefit analysis is a method used to assess the desirability of projects when it is necessary to take both a long and a wide view of the impact of a proposed project on the general welfare of a society.[32] It calls for an enumeration and evaluation of all the relevant costs and benefits the project may generate and for choosing the alternatives that maximize the present value of all benefits less costs, subject to specified constraints and given specified objectives. Cost-benefit analysis is very useful when all the economic impacts of a project, indirect as well as direct effects, have to be considered. It is a favorite method of analysis by governmental agencies for assessing the desirability of particular program expenditures and/or policy changes. In fact, it has been formally adopted into U.S. federal government budgetary procedures under the Planning-Programming-Budgeting System (PPBS).[33] It acts as a structure for a general theory of government resource allocation. Above all, it is a decision technique whose aims are first to take all effects into consideration and second to maximize the present value of all benefits less that of all costs, subject to specified constraints. This brings into focus the major considerations of cost-benefit analysis:

1. What are the objectives and constraints to be considered?
2. Which costs and benefits are to be included?
3. How are the costs and benefits to be valued?
4. What are the investment criteria to be used?
5. Which discount rate should be used?

OBJECTIVES AND RELEVANT CONSTRAINTS

The main objective of cost-benefit analysis is to determine whether or not a particular expenditure is economically and socially justifiable. The basic criteria used in cost-benefit analysis is an efficiency criterion is Pareto optimality. A program is said to be Pareto efficient if at least one person is made better off and no one is made worse off. This criterion is too strong and too impractical for cost-benefit analysis, however, given that few programs are likely to leave some individuals better off and no one worse off. A weaker notion of efficiency, known as the Kaldor-Hides criterion, is generally used for cost-benefit analysis. Under this criterion, also known as the potential Pareto improvement criterion, a program is acceptable if it is Pareto optimal or if it could redistribute the net benefits to everyone in the community so that everyone is at least as well off as they were before the initiation of the program.[34] Basically, a program is efficient and should be undertaken if its total discounted societal benefits exceed the total discounted costs.

Besides the objectives of cost-benefit analysis, which are basically intended to maximize society's wealth, it is important to recognize some of the constraints. Eckstein provided a helpful classification of constraints.[35] These include:

1. *Physical constraints*: The program alternatives considered may be constrained by the state of technology and more generally by the production function, which relates the physical inputs and outputs of a project.
2. *Legal constraints*: The program alternatives considered must be done within the framework of the law. Examples of legal constraints include property rights, time needed for public inquiries, regulated pricing, the right of eminent domain, and limits to the activities of public agencies.
3. *Administrative constraints*: Each of the alternative programs requires the availability and the hiring of individuals with the right administrative skills.
4. *Distributional constraints*: Any program is bound to generate gainers and losers. The unfavorable effects on income distribution may be alleviated by expressing the objective of cost-benefit analysis as either maximizing the excess of total benefits over total costs subject to constraints on the benefits less costs of particular groups or maximizing the net gain (or minimizing the net loss) to a particular group subject to a constraint relating to total benefits and costs.
5. *Political constraints*: Political considerations may act as constraints, shifting the decision from what is *best* to what is *possible*. Regional differences and presence of various competing interest groups are examples of actors bound to create political constraints on the choice of the best program.
6. *Budgetary constraints*: Capital rationing and evaluating may act as constraints, shifting the objective function from maximizing to suboptimizing of net benefit given a target budget.
7. *Social and religious constraints*: Social and religious taboos are bound to act as constraints, shifting the decision from what is *best* to what is *acceptable*.

ENUMERATION OF COSTS AND BENEFITS

Enumeration of costs and benefits is important in determining which of the costs and benefits of a particular project should be included in a cost-benefit analysis.

Benefits of a project are either direct or indirect. Primary or direct benefits of a project "are those benefits which accrue directly to the users of the service provided by the project." They consist of "the value of goods or services that result from conditions with the project as compared to condition without the project."[36] Indirect or secondary benefits of a project are those benefits accruing to others that the users of the service provided by the project. They are two types: real or technological benefits or pecuniary benefits.[37] Real or technological benefits are those benefits resulting from changes in total production possibilities and consumption opportunities. For example, if a dam creates a reduction in flooding and more pleasant scenery, these benefits are real benefits. Pecuniary benefits are those benefits that alter the distribution of total income without changing its volume. They generally take the form of lower input costs, increased volumes of business, or changes in the land values. *Only direct real benefits should be included; pecuniary benefits should be excluded in the enumeration of the benefits of a project.* Other benefits that are of an intangible nature and difficult to identify should be also considered. Costs of a project are also either direct or indirect. Direct or primary costs of a project are costs incurred directly by the users of the service provided by the project. They include the capital costs, operating and maintenance costs, and personnel expenses required by the project. Indirect or secondary costs are incurred by others than the users of the service provided by the project. They may also be of two types: real or technological and pecuniary costs. *Again, only the real secondary cost should be counted in a cost-benefit analysis.*

Briefly, in enumerating the costs and benefits of a project, the analyst must be careful to distinguish their allocative effects from their pecuniary or distributional effects. In fact, the confusion of pecuniary and allocative effects constitutes a primary defect in many analyses of the efficiency of public projects. The only effects that should be taken into account in enumerating the costs and benefits of a public project are the real or technological externalities, that is, those that affect total opportunities for production and consumption, as opposed to pecuniary externalities, which do not affect total production or consumption.

VALUATION OF COSTS AND BENEFITS

In general, benefits should measure the value of the additional goods or services produced or the value of cost savings in the production of goods or services, while costs should measure the value of real resources displaced from other uses.

Assuming a competitive economy, benefits the costs will be valued on the basis of the observable market prices of the outputs and inputs of the program. More precisely, the benefits will be valued in either the market price of the output of the program or on the amounts users are willing to pay if charged (i.e., the consumers' surplus, which is the difference between the aggregate willingness to pay and the costs of the projects).

Where market prices do not accurately reflect the value of the market transactions to society as a result of externalities, the shadow prices, as adjusted or input prices, may be used. The general principle for estimating shadow prices for the output of public projects is to stimulate what users would be willing to pay if they were charged as if the goods were sold in perfectly competitive markets.

INVESTMENT CRITERIA

Cost-benefit analysis is a method used to evaluate long-term projects. As such the benefits and costs of each project have to be discounted to be comparable at time 0 when evaluation and decision on the projects have to be made. There is a need to rely on some form of discounting in the choice of investment criteria. There are exactly three possible investment or decision criteria: net present value; benefit-cost ratio; and internal rate of return.

Under the net present value, the present value of a project is obtained by discounting the net excess of benefits (B_t) over costs (C_t) for each year during the life of the project back to the present time using a social discount rate. More explicitly,

$$V = \sum_{t=1}^{\alpha} \frac{B_t - C_t}{(1+r)^t}$$

Where
V = value of the project;
B_t = benefit in year t;
C_t = cost in year t;
r = social discount rate; and
α = life of the project.

Basically a project is found acceptable if the present value V is positive. If there are binding constraints on a project (for example, budget appropriation, foreign exchange, private investment opportunity foregone), then the following model proposed by Steiner[38] would be more appropriate:

$$V = \sum_{t=1}^{\alpha} \frac{B_t - C_t}{(1+r)^t} - \sum_{j=1}^{n} p_j k_j$$

where
p_j = shadow price of a binding constraint; and
k_j = number of units of a constrained resource.

Under benefit-cost ratio, the decision criterion is expressed in terms of the ratio of the present value of benefits to the present value of costs (both discounted at the social discount rate). More explicitly, the benefit-cost ratio is:

$$\frac{\sum_{t=1}^{\alpha} \frac{b_t}{(1+r)^t}}{\sum_{t=1}^{\alpha} \frac{c_t}{(1+r)^t}}$$

Basically all projects that are not mutually exclusive with a benefit-cost ratio in excess of 1 are acceptable.

Under internal rate or return, the decision criterion is expressed in terms of the internal rate of return, that is to say, the discount rate will equate the net benefits over the life of the project with the original cost. In other words, 2 is the rate of interest for which

$$\sum_{t=1}^{\alpha} \frac{b_t}{(1+r)^t} - \sum_{t=1}^{\alpha} \frac{c_t}{(1+r)^t} = 0$$

Basically all projects where the internal rate of return exceeds the closer social discount rate are deemed acceptable.

CHOICE OF A DISCOUNT RATE

The choice of a discount rate is important for at least two reasons. A high rate will lead the firm or the government away from the undertaking of the project, while a low rate may make the project more acceptable from a return point of view. Furthermore, a low discount rate tends to favor projects yielding net benefits further into the future relative to projects yielding net benefits further into the future relative to projects yielding more current net benefits. Choosing the appropriate interest rate becomes therefore an important policy question. There are several possible alternative rates.

Given that the discount rate allows the allocation of resources between the public and private sectors, it should be chosen so that it indicates when resources should be transferred from one sector or another. This means that the discount rate should represent the opportunity cost of funds withdrawn from the private sector to be used in the public sector. As Baumol states, "The correct discount rate for the evaluation of a government project is the percentage rate of return that the resources utilized would otherwise provide in the private sector."[39]

These considerations enter the choice of the *marginal productivity of capital as a discount rate in private investment*: (1) an effort to minimize governmental activity; (2) a concern for efficiency; and (3) a belief that the source of funds for government investment in the private sector or that government investment will displace private investment that would otherwise be made.[40]

Social time preference expresses a concern for future generations in the sense that the welfare of the future generations will be increased if investments are made now. It follows that the discount rate should be the *social rate of time preference*, that is to say, the compensation required to induce consumers to refrain from consumption and save. One study committee argued that the federal government should use the "administration's social rate of time discount" to be established by the president in consultation with his advisors, such as the Council of Economic Advisors.[41] The strongest argument for the social rate of time preference was made by Pigou, who suggested that individuals were short-sighted about the future ("defective telescopic faculty") and the welfare of future generations would require governmental intervention.[42]

ADVANTAGES AND LIMITATIONS

There are thousands of cost-benefit analyses of government projects. The popularity of the method is a witness to some of its advantages. There are also some limitations well recognized in the literature. Let's examine some of the advantages and limitations of both. Among the advantages of cost-benefit analysis we may cite the following:
1. It is most effective in dealing with cases of intermediate social goods.[43]
2. It establishes a framework for a reasonably consistent evaluation of alternative projects, especially where the choice set is narrow in the sense that the projects are not only similar but generate the same volume of externalities.
3. It allows one to ascertain the decisions most advantageous in terms of the objectives accepted.

Among its limitations we may cite the following:
1. There are limits within social objectives can be measured in money terms. An example of nonefficiency objectives that are not measureable in dollar terms is an equitable distribution of income.
2. Cost-benefit analysis falls under what is known as partial equilibrium analysis. It is useful in evaluating only projects that have negligible impact outside the immediately affected areas of the economy.
3. There are obvious problems of enumeration and evaluation of the costs and benefits of particular projects.[44] A committee on the House of Representatives, point-assigning dollar terms to them, argued that such estimates are seldom accurate.[45] Similarly, Baram argued that "monetization of environmental and health amenities constitutes an inappropriate treatment of factors that transcend economies.[46]

Cost-Effectiveness Analysis

The difference between cost-effectiveness analysis and cost-benefits analysis is merely a difference of degree and not in kind. While cost-benefit analysis is concerned with quantifying both benefits and costs in money terms and determining the most efficient way to conduct a given program, cost-effectiveness assumes that the outputs of a given program are useful and valuable without attempting to measure their values. Thus, cost-effectiveness analysis may be merely defined as "a technique for choosing among *given* alternative courses of action in terms of their cost and effectiveness in the attainment of *specified* objectives."[47] This definition assumes that the objectives are known and well specified and the only concern is with cost-effectiveness considerations. Consider, however, another definition where cost effectiveness is "a technique for evaluation broad management and economic implications of alternative choices of action with the objective of assisting in the identification of the preferred choice."[48] This last definition implies less well-defined objectives, solutions, and criteria of effectiveness. In any case the methodology will be the same under both approaches.

METHODOLOGY

Before introducing the methodology, we should keep in mind that cost-effectiveness analysis is used generally for projects where the aim is to minimize the costs associated with the attainment of any given objective or objectives. As such it may be outlined as a sequence of general steps:[49]

1. *Definition of objectives*: The basic requirement for cost-effectiveness analyses is that the objectives be *specifiable*.
2. *Identification of alternatives*: Devising various feasible options for accomplishing objectives.
3. *Selection of effectiveness measures*: This step is considered the most difficult in cost-effectiveness analysis since the desirability of a given program may change depending on the types of the effectiveness measure used.[50]
4. *Cost estimates*: The estimation of costs for each alternative, precisely as in cost-benefit analysis.
5. *Selection of a decision criterion*: Two major types of criteria are used in cost-effectiveness analysis: a constant cost criterion, or a least-cost criterion. The constant cost criterion allows one to determine the output that my be achieved from a number of alternative systems, all of which require the same outlay of funds. In short, the constant cost criterion specifies what the analyst can get or his or her money and how to maximize effectiveness at a given cost. The least cost criterion allows one to identify the least expensive option for achieving a certain level of output. In other words, it attempts to minimize cost while attaining a given level of effectiveness. N. M. Singer illustrated adequately the differences between the constant cost and least cost criteria:

   > The differences among the various types of systems analysis can be seen by comparing the operations research problem, to collect refuse with a given fleet of trucks, to studies that would be made under the other methodologies. A least cost study would determine the collection system of minimum cost for the given pick-up locations; that is, the capital and labor inputs would be permitted to vary. A constant cost study would examine the various outputs that could be produced for the cost of the garbage truck fleet: commuter transit if the money were spent on buses, highway safety if the money were spent on roadgrading equipment, education if the funds were spent on schools, and so forth. Finally, a benefit-cost study would estimate the value that consumers place on the garbage pick-up and would then recommend whether or not to undertake the program.[51]
6. *Creation of models*: The next step is to formulate analytical relationships among costs, effectiveness and environmental factors. Given these relationships, the next step is to choose either the alternative that maximizes effectiveness with a given cost or the alternative that minimizes costs given a desired level of effectiveness.

LIMITATIONS

Three limitations of cost-effectiveness analysis are generally considered.[52] First, judgment may be necessary to delineate factors and interrelationships and to interpret the results. Second, it may be difficult to select measures of effectiveness. Third, imperfect information and insufficient input information may distort the analysis. Finally, the analysis is too deterministic and does not account for uncertainty.

Conclusions

This chapter suggested ways of conceptualizing micro social accounting and ways of measuring and evaluating the environmental effects of organizational behavior. A tentative conceptual framework is presented as a way of conceptualizing micro social accounting. This framework rests on proposed objectives, concepts, and qualitative characteristics of micro social accounting. The measurement of the environmental effects of organizational behavior rests on measurement of social costs and social benefits. Various ways of measuring social costs and benefits are presented. The evaluation of social programs rests on two established techniques, namely, cost-benefit analysis and cost-effectiveness.

What is conveyed in this chapter is, first, that a conceptual framework for socio-economic accounting is feasible and, second, that techniques of measurement evaluation of the environmental effects of organizational behavior are available. What remains to be accomplished by corporate firms and interest groups is a trial implementation and "legitimization" of micro social accounting.

Appendix: Determining the Optimal Level of Air Pollution for a Firm

Air pollution is an example of external diseconomy. Its effects are varied:
1. It causes destruction of property values through progressive destruction and premature deterioration of building materials, metals, paint coatings, merchandise, etc.
2. Smoke affects human health adversely.
3. It has an adverse effects on plant and animal life.

The economics of air pollution involves the measurement of the social costs of pollution and the determination of economic solutions to stop it. Wolozin states that the economics of air pollution are largely directed to two broad areas, both difficult assignments:
1. Measuring the costs to individuals and society at large of the diffusive despoiling of the atmosphere (and the corresponding benefits of cleaning it up).
2. Determining economic measures to stimulate and/or coerce polluters to eliminate or at least cut down their emissions of destructive gases and particulate matter.[53]

Relationships Between Costs and Pollution Levels

Air pollution is an external cost of production and consumption. But there are no market forces to compel the user to consider the costs he or she imposes on others; one reason may be the difficulties in estimating fully the social costs of air pollution and the determination of a level of pollution that will be socially acceptable. Wolozin poses the fundamental question: "Can we presume with any confidence to measure the total economic costs of air pollution?"[54] One of the main difficulties is its dimensionality. Air pollution is a multidimensional phenomenon. "Its sources are varied, it affects a multitude of objects, and it can produce a wide variety of changes in behavior."[55]

Another point is the relationship between the total cost of pollution and the level of pollution. Linearity is implied in a paper delivered by Kneese.[56] However, nonlinearity is assumed by both Wolozin and Ridker.[57] Wolozin looks first at the relationship between the costs of abatement and the level of pollution to justify the nonlinearity between the social costs of air pollution and the level of pollution (see Exhibit 7.3). Exhibit 7.3 shows the relationship between various levels of pollution (measured by some composite indicies) and the total cost of control required to reach each level of pollution measured on a horizontal scale. The rationale behind the shape of such a curve is that the costs of abatement would, after a time, have to increase more rapidly to reach a lower level of pollution. Following that argument, Wolozing states that it is possible that the social costs due to pollution are also nonlinear: "An initial range of minimal damage, then a range of rapid rise in damage costs relative to pollution levels followed by a leveling off, even though this might not be reached except near the point of disaster."[58] Such cost behavior would look like that shown in Exhibit 7.4, shows both the cost of control and the cost of pollution. As the level of pollution rises, the costs of pollution (or social costs) will grow larger (nonlinearly). Likewise, the costs of control will be higher to reach a lower level of pollution.

Exhibit 7.5 shows the sum of the costs of pollution and the costs of control and led us to conclude that *the social goal should be to reach that level S of pollution which minimizes the costs of pollution and the cost of control.*[59]

Determining the Optimal Level of Air Pollution

Let us use an example to illustrate the determination of the level of pollution that minimizes the costs of pollution and the cost of control. Let us assume that Exhibit 7.6 lists the value of the annual total social cost that occurs with no abatement and the social cost of control (abatement costs). These estimates are transformed into two curves in Exhibit 7.7, the social cost of pollution curve and the social cost of control curve. The objective is to select the level of abatement that will minimize both the social cost and cost of control of pollution. In this example, that level is at 60 percent abatement, as shown in Exhibit 7.7.

EXHIBIT 7.3: COST OF ABATEMENT

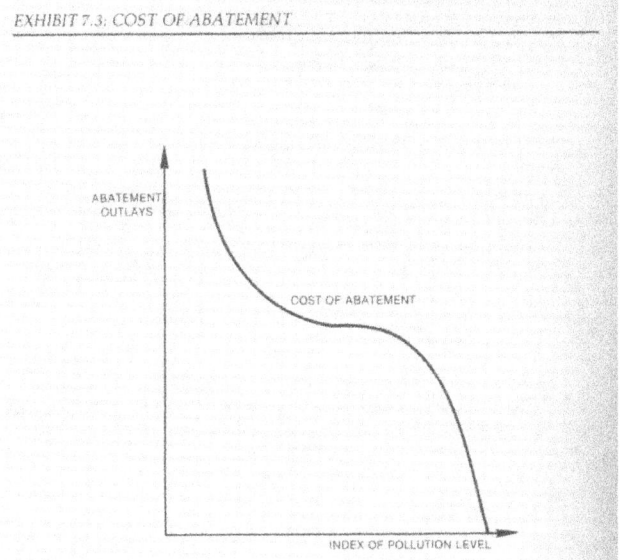

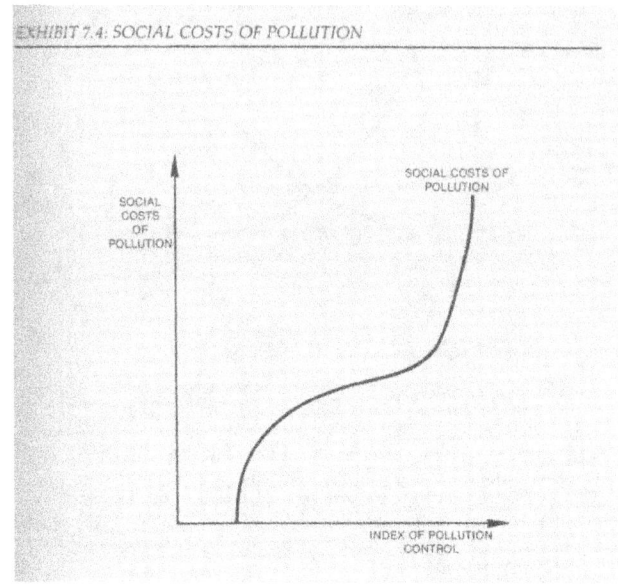
EXHIBIT 7.4: SOCIAL COSTS OF POLLUTION

EXHIBIT 7.5: COST OF CONTROL AND COST OF POLLUTION

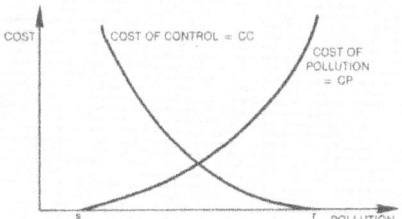

EXHIBIT 7.6: SOCIAL COST OF AIR POLLUTION AND CONTROL

LEVEL OF CONTROL (%)	SOCIAL COST OF POLLUTION (dollars)	SOCIAL COST OF CONTROL (dollars)	TOTAL COST (dollars)
0	500	0	500
10	380	10	390
20	280	20	300
30	210	30	240
40	150	50	200
50	95	80	175
60	65	100	165
70	40	250	290
80	30	300	330
90	20	450	470
100	0	500	500

EXHIBIT 7.7: CC + CP AT A MINIMUM

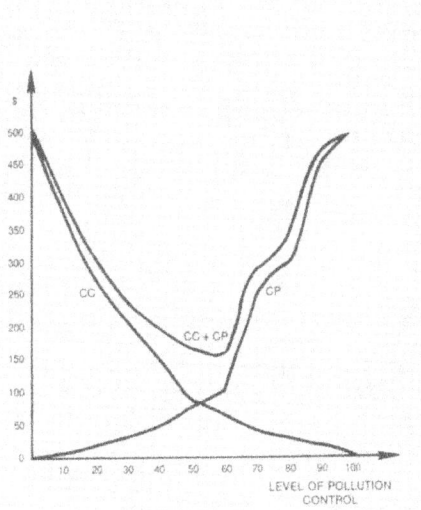

Another way of determining the optimal level of abatement is to consider the benefits and costs of abatement.[60] Net benefit will be the "difference between the benefits received by a community from a reduction in pollution and the costs incurred by the community in reducing the level of pollution."[61] It could be expressed by the following equation: $P_i = B_i - SC_i$, where P_i is the total net benefit, B_i is the total benefit, and SC_i is the total cost of air pollution.[62] *The objective of the technique is to choose that level of pollution which will maximize net benefits. This was found, in economics, to be where the marginal benefits from pollution are equal to the marginal costs of pollution.*

A benefit from a pollution schedule could be obtained by using the data from Exhibit 7.6. For example, with no control, the social costs of air pollution are equal to $500. With 10 percent control, they are equal to $120. As a general rule:

$B_i = SC_o = 100 - SC_i$

Where
i = percent level of control, $0 \leq i \leq 100$; and
SC_i = social cost of air pollution with i level of control.

The results are listed in Exhibit 7.8 and graphed in Exhibit 7.9 and 7.10. The optimal point of control that maximizes net benefits is the point where marginal benefit intersects marginal cost. From Exhibit 7.8, 7.9, and 7.10 this level is 60 percent.

At the firm level the manufacturer wishing to plan by an efficient allocation of resources may add as an additional constraint the reaching of the optimal level of pollution control (as determined above) that minimizes net social benefits. Jackson, Woblers, and Decoursey have used various other methods to determine the optimal level of pollution control to minimize the total cost-effectiveness analysis.[63] They have elaborated a six-step procedure:

1. Examining present emission rate by source category to evaluate existing degree of air pollution controls.
2. Evaluating regional trends make future projections of controlled and uncontrolled emissions.
3. Evaluating emission control trends that have been established in the region.
4. Examining alternate control schemes they may be feasible for application to each source category.
5. Determining emission control costs.
6. Using a technique to determine the control scheme with the optimum cost-effectiveness aspect.

Another example has been the use of linear programming and systems analysis.[64] All these models (cost-benefit analysis, cost-effectiveness analysis, and linear programming models) are intended to determine that level of control which minimizes the total cost of air pollution; the problem remains to define strategies for the estimation of the social costs and costs of air pollution control.

Estimation of the Social Costs of Air Pollution

In order to estimate the social costs of air pollution at a macro or regional level, Ridker developed the following strategy, which I assume could be applied at the firm level.[65] He considered a community where ambient air quality is measured on a scale, for example, annual geometric sulfuration rate. If this rate increases, its effects could be divided into three categories: (1) direct and immediate effects in the absence of adjustments; (2) individual adjustments; and (3) market effects. These three categories constitute different levels of analysis of the social costs of air pollution.

EXHIBIT 7.8: COST-BENEFIT TABLE

EXHIBIT 7.9: DETERMINATION OF MINIMUM COST USING MARGINAL CURVES

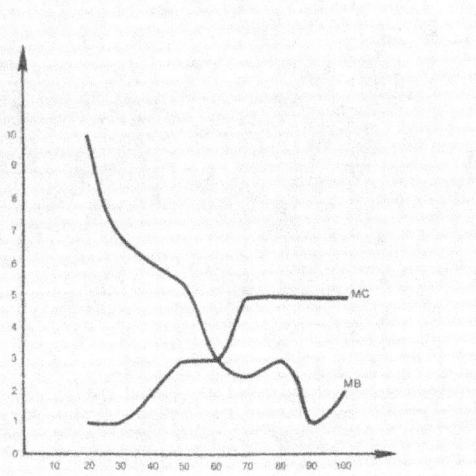

EXHIBIT 7.10: DETERMINATION OF MINIMUM COST USING
TOTAL CURVES

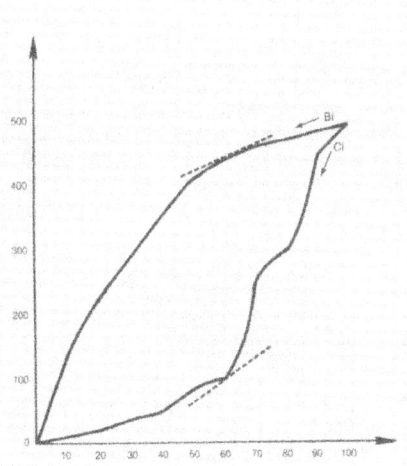

Ridker assumes that in the absence of individual adjustments and social interactions, the first level of social cost estimate will be computed using three types of information. First, it is necessary to determine the damage function per unit of each object affected as a function of the air pollution level.[66] This could be represented by

$$D_i = F_i(S)_i, = (1, \ldots h)$$

Where D_i is a measure of the i type of damage per unit of object affected by the pollution and S is a measure of pollution, SO_2 for example. Second, monetary weight of the cost per unit of damage must be obtained. Third, the number of the objects affected should be available then if C_i is the cost per unit of damage and Q_i is the number of units affected, the social costs of air pollution in the absence of adjustments could be expressed as

$$TC_1 = \sum_{i=1}^{n}(Q_i F_i(S))$$

Ridker refers to possible actions taken by individuals to adjust to the change in environment quality. He gives the following example:
Consider a person who suddenly finds his asthma getting worse because the level of pollution is increasing. On the most general level, he may do nothing, simply suffering the additional discomfort involved; or he may change his behavior in response to a deteriorating environment. The change in his behavior may be of three different types: First, the individual may change the amount of time he spends in the affected area, for example, by taking longer vacations outside the area of his residence; second, ...[67]

Each of the actions taken by the individuals lead to a loss in utility, and the difficulties of measuring its costs is related to the "psychic" character of the possible losses. However, if we do not add the individual adjustments to TC_i, the total social costs of air pollution will certainly be understated.

It may be assumed that any adjustment by an individual has an effect on other individuals. "Perhaps the most important interactions for out purpose are the effects that occur because people are linked together by their purchases and sales in different markets."[68] One example is the increase in the rent in the sector not yet affected by air pollution. Here again there is a measurement problem, and Ridker assumes that the only way to measure the market effect if to estimate the change in consumer and producer surpluses and to sum those surpluses over the affected markets. However, he admits the difficulties of doing so and assumes that the total cost of air pollution could better be understated by TC_1: the direct effects without individual adjustments.

Besides the individual adjustments and market effects mentioned by Ridker, the difficulties of measurement of the social costs of air pollution are numerous. Let us examine some of them:

First, some of the damages are difficult to measure, and the experimental studies used may lack external validity.[69] Haltman, for example, recognizes that it is difficult to establish a quantitative relationship between disease rates and specific pollutant levels. He assumes that the best that can be done is to estimate the average and total costs of these diseases and to suggest roughly the magnitude of the costs that might be the result of air pollution.[70]

Second, useful measurements of economic costs of air pollution must be made "within a specific air shed" and/or specific pollutants.[71] The concept of air shed is very vague.

Third, chronic effects of air pollution are usually less considered than acute effects, while it is known that in the long run they might have a harmful effect on human, animal, and plant life.[72] Usually undetected, these chronic costs of air pollution are uncounted and as such there will be an understatement of the total costs of air pollution.

Fourth, air pollution is not the only externality affecting the environment, and as such it is difficult to estimate the damages inherent only to air pollution. Externalities are multidimensional phenomena with varied sources. Air pollution is an externality and as such "cannot be studied and controlled in isolation, for it is one of a number of interrelated problems affecting the quality of the environment."[73]

The Problem of Control

The economics of air pollution includes two broad areas, the measurement aspect and the control aspect. The control aspect consists of the elaboration of economic and legislative measures toward motivating polluters into controlling air pollution.

The Air Quality Act of 1967 is one of the measures advocated through legislation. In the case of air pollution, the Air Quality Act provided a framework for government industry association to control air pollution. It amended the Air Act of 1963 in the sense that it allowed state control or air pollution problems, thus recognizing the existence of differences in controls of different regions, and it enabled HEW to impose standards of air quality if the state fails to do so.[74]

However, the 1967 Air Quality Act has been criticized for various deficiencies.[75] First of all, it emphasizes the adoption of air quality standards (ambient air standards) when it should call for immediate reduction of industrial emissions. "National industrial emissions standards should precede ambient air standards as a logical and necessary prerequisite to their attainment.[76] Air quality standards define a certain limit to pollution rather than identifying the pollutants and providing rules to stop them. As O'Fallon states, "An ambient air quality standard says in effect that a given pollutant should not exceed a predetermined level in the atmosphere because of aesthetic, economic or health effects. Emission standards, on the other hand, limit the permissible discharge from sources of pollution."[77]

The act also tries to give the states responsibility for enacting a standard and controlling air pollution. But air pollution is a metropolitan problem, and historically local authorities have taken the lead in abating air pollution. This state-oriented approach represents a centralization for problems that are basically different. Air pollution is generated from different cities and as such requires the specific attention of each concerned city. Besides, "it will be difficult for states to bridge the gap of years of experience in this field in order to become full-fledged partners with local and regional agencies.[78]

The Clean Air Act of 1970 protects the air quality in three principal ways. It establishes national ambient air quality standards (NAAQS) and a mechanism, known as the state implementation plan, for meeting these standards. It authorizes emission standards for stationary sources of pollution. It sets various measures, such as exhaust standards, to control pollution from mobile sources.[79]

The Clean Air Amendments of 1977 concern the prevention of significant deterioration in areas with better air quality than the NAAQS require the address the problem of meeting the NAAQS in nonattainment areas. The following requirements were set in nonattainment areas, where air quality does not meet the NAAQS, for entry of a major new firm or modification of an existing firm:

Procuring emission offsets, or emission reductions, from established firms, so as to result in an improvement in air quality; adopting lowest achievable emissions rate technology (LAER), the most stringent control measure used anywhere; demonstrating that pollution control measures (emissions offsets plus LAER) are consistent with reasonable further progress, as defined by the EPA, toward meeting the NAAQS; for photochemical oxidant violations in cases where a five-year extension has been obtained for compliance with the NAAQS, an analysis of alternative sites and other factors which demonstrate that the benefits of the project significantly outweigh its environmental and social costs.[80]

Controlled Training

The Environmental Protection Agency has introduced an economic incentive approach for dealing with air pollution control, which consists of either the *bubbly policy*, the *offset policy*, or *emission reduction banking*.

The bubble policy considers that an imaginary enclosure, or bubble, is set for a plant or a multiplant with a permission for a maximum level of emission. This policy was initiated in December 1979. The offset policy allows major firms to start projects in nonattainment areas provided they offset their emissions with emissions reductions obtained from existing firms. This policy was initiated in December 1976. Emission reduction banking facilitates the use of offsets and bubbles by having in storage and ready for use "emission credits" and by creating a central cleaning facility to facilitate trading. The controlled trading policies constitute examples of a limited market approach. A "true market approach would allow more flexibility for firms in their compliance with the clean air acts. For example, a GAO study suggests the establishment of a market for air pollution entitlements to meet minimum standards of outdoor air quality.[81] Such a market approach to air pollution control would allow the purchase, sale, and use of air pollution entitlements consistent with present standards governing outdoor air quality.

The Economist's View: Effluent Fees

A second approach to environmental problems is taxation, and mainly effluent fees.[82] As one author states, "Corrective taxes and subsidies are deemed to be required in order to satisfy the necessary conditions for optimality when external effects are observed to be present."[83] This has also been advocated strongly by Croker, Mills, and Vickery.[84] They maintain that the objective of effluent fees would be to place all costs resulting from a specific individual action on the individual who caused it. Under this concept an air polluter would be assessed a tax equal to the damages resulting from his productive activities. This tax amount would then represent the marginal costs he imposed on others. This point of view of "internalizing" the social cost of air pollution through a government-levied charge on the polluters has been praised and criticized.

Among its advantages is the fact that a system of efficient fees is flexible. It could be adopted to different situations. For example, fees could increase or decrease depending on the weather conditions, the time of the day, and other factors. Also, under such a system, management rather than government has to take the decision to accept the effluent fees or abate pollution. Implicit in the effluent fees point of view "is recognition that the optimal level of air pollution abatement is closely tied to the technological process involved, with the least cost solution being in many cases a complex combination of process changes and treatment of effluents."[85]

However, some reservations have been raised. A major drawback is seen in the difficulties of measuring and identifying the damages attributable to particular air pollutants, which leads to a degree of skepticism on the efficacy of the existing technology in effectively enforcing an effluent fee system. The difficulties on inspecting, metering, and monitoring air pollution stems from the fact that the small emitters and emitters difficult to meter are large contributors to air pollution.[86] Another reservation is expressed by Wolozin, who questions the belief that taxation has an impact on business policies and human behavior.

To support the contention that externalities can be internalized through effluent fees, proponents generally fall back upon a conventional economic analysis of the nature of business behavior in the modern world, a model of business behavior that has been questioned seriously in the literature on the subject and one that very few economists adhere to rigorously in explaining the behavior of the firm or industry.[87]

This contention of the inapplicability of the neoclassical profit maximization model of business behavior to the kind of situations in which effluent fees have to be used is related to the investment decision in business management to adopt an abatement program and to authorize inherent outlays is lacking and difficult to validate.

In sum, effluent fees are theoretically founded but practically very difficult to enforce. Air pollution cannot be studied and controlled in isolation. It interferes with other factors that affect the quality of the environment, so an overall approach to control externalities directly could be considered and would allow significant economies.

Payments

Besides the effluent fee system, alternative approaches exist to control air pollution, such as payments and direct regulation. Direct regulations have been discusses as part of the legislative process and we best expressed by the Air Quality Act of 1967. Payment is an original type of subsidy to restrict waste disposal. It consists of providing payments to the firm for each amount of waste withheld. In other words, this system will be similar to the effluent fee system in theory but opposite in approach. These payments could take the indirect form of tax credits, investment credit, accelerated depreciation, or a tax write-off of capital cost.[88] They payment system suffers from a major handicap. The concept of paying a polluter is very far from the concept of equitable practice, especially that such payments must be provided through increased personal taxation.

Methods of Control for the Firm

The three general methods of air pollution abatement are mentioned by the technical progress report of the Los Angeles Country Air Pollution Control District.[89]

The installation of control equipment to convert the pollutant gases to a harmless form. This necessitates a cost analysis of the different steps of introducing such equipment.[90] First comes the initial cost of equipment, consisting of the purchase price, freight in, and installation. The second stage is the disruption of normal production during installation, which necessitates overtime, above normal scrap materials and labor, and time for nonproductive and supervisory personnel. Third, the depreciation policy entails new equipment and changes in the present plant. Fourth comes the maintenance, involving full-time or part-time personnel; possible shutdown periods; supplies, bads, etc.; containers (drums or collecting devices for pollutants); pollutant removal costs; and the charges, if any, for dumping (land rental or purchase). Finally, there is the renovation of the present plant, which will have to include space for a collection area as well as other changes.

A second abatement method is the modification or redesign of the basic equipment so as to minimize or eliminate the problem. An example would be the eventual use of crucible furnaces instead of direct flame furnaces in melting operations. Last, a change in the production process is a way of reduce or eliminate the pollutants. An example would be the substituting of natural gas for sulfur-bearing fuel oil.

Notes
1. Meinoff Dierkes and Raymond A. Bauer, *Corporate Social Accounting* (New York: Praeger 1973), p. xi.
2. Kavassen V. Ramanathan, "Toward a Theory of Corporate Social Accounting," *Accounting Review* (July 1976): 519-21.
3. Ibid., pp. 520-521.
4. Ibid., pp. 522-523.
5. Ibid.
6. Financial Accounting Standards Board, "Qualitative Characteristics: Criteria for Selecting and Evaluating Financial Accounting and Reporting Policies," Exposure draft (Stamford, Conn.: FASB, 1979).
7. American Accounting Association, *A Statement of Basic Accounting Theory* (Evanston, Ill.: AAA, 1966), p. 9.
8. American Accounting Association, Committee on Concepts and Standards for External Financial Reports, *Statement of Accounting Theory and Theory Acceptance* (Saratose, Fla.: AAA, 1977), p. 16.
9. American Accounting Association, *A Statement of Basic Accounting Theory*, p. 10.
10. "Conceptual Framework for Financial Accounting and Reporting: Elements of Financial Statements and their Measurements." FASB Discussion Memorandum (Stamford, Conn.: FASB, 1976), p. 1.
11. Robert H. Haveman, "On Estimating Environmental Damage: A Survey of Recent Research in the United States," in Organization for Economic Cooperation and Development, *Environmental Damage Costs* (Paris: OECD, 1976), p. 102.
12. Allen V. Kneese, Robert U. Ayres, and Ralph C. d'Arge, *Economics and the Environment: A Materials Balance Approach* (Baltimore: Johns Hopkins University Press, 1970).
13. Ibid., p. 107.
14. Office of Service and Technology, "Cumulative Regulatory Effects on the Cost of Automotive Transportation (RECAT): Final Report of the *ad hoc* Committee" (Washington, D.C.: Office of Service and Technology, February 28, 1972). Programmers Analysis Unit, *Economic and Technical Appraisal of Air Pollution in the United Kingdom* (Chilton: Berkes, 1971).
15. R. G. Ridker, *Economic Costs of Air Pollution* (New York: Praeger, 1967); P. G. Lave and N.T. Seskin, "Air Pollution and Human Health," *Science* 169:723.
16. R. T. Stickney, N. P. Mueller, and A. S. Spence, "Pollution vs. Rubber," *Rubber Age* 45 (September 1971); Midwest Research Institute, *Systems Analysis of the Effects of Air Pollution on Materials* (Chicago: Midwest Research Institute, January 1970).
17. Ridker also attempted to estimate soiling and deterioration damages by relying on two other approaches: survey of consumers; and survey of the cleaning industry.
18. P. Benedict, M. Miller, and T. Olson, *Economic Impact of Air Pollution Plants in the United States* (Stanford, Calif.: Stanford Research Institute, November 1971); S. Millecan, *A Survey*

of Assessment of Air Pollution Damage to California Vegetation in 1970, (Sacramento: California Department of Agriculture, June 1971).
19. T. Landau, "Statistical Aspects of Air Pollution as It Applies to Agriculture" (Paper presented at the 1971 meeting of the Statistical Societies, Fort Collins, Colo.).
20. R. Diffey, "An Investigation Into the Effect of High Traffic Noise on House Prices in a Homogeneous Submarket" (Paper presented at a Seminar on House Prices and the Microeconomics of Housing, London School of Economics, December 1971).
21. P. Plowden, *The Cost of Noise* (London: Metra Consulting Group, 1970).
22. R. E. Wyzga, "A Survey of Environmental Damage Functions," in *Environmental Damage Costs* (Paris: Organization for Economic Co-Operation and Development, 1974).
23. M. Clawson and J. L. Knetsch, *Economics of Outdoor Recreation* (Baltimore: Johns Hopkins University Press, 1971).
24. Organization for Economic Co-Operation and Development, *Economic Measurement of Environmental Damage* (Paris: OECD, 1976), p. 6.
25. Ibid.,, p. 52.
26. A. Myrick Freeman, Ill., *The Benefits of Environmental Improvement: Theory and Practice* (Baltimore: Johns Hopkins University Press, 1979), p. 4.
27. Ibid., p. 82.
28. M. Kurtz, "An Experimental Approach to the Determination of the Demand for Public Goods," *Journal of Public Economics* 3 (1974): 329-348; Peter Bolrun, "An Approach to the Problem of Estimating Demand for Public Goods," *Swedish Journal of Economics* 1 (March 1971): 94-105.
29. H. R. Bowen, "The Interpretation of Voting in the Allocation of Economic Resources," *Quarterly Journal of Economics* 58 (1963): 27-48.
30. James L. Barr and Otto A. Davis, "An Elementary Political and Economic Theory of the Expenditures of Local Government," *Southern Economic Journal* 33 (October 1966): 149-165; T. E. Borcherding and R. T. Deacon, "The Demand for Services of Nonfederal Governments," *American Economic Review* 67 (December 1972): 891-901; T. C. Bergstrom and R. P. Goodman, "Private Demands for Public Goods," *American Economic Review* 63 (June 1973): 280-296.
31. Ridker, *Economic Costs of Air Pollution*, p. 25.
32. A. R. Prest and R. Turvey, "Cost-Benefit Analysis: A Survey," *Economic Journal* (December 1965): 683-735.
33. PPBS rests essentially on Cost-Benefit Analysis.
34. Another test for potential Pareto improvements is that everyone in society could be made better off by means of a costless redistribution of the net benefits.
35. Otto Eckstein, "A Survey of the Theory of Public Expenditure Criteria," in James M. Buchanan, ed., *Public Finances: Needs, Sources and Utilization* (Princeton: Princeton University Press, 1961).
36. Jese Burkehead and Jerry Miner, *Public Expenditure* (Chicago: Aldine-Atherton, 1971), p. 225.
37. R. N. McKean, *Efficiency in Government Through Systems Analysis* (New York: Wiley, 1958), ch. 8.
38. George A. Steiner, "Problems in Implementing Program Budgeting," in David Novick, ed., *Program Budgeting* (Cambridge: Harvard University Press, 1965)., pp. 87-88.

39. William J. Baumol, "On the Discount Rate of Public Projects," in Robert Haveman and Julius Margolis, eds., *Public Expenditure and Policy Analysis* (Chicago: Markham, 1970), p. 274.
40. Burkhead and Miner, *Public Expenditure*, p. 232.
41. U.S., Bureau of the Budget, *Standards and Criteria for Formulating and Evaluating Federal Water Resources Development* (Washington, D. C.: U.S. Government, 1961), p. 67.
42. A. C. Pigou, *The Economics of Welfare*, 4th ed. (London: Macmillan, 1932).
43. R. A. Musgrave, *Fiscal Systems* (New Haven: Yale University Press, 1969), pp. 797-806.
44. Prest and Turvey, "Cost-Benefit Analysis," pp. 729-731.
45. U.S., House of Representatives, Committee on Interstate and Foreign Commerce, Subcommittee on Oversight and Investigations, *Federal Regulation and Regulatory Reform*, 94th Cong., 2d sess., 1976, ch. 15 (subcommittee print).
46. Michael S. Baram, "Cost-Benefit Analysis: An Inadequate Basis for Health, Safety, and Environmental Regulatory Decision Making," *Ecology Law Quarterly* 8 (1980): 473-531.
47. Barry G. King, "Cost-Effectiveness Analysis: Implications for Accountants," *Journal of Accountancy* (May 1970): p. 43.
48. M. C. Heuston and G. Ogawa, "Observations on the Theoretical Basis of Cost Effectiveness," *Operations Research* (March-April 1966): 242-266.
49. King, "Cost-Effectiveness Analysis," p. 44.
50. William A. Niskanen, "Measures of Effectiveness," in Thomas A. Goldman, ed., *Cost-Effectiveness Analysis* (New York: Praeger, 1967), p. 20.
51. Neil M. Singer, *Public Microeconomics* (Boston: Little, Brown, 1976), p. 320.
52. King, "Cost-Effectiveness Analysis," pp. 48-49.
53. Harold Wolozin, "The Economics of Air Pollution: Central Problems," *Law and Contemporary Problems* 33, no. 2 (Spring 1968): 227.
54. Ibid., p. 288.
55. R. G. Ridker, *Economic Costs of Air Pollution* (New York: Praeger, 1967), p. 13.
56. A. V. Kneese, "How Much is Air Pollution Costing Us in the United States," in *Proceedings: The Third National Conference on Air Pollution* (New York: Public Health Service, 1967).
57. Wolozin, "The Economic Costs of Air Pollution," p. 229; Ridker, *Economic Costs of Air Pollution*, p. 13.
58. Wolozin, "The Economics of Air Pollution," p. 15.
59. Ridker, *Economic Costs of Air Pollution*, p. 4.
60. R. D. Wilson and D. W. Minnotte, "A Cost Benefit Approach to Air Pollution Control," *Journal of the Air Pollution Control Association* (May 1969): 303-323.
61. Ibid., p. 304.
62. Wilson and Minnotte considered first only the cost of control of air pollution. Second, because of the existence of n entities and m reception areas, the cost of control CC_j was set equal to $\sum_{j=1}^{n} CC_j$ where CC_j is the cost of control for the jth of n polluting emitters, and the total benefit B_T equal to $\sum_{i=1}^{m} \sum_{j=1}^{n} B_{ji}$ is the benefit received in the ith of m reception areas due to the control of the jth of the n emitters. Thus the equations for net benefits will be:

$$B_T = \sum_{i=1}^{m}$$

63. W. E. Jackson, H. C. Woblers, and W. Decoursey, "Determining Air Pollution Costs," *Journal of Air Pollution Association* (December 1969): 971-982.

64. A. Louch, "LP Models for Water Pollution Control Programs," *Management Science* (December 1967): 166-181; T. A. Wilson and N. T. Bunyard, "A Systematic Procedure for Determining the Cost of Controlling Particulate Emission from Industrial Sources," in *Proceedings of the Air Control Association* (Ney Work: Pollution Control Association, June 1969).
65. Ridker, *Economic Costs of Air Pollution*, p. 14.
66. Ibid.
67. Ibid., p. 31.
68. Ibid., p. 21.
69. Arthur C. Stern, ed., *Air Pollution* (New York: Academic Press, 1962).
70. Ridker, *Economic Costs of Air Pollution*, p. 30.
71. Ibid., p. 9.
72. Wolozin and Landau, "Crop Damage from Sulfur Dioxide," *Journal of Farm Economics* (October 1966): p. 394.
73. Wolozin, p. 237.
74. N. P. Martin and T. A. Syminton, "A Guide to the Air Quality Act of 1967," *Law and Contemporary Problems* 33 (Spring 1968): 275.
75. John E. O'Fallon, "Deficiencies in the Air Quality Act of 1967, *Law and Contemporary Problems* 33 (Spring 1968): 275.
76. Ibid., p. 277.
77. Ibid., p. 278.
78. Ibid., p. 289.
79. S. Blacker et al., "Measurement and the Law: Monitoring for Compliance with the Clean Air Amendments of 1970," *International Journal of Environmental Studies* 3 (1977): 169.
80. U.S. General Accounting Office, *A Market Approach to Air Pollution Control Could Reduce Compliance Costs Without Jeopardizing Clean Air Goals* (Washington, D.C.: GAO, March 23, 1982), pp. 13-14.
81. Ibid.
82. Norman F. Ramsey, "We Need a Pollution Tax," *Bulletin of Atomic Scientists* (April 1970), 3.
83. J. M. Buchanan, *Cost and Choice* (Chicago: Markham, 1969), p. 70.
84. T. Croker, *Some Economic Aspects of Air Pollution Control with Particular Reference to Polk County, Florida*, U.S. Public Health Service Grant, AP-00389-02 (January 1968), p. 282; J. Mills, "Federal Fiscal Policy in Air Pollution Control," in *Proceedings of the Air Control Association Meeting* (Cleveland, O.: ACAM, June 11, 1967); A. Vickery, "Theoretical and Practical Possibilities and Limitations of a Market Mechanism Approach to Air Pollution Control," in *Proceedings of the Air Control Association Meeting*.
85. George Hagevisk, "Legislating for Air Quality Management: Reducing Theory to Practice," *Law and Contemporary Problems* 33, no. 2 (Spring 1968): 369.
86. Ibid.
87. Kneese, pp. 192-195.
88. Paul R. McDaniel and Alan S. Kaplinsky, "The Use of the Federal Income Tax System of Combat Air and Water Pollution: A Case Study in Tax Expenditure," *Environmental Affairs* 1, no. 9 (April 1971): 12-53.
89. Control of Stationary Sources," Air Pollution Control District, County of Los Angeles, Technical Progress Report, vol. 1, April 1960, p. 4.

90. Alvah Bearse, "Air Pollution: A Case Study," *Management Accounting* (September 1971): 18.

Bibliography
TOWARD A THEORY OF MICRO SOCIAL ACCOUNTING
Beams, Floyd A., and Paul E. Fertig. "Pollution Control Through Social Cost Conversion." *Journal of Accountancy* (November 1971): 37-42.
Bendock, C. M. "Measuring Social Costs." *Management Accounting* (January 1975): 13-15.
Chastain, Clark E. "Corporate Accounting for Environmental Information." *Financial Executive* (May 1975): 45-50.
Churchill, Neil C. "Toward a Theory for Social Accounting." *Sloan Management Review* (Spring 1974): 1-16.
Churchman, C. W. "On the Facility, Felicity and Morality of Measuring Social Change." *Accounting Review* (January 1971).
Linowes, David F. "The Accountant's Enlarged Professional Responsibilities." *Journal of Accountancy* (February 1973): 47-57.
Mason, Alister K. "Social Costs: A New Challenge for Accountants." *Canadian Chartered Accountant Magazine* (June 1971): 390-395.
Ramanathan, Kvassen V. "Toward a Theory of Corporate Social Accounting." *Accounting Review* (July 1976): 516-528.
Ronen, J. "Accounting for Social Costs and Benefits," pp. 317-342. In J. J. Cramer, Jr., and G. H. Sorter, eds., *Objectives of Financial Statements*. N.Y.: American Institute of Certified Public Accountants, May 1974.
Sawin, Henry S. "The CPA's Role in Restoring the Ecological Balance." *Management Advisor* (March-April 1971): 23-29.
Shulman, James S., and Jeffrey Gale. "Laying the Groundwork for Social Accounting." *Financial Executive* (March 1972): 38-52.

EVALUATING SOCIAL PROGRAMS: COST-BENEFIT ANALYSIS
Anderson, Lee G., and Russel F. Settle. *Benefit-Cost Analysis: A Practical Guide*. Lexinton, Mass.: Heath, 1977.
Bailey, Duncan, and Charles Schotta. "Private and Social Rates of Return to the Education of Academicians." *American Economic Review* (March 1972).
Baram, Michael S. "Cost-Benefit Analysis: An Inadequate Basis for Health, Safety, and Environmental Regulatory Decision Making." *Ecology Law Quarterly* 8 (1980): 473-531.
Baumol, William J. "On the Discount Rate for Public Projects." In Robert Haveman and Julius Margolis, eds., *Public Expenditures and Policy Analysis*. Chicago: Markham, 1970.
___. "On the Social Rate of Discount." *American Economic Review* (September 1968).
Eckstein, Otto. "A Survey of the Theory of Public Expenditure Criteria." In James M. Buchanan, ed., *Public Finances: Needs, Sources and Utilization*. Princeton: Princeton University Press, 1961.
Gramlich, Edward M. *Benefit-Cost Analysis of Government Programs*. Englewood Cliffs, N.J.: Prentice-Hall, 1981.
Hanke, Steve H. "On the Feasibility of Benefit-Cost Analysis." *Public Policy* 29, no. 2 (Spring 1981): 147-157.
Kendall, M. G., ed. *Cost Benefit Analysis*. New York: American Elsevier, 1971.

McKean, R. N. *Efficiency in Government Through Systems Analysis*. New York: Wiley, 1958.
Mishan, E. J. *Cost-Benefit Analysis*. New York: Praeger, 1976.
Novick, David, ed. *Program Budgeting*. Cambridge: Harvard University Press, 1965.
Prest, A. R., and R. Turvey. "Cost-Benefit Analysis: A Survey." *Economic Journal* (December 1965): 683-735.
Sassone, Peter G., and William A. Schaefer. *Cost-Benefit Analysis: A Practical Guide*. Lexington, Mass.: Heath, 1977.
Weisbrod, Burton A. "Costs and Benefits of Medical Research: A Case Study of Poliomyelitis." *Journal of Political Economy* (May-June 1971): 527-544.

EVALUATING SOCIAL PROGRAMS: COST-EFFECTIVENESS ANALYSIS
Committee on Accounting for Not-For-Profit Organizations. "Report of the Committee." *Accounting Review*, supplement, 46 (1971): 81-164.
Committee on Measure of Effectiveness of Social Programs. "Report of the Committee." *Accounting Review*, supplement, 47 (1972): 337-398.
Committee on Nonfinancial Measures of Effectiveness. "Report of the Committee." *Accounting Review*, supplement 46 (1971): 165-212.
Committee on Not-for-Profit Organizations, 1972-73. "Report of the Committee." *Accounting Review*, supplement, 49 (1974): 225-249.
Goldman, Thomas A. *Cost-Effectiveness Analysis*. New York: Praeger, 1967.
Heuston, M. C., and G. Ogawa. "Observations on the Theoretical Basis of Cost Effectiveness." *Operations Research* (March-April 1966): 242-266.
King, Barry G. "Cost-Effectiveness Analysis: Implications for Accountants." *Journal of Accounting* (May 1970).
Singer, Neil M. *Public Microeconomics*. Boston: Little, Brown, 1976.
Sorenson, James E., and Hugh D. Grove. "Cost-Outcome and Cost-Effectiveness Analysis: Emerging Nonprofit Performance Evaluation Techniques." *Accounting Review* (July 1977): 658-675.

MEASUREMENT IN MICRO SOCIAL ACCOUNTING
Barr, James L., and Otto A. Davis. "An Elementary Political and Economic Theory of the Expenditures of Local Government." *Southern Economic Journal* 33 (October 1966): 149-165.
Bergstrom, T. C., and R. P. Goodman. "Private Demands for Public Goods." *American Economic Review* 63 (June 1973): 280-296.
Bohn, Peter. "An Approach to the Problem of Estimating Demand for Public Goods." *Swedish Journal of Economics* 1 (March 1971): 94-105.
Borcherding, T. E., and R. T. Deacon, " The Demand for Services of Nonfederal Governments." *American Economic Review* 67 (December 1972): 891-901.
Bowen, H. R. "The Interpretation of Voting in the Allocation of Economic Resources." *Quarterly Journal of Economics* 58 (1963): 27-48.
Clawson, M., and J. L. Knetsch. *Economics of Outdoor Recreation*. Baltimore: Johns Hopkins University Press, 1971.
Feenberg, D., and E. S. Mills. *Measuring the Benefits of Water Pollution Abatement*. New York: Academic Press, 1980.

Freeman, A. Myrick, III. *The Benefits of Environmental Improvement: Theory and Practice.* Baltimore: Johns Hopkins University Press, 1979.
___. "On Estimating Air Pollution Control Benefits from Land Value Studies." *Journal of Environmental Economics and Management* 1 (May 1974): 74-83.
Hause, John C. "The Theory of Welfare Cost Measurement." *Journal of Political Economy* 6 (December 1975): 1145-1182.
Kapp, K. William. *Social Costs of Business Enterprise.* New York: Asia Publishing House, 1963.
Kneese, Allen V., Robert U. Ayres, and Ralph C. d'Arge. *Economics and the Environment: A Materials Balance Approach.* Baltimore: Johns Hopkins University Press, 1970.
Kurtz, M. "An Experimental Approach to the Determination of the Demand for Public Goods." *Journal of Public Economics* 3 (1974): 329-48.
Organization for Economic Co-Operation and Development. *Economics Implications of Pollution Control.* Paris: OECD, 1974.
___. *Economic Measurement of Environmental Damage.* Paris: OECD, 1976.
___. *Environmental Damage Costs.* Paris: OECD, 1974.
Plowden, P. *The Cost of Noise.* London: Metra Consulting Group, 1970.
Ridker, R. G. *Economic Costs of Air Pollution.* New York: Praeger, 1967.

8
MACRO SOCIAL ECONOMICS

Social accounting has been appropriately defined as representing "the application of accounting concepts and standards to the collection, complication, and presentation of aggregate data for a national economy."[1] In our context the scope is that part of social accounting interested in the evaluation, measurement, and disclosure of the social performance of nations, i. e., national social performance. Micro social accounting, as presented in Chapters 6 and 7, is more oriented toward the evaluation, measurement, and disclosure of the social performance of firms. Social accounting has taken over main routes toward this evaluation, measurement, and disclosure of national social performance. The routes are the social indicators movement, the refinement efforts in national income accounting, and the increasing role of accounting in achieving economic development. This chapter will examine each of these routes.

Social Indicators

Social indicators constitute one of the routes chosen in macro social accounting toward the evaluation, measurement, and disclosure of national social performance. The approach consists in focusing on a number of social issues to which "measures" are assigned to depict the extent of improvement in these issues. The approach has generated a rich literature on an international scale aimed at producing, testing, and refining an array of "social indicators" on all possible issues of interest to a particular society, nation or government.

Social indicators have been described as mere statistics that reflect the human condition and that may be helpful to plan for social change. They go beyond economic indicators with their greater orientation toward the needs and goals within the full range of human social activities and a greater emphasis on all the social concerns, processes, and systems deemed essential for an adequate living standard and quality of life. They are essential to an assessment of the state and changing conditions of society, a discovery of the potential and actual social problems, and an evaluation of the effects of social policies and programs. As such they are a basic component of a macro social accounting aimed at measurement, evaluation, and monitoring of social performance of macro economic units, from cities to entire governments. In what follows the origins of the social indicator movement, the nature of social indicators, the construction of social indicators, the actors involved in the production of social indicators, the research approaches and functions of social indicators, and examples of social indicators are examined.

ORIGIN OF THE SOCIAL INDICATOR MOVEMENT

For good reason, the origins of the movement for the production and use of social indicators are generally traced back to biblical times. Concern with social justice and the application of new statistical techniques spurred the social indicators movement. The movement truly emerged, however, in 1966, when the National Aeronautic and Space Administration became concerned with the social effects of its space exploration program and R. A. Bauer and his colleagues examined the need to anticipate the consequences of rapid technological change through a comprehensive system of what they called social indicators.[2] This was follows by the publication of *Toward a Social Report* and Senator W. Mondale's Full Opportunity and Social Accounting Act of 1967.[3] From there the social indicator movement found followers in many nations and international organizations and established itself as a legitimate research field of relative independence in the social sciences. This effort is evident in the surge of assessments and bibliographical publications,[4] a special newsletter (*Social Indicators Newsletter*) and a specialized journal (*Social Indicators Research*).

NATURE OF SOCIAL INDICATORS

There is no agreed definition of social indicators. Various definition are provided in the literature.

Social indicators are "quantitative data that serve as indices to socially important conditions of society."[5]

Social indicators are "statistics, statistical services, and all other forms of evidence that enable us to assess where we stand and are going with respect to our values and goals, and to evaluate specific programs and determine their impact."[6]

Social indicators are "statistics which measure social conditions and changes there-in over time for various segments of the population. By social conditions, we mean both the external (social and physical) and the internal (subjective and perceptional) context of human existence in a given society."[7]

"Social indicators and social statistics are facts about society in a quantitative form. But social indicators involve not only quantitative measurement of an aspect of the social but also its interpretation in relation to some norm against which statistic represents advance or retrogression."[8]

The first common characteristic of these definitions is their reference to the functions of the social indicators, which are essentially to measure social changes and conditions. The second common characteristic of these definitions is their reference to the nature of the social indicator as a kind of statistic. *From these two characteristics we may summarize the nature of social indicators as generally quantative constructs designed to monitor, measure, and/or report social conditions and changes.*

Following a social indicator model introduced and elaborated by Land, these constructs may be categorized in one of several types of social indicators:[9]

1. *Policy instruments descriptive indicators:* These are exogenous descriptive variables that are maniplable by social policy. By exogeneous it is meant that they are outside the social system model, a system of relationships connecting all variables and containing analytical indicators.
2. *Nonmanipulable descriptive indicators:* These are exogenous descriptive variables that are not manipulable by social policy.
3. *Output or end product descriptive indicators:* These are endogenous descriptive variables that define the social conditions being measured and are the consequences of the social processes embodied within the model.
4. *Side-effect descriptive indicators:* These are endogenous descriptive variables that influence or are influenced by, but do not define, the social conditions and social processes under consideration.

Land emphasizes also that the relationship between these indicators is more of an ideal rather than an actual description of the state of social indicators research.[10]

Social indicators as quantitative constructs generally meet some qualitative characteristics as well:

1. Social indicators are generally normative, in the sense that any move in a particular direction may be interpreted as either good or bad.
2. Social indicators generally relate to outputs rather than inputs of social programs.
3. Social indicators are generally comprehensive and aggregate measures.
4. Social indicators should be genuinely "indicative" of something in the sense that they should relate to economic theories and fit into models, whether explanatory or predictive.[11]
5. Social indicators relate to subjects for which problems of measurement are not impossible to handle.
6. Social indicators should tap questions of importance to the general public and related to shared goals. "Good health, better education, lower crimes rates, improved streets and lighting, and less traffic congestion are goals over which there would be reasonably limited disagreement, even though questions of relative priority inevitably persist."[12]
7. Social indicators are best showing the direct and indirect effects of alternative policies when they are integrated into a model. This last characteristic argues for analytical as opposed to descriptive indicators. This view is also supported as follows:

In summary, development of a social indicator science requires that concentration be on explanatory, not descriptive, models of social subsystems and attendant indicators. These models should leave operationalized concepts and casual relationships expressed in proportions which will be empirically tested to establish whether linkages exist between indicators and other unobservable variables.[13]

CONSTRUCTION OF SOCIAL INDICATORS

The construction of social indicators ought to rely on a theoretical or formal approach to be able to provide power and precision in its measurement. This approach ought to be deductive, going from the abstract and general to the simple and particular. Such a model has been proposed by Carley[14] and includes the following steps: "development and statement of a theoretical proposition; formulation of an explicit casual model in words and/or some type of diagram, for example, a path diagram; operationalization, that is, the statement in measurable terms of the postulated relationships between social indicators and empirically defined variables, for example, in a system of equations; testing, and perhaps retesting, of the model."[15]

This model allows, for one thing, for the continued development and improvement of social indicators and social theory. Each of the steps requires clear and rigorous thinking including a precise statement of the theoretical proposition, a carefully defined casual model of the various social relationships underlying the concept being measured, a translation of the relationships into operational and empirically testable forms, and a continuous testing of the model. The "operationalization" step rests on making various computational or procedural choices as follows:

1. The construction and interpretation of social indicators generally follows accepted statistical standards.
2. The fact that most indicators may behave in linear or curvilinear forms does not preclude that some indicators may not always fit a well-behaved trend.
3. Ordinal measurement generally used for social indicators requires setting standards of adequacy and around that grade of inadequacy and abundance.
4. When percentage and index numbers are used to screen social indicators, the choice of the base period is important given the way it may affect the interpretation of the social indicators.
5. Indicators may be either open-ended in growth, such as population, or related to a maximum, such as mortality.
6. Indicators may be either "objective" indicators based on numerical counts of people, money, and things or "subjective" indicators based on the appraisal of interviewed persons.
7. Indicators may be constructed for al types of goods: free goods, public goods, consumer goods, and/or capital goods.
8. The difficulties with finding indicator units and valuation of intangibles applies also to social indicators.
9. International comparison of indicators may be hampered by the calculation of purchasing power parties that may justify the use of nonmonetary indicators of production and consumption.
10. Social indicators are the result of aggregation of a mass of information into a single or several series.
11. Social indicators should be empirically correlated into the constituent variables of a social concern they are supposed to measure.
12. Social indicators may be based on either implicit weighing through selection and scaling or explicit weighing.[16]

ACTORS IN THE PRODUCTION OF SOCIAL INDICATORS

Various actors are involved in the production of social indicators, including supranational and national agencies, scientific institutions, and individuals.

Of the supranational agencies, the United Nations, the Organization for Economic Co-Operation and Development, the European Community, and the Council for Mutual Economic Assistance are very much involved in the production of social indicators. For example, the UN interest started with attempts to define and measure standards and levels of living,[17] before moving to developing a socio-economic system including a data base and procedures for determining indicators and finally extending the system into a system of demographic and social statistics (SDSS).[18] The SDSS system used principles of economic bookkeeping to suppress the socio-economic state of the population and its change over time as a set of demographic accounts in the form of an input-output matrix. The data pertain mainly to demographic structure, housing, public order, use of time, and social mobility. The most interesting development in the construction of social indicators is achieved by the OECD and will be reviewed later in this chapter.

National agencies in various countries are continuously developing national compendias of social indicators and social reports. A list of national compendia of social indicators and social reports is shown in Exhibit. 8.1.

Similarly, various scientific institutions and individual researchers are involved in social indicator research. In Sweden, two theoretical approaches have been used, one characterized by a conception of welfare based on command over resources[19] and one based on a consideration of needs.[20] This translated on a practical level in welfare or level-of-living surveys in Sweden,[21] as well as in England,[22] Norway,[23] Austria, and West Germany.

RESEARCH APPROACHES AND FUNCTIONS OF INDICATORS

The term *social indicator* is not associated with a single specific research proposal. The number of approaches for systems of social indicators is on the rise. Most of them attempt to operationalize and measure the components of a multidimensional conception of welfare. Examples include the development of a net national welfare index by the Economic Council of Japan, which measures the annual value of the total economic production available for final consumption,[24] the development of a level-of-living index, or index of measureable welfare, in natural units of goods and services by Jan Drewnovsky,[25] the development of a social indicators battery by J. Q. Wilson for the purpose of ascertaining differences in the quality of life in the United States,[26] the attempt by Nestor E. Terleckyj to calculate the improvements in the quality of life with thirty-one selected programs in relation to twenty-one national goals and relying on a large-scale input-output maxtrix,[27] the development at the UN of a system of social and demographic statistics to encourage the national statistical bodies to systematize their entire social statistics in the direction of an integrated system of "stocks" and "flows,"[28] and the development by Erik Allardt of a welfare model of national development based on the theory of social systems, the theory of social structure, and the theory of needs.[29] These are only examples and are far from exhaustive of all the approaches to social indicator research. It is generally accepted to classify this research into three distinct approaches: those concerned with measuring the quality of life and welfare; those concerned with monitoring social change and socio-economic development; and those concerned with forecasting social events and evaluation research.[30]

In fact, these three areas follow the main aspects of social reporting, namely, welfare measurement, observation of a social change, prognosis of a social change without intervention, social policy planning to steer society in desired direction, and monitoring of planning performance.[31] V. H. Horn used this sequence to specify the most exhaustive list of the different functions of social indicators as follows:

EXHIBIT 8.1: LIST OF NATIONAL COMPENDIA OF SOCIAL
INDICATORS AND SOCIAL REPORTS

Country	Title, Date	Editor
Australia	Social Indicators; 1976, 1978	Australian Bureau of Statistics
Austria	Indikatoren zur gesellschaftlichen Entwicklung; 1976	Österreichisches Statistisches Zentralamt
	Soziale Ungleichheit in Österreich; 1979	
Brazil	Indicadores sociais para areas urbanas; 1977	Departamento e Indicatores Sociais
	Relatorio des indicadores sociais; 1979	
Canada	Perspective Canada; 1974, 1977	Statistics Canada
Colombia	Compendio de Indicadores Sociales; 1977	Departemente Administrative National de Estadistica
Denmark	Levevilkar i Danmark; 1976, 1979	Danmarks Statistik and Socialforskningsinstitutet
Fiji	Social Indicators for Fiji; annually since 1973	Bureau of Statistics
Finland	Levnadsforhallanden: 1950-1975; 1977	Statistikcentralen
France	Données sociales; 1973, annually since	Institut National de la Statistique et des Etudes Economiques (INSEE)
Germany (Fed.Rep.)	Gesellschaftliche Daten; 1973, 1977	Bundesministerium für Arbeit und Sozialordnung
	Basisdaten; 1974	Verlag Neue Gesellschaft GmbH
	Soziologischer Almanach; 1975, 1979	Sozialpolitische Forschergruppe Frankfurt/Mannheim (SPES-Projekt)
	Lebensbedingungen in der Bundesrepublik; 1977	
India	Social and Economic Indicators; (in preparation)	Central Statistical Organization
Indonesia	Social Indicators; annually since 1971	Central Bureau of Statistics
Israel	Society in Israel: Selected Statistics; 1976	Central Bureau of Statistics
Italy	Statistiche Sociali; 1975	Instituto Centrale die Statistica
Japan	Whitepaper of National Life: 1973 (1975)	Economic Planning Agency
Kenya	Social Perspectives; 1976	Central Bureau of Statistics
Malaysia	Socio-economic indicators and National Policy: Malaysia; 1974	Department of Statistics
Netherlands	Social and Cultural Report; 1974 1976, 1978	Sociaal en Cultureel Planbureau
New Zealand	Social Trends in New Zealand; 1977	Department of Statistics
Norway	Sosialt Utsyn; 1974, 1977	Statistisk Sentralbyra

EXHIBIT 8.1 (continued)

Panama	Indicadores Economicos y Sociales; 1970	Direción de Estadistica Censo
Philippines	Measuring the Quality of Life: Philippine Social Indicators; 1974	Development Academy of the Philippines
Spain	Espana Panoramica Social; 1974	Instituto National des Estadistica
Sweden	Levnadsföhållanden Arsbok; 1975	Statistiska Centralbyran
Switzerland	Almanach der Schweiz; 1978	Soziologisches Institut der Universität Zürich
Trinidad u. Tobago	Social Indicators; 1975	Central Statistical Office
United Kingdom	Social Trends: annually since 1970	Central Statistical Office
United States	Social Indicators; 1973, 1977	Office of Management and Budget

SOURCE: W. Glatzer, "An Overview of the International Development in Macro-Social Indicators," *Accounting, Organizations and Society* (September 1981): 129. Reprinted with permission.

SOCIAL PROCESS	FUNCTIONS OF SOCIAL INDICATORS
Assessment of welfare elements	Cognition
Observation of welfare trends	Analysis
Clarification of societal interaction	Conceptualization
Prognosis of trend without intervention	Projections
Formulation of social policy alternatives, including priority-rating and trade-offs	Operationalization, direction
Social Policy decision	Classification and targeting
Audit of planning progress	Monitoring
Review of plan performance	Retrospective analysis

Each of these functions constitute a legitimate avenue in social indicator research.[32]

THE OECED LIST OF SOCIAL INDICATORS

The OECD list of social indicators was intended to measure and report changes in the relative importance of the social demands, aspirations, and problems that are, or could become in the decade ahead, major concerns of the socio-economic planning process. They are to be viewed as an initial framework subject to any improvements to be brought by member countries. Seven major criteria were used in the final selection of social indicators. The social indicators should:

(a) Be output-oriented or designed to describe a final social outcome, leaving to other statistics the quantification of inputs, through puts or intermediate outputs;
(b) Be relevant to policy- i.e., descriptive of prevailing social conditions which are potentially amenable to improvement through collective actions or public policy;
(c) Be applicable over a long period of time in a substantial number of member countries. Actual values of the indicators may of course differ widely over time and access the whole OECD area;
(d) Apply to conditions of individual well-being, excluding a number of "indivisible public goods," however desirable these are as an aspect of welfare;
(e) Be independent of particular institutional arrangements, so as to be reasonably comparable between countries and over time;
(f) Form part of a comprehensive grid portraying all areas of social concerns;
(g) Correspond closely to the social concern to which they relate, yet be more than a narrow description of social phenomena;
(h) Form an integrated framework of definitions, specifications, statistical guidelines, and disaggregations which should be compatible with other important sets of social and demographic statistics.[33]

Based on these criteria a tentative list of eight social concerns and thirty-three indicators was developed. Exhibit 8.2 supplies the list of social concerns and indicators. The indicators present systematically selected statistical measures of individual well-being that can be influenced by social policies and community actions.[34] To give meaningful basic information on the level of individual well-being, some disaggregations are presented as suggestions. The purposes of disaggregation relates to normative considerations, explanatory requirements, and program monitoring and evaluation.[35] Examples of standard disaggregations include age, sex, household type, socio-economic status, community size, ethnic group, citizenship, region, branch of economic activity, occupation, type of activity, working hours, level of education, tenure status, and/or age of dwelling.

EXHIBIT 8.2: THE OECD LIST OF SOCIAL INDICATORS

SOCIAL CONCERN	INDICATOR
Health	
Length of life	Life expectancy
	Perinatal mortality rate
Healthfulness of life	Short-term disability
	Long-term disability
Education and Learning	
Use of educational facilities	Regular education experience
	Adult education
Learning	Literacy rate
Employment and Quality of Working Life	
Availability of employment	Unemployment rate
	Involuntary part-time work
	Discouraged workers

EXHIBIT 8.2 (continued)

SOCIAL CONCERN	INDICATOR
Quality of working life	Average working hours
	Travel time to work
	Paid annual leave
	Atypical work schedule
	Distribution of earnings
	Fatal occupational injuries
	Work environment nuisances
Time and Leisure	
Use of time	Free time
	Free time activities
Command Over Goods and Services	
Income	Distribution of income
	Low income
	Material deprivation
Wealth	Distribution of wealth
Physical Environment	
Housing conditions	Indoor dwelling space
	Access to outdoor space
	Basic amenities
Accessibility to services	Proximity of selected services
Environmental nuisances	Exposure to air pollutants
	Exposure to noise
Social Environment	
Social attachment	Suicide rate
Personal Safety	
Exposure to risk	Fatal injuries
	Serious injuries
Perceived threat	Fear for personal safety

SOURCE: Organization for Economic Co-Operation and Development, *The OECD List of Social Indicators* (Paris: OECD, 1982), p. 13. Reprinted with permission.

National Income Accounting

National income accounting toward the evaluation, measurement, and disclosure of national performance. The first approach taken in national income accounting was to rely on a system of national accounts to measure macro economic indicators such as the gross national product. Given the limitations and narrow scope of the GNP, the second approach aims to providing a better measure of social well-being.

National income accounting is the set of rules and techniques for measuring the total flow of output (parts and services) produced and the total flow of inputs (factors of production) used by the economy. It relies on a system of national accounts to measure macro economic indicators such as the gross national product (GNP). Basically, the statement produced is similar to the conventional income statement for a profit-oriented firm. One side of the report shows the total value of the nation's output, classified in terms of its distribution to the four major sectors of the national economy. The other side details the changes against the aggregate national output and includes, therefore, the income accruing to the various factors of production (wages, rent, interest, and profits). The four sectors of the economy considered by the national accounting system are business, consumers (or households), government, and the rest of the world. The aggregate data from each of these sectors are consolidated in order to provide the data for both the national income and product account. The following rules are important to an understanding of the results of national income accounting:

1. The government outputs are valued at the cost of the input needed to produce them.
2. Inventories are treated as if they were "purchased" by the firms producing them.
3. A firm's output is defined to be its value added, that is to say, the value of output minus the value of the inputs it purchased from other firms.
4. Finally, current market prices are used in measuring the value of the economic output.

CONVENTIONALLY MEASURED GNP

As stated earlier, the value of the output of the economy can be measured either as the sum of the values of the final products or as the sum of the payments to the various factors of production. In either case the value of the output of the national economy is best exemplified and known as the GNP of the nation. As conventionally known, the GNP is the sum of the values of all final goods and services produced in a specific period of time (usually a year) and valued at current market prices.

Two ways have been devised for the measurement of the GNP. The first method measured the GNP as the sum of all final goods and services:

$$GNP = C + I + G + EX - IM$$

Where
C = sales of goods and services to consumers;
I = gross sales of products to business for final use of producers' (capital) goods, including inventory changes;
G = sales of goods and services to government;
EX = exports;
IM = imports.

Exhibit 8.3 shows the GNP as the sum of final demands. The second method measures the GNP as the sum of all factor payments, in other words, as the sum of all the incomes in the economy:

EXHIBIT 8.3: GNP IN 1981 AS THE SUM OF FINAL DEMANDS

ITEM	AMOUNT (billions of dollars)	
Personal consumption expenditures	1,858.1	
Gross private domestic investment	450.6	
Government purchases of goods and services	589.6	
Net exports	23.8	
Exports		366.7
Imports		342.9
GNP	2,922.2	

SOURCE: U.S. Department of Commerce

$$GNP = W + R + I + P + T + X + D$$

Where
W = wages;
R = rental income of persons;
I = net interest paid to households;
P = profits;
T = indirect business taxes;
X = business transfer payments;
D = depreciation or capital consumption.

Exhibit 8.4 shows the GNP as the sum of incomes. Through some recombinations, some other useful macro-economic measurements may be derived as follows:

Net National Product	= GNP − Depreciation
National Income	= W + R + I + P
Personal Income	= National Income − (Corporate Profit Taxes + Retained Earnings + Payroll Taxes) + Transfer Payments.
Disposable Personal Income	= Personal Income − Personal Taxes.

Both methods of measurement constitute the parts of a dualistic system intended to measure the output of a nation. Both, however, suffer from some limitations as follows. First of all, the GNP includes only market activity and does not include nonmarket activities are not conducted in organized markets. Secondly, the GNP does not include illegal activities; even though some of those activities produce goods and services, few are sold on the market generating factor incomes. In addition, the GNP does not include illegal activities; even though some of those activities produce goods and services, few are sold on the market generating factor incomes. In addition, the GNP does not include factors affecting human welfare. For example, leisure is not included, although it is important for well-being. In brief, the GNP is not a measure of well-being. Also, the GNP includes good as well as bad activities. For example, the outlays necessary to correct the effect of a disaster may cause the GNP to rise. Finally, most of the undesirable effects of economic activities are not deducted from the GNP to give a better measure of the net increase in economic welfare.

TOWARD A BETTER MEASURE OF GNP

As stated earlier, the GNP is a measure of the nation's annual production of goods and services. It fails, however, to measure adequately social well-being. Accordingly, various attempts have been made to modify conventionally measured GNP to obtain a better measure of social well-being. First, Nordhaus and Tobin developed a measure of economic welfare as a result of a rearrangement of items in the national accounts and addition of items not covered in the GNP computations; household work, leisure, and the services consumers derive from the durable goods such as auto, boats, and appliances.[36] A correction is also made for the "disamenities of urbanization," which include "litter, congestion, noise, insecurity, large buildings, and advertisements offensive to taste."

EXHIBIT 8.4: GNP IN 1981 AS THE SUM OF INCOMES

ITEM	AMOUNT (billions of dollars)	
Compensation of employees (wages)		1,771.7
Net interest		215.0
Rental income		33.6
Profit		323.4
Corporate profits	189.0	
Proprietors' income	134.4	
National income		2,343.7
Indirect business taxes and miscellaneous items		257.0
Net national product		2,600.0
Depreciation		321.5
GNP		2,922.2

SOURCE: U.S. Department of Commerce

Second, as stated earlier in the social indicators section, the Economic Council of Japan has developed a net national welfare (NNW) measure to account for the impact on the environment.[37] As in Nordhaus and Tobin, the NNW is a rearrangement of national accounts items, added to imputations for the services of government capital, consumer durables, leisure, and other nonmarket activities, and corrected for "urbanization" and "environmental maintenance costs," that is, the costs of operating and maintaining pollution control equipment plus the annualized capital costs of purchasing it.

Other attempts were made to provide a framework of modifying the traditional account structure in order to measure, the environmental changes. First, Olson suggested that the GNP be reduced by an amount equal to the social damage from pollution.[38] Second, Herfindahl and Kneese suggested that a surrogate for the social damage from pollution is the pollution control expenditures and as such they should be deducted to reduce the GNP.[39] Third, Marin also concluded that if we want national income to conform more closely to theoretical concepts of welfare indices, then we need to include a proxy for the environmental services that would not be completely free goods if it were possible to overcome their inherent non-marketability.[40] The least unsatisfactory proxy considered for Marin would be the spending on environmental protection. Finally, Peskin, building on earlier work,[41] suggested a procedure for modifying the conventional income and product accounts so that they can capture certain features of the environment that are presently ignored.[42] It is based on a framework that views the environment as a separate sector subject to both "environmental services" and "environmental damages." As a result, two entries are required to account for these services and damages into a national accounting structure:

One will describe the productive services the environment provides to business and other consumers of environmental services. This will be entered on the lefthand side of the business accounts and the consolidated national account, along with the other productive inputs. A second entry will describe any loss of environmental services or damage to consumers resulting from the use of the environment by business and other sectors. Since this damage can be viewed as a "bad" produced by the business (as opposed to a "good"), it will be entered negatively on the righthand side of the business accounts and the consolidated national account, along with the other components of output. Since, in general, these two entries will not be equal, a balancing entry will be required if accounting balance is to be maintained.[43]

Pesking has shown that the modified GNP can be defined alternatively as conventional GNP less damages, conventional GNP plus environmental services, and conventional GNP plus net environmental benefit. Efforts to design and implement this modified accounting framework are underway.[44]

OTHER POSSIBLE IMPROVEMENTS IN NATIONAL INCOME ACCOUNTING

More and more economists are arguing that the government should keep its books like a business. As a first step the government should adopt a complete balance sheet and income statement that would separate its long-term investment in physical assets from its operating expenses, adjust its assets and debts for inflation, and clarify the way it records nontax revenues and outlays. In addition the government should add a capital account to the government budget that would separate long-term investments from operating squares.

The complete balance sheet would require a detailed inventory of the nation's land and mineral holdings as well as a list of the condition and expected life span of buildings and a complete record of its finances and investments. These assets and liabilities should be adjusted for inflation to reflect the real net worth of the nation.

Accounting and Economic Development
The increasing role of accounting in economic development and social planning constitutes the third route in macro social accounting toward the evaluation, measurement, and disclosure of national social performance. The problem of economic development is central of all economies in general and particularly important to the developing economies. Because all approaches to economic development rest on some form of development planning and adequate supply of relevant information, accounting is bound to play a vital role in economic development. In what follows the developing economies, the barriers and impediments to economic development, the approaches to development, the role of accounting in economic development, and the elements influencing the development of accounting are examined.

THE DEVELOPING ECONOMIES
The developing economies form a third element in a world power structure dominated by the technologically more advanced nations of the Atlantic bloc and the European Communist bloc. This third element has been seen for a long time as the "commonwealth of poverty," in spite of its niche and complex cultures, its immense human resources, and its possession of much of the world's metallic minerals, water power, oil and coal, timbers, and potential cropland. It is also seen as a universe of radical scarcity: "The Third World is a universe of radical scarcity. Defining and determining every dimension of men's relationships to each other. . . the inadequacy of the means of livelihood is the first and distinguishing truth of this area."[45]

In effect, for much of the Third World real GNP per capita is under $200, the daily intake of calories is under 2,200, and the daily intake of animal protein is under 15 grams. Added to this poverty is a legacy of warped economics facing continuous environmental difficulties-poor soils, erratic climates, floods and droughts, and diseases. This is particularly serious given that the economics of the Third World are plagued by two distortions: a grossly inflated agricultural sector and an overexpanding tertiary sector. In general, these countries are characterized by low per capita real income, limited stock of capital goods, dominance of subsistence agriculture, and relatively low levels of education and wealth. The rate of economic growth in these economies appears to be dependent on the rate of capital formation, the incremental capital output ratio, technological change, the growth of the labor force, and a favorable social and political environment.

To escape from this vicious cycle of underdevelopment, the Third World countries have begun searching for a new economic and social identity. In fact, since acquiring their independence, most developing economies have begun a major effort to improve their economic situations. Economic development is now the primary goal in the developing economies. It is understood to include both economic growth and social and institutional changes. The strategies adopted to spur economic development in the developing economies have been either of the kind putting a primacy on economic growth or of the kind emphasizing socio-economic development.

BARRIERS AND IMPEDIMENTS TO ECONOMIC DEVELOPMENT
There seems to be a consensus on the factors contributing to the economic problems of the developing countries, which include rapid population growth, resource limitations, and inefficiency in resource use.

Rapid population growth is an important concern for the developing countries. The growth in population has been further stimulated by improvements in health care and the radification of major epidemic diseases. The improvement in health care has averted the doom predictions, known as the iron law of population growth, as envisioned by Malthus. Population growth remains serious, however, leading economists to talk about the "critical minimum effort" needed to increase capital quickly enough so that the increase in output exceeds the increase in population.

With respect to resources limitations, economic development must rest on an adequate presence of financial and physical capital, social-overhead capital, and human capital. Physical capital in terms of natural resources endowment is important for economic development, but its presence has never been an absolute precondition for economic growth. It needs to be complemented with an adequate supply of financial, social-overhead, and human capital.

Financial capital plays a vital role in economic development by spurring investment. It may be generated internally through the savings of households and firms if a healthy banking climate is maintained in the country. In most cases, the developing countries have to rely on external funding of their major projects.

The social-overhead capital of a country is also known as the infrastructure of the economy. It is composed of the system of supporting services, such as transportation and communications, necessary to an efficient conduct of the economy. Consequently, a dependable social-overhead capital is vital to the economic development of the developing countries. A precondition to economic development is a high-quality system of education, training, and health.

The developing countries are also plagued by an inefficient use of resources, both in terms of allocative efficiency and X-efficiency. Allocative efficiency results from the use of a nation's resource to make the wrong products. X-efficiency, to use a term introduced by Professor Harvey Liebenstein,[46] arises wherever resources are sued poorly even in making the right product. The source of X-efficiency may be inadequate education, poor health, traditions, institutions, habitual ways of producing, custom, or cultural attitudes. The presence of X-efficiency in the developing countries is evident in the enormous differences in productivity from country to country in particular industries using the same technology.

It is generally believed that entrepreneurship is a vital ingredient for economic development. The lack of entrepreneurship in most developing countries is generally seen as one of major ingredients to a maintained economic growth. Entrepreneurship is "a combination of the following attributes: imagination, daring, willingness to take risks, a sense of timing, and an ability to recognize profitable opportunities, all driven by a love of money, power, or some other such goal, which together combine to make up the quality of business leadership."[47] Besides the lack of entrepreneurship, the lack of political stability and of political freedom and civil liberties may act as a major barrier to economic growth. Instability may discourage local and foreign direct investment because of the constant fear of nationalization, harassment, and a poor business climate.

Approaches to Development

Two major approaches have been applied to development in the developing countries.[48] The first strategy aimed at a high push to be achieved by a high rate of growth and industrialization leading to a high rate of growth in per capita income. This view was reinforced by the works of Harrod and Domar, which transformed development into a process of growth resting on a few quantifiable variables,[49] and by Rostow's theory of stages of economic growth and the idea of a take-off.[50] The process of economic development consisted of transforming the underdeveloped societies from an ascriptive, particularistic, and functionally diffuse pattern to a pattern characterized by achievement, universalism, and functional specificity.[51] As stated by Islam and Henault, an "underdeveloped society thus suffers from a lack of social and geographic mobility, a lack of division of labor, emphasizes status rather than achievement, and consequently leads to low productivity."[52] This first strategy called for a direct involvement of the government in achieving industrialization and urbanization and in maintaining a high rate of sustained economic growth through the "planning" process.

Planning is seen as the essential ingredient of any development policy. At the micro level, the "technology gap" was to be reduced by a transfer of relevant techniques and procedures taken from the Western countries. All the projects were to be conducted systematically using "development administration" as a way of designing, implementing, and evaluating policies and programs leading to socio-economic changes. It relied on what is known in UN technical assistance circles as MMT (modern management technology), which refers to techniques such as linear programming, CPM, PERT, Quering theory, long-range planning and forecasting network analysis, modeling, and cost-benefit analysis. The total impact of this first strategy is far from perfect. For example, Islam and Henault state:

In our opinion, the net overall result of this gigantic effort of international and foreign-aid giving agencies in the area of administrative development was over-bureaucratization, excessive controls and regulation of the economy, proliferation of bureaucratic structures, increase in the size of bureaucracies, and excessive concentration of power in the hands of the administrative elites. The impact of these factors on development at best remains questionable. In fact, the balance may tip toward the negative rather than the positive side.[53]

The second strategy is usually traced back to the institutional school of Ayres, Veblen, and Myrdal, with their emphasis on the social and institutional preconditions for progress. Here the growth models of the first strategy were replaced by a new ideology of development. The main elements of this new ideology are supposed to include need orientation, endogenous, self-reliant, ecologically sound motives and be based on agricultural transformation.[54] The approach moves from a largely economic perspective to a wider, all encompassing, socio-economic one aimed at the fulfillment of all basic needs: adequate nutrition, health, clean water, and shelter. The advocates of this second strategy are generally influenced by the center-periphery thesis in dependency theory, which holds that under-development is a function of one society's dependence on another. This explains their constant demands for a new international economic order based on both a global redistribution of economic surpluses and major changes in the productive relations within the periphery sector.[55] In fact, a major cause of discontent in the center-periphery thesis (also known as the North-South controversy) is the price of commodities, which the periphery countries consider to be unfairly low and unstable.

The second strategy views development in terms of the fulfillment of basic needs, which have been eloquently defined as follows:

The concept of basic needs bring to any development strategy a heightened concern with meeting the consumption needs of the whole population, particularly in the areas of education and health, but also in nutrition, housing, water supply, and sanitation. In formulating policies aimed at reducing poverty, a good deal of attention has generally been paid to restructuring the patterns of production and income so that they benefit the poor. But similar attention has not been devoted to their needs for public services.[56]

The concept of basic needs was justified by the failure of the three types of justification used for the emphasis on a country's economic growth as the principal performance indicator. First, income did not automatically trickle down to the poor; second, governments did not always take steps to reduce poverty; third, a period of inequality is not needed in the early stages of development.[57] The concept of basic needs is also perceived as a positive concept and has a broad appeal, politically and intellectually.

The performance of developing countries in meeting basic needs varies from one country to another. Frances Stewart used life expectancy as the single most significant indicator of performance on basic needs.[58] She compared achievement in life expectancy with what may have been predicted on the basis of a country's level of income per capita as a way of classifying countries' performance. Three types of economies turned out to be notably successful: the rapidly growing, market-oriented economies; the centrally planned economies; and the "misled" economy with welfare intervention. The less successful cases are evident in three categories of developing economies: the very poor economies; the economies with rapid growth but without substantial poverty reduction; and the economies with moderate growth and moderate poverty impact. It is accepted, however, that most developing countries have made some progress in meeting basic needs, such as education, basic health, nutrition, water and sanitation, and shelter.

But is it possible that policies aimed at providing the poor and neglected with basic goods and services are the cause for a sacrifice of productive investments and economic growth? Proponents of the basic needs approach argue on the basis of theoretical and empirical evidence that providing for basic needs can improve growth performance. In short, "investing in people may be a good way to both eliminate the worst aspects of poverty and to increase the growth rate of output."[59]

ROLE OF ACCOUNTING IN ECONOMIC DEVELOPMENT

Accounting functions at two levels in the economic development process: the micro level and the macro level.

At the micro level, accounting will be first helpful to corporations and micro-governmental units in the measurement, reporting, and disclosure of information in their financial position and performance. It will also be helpful in the collection and transformation of economic and social data and the dissemination of relevant data for decision making by the same micro units.

At the macro level, accounting will be first helpful to governments and nations in the measurement, reporting, and disclosure of national economic performance. It will be also helpful in the measurement of social indicators to assess the adequacy of the performance of planning in all the national areas of concern to the country, including education and health.

In short, the role of accounting in economic development goes beyond the mere measurement of economic activity at the micro and macro levels; more explicitly, to acquire socio-economic dimension, accounting is to serve in the full implementation of economic development planning by providing the relevant information for their execution. Enthoven suggests seven contributions that accounting can make to development planning:

1. Definition, classification, and valuation of transactions and stocks for all social accounts, in particular the national income and input-output accounts;
2. Assessment of, and changes in, the components of input-output data, capital coefficients, and shadow prices, the latter being the equilibrium of true factors of production;
3. A uniform and standardized system of industrial accounts that would assist in obtaining more comparable data and coefficients for different countries;
4. Up-to-date cost accounting procedures for cost-benefit calculations at various sector levels;
5. Assistance in estimating future financial results and determining how these will affect investments and the planning pattern;

6. Assistance in devising economic policies, measures, and programs; this may include help in elaborating tax or incentive provisions and other administrative policies to stimulate industrial growth;
7. Control and audit of the plan, and reporting its results.[60]

In fact, a review of the relevant international accounting literature suggests the following main roles accounting may have with regard to economic development:
1. The skills and techniques that make up accounting are essential to the development of commerce, industry, and public administration.
2. Economic development rests on successful industrialization and the efficient mobilization of capital. Accounting can help in evaluating the success of both endeavors, as stated by Seidler: "Enterprise accounting is a supplier of information, a device for increasing the efficiency of resource allocations, and a mechanism for controlling productive operations. It seems logical that these skills, normally considered to be tools of private enterprise management, should be equally useful to the management of the development process."[61]
3. Through the production of reliable and timely information, accounting is essential to the efficient functioning of a capital market necessary, a) to channel funds for development and investment, b) in the collection of taxes, and c) the efficient allocation of scarce resources.
4. Accounting information is needed by government, capital markets, and business firms in developing nations. First, government needs such information for implementing public policy, controlling, and regulating private enterprise, controlling economic cycles, analyzing expenditures for social overhead, measuring national income, constructing input-output and flow of funds systems, disseminating information, and, finally, collecting income taxes.
5. Accounting information is seen as vital to the emergence of a domestic private capital market, a domestic public capital market, and external private capital market, an external public source of capital, and a capital market consisting of funds from international agencies.
6. Accounting information is necessary to assist management in its custodial functions, operating decisions, control of subsidiaries and branches, personnel control, real income measurement, budgeting and forecasting, and special management problems.
7. Finally, economic development depends on an efficient use of a country's economic resources. It rests on development planning to guide the efficient use of these resources. It rests on development planning to guide the efficient use of these resources. To be successful, development planning should be supported by an adequate supply of information, which is one of the prerogatives of accounting. This last point is eloquently addressed by Mirghani:

Since development planning represents a system of decision making under conditions of great uncertainty, it should be supported by an information system capable of generating the types of information necessary for reducing the amount of uncertainty surrounding the economic choices that must be made. The development planning process can be likened to the resource allocation process in a microorganization. The management of any organization would attempt to select the package of alternative uses that would yield maximum benefits in view of the constraints operating in that organization's specific environment. Such an exercise would not be fruitful without an information system that would enable management to make rational choices among alternative uses.[62]

ELEMENTS INFLUENCING THE DEVELOPMENT OF ACCOUNTING

That accounting objectives, standards, policies, and techniques differ among countries is an established fact in international accounting. As a result, the comparative accounting literatures includes various attempts to classify the patterns in the world of accounting in different historical "zones of accounting influence." A general explanation for the various zones of accounting influence obtained is that the accounting objectives, standards, policies, and techniques result from the environmental factors in each country, and if "these environmental factors differ significantly between countries, then it would be expected that the major accounting concepts and practices in use in various countries also differ."[63]

Attempts have been made to identify the environmental conditions likely to affect the determination of national accounting principles.[64] In general, these attempts have assumed that cultural, social, as well as economic factors may explain the differences in accounting principles and techniques between various countries. A more general model of the elements influencing the development of accounting is shown in Exhibit 8.5. It shows reporting and disclosure adequacy of a given country as being influenced by its political, economic, and demographic environment.[65]

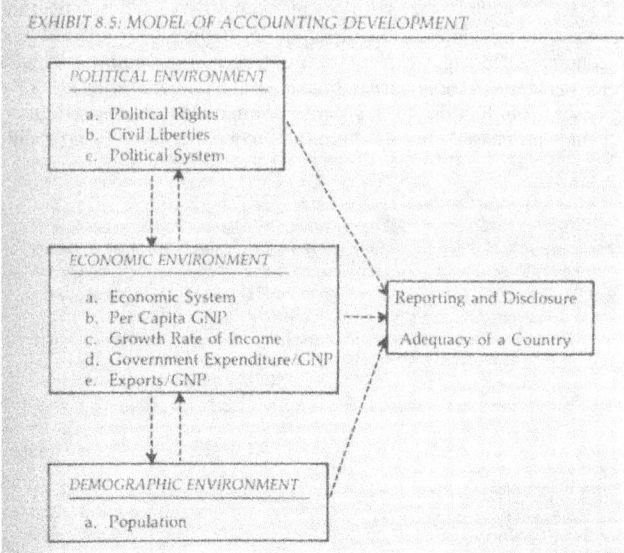

The degree of political freedom in a country is important to the development of accounting in general and reporting and disclosures in particular. When people cannot choose the members of government or influence government policies, they are less likely to be able to create an accounting profession based on the principle of full and fair disclosure. Political repression involves a general loss of freedom, which may hinder to some extent the development of the accounting profession. There is likely to be a negative relationship between accounting freedom to report and disclose and political freedom. As Exhibit 8.5 shows, the degree of political freedom in a given country is assumed to depend on the degree of political rights, civil liberties, and type of political system. Violations of political rights and civil liberties associated with various forms of political structure restrict political freedom in general and may act as a hindrance to the tradition of a full and fair disclosure.

The economic environment is also important to the development of accounting in general and reporting and disclosure in particular. Economic development consists of economic growth and various structural and social changes. One of these structural and social changes is the need for financial and reporting devices to measure the performance of each sector of the economy in terms of efficiency and productivity. H. D. Lowe notes that, from a historical point of view, accounting development is an evolutionary process dependent upon and interwoven with economic development.[66] Similarly, Elliot, Larrea and Rivera state that the "social function of accounting, to measure and to communicate economic data, cannot be considered simply as the effect of economic development, but should be considered a valuable tool for promoting the development process."[67] However, economic development may be achieved by various forms of economic policies, depending on the type of economic system chosen, the level and growth rate of income, the extent of government intervention and expenditures, and the level of exports. Each of these factors may imply a specific impact on accounting development.

Ceteris paribus, a capitalist system may be more favorable to accounting development than other economic systems. In a capitalist economic system the survival of private enterprises depends not only on the production of goods and services but adequate information to various interest groups from investors and creditors to the capital market in general. In a similar vein, Quereshi draws attention to the relationship among financial accounting, capital formation, and economic development:

The choice is based on the idea that financial reporting, capital markets, and capital formation interrelate. Capital formation, a strategic formation in economic development, is closely dependent upon financial mechanisms and institutions. Studies by such eminent monetarists such as Kuznets, Goldsmith, and McKinnon provide a convincing evidence of the parallel between the development of capital markets and economic growth. The development and proper functioning of capital markets in turn is intimately related to the availability of financial information which is provided by the accounting function of reporting.[68]

In addition, the higher the level and growth of income, the higher the political and economic freedom, and as suggested in the preceding arguments, the better the adequacy of reporting and disclosure. This may apply to any economic system, since economic growth in some socialist countries has often been followed by an effort to liberalize the regimes.

Furthermore, the higher the level of government expenditures, the higher the level of government intervention and the better the adequacy of reporting and disclosure. Government intervention is dictated by a need to provide economic security to all classes of society and takes the form of industry and opportunity creation. Because government is assumed to be accountable to the people, its intervention may be followed by an effort to report and disclose and may be favorable to the development of an accounting profession and a reporting and disclosure tradition. This is applicable to any economic system. In the United States, a capitalist economic system, governmental agencies all employ accounting as a tool to accomplish the regulatory mandate placed upon them by Congress. The socialist countries have developed unique accounting systems and procedures in the furtherance of their own centrally managed economies. Finally, the role of governments in developing accounting principles and providing legal authority is assumed to result in a higher reliability of financial disclosures in the developing countries. As stated by Jaggi, the "interference by governments may be essential to ensure higher reliability (which is vital for the expansion of industries in these countries), for creating public confidence and trust in corporations, for creating an atmosphere where industrialization can progress, and for making economic and social decisions."[69]

Lastly, the higher the level of exports, the higher the need for better reporting and disclosure. Free trade policies in general and export promotion in particular increase the cooperation with other countries, the flows of human and physical capital, and the need for comparable reporting and disclosure adequacy. For example, Kraayenhof argues that the international flow of capital for financing and participation creates more interest in the soundness of financial presentations and the intelligibility of the explanatory notes.[70]

The number of people in a given country could also be important to the development of accounting. The larger the population, the higher the number of people interested in the accounting profession, who feel the need for a well-developed accounting profession and the need for full and fair disclosure. For example, India, Egypt, and Pakistan, which are usually classified as developing countries, have developed accounting professions and also well-developed systems for accounting education.

Macro social accounting encompasses the subfields of social indicators, national economic accounting, and the effective use of accounting in economic development. Much work remains to be done in each of these subfields before reaching an effective evaluation, measurement, and disclosure of national social performance.

Notes

1. Dhia D. Alhashim, "Social Accounting in Egypt," *The International Journal of Accounting, Education and Research* 12, no. 2 (Spring 1977): 128.

2. R. A. Bauer, ed., *Social Indicators* (Cambridge: MIT Press, 1966).

3. U. S., Department of Health, Education, and Welfare, *Toward a Social Report* (Washington, D.C.: 1965).

4. Leslie D. Wilcox et al., *Social Indicators and Social Monitoring: An Annotated Bibliography* (Amsterdam: Elsevier Scientific, 1972); and Kenneth C. Land, "Social Indicator Models: An Overview," in Kenneth C. Land and Seymor Spilerman, eds., *Social Indicators Models* (New York: Russell Sage Foundation, 1975).

5. A. D. Biderman, "Social Indicators and Goals," in *Social Indicators*, p. 69.

6. R. A. Bauer, "Detection and Anticipation of Impact: The Nature of the Task," in Bauer, *Social Indicators*, p. 1.

7. Kenneth C. Land, "Theories, Models and Indicators of Social Change," *International Social Science Journal*, no. 1 (1975).

8. P. M. Hauser, *Social Statistics in Use* (New York: Russell Sage, 1975).

9. Kenneth C. Land, "On the Definition of Social Indicators," *American Sociologist* (November 1971): pp. 322-325; Land, "Social Indicator Models: An Overview."

10. Land, "Theories, Models and Indicators of Social Change," p. 35.

11. Sir Claus Moser, "Social Indicators: Systems, Methods and Problems, *Review of Income and Wealth* (June 1973): 135-136.
12. Terry Nichols Clark, "Community Social Indicators: From Analytical Models to Policy Applications," *Urban Affairs Quarterly* (September 1973): 6.
13. Michael J. Carley, "Social Theory and Models in Social Indicator Research," *International Journal of Social Economics* 6, no. 1 (1979): 42.
14. Ibid., pp. 33-44.
15. Ibid., p. 42.
16. R. V. Horn, "Social Indicators: Meaning, Methods and Applications," *International Journal of Social Economics* 7, no. 8 (1980): 440-441.
17. United Nations, *International Definition and Measurement of Standards and Levels of Living*, (1V, 5., New York, 1954); United Nations, *International Definition and Measurement of Levels of Living, An Interim Guide*, (1V, 7. New York, 1961).
18. United Nations, *Social and Demographic Statistics: Draft Guidelines on Social Indicators*, (New York: United Nations, 1976); *United Nations, Toward a System of Social and Demographic Statistics*, prepared by Richard Stone, ST/STAT. 68 (United Nations, 1973).
19. Sten Johansson, "The Level of Living Survey: A Presentation," *Acta Sociologica* (1973); *Toward a Theory of Social Reporting* (Stockholm: Swedish Institute for Social Research, 1976).
20. Erik Allardt and Hannu Uusitalo, "Dimensions of Welfare in a Comparative Study of the Scandinavian Societies," *Scandinavian Political Studies* (1972).
21. Johansson, "The Level of Living Survey."
22. J. P. Roos, "The Way of Life in Social Change: A Comparative Study," *Acta Sociologica* (1978).
23. Stein Ringen, *An Introduction to the Level of Living Study*, Memorandum no. 23 (Bergen, Norway, 1973).
24. Economic Council of Japan, *Measuring Net National Welfare of Japan* (Tokyo: Economic Research Institute, 1973).
25. Jan Drewnovsky, *Studies in the Measurement of Levels of Living and Welfare*, UNRISD Report, no. 703 (Geneva: United Nations, 1970).
26. John Q. Wilson, *Quality of Life in the United States* (Kansas City, Mo.: Midwest Research Institute, 1969).
27. Nestor Terleckyj, *Elements of Possibilities for Improvements in the Quality of Life in the USA, 1971-1981* (Washington, D. C.: National Planning Association, 1978).
28. United Nations Secretariat, *Toward a System of Social and Demographic Statistics*, ST/STAT, 68 (New York: United Nations, 1973).
29. Erik Allardt, "A Welfare Model for Selecting Indicators of National Developments," *Policy Sciences* 4 (1973): 63-74; Erik Allardt, "Individual Needs, Social Structures and Indicators of National Development," in Einsenstadt and Rokkan, eds., *Building States and Nations*, vol. 1 (Beverly Hills, Cal.: Sage, 1973), pp. 259-273.
30. Wolfgang Glatzer, An Overview of the International Development in Macro Social Indicators," *Accounting, Organizations and Society* 6, no. 3 (1981): 224.
31. W. Zapf, "Soziale Indikatoren: Eine Zwischenbilanz," *Allgemeines Statistisches Archiv* 1 (1976): 432.
32. Horn, "Social Indicators," p. 432.
33. Organization for Economic Co-Operation and Development, *Measuring Social Well-Being: A Progress Report on the Development of Social Indicators* (Paris: OECD, 1982), p. 10.

34. Ibid., p. 12.

35. Organization for Economic Co-Operation and Development, *Measuring Social Well-Being: A Progress Report on the Development of Social Indicators* (Paris: OECD, 1976), pp. 31-33.

36. W. Nordhaus and J. Tobin, "Is Growth Obsolete?" in F. Thomas Juster, ed., *Economic Growth* 1972.

37. Economic Council of Japan, NNW Measurement Committee, "Measuring National Welfare of Japan" (Report prepared for the Japanese Ministry of Finance, Tokyo, April 30, 1974).

38. M. Olson, "The Treatment of Externalities in National Income Statistics," in L. Wings and A. Evnas, ed., *Public Economics and the Quality of Life*, 1977.

39. O. Herfindahl and A. Kneese, "Measuring Social and Economic Change: Benefits and Costs of Environmental Pollution," in M. Moss, ed., *Measurement of Economic and Social Performance*, 1973.

40. A. Marin, "National Income, Welfare, and the Environment."

41. H. M. Peskin and J. Peskin, "The Valuation of Nonmarket Activities in Income Accounting," *Review of Income and Wealth* 71 (March 1978); and H. M. Peskin, "A National Accounting Framework for Environmental Assets," *Environmental Economics and Management* 255 (1976).

42. H. M. Peskin, "National Income Accounts and the Environment," in H. M. Peskin, P. R. Portney, and A. V. Kneese, eds., *Environmental Regulation and the U.S. Economy* (Baltimore: Johns Hopkins University Press, 1981).

43. Ibid., p. 84.

44. H. M. Peskin, "Accounting for the Environment," *Social Indicators Research* 191 (September 1975).

45. *New Left Review* (1963): p. 4.

46. H. Liebenstein, "Allocative Efficiency v. X-Efficiency," *American Economic Review* (June 1966): 352-415.

47. W. J. Baumol and A. S. Binder, *Economics: Principles and Policy*, 2nd ed. (New York: Harvourt Brace Jovanovich, 1982), p. 760.

48. Nasir Islam and Georges M. Henault, "From GNP to Basic Needs: A Critical Review of Development and Development Administration," *International Review of Administrative Sciences* 2 (1979): 253-267.

49. Ibid.

50. W. W. Rostow, "The Stages of Economic Growth," *Economic History Review* (August 1959).

51. Talcott Parsons, *The Social System* (Glencoe, Ill.: Free Press, 1951).

52. Islam and Henault, "From GNP to Basic Needs," p. 254.

53. Ibid.

54. Marc Nefron, "Introduction," in Marc Nefron, ed., *Another Development: Approaches and Strategies*, (Uppsala: Dag Jammarskjold Foundation, 1977), p. 10.

55. Benjamin J. Cohen, *The Question of Imperialism: The Political Economy of Dominance and Dependence* (New York: Basic Books, 1973).

56. Mahbub Ul Haq, "An International Perspective on Basic Needs," in World Bank, *Poverty and Basic Needs* (September 1980): 32.

57. Paul Streeten, "From Growth to Basic Needs," in Work Bank, *Poverty and Basic Needs.*, p. 6.
58. Francis Stewart, "Country Experience in Providing Basic Needs," in Work Bank, *Poverty and Basic Needs*, p. 9.
59. Norman L. Hicks, "Is There a Tradeoff Between Growth and Basic Needs?" in World Bank, *Poverty and Basic Needs*, p. 25.
60. Adolph J. H. Enthoven, *Accountancy and Economic Development Policy* (Amsterdam: North Holland, 1973), pp. 168-169.
61. Lee J. Seidler, *The Function of Accounting in Economic Development: Turkey as a Case Study* (New York: Praeger, 1967), p. 7.
62. Mohamed A. Mirghani, "A Framework for a Linkage between Microaccounting and Macroaccounting for Purposes of Development Planning in Developing Countries," *International Journal of Accounting, Education and Research* 18, no. 1 (Fall 1982): 57-68.
63. Werner G. Frank, "An Empirical Analysis of International Accounting Principles," *Journal of Accounting Research* (Autumn 1979): 593.
64. F. D. S. Choi and G. G. Mueller, *An Introduction to Multinational Accounting* (Englewood Cliffs, N. J.: Prentice-Hal, 1978).
65. Ahmed Belkaoui, "Economic Political and Civil Indicators and Reporting and Disclosure Adequacy: An Empirical Investigation," *Journal of Accounting and Public Policy* (Winter 1983).
66. H. D. Lowe, "Accounting Aid for Developing Countries," *Accounting Review* (April 1967): 360.
67. E. L. Elliot, J. Larrea, and J. M. Rivera, "Accounting Aid to Developing Countries: Some Additional Considerations," *Accounting Review* (October 1968): 764.
68. Mahmood A. Quereshi, "Economic Development, Social Justice and Financial Reporting: Pakistan's Experience with Private Enterprise," *Management International Review* (1975): 71.
69. B. L. Jaggi, "The Impact of the Cultural Environment of Financial Disclosure," *International Journal of Accounting, Education and Research* (Spring 1975): 84.
70. J. Kraayenhof, "International Challenges in Accounting," *Journal of Accountancy* (January 1963): 36.

Bibliography
SOCIAL INDICATORS
Allardt, Erik. "A Welfare Model for Selecting Indicators of National Developments." *Policy Sciences* 4 (1973): 63-74.
Andrews, F. M., and S. Withey. *Social Indicators of Well-Being*. New York: Plenum, 1976.
Bauer, R. A., ed. *Social Indicators*. Cambridge: MIT Press, 1966.
Carley, Michael J. "Social Theory and Models in Social Indicator Research." *International Journal of Social Economics* 6, no. 1 (1979).
Cohen, W. B. "Social Indicators: Statistics for Public Policy." *American Statistician* 22 (October 1968).
Economic Council of Japan, *Measuring Net National Welfare of Japan*. Tokyo: Economic Research Institute, 1973.
Hauser, P. M. "Assessment of Living Levels, the S. I. Approach." *International Journal of Social Economics*, no. 3 (1978).
___. "From Social Statistics to Social Indicators." *Australian Journal of Statistics* 20, no. 2 (1978).

___. *Social Statistics in Use*. New York: Russell Sage, 1975.
Horn, R. V. "Social Indicators for Development Planning." *International-Labour Review* 6 (1975).
___. "Social Indicators: Meaning, Methods and Applications." *International Journal of Social Economics* 7, no. 8 (1980).
Johansson, Sten. "The Level of Living Survey: A Presentation." *Acta Sociologica* (1973).
Land, Kenneth C. "On the Definition of social Indicators." *American Sociologist* (November 1971): 322-325.
___. "Theories, Models and Indicators of Social Change." *International Social Science Journal*, no. 1 (1975).
___, and Symor Spilerman, eds. *Social Indicators Models*. New York: Russell Sage Foundation, 1975.
Moser, Sir Claur. "Social Indicators," *Review of Income and Wealth* 19 (1973): 133-144.
___. "Social Indicators: Systems, Methods and Problems." *Review of Income and Wealth* (June 1973): 135-136.
Olson, A. M. "The Plan and Purpose of the Social Report." *Public Interest* 15 (1969).
Organization for Economic Co-Operation and Development. *The OECD List of Social Indicators*. Paris: OECD, 1982.
Rice, S. "Social Accounting and Statistics." *Public Administration Review* 27 (1967): 169-174.
U. S. Department of Health, Education, and Welfare. *Towards a Social Report*. Washington, D. C.: 1965.
Wilcox, Leslie D., et al. *Social Indicators and Social Monitoring: An Annotated Bibliography*. Amsterdam: Elsevier Scientific, 1972.
Zapf, W. "Systems of Social Indicators." *International Social Science Journal* 27, no. 3 (1975).

NATIONAL INCOME ACCOUNTING

Nordhaus, W., and J. Tobin. "Is Growth Obsolete?" In F. Thomas Juster, ed., *Economic Growth* 1972.
Peskin, H. M. "Accounting for the Environment." 2, *Social Indicators Research* 191 (September 1975).
___. "A National Accounting Framework for Environmental Assets." 2, *Journal of Environmental Economics and Management* 255 (1976).
___, and J. Peskin. "The Valuation of Nonmarket Activities in Income Accounting." *Review of Income and Wealth* 71 (March 1978).
Peskin, J. M., P. R. Portney, and A. V. Kneese. *Environmental Regulation and the U.S. Economy*. Baltimore: Johns Hopkins University Press, 1981.

ACCOUNTING AND ECONOMIC DEVELOPMENT

Belkaoui, Ahmed. "Economic, Political and Civil Indicators and Reporting and Disclosure Adequacy: An Empirical Investigation." *Journal of Accounting and Policy* (Winter 1983).
Elliot, E. L., J. Larrea, and J. M. Rivera. "Accounting Aid to Developing Countries: Some Additional Considerations." *Accounting Review* (October 1968).
Enthoven, Adolf J. H. *Accounting and Economic Development Policy*. Amsterdam: North Holland, 1973.

Frank, Werner G. "An Empirical Analysis of International Accounting Principles." *Journal of Accounting Research* (Autumn 1979).

Haq, Mahbub Ul. *The Poverty Curtain: Choices for the Third World*. New York: Columbia University Press, 1976.

Islam, Nasi, and George M. Henault. "From GNP to Basic Needs: A Critical Review of Development and Development Administration." *International Review of Administrative Sciences* 2 (1979): 253-267.

Jaggi, B. L. "The Impact of the Cultural Environment on Financial Disclosure." *International Journal of Accounting, Education and Research* (Spring 1975).

Kraayenhof, J. "International Challenges in Accounting." *Journal of Accountancy* (January 1963).

Lowe, H. D. "Accounting Aid for Developing Countries." *Accounting Review* (April 1967).

Mehmet, Ozay. *Economic Planning and Social Justice in Developing Countries*. London: Croom Helm, 1978.

Mirghani, Mohamed A. "A Framework for a Linkage Between Microaccounting and Macroaccounting for Purposes of Development Planning in Developing Countries." *International Journal of Accounting, Education and Research* 18, no. 1 (Fall 1982): 57-68.

Myint, Hla. *The Economics of Developing Countries*. New York: Praeger, 1965.

Needles, Belverd E., Jr., "Implementing a Framework for the International Transfer of Accounting Technology," *Journal of Accounting, Education and Research* (Fall 1976): 47-62.

Quereshi, Mahmood A. "Economic Development, Social Justice and Financial Reporting: Pakistan's Experience with Private Enterprise." *Management International Review* (1975).

Samuels, J. M., and J. C. Oliga. "Accounting Standards in Developing Countries." *International Journal of Accounting, Education and Research* (Fall 1982): 69-114.

Scott, George M. *Accounting and Developing Nations*. Seattle: University of Washington Press, 1970.

Seidler, Lee J. *The Function of Accounting in Economic Development: Turkey as a Case Study*. New York: 1967.

9
SOCIAL AUDITING

Public demand for socially oriented programs of one kind or another and for measurement and disclosure of the environmental effects of organizational behavior has created pressure for a form of social auditing of the activities of corporations. Given the novelty of the phenomena and the lack of generally accepted procedures, social auditing tends to take forms to accommodate the various views about the ways firms should respond to their social environment. The purpose of this chapter is to provide a general definition of social auditing and to clarify the differences between the various forms of social audits advocated in practice and in the literature.

Definition of Social Auditing

As with any other new management term or technique that has not yet gained general acceptance, the social audit has been applied to a variety of activities. Blake, Frederick and Myers list the following practices as applicable to a social audit:

(1) An inventory of a company's "social" programs; (2) an inventory of its social "impacts'"; (3) cost estimates of various company activities thought to have special social significance; (4) the results of surveys of various company practices regarding environmental pollution, employment discrimination, occupational health and safety, and so on, undertaken at the behest of government regulatory agencies; (5) critical reports or surveys made by persons or organizations external to a company or industry, usually dealing with some particular area of social concern such as sexual discrimination; (6) attempts to determine the attitudes of various groups important to the corporation, such as stockholders, customers, employees, and others; and (7) several other so-called "social-audit" efforts.[1]

Similarly, the term has been given various definitions. Bauer and Fenn define social audit as "*a commitment to systematic assessment of and reporting on some meaningful, definable domain of a company's activities that have social impact.*"[2] Their focus is on the assessment and evaluation of corporate social programs. Dilley defines the social audit as "an investigation of an enterprise's performance as a member of the community in which it has its primary impact; such investigation consisting of the preparation of an inventory of the socially relevant activities of the enterprise, quantification (to the extent possible) of the social cost and benefits resulting from those activities, and compilation of other quantitative information providing insight into the social performance of the enterprise."[3] From both definitions it appears that the social audit- much like the financial audit- is an identification and examination of the activities of the firm in order to assess, evaluate, measure, and report their impact on their immediate social environment. Each of the elements of this definition requires further clarification:

1. *Identification* assures a tracking down and inventory of all the firm's activities having potential impact on the firm's environment. Identification will result in a definition of the social dimensions of the firm's activities in terms of social costs or social benefits depending on the nature of their impact on the social environment.
2. *Assessment and evaluation* imply the categorization of the firm's impact on its environment as either positive social benefits or negative social costs.
3. *Measurement* implies the assignment of quantitative or qualitative score to the social costs and benefits identified in assessment and evaluation.
4. *Reporting* assumes the disclosure of the firm's performance as measured.

This definition meets some of the purposes leading companies to undertake social audits. A recent survey identified the principal reasons corporations have undertaken assessments of their social activities.[4] By order of priority these are (1) to examine what the company is actually doing in selected areas; (2) to appraise or evaluate performance in selected areas and to identify those social programs that the company feels it ought to be pursuing; (3) to inject into the general thinking of managers a social point of view; (4) to determine areas where the company may be vulnerable to attacks; (5) to ensure that specific decision-making processes incorporate a social point of view; (6) to meet public demands for corporate accountability in the social area; (7) to inform the public of what the company is doing; (8) to identify the social efforts that the company feels pressure to undertake; (9) to offset irresponsible audits made by outside self-appointed groups; (10) to increase profits; and (11) others. All these purposes fit within the general framework provided by this definition, which is *the identification, assessment and evaluation, measurement, and reporting of the environmental effects of organizational behavior.*

Types of Social Audits

There is a proliferation of social audits proposed in the literature and in practice. They differ in terms of objectives, methodologies, and results. The following types of audits will be examined: social process/program management audit; macro-micro social indicator audit; social performance audit; social balance sheet and income statement; energy accounting and auditing; comprehensive auditing; environmental auditing; and human resource accounting.

SOCIAL PROCESS/PROGRAM MANAGEMENT AUDIT

The social process audit or program management audit, associated mainly with the Bank of America, is an attempt to measure the effectiveness of those activities of the corporation incurred largely for social reasons and to develop an internal management information system that will allow management to better evaluate and administer these special socially oriented programs. For example, the Bank of America initially selected the following four social programs to be audited:
1. *The New Opportunity Loan Program*- reduced home loan terms to low-income borrowers.
2. *The SBA-Minority Enterprise Program*- liberalized terms for minority entrepreneurs.
3. *The "Banking on People" Program*- our NAB hard-core hiring and upgrading effort.
4. *The Student Loan Program.*[5]

The bank set to determine whether or not these program objectives had been met.

The social process audit or program management audit generally contains three elements:
1. *Historical Perspective*: The auditor analyzes the actual reasons for a particular social program and the original objectives of the program, which help the formulation of realistic objectives and assess future possibilities.
2. *Cost Analysis*: The auditor compiles the costs resulting from the adoption of each program. These costs are generally comprised of the direct costs, allocated costs, and opportunity costs associated with each program.
3. *Benefit Analysis*: The auditor compiles the social benefits of each program that can be quantified. Where quantification is not possible, surveys may be conducted to determine from those affected by the programs whether or not the objectives have been met.

A similar "process audit" is proposed by Bauer and Fenn in the *Corporate Social Audit.*[6] Their method involves four steps:
1. An assessment of circumstances under which social program being audited came into being.
2. Explicate the goals of the social program.
3. Specify rationale behind the program.
4. Describe (quantitatively where possible) what is being done as opposed to what the rationale says ought to be done.[7]

The objective of these steps is to help the company assess and evaluate their social programs systematically. In fact, Bauer, Cauthorn, and Warner went one step further and proposed a management process audit manual for assessing the organizational readiness of a firm to implement organization wide policy in the area of recent social concerns.[8] The manual

included four sections. The skeletal structure of each section is a main research question followed by procedural questions to be answered by the data. The main questions are as follows:
1. What issue or issues are to be investigated?
2. What is the background of the industry and firm? Is any comparative data available on industry performance on social issues?
3. Is there evidence of top-level concern for each social issue, and to what extent has the concern been translated into a corporate commitment to deal with the issue?
4. Has corporate policy been developed on the social issue?
5. Is there a staff specialist responsible for managing response to the social issue, or is this function being performed on an ad hoc basis? Is there a staff specialist, what is he doing, and how is he carrying out the function?
6. Can the corporate information system measure an individual manager's performance on social issues as well as progress for the company as a whole?
7. What programs exist in the company to deal with social issues?
8. Has the response to the social issue been integrated into the company's standard operating procedure?

Each of these questions may be answered in whole or in part by literature sources, reading the files of the firm, or inspecting the plants. The rationale for each research question was stated as follows:

The purpose of each research question is to establish the status of various aspects of the firms and its management system for handling social issues. Since many types of evidence may be brought to bear, and since it is impossible for us to forsee every contingency that might arise, we have concluded that the intelligent user of this manual can handle these contingencies if the rationale and intent of the research question is clear.[9]

MACRO-MICRO SOCIAL INDICATOR AUDIT

The macro-micro social indicator audit consists of evaluating the company's social performance by a comparison of micro social and macro social indicators.

Macro social indicators are measures of the adequate level of certain needs that should be met in conformity with social goals that a community has set for itself. These needs cover health and safety, education, housing, cultural activity, and other items deemed important to the general welfare of the community. Micro social indicators are measures of the performance of the corporation in those areas measured by the macro social indicators. The comparison of micro social and macro social indicators may be used to assess the quality of the social performance of the organization and constitute the essence of the macro-micro social indicator audit. Two good examples of this type of audit exist, the one used by the First National Bank of Minneapolis and the one proposed by Preston and Post.[10]

First National Bank applied the social indicator approach to corporate community involvement. Their annual report disclosed the following aspects of the quality of life in the Twin Cities: housing, education, public safety, income, job opportunities, health, transportation, participation, environment, culture, human relations, and community investment. It then measures, through the use of macro-micro social indicators, the quality and the quantity of the bank's activity in each area. An example of the bank's annual report is shown in Exhibit 9.1. One author reported two severe limitations to this bank's social unit.

The first is the reliability of the social indicators themselves: Does an increase in the number of high school graduates going to college really indicate higher quality education? Does an increase in home ownership really indicate better housing? This type of basic question has been troubling social scientists for years. The second limitation is that it will be next to impossible for these banks to determine what impact their individual programs have had on changes observed in the community. There are so many variables at work in any community that the input of one company will more than likely be highly obscured.[11]

EXHIBIT 9.1: FIRST NATIONAL BANK OF MINNEAPOLIS:
1974 INTERNAL SOCIAL-ENVIRONMENTAL AUDIT

		1974 Performance Level	Net Percentage Performance Differential 73-74	1974 Objectives	1974 Social Performance Index	1975 Objectives
Housing 1	1. Number of residential mortgage loans originated in 1974 to families living in a.) Minneapolis b.) Suburbs & St. Paul	a.) 360 b.) 967		+ +	↑ ↓	a.) 360 b.) 967
	2. Dollar amount of residential mortgage loans originated in 1974 to families in a.) Minneapolis b.) Suburbs & St. Paul	a.) $8,881,000 b.) $29,324,000		+ +	↓ ↓	a.) $8,881,000 b.) $29,324,000
	3. Number of outstanding home improvement loans made to families living in a.) Minneapolis b.) Suburbs & St. Paul	a.) 387 b.) 744				a.) 655 b.) 878
	4. Ratio originated residential mortgage loans to bank's total resources	1.50				1.50
	5. Foundation contribution	$10,000		$10,920	92	$10,000
Education 2	1. Number of classes taken by employees paid by bank a.) internal b.) external	363 164 199		+ +	↑ ↓	
	2. Number of employees in bank college gift matching program	45		+	↓	59
	3. Employee community involvement man-hours per month	1,129		+	↓	1,241
	4. Foundation contribution to educational institutions	$51,750		$50,006	1.03	$55,000
Public Safety 3	1. Accidents on bank premises involving employees – 1974 (Does not include sports)	26				26
	2. Accidents involving non-employees	14				14
Income 4	1. Clerical employees – monthly income related to area-wide averages	1:1.01				1:1
	2. Clerical employees – composite productivity related to base 1973	1.1.05				1:1.10
Job Opportunities 5	1. Percent officers, managers and professionals (EEO defined) a.) women b.) racial minority	a.) 19.6 b.) 3.5		+ +	↓ ↓	a.) 23.6 b.) 4.2
	2. Percent of job categories posted	77		79	1.03	77
Health 6	1. Estimated commitment to treatment of alcoholism a.) money b.) man-hours	a.) $5,460 b.) 722		+50% +100%	.61 1.39	
	2. Number of days missed due to health problems per capita a.) women b.) men	a.) 3.43 b.) 1.85		a.) 5.0 b.) 2.3	a.) 1.7 b.) 4.3	a.) 3.43 b.) 1.85
	3. Prepaid health services (HMO) as employee health option a.) services offered b.) dollar c.) man-hours	a.) 0 b.) $1,000 c.) 141		+ +	↓ ↓	a.) 0 b.) $1,500 c.) 150
Transportation 7	1. Percent employees taking bus to work	61		50	1.22	65
	2. Percent employees who come to work in car pools	17		30	.56	20
	3. Percent employees who drive to work alone	15		15	.79	15
Participation 8	1. Man-hours per month spent by employees in community activity a.) on bank time b.) non-bank time	4,632 585 4,047		+ 380 +	1.54 ↓	5,095 643 4,451
	2. Percent employees donating to United Way	83		+	↓	85
	3. Percent employees voting Nov. 74	75				

EXHIBIT 9.1: (Continued)

		1974 Performance Level	Net Percentage Performance Differential 73-74 (+)	1974 Objectives (b)	1974 Social Performance Index (e)	1975 Objectives (d)
Environment 9	1. Percent office paper which is recycled	16	1%	+	6	18.5
	2. Energy consumed by bank					
	a.) steam	44,727,500		44,355,075	99	44,727,500
	b.) electric (in kilowatt hours 1-1-74 to 12-31-74)	13,095,560	-15%		91	13,095,566
	3. Loan commitments to firms dealing in anti-pollution equipment	$8,362,000				
	4. Community involvement commitment in man-hours per month	163				166
	5. Foundation contribution	$5,090		$8,037	63	$5,000
Culture 10	1. Level of commercial line commitments to cultural institutions	$4,000,000				$4,000,000
	2. Community involvement — man-hours/month	333				376
	3. Foundation contribution	$115,200		$113,514	99	$133,200
Human Relations	1. Number minority business loan applicants	56	10%	6		
	2. Percent approved installment loan applications					
	a.) women	62				63
	b.) men	63	-9%			63
	3. Level of minority business purchases	$163,930		$45,840	1.01	149,000
	4. Community involvement — man-hours/month	803		+		882
	5. Foundation contribution	$20,500		$18,250	1.12	$22,500
Community Investment 4	1. Commitment to lend money to businesses		10%			
	a.) Minneapolis	$284,936,000				$284,936,000
	b.) Suburbs and St. Paul	$296,127,000				$296,127,000
	2. Commitments to lend money to civic minorities at other than market terms					
	a.) number	8				
	b.) amount	$5,700,000				$8,700,000
	3. Dollar volume of commercial mortgage loans originated in					
	a.) Minneapolis	$1,140,000				
	b.) Suburbs and St. Paul	$3,302,000				
	4. Dollar volume commercial construction and land development loans					
	a.) Minneapolis	$4,680,000				
	b.) Suburbs and St. Paul	$20,905,000		+		
	5. Estimated dollar value of personal loans outstanding/total personal savings deposits	$209,500,000/$233,563,000		+		
	6. Total Foundation Contribution	$421,300		$420,000	1.0	$445,300
Consumer Protection and Services	1. New consumer services offered	4				
	2. Diversity of perspectives — percent of Board members without a primary background as a business executive	8		+		
	3. Student loans originated in 1974					
	a.) number	a.) 175				a.) 2,000
	b.) dollar volume	b.) $1,877,000				b.) $1,877,000

SOURCE: Reprinted with permission.

The macro-micro social indicator audit rests on the main assumption that social indicators can be developed to reflect the impact of various areas on the overall "quality of life" and that the activities of business firms may be traced to discover their impacts on these indicators. This presents problems related to both the availability and reliability of the social indicators. Use of the macro-micro social indicator units has, however, certain benefits, namely, in allowing all firms to compare their activity to a rational set of goals and indicators ensuring consistency and comparability of the reports of various business organizations.

SOCIAL PERFORMANCE AUDIT

The social performance audit is also known as the corporate rating approach. It results from the attempt by various concerned organizations to evaluate, compare, and rank leading corporations in their efforts to respond to social and environmental demands. These corporate social ratings are mainly initiated by church groups, universities, mutual funds, and other "ethical" investors concerned about being "socially responsible" in their portfolio choices.[12]

Each of these groups has determined its own form of rating system aimed generally at evaluating the environmental impact of organizational behavior and the adequacy of the organization's responses. The most prevalent method is to use opinion polls, in which respondents are asked to rate the social performance of corporations.[13] Two organizations are known to have adopted more rigorous types of social performance audit, the Council on Economic Priorities (CEP), a public-interest research organization, and the Interfaith Center on Corporate Responsibility (ICCR), affiliated with the National Council of Churches.

The social performance audits performed by the CEP consist of in-depth factual analysis and reporting of the performance of selected firms and industries with respect to some particular area of social concern. The council has performed various audits, including pollution in the steel industry, the pulp and paper industry, and electric power-generating installations; minority personnel practices of selected banks; and companies active in the production of antipersonnel weapons.[14]

The social performance audits performed by the ICCR are intended to influence the portfolio decisions of member church organizations. It combines a concern for social performance with an "active" concern for social justice. The second concern consists of denouncing and opposing companies operating in South Africa and companies that discriminate against women and minorities in corporate personnel practices. The ICCR strategy is characterized by its activism in political and social areas.

SOCIAL BALANCE SHEET AND INCOME STATEMENT

The main idea in this type of audit is the preparation of a social balance sheet and social income statement that would be similar in format to the ones in the conventional financial statements and that would include in addition social information. There are two versions of this type of social audit, one proposed by Abt Associates, Inc., and one suggested by David F. Linowes.

The proposal of Abt Associates, a management consulting firm, is to compute and disclose the results of all the transactions of the firm with its social environment. The balance sheet would include a list of the social assets on one side and a list of the social commitments, liabilities, and equity on the other side. The income statement would include the social benefits, the social costs, and the net social income provided by company operations to the staff, community, general public, and clients. To illustrate the proposal, Abt Associates sponsored a social audit of its own activities and disclosed the results in the annual reports for 1971, 1972, 1973, and 1974. An example of Abt's social audit is shown in Exhibit 9.2. As may be seen in the exhibit, the intent of Abt's social audit is to quantify and assign a dollar figure to all social impacts. In fact, Clark Abt, the president of Abt, Associates, reports,

The basic concept used in the social audit to measure social benefits and costs to employees, communities, clients, and the general public is adopted from accounting practice. A thing Is assumed to be worth what is paid for it, or what it costs, or the value received from it. This practice assumes all social impacts such as health, security, equality, environment, etc., can be expressed in terms of the money the people concerned have actually paid for the benefits or services, and what they have actually paid to avoid equivalent costs.[15]

The proposal of David F. Linowes, a certified public accountant , is similar in format to the Abt proposal but differs in content by being restricted to expenditures undertaken voluntarily to improve the welfare of employees and the public, product safety, or environmental conditions. The expenditures required by law or union contract are not included because they are perceived as both mandatory and necessary costs of doing business.[16] Several rules are proposed that help to identify socio-economic items to be included into the socio-economic operating statement (SEOS) as follows:

- If a socially beneficial action is required by enforceable law and regulation, it is not included on a SEOS statement.
- If a socially beneficial action is required by law, but is ignored, the cost of such item is a "detriment" for the year. The same treatment is given an item if postponed, even with governmental approval.
- A prorated portion of salaries and related expenses of personnel who spend time in socially beneficial actions or with social organizations is included.
- Cash and product contributions to social institutions are included.
- The cost of setting up facilities for the general good of employees or the public, if done without union or government requirement, is included.
- Expenditures made voluntarily for the installation of safety devices on the premises or in products and not required by law or contract are included.
- Neglecting to install safety devices which are available at a reasonable cost is a "detriment."
- The cost of voluntarily building a playground or nursery school for employees and/or neighbors is included.
- The cost of relandscaping strip-mining sites or other environmental eyesores, if not required by law, is included.
- Extra costs of designing and building business facilities of unusually high beauty, health, or safety standards are included.[17]

These items, either positive or negative social actions and inactions, are then classified on a SEOS into three groups: relations with people; relations with environment; and relations with product. An example of a SEOS is shown in Exhibit 9.3. It shows separate accounts for activities "relating to people," with a "net improvement" balance of $16,000 and those involving "relations with environment" with a "net deficit" of $97,000. It is notable that no attempt was made to combine the two figures.[18]

There are two obvious difficulties with this type of social audit. First, it may be difficult to estimate the dollar value of some of the social benefits and costs. Second, the SEOS generated by the firm views the situation from the firm's point of view. As a consequence, benefits and costs are seen from *its* perspective, and the "benefits" it estimates may appear as "costs" elsewhere in the system. This is a normal state of affairs with respect to routine accounting principles, which aim at measurement of the status of a single organization vis-à-vis the rest of the world. However, it is not an appropriate format for evaluating and comparing the *net* social benefits generated by different organizations."[19]

EXHIBIT 9.2. ABT ASSOCIATES, INC.:
SOCIAL AND FINANCIAL BALANCE SHEET 1973

Assets		1973	1972
1.	Staff Assets		
	Staff Available Within One Year (note 1)	$ 6,384,000	$ 4,166,000
	Staff Available After One Year (note 1)	15,261,000	12,567,000
	Training Investment (note 2)	2,051,000	971,000
		23,696,000	17,704,000
	Less Accumulated Training Obsolescence (note 2)	503,000	248,000
	Total Staff Assets	$23,193,000	$17,456,000
2.	Organizational Assets		
	Creation and Development of Organization		
	Research (note 3)	$ 437,000	$ 352,000
	Child Care (note 4)	7,000	7,000
	Social Audit (note 4)	32,000	18,000
	Total Organizational Assets	$ 476,000	$ 377,000
3.	Use of Public Goods		
	Public Services Paid For Through Taxes (Net of Consumption) (note 5)	$ 365,000	$ 160,000
4.	Financial Assets (note 9)		
	Cash	$ 91,000	$ 365,000
	Accounts Receivable, Less Allowance for Doubtful Accounts	2,083,000	1,285,000
	Unbilled Contract Costs and Fees	1,789,000	1,539,000
	Other Current Financial Assets	42,000	46,000
	Other Long-Term Financial Assets	39,000	89,000
	Total Financial Assets	$ 4,044,000	$ 3,324,000
5.	Physical Assets (note 9)		
	Land	$ 310,000	$ 307,000
	Buildings	1,710,000	1,737,000
	Improvements	222,000	152,000
	Equipment, Furniture and Fixtures	242,000	137,000
		2,484,000	2,333,000
	Less Accumulated Depreciation	204,000	111,000
		2,280,000	2,222,000
	Office Building Under Construction	225,000	—
	Total Physical Assets	$ 2,505,000	$ 2,222,000
	Total Assets	$30,583,000	$23,539,000

Social assets and liabilities are identified in lightest type.

Liabilities and Equity	1973	1972
1. Staff Liabilities		
Staff Wages Payable (note 6)	$23,193,000	$17,456,000
2. Organizational Liabilities		
Organizational Financing Requirements (note 7)	$ 563,000	$ 351,000
3. Public Liabilities (note 8)		
Environmental Resources Used Through Pollution:		
Paper	$ 11,000	$ 5,000
Electricity	76,000	41,000
Commuting	37,000	20,000
Total Public Liabilities	$ 124,000	$ 66,000
4. Financial Liabilities (note 9)		
Notes Payable (Short Term)	$ 514,00	$ 1,112,000
Accounts Payable	1,081,000	539,000
Accrued Expenses	875,000	596,000
Federal Income Taxes	109,000	78,000
Deferred Federal Income Taxes	52,000	35,000
Notes Payable (Long Term)	1,092,000	757,000
Leasehold Interest in Property	128,000	127,000
Total Financial Liabilities	$ 3,851,000	$ 3,244,000
Stockholders' Equity (note 9)		
Common Stock	$ 295,000	$ 295,000
Additional Paid-In Capital	1,491,000	1,491,000
Retained Earnings	912,000	516,000
Total Stockholders' Equity	$ 2,698,000	$ 2,302,000
Society's Equity		
Society's Equity Generated by Increases (Decreases) in Net Social Assets (note 10)	$ 154,000	$ 120,000
Total Liabilities and Equity	$30,583,000	$23,539,000

Note 1
Company staff is considered a social asset. Valuation of the asset is based on year-end payroll, discounted to present value, the discount rate being a function of mean staff tenure (averaged over previous years) and salary profiles over time. Discount rate for 1973 was .9604 for staff available within one year (1972: .9634) and 2.296 for those available after one year (1972: 2.906), based on a mean staff tenure of 3.8 years (1972: 4.6 years).

Note 2
Training investment has been estimated from a staff survey conducted in January 1974. 1973 training expenditures, identified in the Social and Financial Income Statement, have been added to the 1972 balance. Training obsolescence is based on a straightline depreciation of training investment over the mean staff tenure.

Note 3
Creation and development of organization is equated to the replacement cost of paid-in capital, computed by weighing the capital stock account from 1965 (the year of the company's founding) to the present by the deflator for Gross Private Fixed Investment. The replacement cost of total paid-in capital less actual cost constitutes a social asset.

Note 4
Investments in research in child care and the social audit by the company accrue as a social asset.

EXHIBIT 9.2 (continued)

Note 5
Taxes paid by the company are considered a social contribution or benefit, while public services consumed by the company are considered social costs. When the company does not consume public services equal to taxes paid, a net social asset is produced. The change in this asset from 1972 to 1973 is equal to the difference between the value of public services consumed and total taxes paid, as identified in the Social and Financial Income Statement.

Note 6
This amount does not constitute a liability in the legal sense. It is a liability contingent upon future utilization of staff on contract or administrative tasks.

Note 7
The company's financing requirements are considered to be an opportunity cost to society. This cost is equated to the difference between mean borrowing during the year and year-end borrowing.

Note 8
The use of environmental resources through pollution generated by company operations is considered a cumulative social liability. The change between 1972 and 1973 figures is equal to the social costs identified in the Social and Financial Income Statement.

Note 9
Financial and physical assets, financial liabilities and stockholders' equity are items conventionally accounted for. The individual line items are the same as in the Financial Balance Sheet; they have been rearranged and rounded off for integration into the social balance sheet.

Note 10
Society's investment in the company is created by recognizing the difference between the net increase in the value of social assets and social liabilities.

Note 11
Conventional financial accounting fails to adjust for public services flowing from society to the corporation. These public services constitute a social cost, corresponding to an "invisible subsidy" to the company — which is offset by conventionally accounted tax payments. Federal and state public services consumed by the company are calculated by multiplying the ratio of company revenues to total federal or state corporate revenues times the total of federal or state corporation tax collections. The company's share of local services consumed is computed by multiplying the ratio of the average daily work force of the company to total local population by total local taxes, subtracting the share of the local budget going to education (30.6% in 1973; 29% in 1972) since the staff does not use local public education.

Note 12
In its operations, the company contributes to the degradation of environmental resources through pollution. The cost of pollution abatement is considered analogous to public services provided by society.

Note 13
The company consumed 1,723,593 kWH of electric power in 1973 and 1,542,524 kWH in 1972. The cost of abatement of air pollution created by the production of this power is estimated at $.02 per kWH.

Note 14
The company generated 1,727,440 commuting trip miles in 1973 and 783,750 miles in 1972 (3,622 and 3,438 per staff member, respectively). The cost of abatement of air pollution caused by automobile commuting is estimated at $.01 per mile.

Note 15
A substantial portion of the company's activities are expressed in tangible form through the printed word. The company used 170 tons of paper in 1973 and 102 tons in 1972. The cost of

abatement of water pollution created by the manufacture of this paper is estimated at $35 per ton.

Note 16
The most significant development in the company has been the increase in staff. Total number of employees (in annual average full-time equivalents) increased from 228 in 1972 to 477 in 1973. This increase is reflected in the totals reported in the social and financial income statement. Figures are therefore reported in terms of per employee in the footnotes to clarify qualitative developments.

Note 17
Total annual payroll has been broken down into pay for time worked, vacation and holidays, and sick leave. As a cost to the company, salaries for time worked have been broken down further into compensation for work and training investment (see Note 21).

Abt Associates, Inc.
Social and Financial Income Statement 1973*

Benefits (Income)		1973	1972
1.	To Company/Stockholders		
	Contract Revenues and Other Income	$15,224,000	$ 6,995,000
	Federal Services Consumed (note 11)	195,000	129,000
	State Services Consumed (note 11)	80,000	46,000
	Local Services Consumed (note 11)	32,000	22,000
	Environmental Resources Used Through Pollution (note 12)		
	Electricity (note 13)	35,000	31,000
	Commuting (note 14)	17,000	10,000
	Paper (note 15)	6,000	4,000
	Total	$15,589,000	$ 7,237,000
2.	To Staff (note 16)		
	Salaries for Time Worked (note 17)	$ 5,399,000	$ 2,688,000
	Career Advancement (note 18)	602,000	332,000
	Vacation and Holidays (note 17)	571,000	298,000
	Health and Life Insurance (note 19)	361,000	140,000
	Sick Leave (note 17)	127,000	53,000
	Parking (note 20)	124,000	59,000
	Food Services (note 21)	51,000	24,000
	Quality of Work Space (note 22)	16,000	25,000
	Child Care (note 23)	11,000	5,000
	Credit Union (note 24)	8,000	4,000
	Total	$ 7,270,000	$ 3,628,000
3.	To Clients/General Public		
	Value of Contract Work at Cost (note 35)	$15,224,000	$ 6,995,000
	Staff Overtime Worked but not Paid (note 36)	1,056,000	883,000
	Federal Taxes Paid by Company	349,000	272,000
	State and Federal Tax Worth of Net Jobs Created (note 37)	327,000	174,000
	State Taxes Paid by Company	100,000	62,000
	Contributions to Knowledge (Publications) (note 38)	54,000	18,000
	Total	$17,110,000	$ 8,404,000

Benefits (Income)	1973	1972
4. To Community		
Local Taxes Paid by Company	$ 63,000	$ 71,000
Local Tax Worth of Net Jobs Created (note 39)	52,000	40,000
Environmental Improvements (note 40)	18,000	22,000
Total	$ 133,000	$ 133,000

Costs (Expenditures)	1973	1972
1. To Company/Stockholders		
Salaries Paid (Exclusive of Training Investment and Fringe Benefits (notes 17, 25)	$ 4,319,000	$ 2,150,000
Training Investment in Staff (notes 17, 25)	1,080,000	538,000
Direct Contract Costs (note 26)	5,596,000	1,921,000
Overhead/General and Administrative Expenditures Not Itemized (note 26)	1,649,000	925,000
Vacation and Holidays (note 17)	571,000	298,000
Improvements, Space and Environment (note 27)	384,000	151,000
Federal Taxes Paid (note 26)	349,000	272,000
Health and Life Insurance (note 19)	201,000	96,000
Sick Leave (note 17)	127,000	53,000
State Taxes Paid (note 26)	100,000	62,000
Local Taxes Paid (note 26)	63,000	71,000
Food Services (note 21)	51,000	24,000
Child Care (note 27)	11,000	5,000
Company School and Tuition Reimbursement (note 28)	2,000	1,000
Miscellaneous and Public Offering of Stock (note 26)	154,000	23,000
Interest Payments (note 26)	171,000	107,000
Income Foregone on Paid-In Capital (note 29)	276,000	276,000
Total	$15,104,000	$ 6,973,000
2. To Staff		
Opportunity Costs of Total Time Worked (note 30)	$ 6,455,000	$ 3,571,000
Absence of Retirement Income Plan (note 31)	58,000	43,000
Layoffs and Involuntary Terminations (note 32)	31,000	15,000
Inequality of Opportunity (note 33)	11,000	26,000
Uncompensated Losses Through Theft (note 34)	1,000	1,000
Total	$ 6,556,000	$ 3,656,000
3. To Clients/General Public		
Cost of Contracted Work	$15,224,000	$ 6,995,000
Federal Services Consumed (note 11)	195,000	129,000
State Services Consumed (note 11)	80,000	46,000
Environmental Resources Used Through Pollution (note 12)		
Electricity (note 13)	35,000	31,000
Commuting (note 14)	17,000	10,000
Paper (note 15)	6,000	4,000
Total	$15,557,000	$ 7,215,000
4. To Community		
Local Services Consumed (note 11)	$ 32,000	$ 22,000
Total	$ 32,000	$ 22,000

Net Income		1973	1972
1.	To Company/Stockholders: Financial	$ 396,000	$ 298,000
	Social (note 41)	89,000	(34,000)
2.	To Staff (note 42)	714,000	(28,000)
3.	To Clients/General Public	1,553,000	1,189,000
4.	To Community (note 43)	99,000	111,000
	Total Net Social Income	$ 2,455,000	$ 1,238,000
	Total Net Social and Financial Income Generated by Company Operations	$ 2,851,000	$ 1,536,000

Note 18
Career advancement is expressed as the added earning power from salary increases for merit or promotion. The annualized salary increases in 1973 amounted to $602,000, as compared to $332,000 in 1972; the average increases per employee were $1,262 in 1973 and $1,456 in 1972.

Note 19
The value of health and life insurance provided by the company is assumed to be equal to the cost of purchasing comparable coverage individually by full-time staff. For each dollar spent, the company generates $1.80 of benefits per employee. Benefits per employee amount to $757 in 1973 and $614 in 1972.

Note 20
The company offers free parking to employees at all its locations. This constitutes an "invisible income" to staff, corresponding to the savings in terms of parking costs over alternative locations. Free parking privileges are assumed to be worth $30 per month. Benefits per employee have remained virtually unchanged (1973: $260, 1972: $259).

Note 21
The company subsidizes the operation of food services on its premises, in the interest of work efficiency and staff congeniality, saving the time and public resources otherwise needed to commute to other eating facilities. The average value of subsidies per employee has increased slightly from $105 in 1972 to $107 in 1973.

Note 22
The company provides its employees with floor space exceeding industry standards (average of 90 square feet/employee). The value of actual square footage in excess of industry standards has been estimated at $6.50/square foot. As a result of company employment growth, the average benefit per employee has decreased from $111 in 1972 to $33 in 1973.

Note 23
The company subsidizes the operation of a day-care center on its premises, in the interest of working parents of pre-school children. The average value of subsidies per employee has remained stable (approximately $22.50).

Note 24
The Abt Associates Employees Federal Credit Union provides benefits to staff in the form of lower interest rates for loans and higher dividends for deposits than commercially available. The value of these benefits has been estimated at $8,000 for 1973 and $4,000 for 1972. The average benefit per employee has been approximately $18 for both years.

Note 25
The staff survey indicates that company employees spend an average 20% of their time in training, decreasing from a high of 25% during the first year to about 15% by the fourth year.

This percentage has been applied to total salaries for time worked to delineate training investment.

Note 26
Figures have been taken from the financial income statement, adjusted for itemized expenditures.

Note 27
Actual expenditures on building maintenance.

Note 28
The company encourages employees to take courses at local universities related to the work performed by offering a 50% tuition subsidy to qualified staff.

Note 29
"Income Foregone on Paid-In Capital" has been estimated as the opportunity cost to stockholders of having paid-in capital tied up in the company. The opportunity cost is equivalent to the expected return on an investment in a medium-risk venture, estimated at 12%.

Note 30
The opportunity cost of work to staff is equivalent to salaries received for regular working hours plus the value of overtime worked but not paid.

Note 31
Currently, the company does not offer retirement income to its employees. In the staff survey conducted in January, 1974, 73% of the respondents indicated a strong interest in a retirement income plan. Its absence therefore constitutes an opportunity cost to staff in terms of benefits routinely available in other employment. The average annual cost of purchasing a standard retirement income plan outside the company has been estimated at $1,935. For 1973, 30 employees were eligible for a standard retirement income plan, compared to 22 in 1972.

Note 32
The cost of layoffs and involuntary terminations to staff is estimated to be one month's salary to each terminee, based on the assumption that the mean time to next employment is one month. The average cost per employee has decreased slightly from $66 in 1972 to $65 in 1973, as has the percentage of employees involuntarily terminated from 6.9 to 6.5 percent.

Note 33
Inequality of opportunity is defined in terms of the costs to individuals of the income loss equal to the difference between what the minority or female individual earns and what a non-minority or male individual doing the same job with the same qualifications earns. The social cost of inequality of opportunity was incurred entirely by women, as a result of a strongly discriminatory labor market that company policy was not completely able to overcome within national wage-price constraints. However, company efforts in 1973 led to an absolute decrease in the total cost of the inequality of opportunity from $26,000 in 1972 to $11,000 in 1973, corresponding to a decrease in the per employee cost from $114 in 1972 to $23 in 1973.

Note 34
Prior to the establishment of security measures, employees have suffered losses through theft of personal property. In some instances, employees were not reimbursed for such losses. This cost per employee was reduced by half in 1973.

Note 35
A survey of clients indicated that the evaluation of contract value at cost understates the true value to the general public of the work performed by the company. Clients estimated that the actual value of contracts exceeded cost by a factor of up to nine. However, the response rate for this survey was insufficient for reliable statistical estimates of the actual value of

contracts to clients or the general public. The figures reported indicate a slight increase in contact value per employee ($32,000 in 1973 vs. $31,000 in 1972).

Note 36
The 1972 social audit showed an average overtime for professional staff of 33% over regular working hours. Partially in response to that finding, reduction of excessive overtime became company policy. The 1973 staff survey showed a decrease of overtime to 20% of regular working hours. The monetary value of unpaid overtime per employee decreased from $3,873 in 1972 to $2,214 in 1973. The total value of overtime constitutes an "invisible subsidy" of clients an the general public by company staff.

Note 37
The expansion of the company has created 218 additional jobs. The tax value of these additional jobs for the federal and state governments has been computed as 20% of the average starting salary of $12,000, weighted by the proportion of a full year that these (net) new jobs have been effective.

Note 38
Publications by company staff constitute additions to the stock of social knowledge. These contributions are evaluated at the average market rate for similar publications. The average value per employee increased from $79 in 1972 to $113 in 1973, reflecting an increase of publications from one for every fourth employee to one for every third employee.

Note 39
The local tax worth of net jobs created has been computed as the additional revenue to the community in terms of sales taxes, excise taxes on cars, and real estate taxes for private homes.

Note 40
The company contributed to aesthetic improvements of the environment through landscaping ($8,000 in 1973) and the paving over of a dirt lot for a parking lot (rental value of 1973: $10,000). These improvements constitute a benefit to the community.

Note 41
The 1972 net social loss to the company/stockholders results from the relatively high opportunity cost of paid-in capital which was not entirely offset by social contributions to the operations of the company.

Note 42
The change from a net social loss to staff in 1972 ($123 per employee to a social gain in 1973 ($1,497 per employee) is largely a result of the company's success in decreasing the extent of overtime worked but not paid. In addition, this change reflects improvements in the social efforts by the company.

Note 43
The slight decrease in the net social income to the community can be attributed to the fact that physical improvements (new building, landscaping) following the employment expansion of the company have begun late in 1973 and will therefore become effective in 1974 only, while the social costs of increased use of public services from the expanded staff have been immediate.

EXHIBIT 9.3: XXXX CORPORATION: SOCIO-ECONOMIC OPERATING STATEMENT FOR THE YEAR ENDING DECEMBER 31, 1971

I. RELATIONS WITH PEOPLE:
  A. *Improvements:*
    1. Training program for handicapped workers $ 10,000
    2. Contribution to educational institution   4,000
    3. Extra turnover costs because of minority hiring program   5,000
    4. Cost of nursery school for children of employees, voluntarily set up   11,000
    Total improvements $ 30,000
  B. *Less: Detriments*
    1. Postponed installing new safety devices on cutting machines (cost of the devices) $ 14,000
  C. Net improvements in people actions for the year $ 16,000

II. RELATIONS WITH ENVIRONMENT:
  A. *Improvements:*
    1. Cost of reclaiming and landscaping old dump on company property $ 70,000
    2. Cost of installing pollution control devices on Plant A smokestacks   4,000
    3. Cost of detoxifying waste from finishing process this year   9,000
    Total improvements $ 83,000
  B. *Less: Detriments*
    1. Cost that would have been incurred to relandscape strip-mining site used this year $ 80,000
    2. Estimated costs to have installed purification process

EXHIBIT 9.3: (Continued)

to neutralize poisonous liquid being dumped into stream	$100,000
	$180,000
C. Net deficit in environment actions for the year	($ 97,000)
III. RELATIONS WITH PRODUCT:	
A. *Improvements:*	
1. Salary of vice-president while serving on government Product Safety Commission	$ 25,000
2. Cost of substituting leadfree paint for previously used poisonous lead paint	9,000
Total improvements	$ 34,000
B. *Less: Detriments*	
1. Safety device recommended by Safety Council but not added to product	22,000
C. Net improvements in product actions for the year	$ 12,000
Total socio-economic deficit for the year	($ 69,000)
Add: Net cumulative socio-economic improvements as of January 1, 1971	$249,000
Grand total net socio-economic actions to December 31, 1971	$180,000

SOURCE: Linowes, David F., "An Approach to Socio-Economic Accounting," *Conference Board Record* (November 1972):58–61. Used by permission.

ENERGY ACCOUNTING AND AUDITING

Energy accounting is the reporting and disclosing of the results of conservation of energy in the manufacturing process and improvements of the energy efficiency of products. As a result many companies have started resorting to the use of "energy audits" as part of the conservation effort. For example, Dow Chemical Company ahs installed an energy monitoring and reporting system as part of its established cost accounting system.[20] Dow's system is designed to determine first how much energy is consumed by each of its divisions on a monthly basis, which is disclosed in a monthly Btu report, and second the energy value of its input in Btus, which is disclosed in a division energy input report. This last computation includes the Btu value of raw material purchased and transferred and the fuels and power consumed in production which allows Dow to figure out the total energy consumed in Btus and report the result to the Chemical Manufacturers Association. The Chemical Manufacturers Association reports the same statistics for the entire industry to the Department of Energy.

Three major problem areas are reported to affect energy accounting data significantly. These are (1) which energy flows are to be accounted for; (2) energy quality differences; and (3) the method of accounting to be used in accounting for the energies.[21]

The first problem is to identify the various flows of energy to be included and accounted for. A tentative list may include *primary natural energy* such as solar and tides and waves, *primary stored solar energy* such as wood, fossil fuels, and uranium, and *indirect energies* such as wind, rain (dilutant and flowing water), carbon, hydrogen, oxygen, nitrogen, metallic ores, electricity, processed goods, labor and other purchased services, and information and technology.[22]

The second problem refers to the differences in the quality of the various forms of direct and indirect sources of energy. Kilocalories are used to measure the heat produced by energy. They do not, however, measure the quality of the energy. To measure the quality of the energy from different sources it is necessary to develop energy quality factors in terms of coal equivalents, i.e., the amount of kilocalories of heat for the identified energy type to be equivalent to one kilocalorie of coal. For example, it takes 3,140 kilocalories of uranium-235 as mined in order to produce the same work as 1 kilocalorie of coal.

The third problem refers to the choice of an appropriate method of energy accounting. Boyles identified two separate and distinct methods of energy accounting, the heat equivalent method and the energy-expended method. They are defined as follows:

The heat equivalent method involves determining the heat that results when the output under investigation is burned or otherwise used to perform work. . . .

The energy-expended method of energy accounting values a good or service in terms of the total energy expended in order to create it.[23]

It may be suggested that the energy accountant choose one of these methods and for the sake of comparability use that method consistently for each step of his or her analysis. The heat equivalent method may appear, however, to be the most useful energy accounting concept because "expressing both the input and output in terms of their respective ability to perform work when burned makes it easy to determine how much potential energy is degraded by the energy transformation process."[24]

COMPREHENSIVE AUDITING

Comprehensive auditing started as a unique concept for auditing in the public sector both in Canada and the United States, and now extended to the private sector.[25] It is basically an extension of the audit function to *all* phases of management as part of a comprehensive accountability for corporate behavior.

In Canada, the comprehensive audit arose from the need for Parliament and the government to have effective control over the public purse. As a solution the Canadian government created in 1978 the new post of comptroller general of Canada and in 1977 extended the auditor general's mandate to include a review of the economy, the efficiency, and the effectiveness which the government manages the resources placed at its disposal. The concept embodied in these areas became known as *value for money auditing* and a major component of comprehensive auditing. The three areas were defined by the Office of the Auditor General as follows:

1. *Economy* refers to the terms and conditions under which entities acquire human and material resources. An economical operation requires that these resources be obtained in appropriate quality and quantity at the lowest cost.
2. *Efficiency* refers to the relationship between goods or services produced and the resources used to produce them. An efficient operation produces the maximum output for any given set of resource input, or it has minimum inputs for any given quantity and quality of output produced.
3. *Effectiveness* concerns the extent to which a program achieves its goods or other intended effects.

The Canadian version of comprehensive auditing includes five separate but closely interrelated components or modules- financial controls, reporting, attest and authority, management controls, and EDP controls, or FRAME. They are defined by the Office of the Auditor General as follows:

1. *Financial controls.* An evaluation of the controls over revenues, expenditures, assets, and liabilities, including the organization of the financial function and its place in the general management structure. It goes beyond the internal control function to include a review of the qualifications and suitability of financial personnel to the needs of the organization, the appropriateness of the accounting systems and procedures, and the appropriateness and adequacy of budgeting and financial reporting systems.
2. *Reporting*: An evaluation of the nature, content, adequacy, reliability, and timeliness of financial and related nonfinancial information presented in reports. The nonfinancial information referred to includes reporting on performance indicators, which reaches considerably beyond the reporting on the traditional profit measure.
3. *Attest and authority.* The expression of an opinion on financial statements and verification of parliamentary, governmental, and other authority for expenditures.
4. *Management controls.* An evaluation of the system of management information and controls, including the internal audit/ evaluation/ review functions, to ensure due regard to economy, efficiency, and effectiveness- in short, value-for-money auditing.
5. *EDP controls.* An evaluation of controls over financial and other information processed by computers and of management controls over the use of computer-related resources.[26]

Comprehensive auditing has been successfully applied to Canadian governmental departments and agencies and Canadian Crown corporations by the Office of Auditor General in Canada.

There are some issues to be resolved before comprehensive auditing becomes well established. First of all, Churchill and his colleagues mention the fact that comprehensive audits may change the auditor-client relationship.[27] First, the auditor rather than the client determines the scope and the timing of the audit. Second, the comprehensive audit results in a report by the auditors followed by management comments rather than a report by management "attested to" by the auditor.

Secondly, some of the Canadian Crown corporations audited raised the objection that comprehensive auditors would be presuming to second-guess management decisions and that in

any case the auditors are not qualified to pass judgment on most managerial decisions. The auditor response was that the comprehensive audit is not interested in the decisions per se but in the processes that support the decisions- that is, management systems for planning and control. Allard stated the auditor's position:
Comprehensive auditing, therefore, focuses on management systems rather than on transactions or events. They may cite transactions or events to buttress a finding made with respect to a management system, but the event is of secondary importance. It is not, therefore, a question of questioning management judgments, but rather a question of assessing the quality of processes and information on which that judgment is based. Since the decision is not the focus of the enquiry, it is unlikely that hindsight would enter significantly into that assessment.[28]

With respect to the qualifications of the comprehensive auditors, it is generally understood that the audit teams will include qualified specialists in the various management disciplines under examination. In any case it is up to the board of directors to select these people the way they select other consultants.

ENVIRONMENTAL AUDITING

In view of the continuing discoveries of illegal chemical dumping and the efforts by some firms to avoid strict U.S. environmental regulations by shipping hazardous waste abroad, there has arisen a general public consensus that environmental auditing is necessary. For example, the SEC showed its intent to enforce its disclosure requirements in consent degree actions involving the Allied Corporation in 1977, the United States Steel Corporation in 1979, and the Occidental Petroleum Corporation in 1980. In the latter two cases, the SEC ordered the companies to retain environmental consulting firms to prepare some form of regulatory compliance audits. Corporations have been also asked to disclose in their registration statements any environmental litigation that could have significant impact on earnings, and since July 1973 they are required to disclose any material expenditures, earnings, and the company's competitive position.[29] As a result, many companies have established environmental auditing programs, often with assistance from consulting or accounting firms such as Little, Booze, Allen and Hamilton or Coopers and Lybrand, to name two.[30]

Environmental auditing is basically a verification or validation of compliance with environmental laws, such as the Occupational Safety and Health Act, the Toxic Substances Control Act, and other laws passed to protect the environment. It has been conducted at two possible levels. A first level may be for the accounting firm or the consulting firm to provide an environmental "comfort" letter to its clients, similar to the regular auditor's opinion letter, which states that the firm has examined its client's policies and procedures for monitoring compliance with environmental laws and pinpoints the existence or or the absence of violations.[31] A second level may be an all-out audit, where the accounting or consulting firm makes a thorough and independent analysis of compliance with environmental laws, such as sending technicians into factories and properties to examine such things as air and water emissions and ground-water contamination.

HUMAN RESOURCE ACCOUNTING

Users may need to have adequate information about one "neglected" asset of a firm- the human asset. More specifically, investors may greatly benefit from a knowledge of the extent to which the human assets of an organization have been increased or decreased during a given period. The conventional accounting treatment of human resource outlays consists of *expensing* all human capital formation expenditures, while similar outlays on physical capital are *capitalized.* A more valid treatment would be to capitalize human resource expenditures in order to yield future benefits and reveal when such benefits can be measured. In fact, this last treatment has created a new concern with the measurement of the cost or value of human resources to an organization and the development of a new field of inquiry in accounting known as *human resource accounting.*

Broadly defined human resource accounting is: "the process of identifying and measuring data about human resources and communicating this information to interest parties."[32] This definition implies three major objectives of human resources accounting: identification of "human resource value": measurement of the cost and value of people to organizations; and investigation of the cognitive and behavioral impact of such information.

Human resource accounting has led to a few applications, such as those of R. G. Barry Corporation, Touche Ross and Company, and a Midwest branch of a mutual insurance company.[33] In spite of the lack of enthusiasm of many firms for disclosing the value of their human assets, more empirical studies investigating the cognitive and behavioral impact show a favorable predisposition of users to the human resource accounting information.[34] One may wonder, in fact, why R. G. Barry Corporation, a small shoe-manufacturing company listed on the American Stock Exchange, would develop a human resource accounting system. As one of its officers rhetorically observed: "Why in the world is a little company with good- but unspectacular- growth, good- but unromantic- products, good- but unsophisticated- technology, good- but undramatic- profitability interested in the development of a system of accounting for the human resources of the business? This is a fair question and deserves an answer."[35]

To answer this question and any similar questions asked by other corporations, we may cite three facts. First, capitalization of human resource cost is conceptually more valid than the expensing approach. Second, the information on "human assets" is likely to be relevant to a great variety of decisions made by external or internal users or both. And third, accounting for human assets constitutes an explicit recognition of the premise that people are valuable organizational resources and an integral part of a mix of resources.

The concept of human value may be derived from the general economic value theory. Like physical assets, individuals or groups may be attributed a value because of their ability to render future economic services. In line with the economic thinking that associates the value of an object with its ability to render benefits, the individual or group value is usually defined as the present worth of the services rendered to the organization throughout the individual's or the group's expected service life.

How do we determine the value of a human asset? To measure and disclose "human resource value," we need a theoretical framework, or "human resource value theory," to explicate the nature and determinants of the value of people to an organization. Basically, two models exist of the nature and determinants of human resource value, one advanced by Flamholtz and one by Likert and Bowers.[36]

In Flamholtz's model, the measure of a person's worth is his or her expected realizable value. Flamholtz's model suggests that such a measure of individual value results from the interaction of two variables: the individual's expected conditional value, and the probability that the individual will maintain membership in the organization.

Conditional value is the amount the organization would potentially realize from a person's services. It is a multidimensional variable comprising three factors: productivity, transferability, and promotability. The elements of conditional value are perceived to be the product of certain attributes of the person and certain dimensions of the organization. Two individual determinants are identified as important, the person's skills and "activation level." Similarly, the organizational determinants that interact with the individual values are identified as the organizational role of the individual and the "rewards" that people expect from the different aspects of their membership in a firm. The probability of maintaining the organizational membership is considered to be related to a person's degree of job satisfaction.

While Flamholtz's model examined the determinants of an individual's value to an organization, Likert and Bower's model examined the determinants to group value. Intended to represent the "productive capability of the human organization of any enterprise or unit within it,"[37] the model identifies three variables that influence the effectiveness of a firm's "human organization":

1. *Casual* variables are independent variables that can be directly or purposely altered or changed by the organization and its management and that, in turn, determine the course of developments within an organization. These casual variables include only those that are controllable by the organization and its management. General business conditions, for example, although an independent variable, are not viewed as casual since they are not controllable by the management of a particular enterprise. Casual variables include the structure of the organization and management's policies, decisions, business and leadership strategies, skills, and behavior.
2. *Interviewing* variables reflect the internal state, health, and performance capabilities of the organization, that is, the loyalties, attitudes, motivations, performance goals, and perceptions of all members and their collective capability for effective action.
3. *End-result* variables are the dependent variables that reflect the results achieved by the organization, such as its productivity, costs, scrap loss, growth, share of the market, and earnings.[38]

The model states that certain casual variables induce certain levels of intervening variables, which yield certain levels of end-result variables. The casual variables are managerial behavior, organizational structure, and subordinate peer behavior. The intervening variables are such organizational processes are perception, communication, motivation, decision making, control, and coordination. The end-result variables are health and satisfaction and productivity and financial performances.

Human assets measurement methods based on monetary measures are historical or acquisition cost, replacement cost, opportunity cost, the compensation model, and adjusted discount future wages. The principal nonmonetary measure is the "survey of organizations."

The historical, or acquisition, cost method consists of capitalizing all the costs associated with recruiting, selecting, hiring, and training and then amortizing these costs over the expected useful life of the asset, recognizing losses in case of liquidation of the asset or increasing the value of the asset for any additional cost expected to increase the benefit potential of the asset. Similar to any of the conventional accounting treatments for other assets, this treatment is practical and objective in the sense that the data are verifiable.[39]

Several limitations exist, however, to the use of these measurements. First, the economic value of a human asset does not necessarily correspond to its historical cost. Second, any appreciation or amortization may be subjective, with no relation to any increase or decrease in the productivity of the human assets. Third, because the costs associated with recruiting, selecting, hiring, training, placing, and developing employees may differ from one individual to another within a firm, historical cost does not result in comparable human resource values.

The replacement cost method consists of estimating the costs of replacing a firm's existing human resources. Such costs include all the costs of recruiting, selecting, hiring, training, placing, and developing new employees to reach the level of competence of existing employees. The principal advantage of the replacement cost method is that it is a good surrogate for the economic value of the asset in the sense that market considerations are essential in reaching a final figure. Such a final figure is also generally intended to be conceptually equivalent to a notion of a person's economic value.[40]

Several limitations exist, however, to the use of the replacement cost method. First, a firm may have a particular employee whose value is perceived as greater than the relevant replacement cost. Second, there may be no equivalent replacement for a given human asset.[41] Third, as noted by Likert and Bowers, managers asked to estimate the cost of completely replacing their human organization may have difficulty in doing so, and different managers may arrive at quite different estimates.[42]

Hekimian and Jones proposed the opportunity cost method to overcome the limitations of the replacement cost method.[43] They suggested that human resource values be established through a competitive bidding process within the firm, based on the concept of "opportunity" cost. More specifically, using this method, investment center managers bid for the scarce employees they need to recruit. These "scarce" employees all come from within the firm and include only those who are the subject of a recruitment request by an investment center manager. In other words, employees not considered "scarce" are not included in the human asset base of the organization.

Obviously, several limitations exist to the use of the opportunity cost method. First, the inclusion of only "scarce" employees in the asset base may be interpreted as "discriminatory" by the other employees. Second, the less profitable divisions may be penalized by their inability to outbid for the recruitment of better employees. Third, the method may be perceived as artificial and even immoral.[44]

Given the uncertainty and the difficulty associated with determining the value of human capital, Lev and Schwartz suggest the use of a person's future compensation as a surrogate for his or her value.[45] Accordingly, the "value of human capital embodied in a person of age t is the present value of his remaining future earnings from employment." This valuation model is expressed as:

$$V_t = \sum_{t=1}^{T} \frac{I(t)}{(1+r)^{t-r}}$$

where
V_t = the human capital value of a person I years old,
$I(t)$ = the person's annual earning up to retirement,
r = a discount rate specific to the person,
T = retirement age.

Because V_t is an ex-post value, given that I(t) is obtained only after retirement and because V_t ignores the possibility of death before retirement age, Lev and Schwartz refined the valuation model as follows:

$$E(V^*_T) = \sum_{t=1}^{T} P_t(t+1) \sum_{t=i}^{t} \frac{I^*_t}{(1+r)^{t-i}}$$

where
I^*_t = the future annual earnings,
$E(V^*_T)$ = the expected value of a person's human capital,

Pt(t) = the probability of a person dying at age t.

The principal imitation of the compensation model is the subjectivity associated with the determination of the level of future salary, the length of expected employment within the firm, and the discount rate.

Hermanson proposed using an adjusted compensation value as a proxy of the value of an individual to a firm.[46] The discounted future wages are adjusted by an "efficiency factor" intended to measure the relative effectiveness of the human capital of a given firm. This efficiency factor is measured by a ratio of the return on investment of the given firm to all other firms in the economy for a given period. It is computed by the following expression:

$$\text{Efficiency Ratio} = \frac{5\frac{RF_0}{RE_0} - 4\frac{RF_1}{RE_1} - 3\frac{RF_2}{RE_2} - 2\frac{RF_3}{RE_3} - \frac{RF_4}{RE_4}}{15}$$

where
RF_i = the rate of accounting income on owned assets for the firm of the year i.
RE_i = the rate of accounting income on owned assets for all firms in the economy for the year i.
i = years (0 to 4).

The justification for this ratio rests on the thesis that differences in profitability are due primarily to differences in human asset performance. Thus, it is necessary to adjust the compensation value by the efficiency factor.

Many nonmonetary measures of human assets may be used to measure human assets, such as simple inventory of skills and capabilities of people, the assignment of rating or rankings to individual performance, and measurement of attitudes. The most frequently used nonmonetary measure of human value is derived from Likert and Bowers' model of the variables that determine "the effectiveness of a firm's human organization." A questionnaire based on the theoretical model, called "survey of organizations," was designed to measure the "organizational climate."[47] The results of such a questionnaire may serve as a nonmonetary measure of human assets by portraying employees' perceptions of the working atmosphere in the firm.

THE CONSTITUENCY GROUP ATTITUDES AUDIT

Our pluralistic and democratically organized society is comprised of various groups having various goals and various criteria for evaluating a corporation's behavior. The constituency group attitudes audit is suggested as a way of identifying and measuring the attitudes and preference of these groups for corporate actions and the relative strength of these groups to compose social pressures on the corporation. The benefit of such an approach is eloquently stated by A. D. Shocker and S. Prakash Sethi:

This information should incorporated into its decision-making strategies so that it maximizes social satisfaction, sustains incentives for its stockholders to continue investing in it, and mobilizes its resources efficiently so that its traditional constituent groups, e.g., employees, creditors, suppliers, and buyers, are satisfied with its performance.[48]

In the same article, Shocker and Sethi outlined the procedures for implementing a corporate constituency attitudes audit. The methodology includes five steps:[49]

First, the corporate constituency reference groups whose priorities are to be monitored are identified. This is a difficult step because it may require including groups hostile to the firm and its short- and long-term objectives.

Second, the criteria or dimensions potentially important to those groups and capable of being affected by the organization are specified. These dimensions may be either qualitative or quantitative and vary depending on the groups whose opinions are sought.

Third, a number of "social profits" intended to represent different combinations and levels of these dimensions are prepared. These profits should be realistic and comparable to each other.

Realism requires that each profile be believable to the key individuals who will be asked to evaluate it, i.e., the individual must believe that the firm could accomplish the depicted combinations of levels of social benefit and cost in the time frame specified. Comparability requires that all profiles be premised on approximately the same level of the firm's resources, so that they appear to be true *alternatives*, e.g., a situation in which one dominates one another on all dimensions should be avoided.[50]

Fourth, the group preferences among alternative profiles and satisfaction with the level of social good represented by each profile are determined by asking the respondent to state a preference for one profile when the profiles are presented to him in airs.

Fifth and last, the preference judgments are analyzed to determine priorities for the different social dimensions implied by the groups' preference judgments, and the satisfactions are analyzed to determine the social good. The procedure used is similar to those used in the marketing field for determining consumer choices among alternative products. A group's utility for any profile is computed as the weighted sum of the attitudes of that profile. The higher the utility, the more preferred is the profile.

The utility function may be computed according to two possible mathematical forms. In one model the utility is simply the sum of the weighted attitudes of the stimulus profile:

$$u_j = \sum_{p=1}^{t} w_p y_{jp}$$

where
y_{jp} = a measure of the jth profile on the pth social dimension (p = 1,2,3,...t);
w_p = a measure of the importance (priority) attached to the pth dimension by the individual (group);
u_j = a measure of the utility of the jth profile for the individual (group).

In another model, the utility is inversely related to the sum of the weighted distances between a criterion value for each dimension and the actual level of the profit and each dimension:

$$U_j = a/d_j$$

Where
$d_j = (\sum_{p=1}^{t}(x_p - y_{jp})^2 w_p)^{1/2}$ = a weighted measure of the distance between the jth profile and the criterion.
x_r = a measure of the group's goal or criterion value for the pth dimension.
$a = 1 \sum_{j=1}^{n}(\frac{1}{d_j})$ = a constant for any prespecified set of n profiles. The effect of this constant is to standardize a group's utilities so they sum to unity.

A similar procedure is used by Daniel Yankelovich, Inc., to measure public expectations of public behavior![51]

Future of Social Auditing

As the need for social measurement and reporting increases with a greater acceptance of socio-economic accounting, social auditing may become as standard and as rigorous as financial auditing. The professional designation of social auditor will be needed to qualify the people involved in the social audit and asked to examine the validity of the social data prepared by the firm. Before these developments become a reality, there may be a need for a change of value and attitudes so that they become more favorable to a measurement and reporting of the social performance of firms. Only when these social changes become effective would it be then possible to motivate the effort to develop techniques of measuring, recording, disclosing, and verifying the social performance of a firm.

Apart from the social changes, there emerges an ideological transformation of business managers to respond to the call for action in promoting social goals rather than being restricted to the profit motive. The ideological transformation follows the erosion of the traditional American ideological transformation follows the erosion of the traditional American ideology-individualism, property rights, competition, the limited state, and scientific specialization and fragmentation- derived from John Locke's natural laws and the shift from an individualistic attitude to a *communitarian idea*, in which the individual sense of identity depends on the things with which he or she is associated.[52] In response to this ideological transformation and the communitarian attitudes of people, the social audit will be more needed in the future as part of the action and response model of corporate enterprises, community groups, and individuals. Before this prediction becomes a reality, there is a need for solutions to overcome some of the obstacles confronted by the corporations that undertook social audits. Among these obstacles suggested, by order to importance, are (1) the general decline in continuous pressure on business to undertake social programs; (2) the danger to the company in publishing the results of social audits; (3) the inability to develop consensus on ways to organize information; (4) the inability to develop consensus as to what activities shall be covered; (5) the inability to make credible cost-benefit analysis to guide company actions; and (6) the inability to develop measures of performance that everyone will accept.[53]

Notes

1. David Blake, William Frederick, and Mildred S. Myers, *Social Auditing: Evaluating the Impact of Corporate Programs* (New York: Praeger, 1976), pp. 2-3.

2. Raymond A. Bauer and Dan H. Fenn, Jr., *The Corporate Social Audit* (New York: Russell Sage Foundation, 1972). Emphasis in the original.

3. Steven C. Dilley, "What is Social Responsibility? Some Definitions for Doing the Corporate Social Audit," *Canadian Chartered Accountant Magazine* (November 1974): 26.

4. John J. Corson, George A. Steiner, and Robert C. Meehan, *Measuring Business's Social Performance: The Corporate Audit* (New York: Committee for Economic Development, 1974), p. 33.

5. Bernard L. Butcher, "The Program Management Approach to the Corporate Social Audit," *California Management Review* (Fall 1973): 14.

6. Bauer and Fenn, *The Corporate Social Audit*.

7. Raymond A. Bauer and Dan H. Fenn, Jr., "What Is a Corporate Social Audit?" *Harvard Business Review* (January-February 1973): 47.

8. Raymond A. Bauer, L. Terry Cauthorn, and Ranne P. Warner, "The Management Process Audit Manual," in Lee E. Preston, ed., *Research in Corporate Social Performance* (Greenwich, Conn.: JAI Press, 1978).

9. Ibid., p. 266.

10. Lee E. Preston, and James E. Post, *Private Management and Public Policy: The Principle of Public Responsibility* (Englewood Cliffs, N.J.: Prentice-Hall, 1975), chs. 6, 8.

11. Butcher, "The Program Management Approach to the Corporate Social Audit," p. 12.

12. A. Belkaoui, "The Impact of Socio-Economic Accounting Statements on the Investment Decision: An Empirical Study," *Accounting, Organizations and Society* (1980): 263-268; A. Belkaoui, "The Impact of the Disclosure of the Environmental Effects of Organizational Behavior on the Market," *Financial Management* (Winter 1976): 26-31; Bevis Longstreth and H. David Rosenbloom, *Corporate Social Responsibility and the Institutional Investor* (New York: Praeger, 1973).

13. "Corporate Ratings from Xerox to Con Ed," *Business and Society* 5, no. 12 (1972): 1; "How Social Responsibility Became Institutionalized," *Business Week* (June 30, 1973): 74-82.

14. Among the Council on Economic Priorities Studies are *Paper Profits: Pollution in the Pulp and Paper Industry* (Cambridge: MIT Press, 1972); *Paper Profits: Pollution Audit 1972* (Cambridge: MIT Press, 1972); and *The Price of Power: Electric Utilities and the Environment* (Cambridge: MIT Press, 1973). See also Council on Economic Priorities, *Economic Priorities Report*, a bimonthly report.

15. Clark Abt, "Managing to Save Money While Doing Good," *Innovation* (January 1972): xxvii.

16. David F. Linowes, "An Approach to Socio-Economic Accounting," *Conference Board Record* (November 1972): 59.

17. David F. Linowes, "Let's Get on with the Social Audit: A Specific Proposal," *Business and Society Review* (Nov. 1978): 40.

18. A. B. Toan, Jr., "Social Measurement," *New York Times*, March 18, 1973, p. 14.

19. Preston and Post, *Private Management and Public Policy*, p. 136.

20. Morris Gartenberg, "How Dow Accounts for Its Energy Use," *Management Accounting* (March 1980): 10-12.

21. Jesse V. Boyles III, "Energy Accounting," *Management Accounting* (February 1979): 35-41.

22. Ibid., p, 36.

23. Ibid., p, 38.

24. Ibid., p. 39.

25. James J. McDonell, " Auditing the Government of Canada: A Centennial Conspectus," *Chartered Accountant Magazine* (December 1978): 22-31; Neil C. Churchill et al., "Developments in 'Comprehensive Auditing' and Suggestions for Research," *Symposium on Auditing Research II* (University of Illinois at Champaign-Urbana, 1977).

26. J. Claude Allard, "Comprehensive Auditing in Crown Corporations," *Chartered Accountant Magazine* (February 1981): 38-39.

27. Churchill et al., "Developments in 'Comprehensive Accounting' and Suggestions for Research," pp. 202-203.

28. Allard, "Comprehensive Auditing in Crown Corporations," p. 39.

29. Securities Act Release No. 33-5386, see *Wall Street Journal*, April 23, 1973.

30. Len Ackland, "Auditing for Hazards on the Rise," *Chicago Tribune*, July 8, 1981, sec. 3, p. 5.

31. Lee Harrison, "Big Business's Pollution Problems," *New York Times*, May 17, 1981, pp. 8-9.

32. Committee on Human Resource Accounting, "Committee Reports," *Accounting Review*, supplement, 48 (1973): 169.

33. R. L. Woodruff, "Human Resource Accounting," *Canadian Chartered Accountant* (September 1970): 2-7; M. O. Alexander, "Investments in People," *Canadian Chartered Accountant* (July 1971): 38-45; E. Flamholtz, "Human Resource Accounting: Measuring Positional Replacement Costs," *Human Resource Management* (Spring 1973): 8-16.

34. N. S. Elias, "The Effects of Human Asset Statements on the Investment Decision: An Experiment," *Journal of Accounting Research*, supplement, 10 (1972): 215-233.

35. Woodruff, "Human Resource Accounting," p. 2.

36. E. Flamholtz, "Toward a Theory of Human Resource Value in Formal Organizations," *Accounting Review* (October 1972): 666-678; R. Likert and D. G. Bowers, "Improving the Accuracy of P/L Reports by Estimating the Change in Dollar Value of the Human Organization," *Michigan Business Review* (March 1973): 15-24.

37. Likert and Bowers, "Improving the Accuracy of P/L Reports," p. 15.

38. Ibid., p. 17.

39. N.W.E. Glautier and B. Underdown, "Problems and Prospects of Accounting for Human Assets," *Management Accounting* (March 1973): 99.

40. E. Flamholtz, *Human Resource Accounting* (Los Angeles: Dickenson, 1974), p. 190.

41. I. S. Hekimian and J. G. Jones, "Put People on Your Balance Sheet," *Harvard Business Review* (January-February 1967): 108.

42. R. Likert and D. G. Bowers, "Organizational Theory and Human Resource Accounting," *American Psychologist* 24, no. 6 (1969): 588.

43. Hekimian and Jones, "Put People on Your Balance Sheet," pp. 108-109.

44. D. Elovitz, "From the Thoughtful Businessman," *Harvard Business Review* (May-June 1967): 59.

45. B. Lev and A. Schwartz, "On the Use of the Economic Concept of Human Capital in Financial Statements," *Accounting Review* (January 1971): 105.

46. R. H. Hermanson, "Accounting for human Assets," Occasional Paper no. 14, Bureau of Business and Economic Research, Graduate School of Business Administration, Michigan State University, 1964.

47. J. C. Taylor and D. C. Bowers, *The Survey of Organizations* (Ann Arbor, Mich.: Institute for Social Research, 1972).

48. Allan D. Shocker and S. Prakash Sethi, "An Approach to Incorporating Social Preferences in Developing Corporate Action Strategies," in S. P. Sethi, ed., *The Unstable Ground: Corporate Social Policy in a Dynamic Society* (Melville, 1974), p. 70.

49. Ibid., p. 71.

50. Ibid., p. 73.

51. Daniel Yankelovich, Inc., *Corporate Priorities: A Continuing Study of the New Demands on Business* (Stamford, Conn.: Daniel Yankelovich, 1972), A brochure describing firms' services.

52. George Cabot Lodge, "Business and the Changing Society," *Harvard Business Review* (March-April 1974): 62-64.

53. Corson, Steiner and Meehan, *Measuring Business's Social Performance*, p. 36.

Bibliography

Abt, Clark. "Managing to Save Money While Doing Good." *Innovation* (January 1972).

Allard, J. Claude. "Comprehensive Auditing in Crown Corporations." *Chartered Accountant Magazine* (February 1981): 38-43.
Annual Report, Industrial Energy Efficiency Program, July 1977 through December 1978 (Washington, D. C.: Government Printing Office, 1979).
Bauer, Raymond A., L. Terry Cauthorn, and Ranne P. Warner, "Auditing the Management Process for Social Performance," *Business and Society Review* (June 1975): 39-45.
Bauer, Raymond A., and Dan H. Fenn, Jr. "What Is a Corporate Social Audit?" *Harvard Business Review* (January-February 1973): 37-48.
Blake, David H., William C. Frederick, and Mildred S. Myers, *Social Auditing: Evaluating the Impact of Corporate Programs*. New York: Praeger, 1976.
Blum, Fred. "Social Audit of the Enterprise." *Harvard Business Review* (March-April 1958).
Boyles, Jesse V., Ill. "Energy Accounting." *Management Accounting* (February 1979): 35-41.
Brooks, Leonard J., and William R. Davis. "Some Approaches to the Corporate Social Audit." *Chartered Accountant Magazine* (March 1977): 34-45.
Butcher, Bernard L. "The Program Management Approach to the Corporate Social Audit." *California Management Review* (Fall 1973): 11-24.
Charnes, A., and W. W. Cooper. "Auditing and Accounting for Program Efficiency and Management Efficiency in Not-for-Profit Entities." *Accounting, Organizations and Society* 5, no. 1 (1980): 87-107.
Churchill, N. C., et al., "Comprehensive Audits and Some Suggestions for Research." *Symposium on Auditing Research* (Department of Accountancy, University of Illinois at Urbana-Champaign), 11 (1977).
Churchill, Neil C., and Richard M. Cyert. "An Experiment in Management Auditing." *Journal of Accountancy* (February 1966): 39-43.
Corson, John J., George A. Steiner, and Robert C. Meehan. *Measuring Business's Social Performance: The Corporate Audit*. New York: Committee for Economic Development. 1974.
Council on Economic Priorities. *Efficiency in Death*. New York: Harper & Row, 1970.
Dewhirt, James. "Truest and Fairest: The Case for Social Audits." *Accountant* (August 2nd, 1973): 143-144.
Dilley, Steven C. "What Is Social Responsibility? Some Definitions for Doing the Corporate Social Audit." *Canadian Chartered Accountant Magazine* (November 1974): 24-28.
Feldman, Lawrence. "Societal Adaptation: A New Challenge for Marketing." *Journal of Marketing* (November 1971).
Fetyko, D. F. "The Company Social Audit." *Management Accounting* (April 1975): 31-34.
Gartenberg, Morris. "How Dow Accounts for Its Energy Use." *Management Accounting* (March 1980): 10-12.
Gray, Daniel H. "Methodology: One Approach to the Corporate Social Audit." *California Management Review* (Summer 1973): 108-109.
Hay, Robert D. "Social Auditing: An Experimental Approach." *Academy of Management Journal* (December 1975): 871-877.
Higgins, James M. "A Proposed Social Performance Evaluation System." *Atlanta Economic Review* (May-June 1977): 4-9.
Humble, John. *Social Responsibility Audit: A Management Tool for Survival*. London: Foundation for Business Responsibilities, 1973.
Katugampola, B. "The Energy Audit." *Internal Auditor* (October 1978): 93-95.

Linowes, David F. "An Approach to Socio-Economic Accounting." *Conference Board Record* (November 1972): 58-61.
___. "Let's Get on with the Social Audit: A Specific Proposal." *Business and Society Review/Innovation* (November 1978), pp. 35-42.
McDonell, James J. "Auditing the Government of Canada: A Centennial Conspectus." *Chartered Accountant Magazine* (December 1978): 22-31.
Roth, Harold P. "A New Outlet for Energy Audit Data." *Journal of Accountancy* (September 1981): 68-82.
Ryder, Charles. "Energy Audits and Case Histories." *Energy World* (November 1976).
___. "The Need for an Energy Audit." *Management Accounting* (England) (May 1976).
Sethi, S. Prakash. "Getting a Handle on the Social Audit." *Business and Society Review/Innovation* (Winter 1972-73).
Tipgos, Manuel A. "A Case Against the Social Audit." *Management Accounting* (November 1976): 23-26.
Ullman, Arieh A. "The Corporate Environmental Accounting System: A Management Tool for Fighting Environmental Degredation." *Accounting, Organizations and Society* 1, no. 1 (1980): 71-79.

www.ingramcontent.com/pod-product-compliance
Lightning Source LLC
Chambersburg PA
CBHW070314190526
45169CB00005B/1620